FEDERALISM IN CANADA

FEDERALISM IN CANADA

CONTESTED CONCEPTS AND UNEASY BALANCES

Thomas O. Hueglin

UNIVERSITY OF TORONTO PRESS
Toronto Buffalo London

Toronto Buffalo London
utorontopress.com

ISBN 978-1-4426-3646-0 (cloth) ISBN 978-1-4426-3648-4 (EPUB)
ISBN 978-1-4426-3645-3 (paper) ISBN 978-1-4426-3647-7 (PDF)

Library and Archives Canada Cataloguing in Publication

Title: Federalism in Canada : contested concepts and uneasy balances / Thomas O. Hueglin.
Names: Hueglin, Thomas O., author.
Description: Includes bibliographical references and index.
Identifiers: Canadiana (print) 20200342282 | Canadiana (ebook) 20200342312 | ISBN 9781442636460 (hardcover) | ISBN 9781442636453 (softcover) | ISBN 9781442636484 (EPUB) | ISBN 9781442636477 (PDF)
Subjects: LCSH: Federal government – Canada. | LCSH: Canada – Politics and government. | CSH: Federal-provincial relations – Canada.
Classification: LCC JL27 .H84 2021 | DDC 320.471—dc23

We welcome comments and suggestions regarding any aspect of our publications – please feel free to contact us at news@utorontopress.com or visit us at utorontopress.com.

Every effort has been made to contact copyright holders; in the event of an error or omission, please notify the publisher.

University of Toronto Press acknowledges the financial assistance to its publishing program of the Canada Council for the Arts and the Ontario Arts Council, an agency of the Government of Ontario.

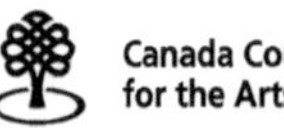

Conseil des Arts
du Canada

Funded by the Government of Canada | Financé par le gouvernement du Canada | Canada

For Yolsun

Contents

PROLOGUE

APPROACHES TO CANADIAN FEDERALISM

The story of Canadian federalism can be told in many ways. All authors bring to this story their personal experiences, opinions, and biases and the way in which they read and understand the literature before them. This book, therefore, begins with a personal account of my apprenticeship travels when I came to this country more than 30 years ago and with an acknowledgement of the literature that first formed my opinion about it. This prologue then proceeds to identify what I see as the underlying dynamic of Canadian federalism and what is meant to weave through the book as its central theme: More than in any other federal system that I have studied, there are deep disagreements about the conceptual or normative meaning of federalism and about how it ought to operate. The prologue ends by explaining in brief the organization and outline of the book.

A Personal Account by Means of Acknowledgement

I came to Canada in the fall of 1983 and thus had just missed out on some of the most tumultuous moments in Canadian history: René Lévesque's first referendum on sovereignty-association, Peter Lougheed's war on the National Energy Program, and of course Pierre Trudeau's constitutional patriation showdown. Yet all I knew about Canada prior to my arrival for what I thought would be a one-year post-doctoral fellowship at Queen's University was that for some reason unbeknownst to me it was a more decentralized federation than most others.

Richard Simeon became my friend and mentor. The first three books he gave me to read were *Canada in Question* by Donald Smiley,[1] *Unfulfilled Union* by Garth Stevenson,[2] and *Prairie Capitalism* by John Richards and Larry Pratt.[3] With the one suitcase I had brought along hardly unpacked, Richard almost immediately dragged me off to the Macdonald Commission in Ottawa where I had to comment on a paper by Kenneth McRoberts. I am not sure what kind of contribution I might have been able to make as a mere novice in all matters Canadian, but I surely added McRoberts's and Dale Posgate's *Quebec: Social Change and Political Crisis*[4] to my reading list, along with Edwin Black's *Divided Loyalties*.[5] Strangely, or perhaps typically, Richard never told me to read his own *Federal–Provincial Diplomacy*, which indeed I read only some time later.[6] Instead he insisted that I read Keith Banting's *The Welfare State and Canadian Federalism*,[7] which first drew my attention to the intractable question of the impact of divided jurisdiction on public policy.

For someone having studied federalism in Germany, this literature was outright bewildering. I read these books like murder mysteries, unable to put them down. There was such a sense of excitement, despair, conflict, crisis, and transition. Much later, another German observer, Arthur Benz, would characterize the difference between German and Canadian federalism as one between "regulatory constitutionalism" and "negotiated constitutionalism."[8] All the excitement was owed to the conflictual nature of negotiation.

---

1 Donald V. Smiley, *Canada in Question: Federalism in the Eighties* (Toronto: McGraw-Hill Ryerson, 1980).

2 Garth Stevenson, *Unfulfilled Union: Canadian Federalism and National Unity*, 5th ed. (Montreal: McGill-Queen's University Press, 2009); first edition published in 1979.

3 John Richards and Larry Pratt, *Prairie Capitalism: Power and Influence in the New West* (Toronto: McClelland and Stewart, 1979).

4 Kenneth McRoberts and Dale Posgate, *Quebec: Social Change and Political Crisis* (Toronto: McClelland and Stewart, 1980).

5 Edwin R. Black, *Divided Loyalties: Canadian Concepts of Federalism* (Montreal: McGill-Queen's University Press, 1975).

6 Richard Simeon, *Federal–Provincial Diplomacy: The Making of Recent Policy in Canada* (1973; Toronto: University of Toronto Press, 2006).

7 Keith G. Banting, *The Welfare State and Canadian Federalism*, 2nd ed. (Montreal: McGill-Queen's University Press, 1987); first edition published in 1982.

8 Arthur Benz, "German Dogmatism and Canadian Pragmatism? Stability and Constitutional Change in Federal Systems," *Polis* 65 (working paper, Fernunversität Hagen, 2008): 31.

It was Black, chair of political studies at Queen's at the time, who insisted that I would not understand Canada without visiting its different regions and therefore set up a small grant for me to travel around the country. During a dinner party at his house, he and Smiley debated vigorously whether I would be allowed to fly out west or whether understanding the country required taking the train. The importance of trains also came up later in another conversation with J.R. Mallory, who was the panel chair when I gave my first paper at one of the annual meetings of the Canadian Political Science Association. Papers had been so much better, Mallory opined, when their authors had still taken the train to these meetings, with more time to write and prepare on the train than now when everybody took the plane.

In the end, I drove. David Elkins, on sabbatical at Queen's, had to fly home because he had become chair of political science at the University of British Columbia, and he offered to pay for the gas if I drove his car back to British Columbia. It came to be a defining road trip. In Winnipeg, I saw the railyards connecting the two halves of the country, in southern Saskatchewan I waded through a solid ground cover of locusts, and in Banff I blew the head gasket of David's aging Datsun 510 (it got repaired and eventually made it all the way to Vancouver). I read J.F. Conway's *The West*[9] along the way and thought of *Small Worlds* by Elkins and Simeon[10] when I crossed from Saskatchewan into Alberta, two provinces a world of political culture apart yet indistinguishable from one dusty Prairie town to the next.

In Calgary, I was shown the new PetroCan building as a sinister symbol of Trudeau's centralist machinations ("American steel and Italian marble"). In Edmonton, I was to meet the already-legendary Peter Meekison, whom I had heard about not only as the "father" of the 1982 amendment formula but also as a harbinger of good because he usually came to the annual conferences at Queen's University's Institute of Intergovernmental Relations with a healthy funding cheque from the government of Alberta.

I approached his vice-presidential suite at the University of Alberta with some trepidation, which was not helped when I saw him standing there, larger than life in suit and tie with a framed photo of the 1981 First Ministers' patriation conference right behind him – signed by "your friend Pierre" (or some such inscription) no less. But Meekison quickly put me at ease, not only by

9 John F. Conway, *The West: The History of a Region in Confederation* (Toronto: Lorimer, 1983).

10 David J. Elkins and Richard Simeon, eds., *Small Worlds: Provinces and Parties in Canadian Political Life* (Toronto: Methuen, 1980).

good-naturedly answering my clumsy questions about western alienation and all that, but by then taking what I thought was a most generous amount of time to tell me about the places I should visit while driving through the Rockies: the continental divide where a stream is parted by a rock with one side flowing toward the Pacific and the other side all the way toward the Atlantic; the Paint Pots in the Kootenays, where Indigenous peoples had met in peace to collect ochre for ceremonial and trade purposes; and the spiral railway tunnel on Kicking Horse Pass, where one can see the head of a long freight train coming out of the tunnel cutting across the tail still going into it.

On the other side of that Pass, in British Columbia, Philip Resnick, the author of *Parliament vs. People*,[11] offered a refreshing critique of Canadian democracy and political culture. I thought it was a bit west-coastish at the time, but it stayed with me as a reminder that the usual critique of Canadian executive federalism as undemocratic is often cast against a rather naively idealistic picture of parliamentary democracy.

Black and Smiley had been right. One could not understand Canada, nor its bewildering literature on federalism, without having seen it, the vast spaces separating one region from the other. In southern Germany, where I grew up, one could drive to five different countries within a few hours. Just to get out of Ontario took almost exponentially more time. With distance came diversity. I began to understand what I had read in Michael Jenkin's *The Challenge of Diversity*: "Whereas political systems in other countries tend to emphasize the traditional divisions between business and labour on economic issues, in Canada *territorial* divisions predominate, and find expression most frequently in federal-provincial, or interprovincial, conflict."[12]

Much later in Saskatoon, during a conference, while reading the local newspaper in the hotel breakfast room every morning during the better part of a week, I found only one single reference to Ottawa, and it was not about federal politics but about whether the local member of parliament had appropriately represented Saskatchewan's interests in the nation's capital. The physical distance between Ottawa and Saskatoon is nearly 3,000 kilometres, and neither city is anywhere near the edge of the country.

---

11 Philip Resnick, *Parliament vs. People: An Essay on Democracy and Canadian Political Culture* (Vancouver: New Star Books, 1984).

12 Michael Jenkin, *The Challenge of Diversity: Industrial Policy in the Canadian Federation* (Ottawa: Science Council of Canada, 1983), 18.

Of course, I went to Quebec. Maybe it was somewhat symptomatic that Black and Smiley had made my trip out west such a priority. There was something almost romantic about the west, almost like a Canadian version of the American frontier mentality. Nobody in English Canada saw the relationship with Quebec as a romance. Most did not understand the language to begin with, even though often pointing out, and not without a measure of disdain, that Québécois films were sometimes shown even in France with French subtitles.

It was Simeon, then, who sent me to see André Bernard at the Université du Québec à Montréal. A few years earlier, Bernard had been asked to provide an English language briefing on the question that had puzzled English Canadians ever since the Quiet Revolution of the 1960s and the rise of the Parti Québécois during the 1970s: What does Quebec want?[13] It became my first serious briefing as well. After Montreal I moved on to Quebec City, where Jean Crête graciously set aside his quantitative instincts and provided much qualitative information about Quebec history and political culture. Back at Queen's, I was told to read Hugh MacLennan's *Two Solitudes*.[14] The iconic status of that novel in English Canada is probably owed to wishful thinking as the story peters out in lukewarm reconciliation just short of assimilation. As in the English Canadian literature on federalism I read, there was a clear understanding of Quebec as a distinct society but less so about what it would take to keep it that way.

With a PhD student and friend at Queen's, Leonard Preyra, I also undertook a camping trip around the Gaspé Peninsula. From Leonard, who had been born in Mumbai, India, I got the first (and at the time rather skeptical) earful about immigrant history and multiculturalism in Canada. Leonard later became an NDP member of the Legislative Assembly in Nova Scotia, where he also served as Minister of Communities, Culture, and Heritage.

Quite ironically, my travel funds ran out before I could visit the Maritimes or Newfoundland. But the posthumously published *Atlantic Canada and Confederation* by David G. Alexander[15] was on my reading list, and Ralph Matthew's *The Creation of Regional Dependency*[16] as well as Paul Philips's *Regional*

13 André Bernard, *What Does Quebec Want?* (Toronto: Lorimer, 1978).

14 Hugh MacLennan, *Two Solitudes* (1945; repr., Toronto: McClelland and Stewart, 1957).

15 David G. Alexander, *Atlantic Canada and Confederation: Essays in Canadian Political Economy* (Toronto: University of Toronto Press, 1983).

16 Ralph Matthews, *The Creation of Regional Dependency* (Toronto: University of Toronto Press, 1983).

Disparities[17] put it into a larger regional political economy context. Janine Brodie's most instructive *The Political Economy of Canadian Regionalism* appeared only a number of years later.[18]

I got a sense of the country, and I got a sense of Canadian political science and its traditions. Back at Queen's, Peter Leslie, just having replaced Simeon as the director of the Institute of Intergovernmental Relations, on occasion took me along Sunday afternoons when he had tea with J.A. Corry, one of the grand old men of Canadian political science, who had significantly contributed to the influential Rowell-Sirois report of 1940[19] and who still lived nearby. The building where I had my office in the political studies department, Macintosh-Corry Hall, bears his name.

More immediately important for my Canadian apprenticeship, however, was Hartmut Kiesling, a German exchange student from the Centre for Canada Studies at Marburg University in Germany, who I shared the office with for the year, who knew infinitely more about Canada than I did, and who more or less served as my personal tutor. Whenever I looked up from one of my books with a puzzled face, he was usually able to clear up my confusion. And then there was Ian Robinson, Simeon's research assistant, who I only stopped debating with while we clashed on the squash court. He usually won the argument, and he broke one of my ribs. He later co-authored *State, Society, and the Development of Canadian Federalism* with Simeon,[20] who thought it was a book that never quite got the recognition it deserved.

Apart from reading books, I also photocopied dozens of articles on Canadian federalism, history, and politics, and a stapler was always close at hand. One day, to demonstrate my greatly improved Canadian cleverness, I put that stapler on the photocopier and then posted the image on my office door with the caption "Harold Innis Memorial Stapler." That caught the attention of John Meisel, who had just returned from his stint as chair of the Canadian Radio-television and Telecommunications Commission. John had a fine sense of humour alongside a lot of seasoned wisdom, and I learned a great deal from him

17 Paul Phillips, *Regional Disparities* (Toronto: Lorimer, 1982).

18 Janine Brodie, *The Political Economy of Canadian Regionalism* (Toronto: Harcourt Brace Jovanovich, 1990).

19 Donald V. Smiley, ed., *Rowell-Sirois Report* (Toronto: Macmillan, 1978), esp. 196–98, footnotes 14 and 28.

20 Richard Simeon and Ian Robinson, *State, Society, and the Development of Canadian Federalism* (Toronto: University of Toronto Press, 1990).

about Canada's place in a world he knew like no other. Included were tales about his time as a refugee in Casablanca, where it was his sister who, in real life, had issued the transit papers for the flights to Lisbon everyone is after in Rick's Café. Meisel also recommended me for the job at Wilfrid Laurier University, where I have been for more than 30 years now.

I did not know yet that just a couple of years later I would teach "staples theory" in my Canadian political economy classes at Laurier. It was Simeon, yet again, who had first alerted me to what was a most formidable Canadian political economy tradition, even though it was already under siege by the hegemonic rise of neoliberal triumphalism. He sent me off to what was at the time still the citadel of neo-Marxist political economy, Carleton University in Ottawa, where I met with Leo Panitch and Glen Williams. Panitch's edited volume on *The Canadian State*,[21] with its chapter contributions by Canada's finest political economy minds, and Williams's entirely captivating *Not for Export*[22] were added to the reading list alongside John Porter's *Vertical Mosaic*[23] classic. I also met up with Reg Whitaker, whose *Federalism and Democratic Theory*[24] had just been published as a discussion paper by the Institute of Intergovernmental Relations, a much-needed reminder that federalism is not just a means to an end.

I had been socialized into political thinking during the 1960s and 1970s, which is to say before the neoliberal obfuscations of social reality were mainstreamed into academic curricula. My inclination was to see the world in terms of class struggle, exploitation, alienation, and dependency. My obsession with federalism, on the other hand, stemmed from having grown up in post-war West Germany, and the promise of a federally united Europe in which the Germans might regain respectability. From the Canadian political economy literature – that is, before it, too, became upstaged by the pious lies of allegedly rational market behaviour – I learned how to see territorial and social divisions as a complex reality of interdependent power relations.

I was first drawn into discussions on federalism and Indigenous self-government by David Hawkes, then associate director of the Institute of

21 Leo Panitch, ed., *The Canadian State: Political Economy and Political Power* (Toronto: University of Toronto Press, 1977).

22 Glen Williams, *Not for Export*, 3rd ed. (Toronto: McClelland and Stewart, 1994).

23 John Porter, *The Vertical Mosaic: An Analysis of Social Class and Power in Canada* (1965; repr., Toronto: University of Toronto Press, 1981).

24 Reg Whitaker, *Federalism and Democratic Theory* (Kingston: Institute of Intergovernmental Relations, 1983).

Intergovernmental Relations, which later led to an invitation to contribute a paper on that topic for the Royal Commission on Aboriginal Peoples (RCAP)[25] where David served as co-director of research. It was during that exhilarating – if ultimately frustrating – time working for the RCAP that I first began to conceptualize "treaty federalism"[26] and constitutional federalism more generally as two distinct traditions and models of federal organization and practice.[27]

I also did not get to visit the north, although I got an earful about it from Michael Whittington at Carleton. If I remember correctly, he was introduced to me as someone who had managed to get himself a research grant that required the use of a canoe as means of transportation. Maybe for that reason, when I read Van Loon and Whittington's *The Canadian Political System*, I paid more attention to the sentence exclaiming that "Canadians are extremely lucky in terms of where they live" than to the sentence later in the book according to which "few subjects are as crucial to an understanding of the Canadian political system as the study of federal-provincial financial or fiscal relations."[28] In fact, given my own predilection for big ideas of institutional design and procedural practice, it took me almost 30 years to realize how true that second sentence was.

I want to acknowledge this literature for two reasons. One is that it accompanied my Canadian apprenticeship and thus pre-formed in important ways what would become my own understanding of Canadian federalism. Moreover, written at a pivotal time of crisis, transformation, and reorientation, I believe these books still provide important guideposts for the understanding of Canadian federalism in general, and for my own discussion of Canadian federalism in this book in particular. In hindsight, they are also important guideposts for what they left out.

After the 1982 constitutional settlement had given recognition to "existing" Indigenous rights, the discussion of federalism and Indigenous self-government was only beginning. And while the literature on Canadian federalism I was given to read generally conveyed a perspective sympathetic to the "Quebec question," it did so from an overwhelmingly English Canadian perspective that rarely engaged

25 Thomas O. Hueglin, "Exploring Concepts of Treaty Federalism: A Comparative Perspective," paper prepared for the Royal Commission on Aboriginal Peoples, 1994.

26 James (sákéj) Youngblood Henderson, "Empowering Treaty Federalism," *Saskatchewan Law Review* 58 (1994).

27 Thomas O. Hueglin, "From Constitutional to Treaty Federalism: A Comparative Perspective," *Publius: The Journal of Federalism* 30, no. 4 (2000).

28 Richard J. Van Loon and Michael S. Whittington, *The Canadian Political System: Environment, Structure, and Process* (Toronto: McGraw-Hill Ryerson, 1984), 3, 266.

directly with its French Canadian counterpart. Two solitudes, as I found out only later, also existed in Canadian political science. I probably did not get the irony, at least not right away, when I mentioned to a member of the political studies department at Queen's that I had applied for a position at Dalhousie University in Halifax, and he approvingly informed me that Dalhousie was probably "the best Canadian university east of McGill."

It also needs to be acknowledged that with few exceptions Canadian political science – and the federalism field in particular – was at the time still firmly in the hands of white men. While David Hawkes first aroused my interest in Indigenous studies, I did not get to meet Indigenous scholars. Nor did I meet any female academics. Truth be told, when Richard Simeon sent me to Ottawa, he told me to speak to Jane Jenson and Leo Panitch (in that order). But Jenson was on sabbatical, and I did not meet her until much later.

Change was on the horizon, though. The political studies department at Queen's boasted more than a handful of exceptional female post-graduate students whose academic careers would contribute to changing the face of Canadian political science soon enough. And a decade later, Jill Vickers would throw out the question as to why women should care about federalism.[29]

What the Canadian literature on federalism left out as well was a more engaged comparative dimension. Ron Watts, who became the undisputed bedrock of comparative federal minutiae in Canada only later, was Queen's University's principal and vice-chancellor at the time, and I had little contact with him. Obsessed with the trials and tribulations of domestic conflict as they were, I got little sense of how Canadians situated themselves and their work in the larger context of a world as much in turmoil as their own. Come to think of it, I probably owed my first steps into a Canadian academic career to the fact that everybody welcomed my contributions as the "refreshing views of an outsider."

I therefore need to acknowledge the central contribution to my Canadian academic apprenticeship of another Queen's professor, Hugh Thorburn, who was not really engaged directly in the federalism field. At the time Hugh was chair of the Research Committee on Socio-Political Pluralism of the International Political Science Association. For some reason, he thought my eclectic comparative views of Canadian federalism somehow connected with a wide range of issues and problems his research group was concerned about.

29 Jill Vickers, "Why Should Women Care about Federalism?" in *Canada: The State of the Federation*, ed. Douglas M. Brown and Janet I. Hiebert (Montreal: McGill-Queen's University Press, 1994).

Through Hugh, who dragged me off to countless international conferences, I made the acquaintance, among many others, of the Polish political scientist Stanislav Ehrlich, who had a more generously pluralist vision of his home country than its current generation of political leaders; of Adolf Bibic, who still harboured dreams that some form of federalism might hold together what was then Yugoslavia; and of Jordi Solé Tura, who had been one of the seven "fathers" of the constitution that established Spain as a de facto federal democratic system in 1978 and who became a friend until his appointment as Spanish Minister of Culture made him all but inaccessible. I surely owe my developing sense of federalism in Canada to the domestic literature I read. But just as surely, I owe to the fact that Hugh Thorburn so generously introduced me to his research group, and hence to a more comparative perspective, that I think of Canadian federalism not only as a model in its own right, but moreover as one that can be instructive in a globalizing world of increasing complexity and diversity.

The other reason why I want to acknowledge this literature is that it harks back to a time when federalism in Canada commanded front-page attention, a time of an unprecedented and unrepeated combination of political conflict as well as foundational argument over the normative meaning of federalism. Through this literature, I caught the tail end of a political drama in which principal actors like Trudeau, Lougheed, and Lévesque, while following different normative scripts, nevertheless shared in common a sense of public duty and responsibility. Accompanying and reflecting on that drama, this literature conveyed to me a sense of federalism as more than just a mechanism for the allocation of powers and resources. Federalism was about first principles, justice, and fairness, and as such it was about accommodating the self-understanding of citizens as "members of both the federal and the sub-state nation simultaneously."[30] Federalism was exciting.

As is well known enough, the drama culminated in a constitutional settlement that at the time appeared acceptable as a reasonable compromise in English Canada but was rejected as outright betrayal in Quebec. Two subsequent attempts at bringing Quebec back into the constitutional fold, the 1987 Meech Lake Accord and the 1992 Charlottetown Accord, failed. Both produced more hype over process than excitement over substance. Prime Minister Brian Mulroney's infamous characterization of his approach to the process as "rolling the dice" became the drama's epitaph.

I remember sitting in front of a television with Richard Simeon listening to Mulroney's victory speech on the night of the 1984 federal election, with

30 Helder de Schutter, "Federalism as Fairness," *Journal of Political Philosophy* 19, no. 2 (2011): 168.

Richard at some point crying out in exasperation "Come on, Brian, *say* something." The torch of Canadian politics had been passed to a new generation of managers of political expediency. The *beau risque* that Lévesque took accepting Mulroney's offer of constitutional inclusion came to nothing with the Meech Lake and Charlottetown accords, not least because an always-fragile common sense of country had ever more given way to fragmented interest calculations. It is no accident that this failure coincided with the rise of neoliberalism and its deregulatory insistence on competitive self-maximization as the only – let alone rational – characteristic of human behaviour. The leading question no longer was "What is good for the country?" but instead became "What's in it for me?"

After Meech and Charlottetown, as already foreshadowed by *And No One Cheered*, a rather lugubrious assessment of the 1982 constitutional settlement edited by Banting and Simeon,[31] the wind was entirely out of the sails of federalist excitement. There were some serious aftershocks, such as the rise of two new political parties in national politics, the western-based Reform Party and the Bloc Québécois, and there was the second Quebec referendum in 1995 that almost succeeded in pushing the country over the cliff of separation.

After that, however, the governments and societies of Canada began to turn their attention from politics to policy, and this also came to be reflected in the work of a new generation of political scientists more concerned with the performance of Canadian federalism than with its foundational premises. This approach has considerably deepened the understanding of how federalism actually works and whether it provides advantages or disadvantages to efficient policymaking. In order to make a point, I may be exaggerating. As one of the most important recent books on Canadian federalism reminds us, the "performance" and "effectiveness" of federalism can never be entirely divorced from its "legitimacy."[32] But at least for the time being, there was little excitement or enthusiasm about Canadian federalism. Instead, federalism was treated in much the same way that Cairns in his contribution to *And No One Cheered* looked at the 1982 constitution, of which he said that it deserved a "restrained half cheer" at best, because "it is the only constitution we have."[33]

31 Keith Banting and Richard Simeon, eds., *And No One Cheered: Federalism, Democracy and the Constitution Act* (Toronto: Methuen, 1983).

32 Herman Bakvis and Grace Skogstad, eds., *Canadian Federalism: Performance, Effectiveness, Legitimacy*, 3rd ed. (Toronto: Oxford University Press, 2012).

33 Alan Cairns, "The Politics of Constitutional Conservatism," in Banting and Simeon, *And No One Cheered*, 55.

Interest in federalism – let alone excitement – is also largely absent for a current generation of political science students who, in the words of Keith Banting, "have never seen a real first ministers summit, never lived through the near-death of a state, never thought about what a national project might mean in the modern era, and tend to think of federalism in the narrowest of instrumental terms."[34] No longer connected to the turbulent times of federalism during the last century, these students are inevitably more interested in what they perceive as the primary reasons for their anxieties about ever-more-elusive prospects of socioeconomic stability: the forces of economic globalization, renewed international conflict, and the spectre of terrorism that can strike anywhere at any time. So they have little patience for the mundane domestic world of power disputes and intergovernmental haggling. Federalism as a defining feature of who they are as Canadians, and where they might go as a country and as a people, is almost entirely off the radar of interest and relevance.

That is unfortunate. The fundamental questions about domestic socioeconomic stability, fairness, and justice, as Garth Stevenson has pointed out with undiminished justification through five editions of *Unfulfilled Union*, "cannot be easily considered or resolved outside the federal context in which they occur."[35] If you are worried about the economy, about jobs, or about your children's education and health, you better turn your attention to how all this unfolds in the context of separate and shared powers. Canada is a federal state, and for a reason. Canada's cultural and socioeconomic diversity does not easily allow for unitary solutions.

For that reason, Canadian federalism should also be of considerable interest to those primarily interested in globalization and the conflicts that come with it as a model case of political accommodation for a larger world of multinationality, ethnic and religious diversity, and conflict. The expertise of Canadian scholars and practitioners of federalism has been sought in places as diverse and distant as South Africa, Cyprus, Ethiopia, Nepal, Sri Lanka, and Yemen. The uneasy positioning of Quebec in Canada serves as a much-studied model for Catalonia in its quest for greater autonomy within the Spanish state. This is not to say that federalism is a cure-all for the diverse conflicts in these countries and their societies, and neither does it suggest that the way in which federalism is organized and practised in Canada has been uncontested. In fact, as I will try to show in this book, contested concepts have been the main animating force of federalism in

34 Personal communication.

35 Stevenson, *Unfulfilled Union*, 2.

Canada. What I would also like to show, however, is that this is not necessarily a bad thing.

In fact, what we can discover by studying federalism in Canada is the futility of modernity's obsession with rationality and closure. From a comparative perspective, Canada has already been called the first postmodern polity,[36] an ongoing conversation in an open-ended process. Federalism can provide guidance to the conversation and structure to the process. That alone should make it exciting.

I had three goals in mind when I started writing this book. First, I wanted to get students interested in the big questions of Canadian federalism again – its history, its dramatic moments of change, and its unresolved conflicts. To this end, I tried to combine systematic inquiry with historical anecdote and, to invite discussion, judgmental commentary.

Second, I wanted to write a book that would give more attention to Quebec's view of Canadian federalism than is usually the case in the English language literature (albeit with important exceptions). To this end, I asked Luc Turgeon to organize a discussion session on the plan of the book with some Francophone colleagues at the University of Ottawa. More than half a dozen attended, and it became one of the best experiences I have ever had as an academic. In particular, I owe to François Rocher the idea of emphasizing contested concepts as the underlying dynamic of federalism in Canada. At the end of an intensive three hours of discussion, I expressed the hope that my book would become acceptable in both English Canada and Quebec. "Careful, Thomas," replied André Lecours laughingly, "you might end up writing a book that is acceptable to neither side."

Third, there had to be a serious and systematic Indigenous perspective. This turned out to be a particularly difficult task. At least until the recognition of "existing aboriginal and treaty rights" in Section 35 of the Constitution Act, 1982, Indigenous peoples were subjected to the impositions of Canadian federalism rather than given an active role in it, and it is still far from clear what role, if any, they would want to assume in the future.

It is with regard to Quebec, however, that I have to add two preliminary and personal observations. One is that before coming to Canada in 1983, I had been intuitively supportive of many European minority movements and their quests for autonomy or outright independence from cultural, religious, or, more

36 Peter Katzenstein, cited in Stephen Clarkson, "The Multi-Level State: Canada in the Semi-Periphery of both Continentalism and Globalization," *Review of International Political Economy* 8, no. 3 (September, 2001).

generally, political domination by the nation-states they were part of. The cases are well known, from Scotland and Northern Ireland to Catalonia and the Basque Country, Corsica and Southern Tyrolia. Yet when it came to Canada, while I was sympathetic to the uneasy place of Quebec in Confederation like most of the English Canadian academics and intellectuals I met, my support for Quebec independence seemed more reluctant. It took me some time to find an explanation.

In part, I subscribe to the view widely held (at least in English Canada) that Quebec would ultimately be better off as a part of the Canadian federation than as a small independent Francophone island in a North American sea of Englishness. I think that this is at least debatable. In part, however, I came to realize that Canada without Quebec was not a place I wanted to be in. Because of Quebec, Canada was, for me, a country forced to be less parochial than many other countries with monocultural inclinations, and it was a federation never allowed to ossify into institutionalized complacency. To be sure, other provinces, notably in the west, have also played their part in this drama of conflict and compromise, but usually, albeit with a few significant exceptions, it has been Quebec taking the lead.

So if Quebec has benefited from Canada in measured proportion, Canada has disproportionately benefited from Quebec, and for me that is not debatable at all. To put it differently: English Canada cannot be as parochial as the United States because of Quebec. But Quebec also cannot be a petty little nation-state because of the rest of Canada. That is the essence of Canadian federalism. And if studying Canadian federalism for 30 years has taught me anything, it is that I am also no longer as supportive of those other independence movements as I once may have been because a federal form of accommodation can provide a better way of securing what is inevitably a compromise between autonomy and interdependence.

The other observation has to do with Quebec nationalism. It is difficult for me, a member of the first generation of post-Nazi Germans, to find anything appealing about nationalism. It was anti-nationalism that made me a federalist and ardent supporter of European integration. In fact, I believe that nationalism in its modern form, with its equation of culture and territory, is essentially a modern fabrication. Medieval kings and princes did not generally care which language their subjects spoke so long as they paid taxes. It was the Industrial Revolution that demanded the monocultural homogenization of national markets in the name of economy-of-scale efficiency. Such nationalism ultimately is incompatible with federalism, which is committed to balancing particular autonomy with universal interdependence. I would concede, however, that there is a qualitative difference between majority and minority nationalism, and that the latter may be justified as long as it serves as a strategic tool of balancing or rebalancing the relationship with the majority culture rather than as an end in itself.

I am grateful to so many friends and colleagues who had to listen to me talking about this book whether they wanted to or not. I cannot possibly mention them all by name. So I won't name any, except Alan Fenna, Luc Turgeon, and Sean Mueller, who read the manuscript and made many valuable suggestions for improvement. There was also encouragement from anonymous reviewers, and patience on the part of the University of Toronto Press for me taking so long. My project outlasted no less than four editors responsible for book acquisition: Michael Harrison, Mat Buntin, Marilyn McCormack, and finally Stephen Jones. Needless to say, Leanne Rancourt proved to be a relentlessly attentive copyeditor.

Last but not least, there were my students in PO374 at Wilfrid Laurier University on whom I tried out the ideas and themes of the book. And there is the current wealth of Canadian academic literature on all things federal, which is as inspiring as were those classical tomes that I began my Canadian journey with so many years ago.

Contested Concepts as the Underlying Dynamic and Central Theme

There is conflict and compromise in all federal systems. The adoption of a federal form of government is itself the result of a compromise between the desire to create or maintain a larger political and economic union and the insistence of the constituent members of that union to retain power over what they perceive to be their own particular affairs. This division of powers between two orders of government inevitably creates friction about who has the right to do what. In all federal systems, therefore, courts play a central role in adjudicating the boundaries of power between the two orders of government, and compromise over conflicting objectives has to be achieved through intergovernmental negotiations. In Canada, however, the roots of friction and conflict go deeper. Canadians cannot even agree on who the original parties to the contract were.[37]

A foundational disagreement over the nature of sovereignty already surfaced during the Confederation debates. Had the new federal government really received all powers of a sovereign state, as John A. Macdonald claimed, or did the

37 See, in particular, Robert C. Vipond, *Liberty & Community: Canadian Federalism and the Failure of the Constitution* (Albany: State University of New York, 1991), as well as Paul Romney, "Provincial Equality, Special Status and the Compact Theory of Canadian Confederation," *Canadian Journal of Political Science* 32, no. 1 (1999).

division of power mean that sovereignty was in fact shared between two orders of government? From this disagreement sprang a first set of contested concepts about the nature of the federation: a centrist concept according to which its primary purpose was to provide all citizens with equal rights and opportunities across the country, and a decentralist concept according to which its primary purpose was to safeguard the diversity of regional communities.

A second set of contested concepts emerged when it quickly became clear that the British North America Act of 1867 had by no means succeeded in dividing powers into watertight compartments of jurisdiction. As Canada's final court of appeal at the time, the British Judicial Committee of the Privy Council, affirmed in one of its first decisions, most powers were in fact overlapping. Especially when the construction of a modern Canadian welfare state in the twentieth century intensified cooperative federalism based on inevitable interdependence between the two orders of government, adherents to a classical or coordinate form of federalism contended that governmental autonomy had to be preserved or even restored.

And finally, a third set of contested concepts indeed focused on the nature of the founding compact of the federation and its original participants. Already in the nineteenth century, and in defence of an overbearing central government, a theory surfaced according to which Confederation was the result of a compact among provinces, and the federal government their creation. Later on, when it saw French language and Catholic education under attack in provinces such as Manitoba and Ontario, Quebec countered with a theory according to which Confederation had instead been the result of a compact among two nations, English and French.

While neither theory could refer to much evidence in historical fact, both fuelled deep disagreement about the structure of the federation – either a symmetrical structure among equal provinces or an asymmetrical one with Quebec distinct from the others. Both theories also delayed the adoption of a domestic amendment formula for half a century after the British Westminster Act of 1931 had granted full sovereignty. From the perspective of the provincial compact theory, some form of super majority as in other federations would suffice for constitutional amendment so long as the formula would not put any region or province in a dominant position. From the perspective of the two-nations compact, Quebec in particular would have to retain veto power over all amendments.

The idea that the underlying dynamic of federalism in Canada has been driven by foundational disagreements and contested concepts about the meaning and operation of federalism is not new. Neither is the observation that the main – but not only – dividing line has been between English Canada and Quebec.[38] The architects of Confederation were deliberately – and perhaps inevitably – ambiguous about the compromise they struck and the character of the union they forged. What deserves more systematic attention, however, is the way in which contested concepts have permeated almost every aspect of Canadian federalism.

Organization and Outline

The book is organized around the three historical cornerstones of Canadian federalism: Confederation (Chapter 2), which first put the country on a trajectory with conflicting expectations of autonomy and interdependence; the crisis of federalism in the wake of the Great Depression (Chapter 4), which challenged the wisdom of the division of powers as originally intended; and patriation (Chapter 7), which finally brought the Canadian constitution home in its entirety by adopting a domestic amendment formula.

Chapter 1 is meant to provide a general introduction to federalism and its key characteristics in the Canadian context. Contrary to unitary states, powers in federal states are divided between two orders of government. Most importantly, this means that the exercise of sovereign power on behalf of the people is shared between these two orders of government rather than concentrated in one central authority. This in turn has two consequences: First, the division of powers as intended by the constitution must be safeguarded, interpreted, and adjudicated by constitutional or supreme courts. Second, because powers are often overlapping rather than mutually exclusive, and to avoid conflict or even litigation, the two orders of government must find compromise through meaningful and constructive intergovernmental relations.

Finally, there are two other characteristics markedly distinguishing federal states from unitary states. One is fiscal imbalance, which essentially means that federal governments raise more revenue than they need for their own programs and the member-units, to varying degrees, depend on fiscal transfers because they raise less revenue than they need for carrying out their responsibilities. The other characteristic is executive dominance at the expense of parliamentary accountability. Particularly in parliamentary federations such as Canada, executive leaders – prime ministers and provincial premiers – can make intergovernmental

38 Herman Bakvis, Gerald Baier, and Douglas Brown, *Contested Federalism: Certainty and Ambiguity in the Canadian Federation* (Toronto: Oxford University Press, 2009), esp. 17–19.

deals behind closed doors because such deals will rarely be contested by their respective legislatures as long as they are in command of a supportive majority.

Chapter 2 properly begins the systematic investigation of federalism in Canada. It examines the way in which the separate British North American colonies were brought together as a federal system, the new Dominion of Canada, under the British North America (BNA) Act of 1867. The main objective of Confederation was to construct and secure Canada as a continental economic union north of the United States. Federalism, with its constitutional division of powers, was a necessary option to accommodate French Canadian language and culture within that union. In terms of how powers were to be divided, the outcome was not much different from other federations: While trade and commerce would go to the federal government, the provinces would retain responsibility for social policy and other matters deemed "local" at the time.

However, the BNA Act deviated from the classical American model of federalism already in existence, not only by professing continued loyalty to the British Empire, but also by a number of unitary provisions overriding the federal division of powers and by the adoption, at the federal level, of a weak second chamber of regional representation that would not pose a serious threat to parliamentary supremacy. By comparison to these complex constitutional arrangements, Indigenous peoples in Canada were simply subjected to the exclusive and complete authority of the federal government.

Chapter 3 turns to judicial interpretation, because almost from the beginning of Confederation crucial debates were played out in the courts about the direction Canadian federalism should take. In the nineteenth century, the British Judicial Committee of the Privy Council (JCPC), the court of final appeal until 1949, established the overlapping nature of powers assigned to the two orders of government in the BNA Act. Responding to the provincial rights movement originating in Ontario, the JCPC's rulings contributed to a more decentralized understanding and practice of Canadian federalism than the quasi-unitary vision Sir John A. Macdonald had championed. In the twentieth century, then, responding in turn to a strengthened sense of national unity and purpose, the decisions of the Supreme Court of Canada (SCC) gave expression to a more centralist recalibration of Canadian federalism. And at the beginning of the twenty-first century, the SCC emphasized the need for intergovernmental cooperation because of the overlapping nature of powers as established by the JCPC a century and a half earlier.

Chapter 4 recounts what was a critical turning point in Canadian federalism. The Great Depression of the 1930s was a systemic crisis of capitalism, the devastating effects of which required massive state intervention for the sake of social stabilization. This crisis of capitalism turned into a crisis of federalism when it became apparent that the provinces did not have the capacity to provide necessary relief, and the federal government did not have the constitutional powers to do so. The eventual outcome of the crisis was a growing involvement of the federal government in social policy and a higher degree of interdependence between the two orders of government.

Challenged by the rise of Prairie populism in the particularly hard-hit west, federal governments dithered with an adequate response. A last-minute attempt at emulating American New Deal legislation was referred to the JCPC where it was rejected on constitutional grounds, as expected. In 1940, all governments finally agreed to a constitutional amendment transferring the responsibility for unemployment insurance to the federal level. Reporting in the same year, the Rowell-Sirois Commission went further, suggesting massive changes to the division of powers, including tax and social policy centralization, not only for the sake of immediate socioeconomic stabilization but also for ongoing Keynesian macroeconomic management. While the provinces vehemently disagreed, effective tax centralization came in the form of tax rental during World War II.

Chapter 5 turns to fiscal relations, which dominated the dynamic of Canadian federalism after World War II. By the 1950s, Quebec under the conservative-nationalist government of Maurice Duplessis had emerged as the federation's main provincial bulwark against centralization. In pointed opposition to the Rowell-Sirois Commission, Quebec's *Tremblay Report* of 1956 demanded a return to the original intentions of the BNA Act, by which it meant massive tax decentralization to secure provincial social policy sovereignty.

The eventual construction of a modern Canadian welfare state resulted from a series of compromises. The centralized tax rental regime gave way to tax sharing, with the federal government successively granting more tax room to the provinces, to the effect that Canada's provinces today can rely on a higher percentage of own revenue than do the member-units in most other federations. Cost sharing rather than policy autonomy became the default model of social policymaking, particularly so in healthcare, where conditions of national uniformity of delivery were attached to transfer payments and where federal unilateralism with regard to changes to the transfer formula remained a matter of provincial discontent. Fiscal equalization in turn became an unconditional obligation for the federal government to ensure that all Canadians have access to equitable public services. Only Indigenous peoples have remained second-class citizens under the Indian Act.

Chapter 6 gives account of the cultural as well as socioeconomic differences that have animated Canadian federalism throughout its history. Although always present at different times and to varying degrees, these differences are discussed midway through the book because they provide an important backdrop for Chapter 7 on patriation, that most dramatic moment in the history of Canadian federalism when a substantive constitutional change package was adopted without the consent of Quebec in 1982.

The distinctiveness of Quebec has, of course, always been the most significant difference among provinces and regions. The Quiet Revolution of the 1960s began a political process of constructing a modern secular Quebec in which Francophone Quebecers would enjoy equal economic opportunity and a homeland in which they could live and function in their own language. Believing that the constraints of Canadian federalism would not allow it to reach these objectives, a new party, the Parti Québécois, led by René Lévesque, began a campaign aimed at a soft version of separatism in the form of sovereignty-association.

At about the same time, discontent mounted in the west. What came to be known as *western alienation* had its roots in John A. Macdonald's first National Policy, which had relegated the west to the status of a resource-producing dependent hinterland. Fiercely opposed to Pierre Trudeau's National Energy Program, Alberta in particular went to battle with Ottawa over the control of oil and gas. A brief outburst of separatism notwithstanding, however, the west wanted in, not out, but with more respect and better representation in Ottawa, which it saw as perennially preoccupied with the accommodation of Quebec.

While the western dependency on central Canadian finance and manufacturing interests was intended as part of the Confederation design, the dependency on fiscal handouts of the Maritime provinces on Canada's eastern seaboard was an unintended if predictable consequence of Confederation and the National Policy. After an initial economic boom, market forces as intended by the National Policy were redirected toward central Canada.

The forced displacement of Indigenous peoples from their traditional lands, finally, was also an intended part of the Confederation and National Policy schemes. "Indians" had to get out of the way to make room for settlement and resource development. Formally, a numbered series of treaties were concluded. What they amounted to was massive land cessation in return for traditional hunting and fishing rights as well as promises of on-reserve education and welfare. More often than not, these promises were broken.

Chapter 7 deals with patriation, the process and outcome of finding agreement on a domestic formula for constitutional amendment, which until 1982 required formal approval by the British government. Several earlier rounds of negotiations to reach agreement had failed, mainly because of Quebec's insistence that as one of Canada's founding nations it should retain veto power over constitutional amendments. In 1980, Pierre Trudeau announced that he would take his constitutional patriation package, which also contained a charter of individual rights and freedoms, to London unilaterally, without the consent of the provinces. Eight provinces including Quebec organized resistance. They successfully intervened in London, which put Trudeau on notice that the British government might not sign off on a constitutional change package unless it came with at least a sufficient level of provincial concurrence. The Gang of Eight, as it came to be known, also produced a constitutional package of its own, which omitted a charter. And it referred to the courts the question whether Trudeau's unilateralism was constitutional. When the Supreme Court of Canada decided that even though unilateral action was not formally unconstitutional it would nevertheless violate constitutional convention, a dramatic last round of negotiations produced an agreement that Quebec was no longer part of.

As adopted and signed off by London, the Constitution Act, 1982, reflected a compromise widely criticized as giving something to everyone and not enough to anyone. Quebec lost its constitutional amendment veto, but provinces would be allowed to opt out from amendments affecting the division of powers. Trudeau got his charter, but certain provisions – such as freedom of expression – could be overridden by a notwithstanding clause that would protect provincial legislation from invalidation by the courts – such as Quebec's language laws, in particular. English and French minority language education rights for all Canadian citizens were exempt from the override but, in a concession to Quebec, they were not extended to immigrants. At the insistence of western provinces, provincial resource ownership was strengthened, but without taking away from the federal government's power to regulate – and tax – out of province transport and trade. At the insistence of Newfoundland, provinces could override labour mobility rights if their unemployment rate was above the national average. Finally, and only after massive protests, existing Indigenous and treaty rights were enshrined in the constitution, but what that meant remained rather unclear.

Chapter 8 follows the trajectory of Canadian federalism since that pivotal moment of constitutional patriation in 1982. Two attempts at bringing Quebec back into the constitutional fold, the 1987 Meech Lake Accord and the 1992 Charlottetown Accord, failed. Continuing regional discontent led to the rise of two new parties at the federal level, the western Reform Party and the Bloc Québécois. In a second referendum in 1995, Quebecers turned down separation by a mere hair's width.

During the referendum campaign, the Quebec premier, Jacques Parizeau, had threatened that the province might withdraw from Confederation unilaterally if the rest of Canada was unwilling to negotiate in the case of a positive referendum outcome. After the referendum, the federal government asked the Supreme Court of Canada whether unilateral withdrawal was constitutional. The court ruled that it was not, but it also held that the rest of Canada had an obligation to negotiate if there was a clear majority on a clear question in favour of separation. Yet it did not specify what it meant by "clear question" or "clear majority." The federal government responded by crafting a so-called Clarity Act, which also avoided answering these questions and instead proclaimed that it would be up to the federal legislature to decide whether it considered a proposed referendum question clear and what it would accept as a clear majority.

Canadians' appetite for constitutional politics faded, and the fortunes of the two separatist party formations, the provincial Parti Québécois, and the federal Bloc Québécois, with it. Political attention turned to the economy, to policy, and with it to fiscal relations. After the federal government's unilateral cuts to transfer payments in 1995, the Social Union Framework Agreement of 1999 was meant to improve intergovernmental dialogue, transparency, and cooperation. In 2003, the Liberal Quebec government of Jean Charest initiated the formation of the Council of the Federation, which institutionalized biannual provincial premiers' conferences with the main objective to reach common positions in negotiations with the federal government.

By comparison, First Ministers' Conferences or Meetings with the prime minister continued to lack institutionalization and regularity. After the western Conservative Prime Minister Stephen Harper took office in 2006, these conferences or meetings, which had played a central role in Canadian federalism throughout most of the twentieth century, were all but discontinued. Harper's intention was to return Canadian federalism to what he thought was its classical form: Each order of government should discharge its responsibilities separately, without interference from the other. The provinces should have a voice in federal politics via a properly elected senate, and if that was not possible, the senate should be abolished altogether. However, formal senate reform as well as outright abolition turned out to be politically impossible under the existing constitutional amendment rules. It remains to be seen whether the informal changes made by Harper's successor, Liberal Prime Minister Justin Trudeau, such as non-partisan senate appointments and non-partisan status of newly appointed senators as independent senators, will result in significant changes to the operation and legitimacy of Canada's second legislative chamber.

Finally, as evidenced by a growing number of land claim agreements, the constitutional recognition of their existing and treaty rights significantly strengthened the position of Indigenous peoples vis-à-vis the governments of Canada. There is now also an acknowledgement that these rights include an inherent right to self-government. Yet again, it remains unclear what this might amount to in the future: Will it include municipality-like status with a limited range of delegated powers, which would not release Indigenous peoples from subordination to federal and provincial law? Or status as a third tier of government with a full range of province-like powers, as envisaged by the Royal Commission on Aboriginal Peoples?

The chapter ends with a brief reflection on a question and answer that would, however, go beyond the scope of this book. This is the question of whether the provincial and territorial boundaries created in the nineteenth century are still appropriate containers of regional identity in the twenty-first century. This question also includes a further question, which is whether unitary governance within provinces and territories adequately reflects a growing south–north, urban–rural divide.

Chapter 9 brings the book to conclusion by reflecting on the conceptual disagreements that have almost perpetually accompanied federalism in Canada. Three of these will be disregarded as either no longer relevant or unhelpful. No longer relevant in particular is the question of whether or not Canadian federalism is centrist in nature, with all powers of sovereignty ultimately emanating from the federal government. If this was John A. Macdonald's idea of faux federalism, then it was already put to rest by the provincial rights movement in the nineteenth century. Also no longer relevant is a debate that animated the deep rivalry between Pierre Trudeau and René Lévesque: whether Canada is a liberal society of individuals, or a community of communities. In a federal system, these are not mutually exclusive concepts. Finally, we put aside the question of whether or not Canada ought to be seen as a multinational federation. Even though multinationalism has gained prominence as a descriptor of culturally diverse societies in recent times, it is ultimately not a helpful concept, not only because it can too easily come with undertones of an exclusive identity that is incompatible with federalism, but also because it has remained a largely theoretical concept with little impact on the actual understanding and functioning of Canadian federalism.

Two other debates that have animated Canadian federalism almost from the beginning, however, are not irrelevant. One is the debate about whether Canada's founding act was a compact among provinces or a compact among two nations. While neither one of these founding assumptions is based on historical fact, both are nevertheless powerful constructs with profoundly different – symmetrical versus asymmetrical – implications for the nature of Canadian federalism. The other debate is about whether Canada should operate as a classical federation, maximizing the autonomy of each order of government, or should embrace cooperation and interdependence as inevitable characteristics of modern governance.

The chapter ends with a critical reflection on treaty federalism, the quintessential form of consent-based Indigenous council governance. As the Royal Commission on Aboriginal Peoples affirmed, the concept of treaty federalism gives expression to a nation-to-nation relationship of Indigenous peoples with the Canadian settler societies.

Chapter One

An Introductory Understanding of Canadian Federalism

Judging by the book titles their academics write, Canadians are not exactly in love with federalism: "unfulfilled union," "divided loyalties," "no one cheered," "Canada in question," "conflict and unity," "constitutional odyssey," "contested federalism" – the list could go on. The point is that these books do not just examine critically Canada's political system as good academic books on the subject should, but that they specifically focus on Canada's federal system as the root cause of discontent. By comparison, Americans simply consider federalism as an uncontested part of their political system.

Part of the Canadian discontent with federalism obviously stems from its inability to reconcile Quebec with the rest of the country so that the (mostly) Francophone province might be reassured that its status as a "distinct society" is not in jeopardy without, however, alienating the (mostly) Anglophone rest of the country in its insistence on the equality of all provinces. But as I want to suggest, a lot of it also has to do with Canadians' understanding of federalism itself, which is likely based on the American model of constitutional federalism with a strong federal government and weak mechanisms of intergovernmental relations. From that narrow comparative vantage point, then, a critical evaluation of Canadian federalism may quickly be reduced to the question of whether the federal government in Ottawa is too powerful or not powerful enough, and the almost constant intergovernmental bickering in Canada must almost inevitably appear to be a systemic defect. In this introductory chapter, therefore, I want to provide an understanding of Canadian federalism from a wider historical, comparative, and systematic perspective that also includes considerations of how federal systems differ from unitary states.

There are about as many definitions of federalism as there are federal systems, but what they all have in common is that in sharp contrast to unitary systems, there is a division of powers between different orders of government. The rationale for this division of powers is to combine autonomy exercised by regional governments in matters considered to be their own affairs with general authority exercised by a central government for purposes considered common to all. As elaborated more extensively elsewhere,[1] this division of powers has a number of institutional, procedural, and normative consequences:

- *Because the division of powers is part of a foundational agreement, it must be underwritten by constitutional guarantees and safeguarded by a supreme constitutional court.* Neither order of government ought to be able to take powers away from the other. This is obviously different from unitary systems such as Britain or France, where all power rests with one government only. It is also different from decentralization, the delegation of self-governing powers to lower levels of government. Such powers are granted by the central government, but they are not constitutionally guaranteed, and they can be revoked.
- *Because central powers create the general framework in which regional governments operate, dual representation in a bicameral legislature should give them a voice in central law making.* This was the great American compromise in 1787: proportional representation of the entire population in a first or parliamentary chamber, and equal representation of the states as constituent entities in a second chamber or senate. It is far from clear, however, whether regional governments have gained a meaningful voice in second chambers unless, that is, their representatives are firmly instructed government delegates, as is the case only in Germany and a few other federal systems. There are some unitary political systems with second or upper legislative chambers, such as Britain with its House of

1 Thomas O. Hueglin and Alan Fenna, *Comparative Federalism: A Systematic Inquiry* (Toronto: University of Toronto Press, 2015).

Lords, but the primary purpose of these chambers is not one of regional representation.

- *Because divided powers typically are exercised in overlapping or even shared jurisdictional spaces, the operation of federal systems requires negotiated compromise by means of intergovernmental relations.* This is what most designers of federal systems overlooked. Given the complexity of modern governance, both orders of government today are active in virtually all policy fields. The extent to which they may infringe upon each other's powers in doing so is the subject matter of intergovernmental tension and conflict. The dynamic of federal systems is thus animated by the question of what constitutes a meaningful balance between central and regional powers – a question obviously absent in unitary systems.
- *Because federalism is at its core an agreement among equal members to share common resources fairly and for the benefit of all, all governments in a federal system have an obligation to act in the spirit of federal comity and social solidarity.* Federal comity means that all governments in a federal system ought to act in a pro-federal manner respectful of each other's rights, interests, and needs. Social solidarity in turn means that the governments of all member-units must be able to provide their citizens with equitable living conditions across the federation without which the commitment to equality would be meaningless. Federal systems are in this way characterized by a social relationship among territorial collectivities. In unitary systems, the paramount relationship is between individual citizens and the state.

Federalism is more than just a form of divided or multilevel governance. Autonomy, membership equality, and social solidarity are normative principles. As we shall see in the following sections, the combination of political form and underlying normative principles make political life in federal systems more complicated, and often more contentious, than in unitary systems.

Shared Sovereignty

The purpose of democratic politics, we might say, is liberty for all. Liberty in a civilized and organized polity, however, as the great French philosopher of law Montesquieu cautioned, is limited "to the right to do everything that the laws permit."[2] In a modern unitary democratic state, the carriers of such liberty are individual citizens with individual rights and obligations. They elect a representative government that is accountable to them and makes legislative decisions by majority vote. As the owners of all rights, the people are the sovereign, and parliament holds supreme power on their behalf. This understanding of modern government had its beginnings with John Locke, who famously wrote:

> When any number of men have so consented to make one community or government, they are thereby presently incorporated, and make one body politick, wherein the majority have a right to act and conclude the rest.[3]

"Any number of men" at the time would include only male, tax-paying property owners, and the Scottish, Welsh, and Irish were not asked for their consent to begin with. Yet Locke's formulation became the template for what we know today as the British Westminster model of representative parliamentary democracy. It eventually became the template of democratic aspiration for modern state formation almost everywhere, including the remaining colonies of British North America after the Americans had gone their own way in 1776.

The problem for the creation of a "body politick" in the part of British North America known as Canada was that "any number of men" spoke two different languages, English and French. And the French had no intention of consenting to the making of "one community," let alone succumbing to majority rule, since if the English did not outnumber them quite yet, it was perfectly clear they soon would. They also had not forgotten that they had become part of Canada not by consent but by conquest, and they had likewise not forgotten that it had been suggested only a few years earlier, by Lord Durham in his famous report of 1839, that the best way of dealing with French Canadians was rigorous assimilation.[4] They still will not forget, which is why "*Je me souviens*," "I remember," can be read on the licence plate of every car registered in Quebec.

Here we have it, then, the entire "question of Quebec" in a nutshell. The historical answer to that question was federalism as pioneered and already

2 Montesquieu, *The Spirit of the Laws* (1748; Cambridge: Cambridge University Press, 1989), IX: 3.

3 John Locke, *Second Treatise of Government* (1690; Indianapolis: Hacket, 1980), VIII: 95.

4 Gerald M. Craig, ed., *Lord Durham's Report* (1839; Toronto: McClelland and Stewart, 1963), esp. 146–52.

practised in the neighbouring United States. What federalism meant in principle was that there would be two sets of constitutionally guaranteed rights: one for the union government to be exercised on behalf of all citizens and one for the constituent member-units of the union to be exercised on behalf of their respective citizenries. Two sets of rights, or powers in the hands of those exercising them, make federal systems dramatically different from unitary ones. Two sets of powers over the same territory raise the question of sovereignty. In order to understand this, we need to turn back to the history of political thought for a moment.

In the English-speaking world, the modern history of the idea of sovereignty begins with Thomas Hobbes. Observing from exile in France the English civil war between king and parliament, a war as much over religion (Anglicans versus Puritans) as over economic advantage (monopolists versus free traders),[5] Hobbes categorically declared "a Kingdome divided in it selfe cannot stand."[6] If England was to return to peace and stability, the traditional regime of power sharing between king and parliament had to be ended. There could only be one supreme power, and Hobbes ultimately did not care whether it was to be a sovereign king or a sovereign parliament.

In England, parliament prevailed. The so-called Glorious Revolution of 1688 for the first time established a constitutional monarchy in which the king still had some prerogatives but no one disputed any longer the supremacy of parliament. The king could rule, but he could do so only with laws made by parliament. As pre-formulated by Locke (see above), this was the beginning of a process at the end of which the undivided powers of sovereignty would be assigned to an elected representative body.

We can now see better the singular importance that the issue of sovereignty and its history played when the first modern federal states were designed, first by the Americans and then by the Canadians, both of whom were keenly aware of this history. Both also subscribed in principle to eminent British jurist William Blackstone's definition of indivisible sovereignty at the time as "a supreme, irresistible, absolute, uncontrolled authority, in which ... the rights of sovereignty reside."[7] In a unitary state, such a definition seemed logical: one territory, (the presumption of) one people, one power of government. But the

5 See Christopher Hill, *The Century of Revolution 1603–1714* (New York: Norton, 1982).

6 Thomas Hobbes, *Leviathan* (1651; Cambridge: Cambridge University Press, 1992), Chapter 18 [92].

7 Cited in Robert C. Vipond, *Liberty & Community: Canadian Federalism and the Failure of the Constitution* (Albany: State University of New York Press, 1991), 23.

definition obviously was much more difficult to reconcile with a federal system in which constitutionally guaranteed powers were to be divided between two orders of government.

In fact, it could not be reconciled at all. As Robert Vipond's analysis has shown, both the Americans and the Canadians sought to circumvent the problem by separating the ownership of sovereignty from its exercise.[8] The Americans grandly ascribed the rights of sovereignty to "we the people," and were then free to construct a complex form of government with multiple checks and balances horizontally between the branches of government and vertically between the two levels of government, the main purpose of which was, as James Madison explained, to make the use of these rights through straightforward majority rule all but impossible.[9] The Canadians in turn suggested that the rights of sovereignty would ultimately remain with the imperial parliament in London. In this way, they could then divide powers between a federal government in charge of building economic union and provincial governments, which, in the case of Quebec, would retain cultural autonomy.

The separation of the ownership of sovereignty from its exercise did not resolve anything. The real question was who, in the case of difference of opinion or open conflict between national and subnational governments, would be able to exercise "supreme, irresistible, absolute, uncontrolled authority"? In the United States, that question eventually was carried into the battlefield. A devastating civil war raged for four years (1861–5). The seceding southern states claiming sovereignty were defeated, and the political language changed from "the United States of America *are*" to "the United States of America *is*."

The Canadian Confederation debates of the 1860s were overshadowed by the events south of the border. For John A. Macdonald, therefore, conservative nation-builder-in-chief and future first prime minister, it was very clear where irresistible power had to be located. Any possibility of "separate sovereignties" had to be avoided. "We have given the general legislature," he declared, "all the powers which are incidental to sovereignty."[10] Nobody was quite sure exactly what that meant, though. For George Brown, leader of the liberal Reform Party in Ontario, it meant that the federal parliament no longer had to deal with "hostile feelings" arising from "sectional questions,"[11] by which he essentially meant

8 Ibid., 27–36.

9 Alexander Hamilton, John Jay, and James Madison, *The Federalist* (1787–8; Indianapolis: Liberty Fund, 2001), No. 51.

10 Janet Ajzenstat et al., eds., *Canada's Founding Debates* (Toronto: Stoddart, 1999), 282–3.

11 Ibid., 289.

that Quebec from now on would have to look after its own financial affairs. George-Étienne Cartier, Macdonald's conservative counterpart in Quebec, vaguely suggested that "on account of the variety of races, local interests, etc., … the federation system … would be found to work well."[12] Only the leader of the more radically liberal Parti Rouge in Quebec, Antoine-Aimé Dorion, gave sharp expression to what he thought it meant and to what has been Quebec's contention ever since: The federal parliament "will have sovereign power, and can do all that it pleases, and may encroach upon all the rights and attributes of the local governments whenever it may think proper."[13]

But it was Cartier's conservative Quebec colleague Joseph Cauchon who enunciated most clearly what sovereignty in a federal system of divided jurisdiction really meant and what Quebec has been insisting on ever since: If sovereignty existed,

> it must be in the constitution. If it is not to be found there, it is because it does not exist … There will be no absolute sovereign power, each legislature having its distinct and independent attributes … The federal parliament will have legislative sovereign power in all questions submitted to its control in the constitution. So also the local legislatures will be sovereign in all matters which are specifically assigned to them.[14]

This is indeed a succinct formulation of the key characteristic that makes federal states fundamentally different from unitary states. But it still does not provide an answer to the question of ultimate authority in the case of disagreement or conflict. In principle, there is no answer to that question. Within the realm of their constitutionally guaranteed powers, the two orders of government are expected to operate side by side, in dual or coordinate fashion, neither interfering with the other. Macdonald even went so far as to suggest that "conflict of jurisdiction and authority" could be avoided altogether.[15]

In practice, such conflicts would arise all too soon. Federal systems had to develop ways to deal with them. As I shall discuss in the following two sections,

---

12 Ibid., 285.

13 Ibid., 311.

14 Ibid., 312; Cauchon's speech is more fully cited in John T. Saywell, *The Lawmakers: Judicial Power and the Shaping of Canadian Federalism* (Toronto: University of Toronto Press, 2002), 8.

15 Ajzenstat et al., *Canada's Founding Debates*, 283.

conflicting matters could be referred to the courts, which would then decide in favour of one or the other order of government. Or, in order to avoid court action, matters could be settled through negotiated intergovernmental compromise and agreement.

Power of the Courts

All democratic political systems based on the rule of law have an independent court system for purposes of civil litigation, criminal justice, and the protection of individual rights. Most also have constitutional courts that can invalidate laws and regulations if they are deemed unconstitutional. What is very different from unitary systems again, however, is that one of the main tasks of constitutional courts in federal systems is to safeguard the division of powers. And since operation as well as legitimacy of federal systems are essentially grounded in the constitutional guarantees of the powers given to each order of government, supreme or constitutional courts play such a central role in these systems that one of the first competent observers of the new federations created in North America, the British jurist and constitutional theorist A.V. Dicey, summed up his assessment by declaring "federalism … means legalism."[16]

It is not all too surprising that this is what struck Dicey as one of the key characteristics of federalism. At the time, Britain had neither a written constitution (and still does not have one today) nor a judicial body that could have challenged the supremacy of the British parliament (a constitutional court was only established in 2005, but it still cannot invalidate legislative acts of parliament). Yet the United States had a Supreme Court, which had long since established itself as a powerful arbiter and adjudicator of American federalism, and there was also a steady stream of Canadians appearing before the Judicial Committee of the Privy Council (JCPC) in London asking to have their constitutional disputes settled.

This needs some explanation. The JCPC was – and still is[17] – a group of so-called Law Lords serving as court of final appeal for the British Empire's colonial territories. Canada's first constitution, the British North America Act of 1867, was in fact not the constitution of an independent country but a statute of British parliament (that would change with the Statute of Westminster in 1931). Hence

16 A.V. Dicey, *An Introduction to the Study of the Law of the Constitution* (1885; London: Macmillan, 1915), 170.

17 See the JCPC's home page at https://www.jcpc.uk.

it was quite obvious to the Canadians that constitutional disputes would also be adjudicated by the JCPC (that would change even later, in 1949).

During the Confederation debates, the Canadians appeared as oblivious to the enormous impact the courts could have and would have on their federal system as the Americans had been – despite the fact that the example of a powerful US Supreme Court was already before their eyes. The main reason for this negligence was probably that the main parties really thought they had gotten what they wanted: on the one hand, a strong central government for national purposes that would reverse, as Macdonald expounded time and again, the American mistake of empowering the provinces with too many rights, yet on the other hand provincial self-rule in local matters as required.

As pointed out by almost every historical account of Confederation, there was surprisingly little debate about the actual division of powers.[18] What is more, the Canadians had little fear that disputes would lead to disunion and open conflict as had happened south of the border. As the colonial union with Britain would not be severed, there was trust that such disputes, should they arise at all, would be settled to everybody's satisfaction by the imperial government. Only Antoine-Aimé Dorion darkly mused that complaints of Lower Canada (Quebec) probably would not be served well that way.[19]

Both the Americans and the Canadians understood full well that in a political system based on constitutionally divided jurisdiction there had to be some dispute-settling mechanism, and that this function would obviously have to be played by a high court of last appeal capable of rendering a final decision. Both did not quite anticipate the central role these high courts would play in co-determining the direction their federations would take. There was – and still is – also a significant difference, though.

Breaking away from Britain and its doctrine of parliamentary supremacy, the Americans invented a new system of government constructed on multiple checks and balances in which the judiciary would simply be one branch of government alongside others. Rarely would the legitimacy of the judiciary and its Supreme Court be questioned as a matter of principle. Not so in Canada, which sought to retain the principle of parliamentary supremacy within a federal system, despite Cauchon's early clarification to the contrary. The contradiction between a sovereign parliament and a tribunal that could declare acts of this parliament invalid remained somewhat camouflaged by the fact that that tribunal was the JCPC,

18 Saywell, *The Lawmakers*, 6.

19 Ajzenstat et al., *Canada's Founding Debates*, 311.

composed of members of the House of Lords and therefore part of the imperial parliament. The imperial parliament hence could be thought of as delegating some of its sovereignty to the federal and provincial parliaments of Canada while reserving ultimate judgment about the proper use of it. But especially since the Supreme Court of Canada became the homegrown adjudicator of all constitutional disputes in 1949, a tension has lingered between the conflicting concepts of parliamentary and judicial supremacy.

This tension can still be discerned. During his tenure, Conservative Canadian Prime Minister Stephen Harper suffered a rather spectacular string of Supreme Court losses. The court told him, for instance, that he could not unilaterally establish a national securities regulator in 2011, and the court declared ineligible his choice of a Supreme Court judge in 2014. At that point, Harper appeared to insinuate that the court's chief justice, Beverley McLachlin, somehow had interfered inappropriately in the process. Harper was reprimanded and urged to apologize by an international commission of jurists. One might well question why the prime minister picked a fight he could not possibly win. But he was undeniably driven by a certain righteousness deeply ingrained in the Canadian political DNA: How can it be that appointed judges can infringe upon the political will of elected parliamentarians?

The same righteousness also explains the long-standing opposition of the provinces to the Charter of Rights and Freedoms, which was added to the constitutional fabric of Canada in 1982. By protecting universal rights of individuals and minority groups, the Charter would further constrain provincial parliamentary sovereignty, the unimpeded right under the constitution to pass legislation deemed to be in the collective interest of a province, because such legislation could now be found in violation of Charter rights.

In terms of federalism, it is the constitutionally guaranteed division of powers that inevitably adds to the power of the courts because only the courts can give legal answers to what is a legal question under the constitution: Who has the power to do what? To varying degrees, all federal systems rely on the courts to resolve conflict over the boundaries of each order of government's powers. But this is not the only way of resolving conflict. As we shall see in the next section, reaching intergovernmental agreement on a compromise over how to exercise or share powers is another.

Sunny Ways of Compromise

As programmatically announced in his 2007 throne speech, Harper intended to practice a classical form of federalism that would respect "the constitutional jurisdiction of each order of government."[20] Behind that intention lurked two strategic considerations: After decades of what had been perceived and resented as federal meddling in provincial affairs, a return to classical federalism would particularly appeal to voters in the west and in Quebec; yet within the constitutional jurisdiction of the federal government, Harper would be free to do as he pleased. It obviously came as an irritant, then, when the Supreme Court repeatedly told him what the boundaries of that federal jurisdiction really were. Parliamentary supremacy obviously had its limits.

Intent as he was on a starkly uncommunicative form of what he called "open federalism,"[21] Harper also shunned almost entirely another key characteristic that distinguishes federal systems from unitary ones: the mostly informal practice of negotiating intergovernmental compromise for the purpose of joint policymaking. During his 10 years in office, Harper only convened two federal–provincial meetings, and both were treated as low-key emergency meetings occasioned by the 2008 world financial crisis. For more than a decade, Canadians had therefore never witnessed the spectacle of a so-called First Ministers' Conference, which had been such a prominent part of Canadian federalism during previous decades.

Canadians probably had all but forgotten about these conferences. It therefore came as a surprise to many when Justin Trudeau, who became prime minister in October 2015, almost immediately embarked on a path of intergovernmental environmental consultation and shortly thereafter took a large contingent of provincial premiers with him to the 2015 United Nations Climate Change Conference in Paris. Some even thought this was just another photo op for a prime minister, who had carried a "sunny ways" slogan around with him like a mantra during much of the electoral campaign. Critics already sharpened their knives with accusations of style over substance. Yet the "sunny ways" slogan was in fact a deliberate reference to a key component of Canadian federalism in practice.

It also was a quote. It came from one those defining moments in Canadian history, the Manitoba school crisis of 1890–6, which brought together three of the main dividing issues that would accompany Canada's trajectory through time:

---

20 Michael Behiels and Robert Talbot, "Stephen Harper and Canadian Federalism: Theory and Practice 1987–2011," in *Challenges for Canadian Federalism*, ed. Michael Behiels and François Rocher (Ottawa: Invenire Books, 2011), 55.

21 See Institute of Intergovernmental Relations, *Open Federalism: Interpretations, Significance* (Kingston: Institute of Intergovernmental Relations, 2006).

religion, culture, and language. It also marked the beginning of the way in which Canadians would proverbially and perennially deal with these issues: "as much as possible under the circumstances."

The province of Manitoba had become Canada's fifth province by a federal act of parliament, the Manitoba Act of 1870. At the time Manitoba was culturally divided between two groups of roughly equal size: the French-speaking Métis people of mixed European and Indigenous ancestry and English-speaking immigrant settlers. As the BNA Act had already done in Section 93(4) for then-existing provinces in 1867, the Manitoba Act sought to protect minority education. In order to guarantee the continuation of two separate school systems in the province, one English and Protestant, the other French and Catholic, it stipulated in Section 22(3) that the "Parliament of Canada may make remedial Laws" in case provincial legislation would "prejudicially affect any right or privilege with respect to Denominational Schools."[22] In 1890, with the English having become the overwhelming majority, the province first abolished French as one of its two official languages and then replaced the dual denominational school system with one system, public and English. The introduction of remedial legislation to restore Francophone education in the province bitterly divided the governing conservatives in Ottawa, and the 1896 federal election was fought over this issue. The Liberal opposition leader Wilfrid Laurier avoided taking a firm stand. But he did distance himself from the confrontational approach of coercing the province into submission by means of imposed remedial legislation, suggesting instead that he would prefer the "sunny way" of reaching an agreement with Manitoba.

Laurier won the election and then negotiated a compromise, the principle of which became a staple of Canadian language policy ever since: Catholic education in the French language would be made available school by school where numbers warranted. In doing so, Laurier also firmly established a tradition of intergovernmental bargaining and compromise as an alternative to the judicial settlement of disputes. Such intergovernmental bargaining over policy issues is that other characteristic that distinguishes (most) federal systems from unitary ones. A government in a unitary state that holds undivided authority obviously does not have to bargain.

In order to understand the central importance of intergovernmental relations in federal systems, we might think of the federal dynamic as a combination

22 Manitoba Act, 1870, available at https://www.solon.org/Constitutions/Canada/English/ma_1870.html.

of "autonomy and interdependence."[23] There will be areas in all federal systems where the different orders of government can operate autonomously, and there will inevitably be areas where their powers will overlap, intersect, or even contradict each other. Just take the already mentioned example of Justin Trudeau's environmental policy initiative. One can surely make a case for "federal power over the environment as a matter of national concern," as the Supreme Court did in 1988 with reference to the "peace, order, and good government clause."[24] But the provinces own natural resources and are autonomous under "property and civil rights" to regulate the industry.

In order to get anything done at all, this interdependence requires cooperation, compromise, and ultimately agreement on some sort of balance of interests. Neither the Americans nor the Canadians foresaw the need for such cooperation. Both thought they had divided spheres of jurisdiction cleanly. Each order of government would discharge its responsibilities separately. If at all, cooperation would happen in the bicameral legislature where legislative action on national projects common to all would require approval in the second and regional chamber.

Hindsight is always easier. American framers and Canadian founders perhaps might have anticipated that legislative participation of second chambers would be driven by political expediency and partisanship rather than collective representation of regional concerns. But when they designed the division of powers in the eighteenth and nineteenth centuries, they could not possibly capture the complexities of modern governance in the twentieth and twenty-first. As already mentioned, the different orders of government in federal systems today are simultaneously active in almost all major policy fields. The only alternative to leaving the resolution of conflicts to the courts is to work out some sort of compromise of power sharing or joint policymaking by means of intergovernmental agreement.

The classic Canadian example is healthcare, entirely in the provincial power domain but as per intergovernmental agreement since 1957 co-financed by the federal government in return for provincial compliance with certain national performance standards. The compromise at the time was that the federal government could use its superior fiscal capacity to demonstrate national leadership in

23 François Rocher, "The Quebec-Canada Dynamic or the Negation of the Ideal of Federalism," in *Contemporary Canadian Federalism*, ed. Alain-G. Gagnon (Toronto: University of Toronto Press, 2012), 98.

24 Gerald Baier, "The Courts, the Constitution, and Dispute Resolution," in *Canadian Federalism: Performance, Effectiveness, and Legitimacy*, eds. Herman Bakvis and Grace Skogstad (Toronto: Oxford University Press, 2012), 82.

a policy field all Canadians cared about strongly, and the provinces received the funds needed to deliver provincial health plans. Of course, as François Rocher reminds us, compromise and agreement or consent are innocuous words behind which lurk power relations not always driven by a commitment to balance or federal comity.[25] In this way, what is "flexible adjustment" to some[26] appears as coercive "imposition" to others.[27]

The point is, however, that there is no way around government interdependence in modern federal systems, and intergovernmental cooperation and compromise are therefore unavoidable. Agreements resulting from such cooperation are a bit like international treaties in that they are not bound by a fixed constitutional framework, and governments operate in a quasi-sovereign space. This is why Richard Simeon called intergovernmental relations "federal-provincial diplomacy."[28]

In order to understand the role intergovernmental relations play in Canadian federalism, it is useful to distinguish two types of federalisms, which in the real world of federations exist side by side on a continuum: classical or constitutional federalism and procedural or treaty federalism.[29] Constitutional federalism primarily relies on a strict division of powers: The two orders of government discharge their responsibilities separately, there is only limited recourse to intergovernmental relations and compromise, and power conflicts are decided by the courts. Procedural federalism in turn, prominently relies on intergovernmental relations to avoid conflict and find solutions by working around the constitutional division of powers through power-sharing agreements and compromise. While the United States provides the purest case of constitutional federalism, we can for now think of Canada as a mixed type of constitutional as well as procedural federalism. Most Canadians would probably agree. Autonomy and interdependence

25 Rocher, "The Quebec-Canada Dynamic," 96–7.

26 Jörg Broschek, "Historical Institutionalism and the Varieties of Federalism in Germany and Canada," *Publius: The Journal of Federalism* 42, no. 4 (2012): 682.

27 Alain-G. Gagnon, "Federal-Provincial and Intergovernmental Relations in Canada," in Gagnon, *Contemporary Canadian Federalism*, 251–2.

28 Richard Simeon, *Federal-Provincial Diplomacy: The Making of Recent Policy in Canada* (Toronto: University of Toronto Press, 2006).

29 See Thomas O. Hueglin, "Comparing Federalisms: Variations or Distinct Models?" in *Federal Dynamics: Continuity, Change, and the Varieties of Federalism*, eds. Arthur Benz and Jörg Broschek (Oxford: Oxford University Press, 2013).

remain contested concepts, however, insofar as there is disagreement over where the balance should be struck.

Fiscal Imbalance

In a unitary state, taxes are collected and then spent on various policy programs as the government of the day sees fit. As the members of every private household do with their credit cards, governments may also borrow and thus spend money they do not really have. Or they may run a surplus by spending less than the annual revenue available to them, thus saving for a rainy day or paying back an already existing debt. Whatever they do, however, will be their undivided responsibility. When in financial disarray, the governments in unitary states have only themselves to blame.

In federal systems, by comparison, all these financial activities will be undertaken by two orders of government. Formally, federal constitutions circumscribe what kind of revenue governments can raise in the form of taxes and on what they can spend it within the range of powers under their jurisdiction. In reality, however, powers to tax and powers to spend are more often overlapping rather than mutually exclusive. And since all governments want to have a reputation of keeping taxes low while generously spending on the programs their electorates want or have come to rely on, "the real distribution of power among governments is in significant measure determined by the complex processes of fiscal relations among governments."[30] Fiscal federalism – in other words, the way public finances are allocated and managed in a federal system – is what much of federalism amounts to in practice. It is also the most problematic aspect of federalism. What is problematic is fiscal imbalance. It has a vertical and a horizontal dimension.[31]

Vertical fiscal imbalance simply means that subnational governments never seem to have enough money for the delivery of the policy programs under their jurisdiction, and they therefore depend on fiscal transfers from the national or

---

30 Richard J. Van Loon and Michael S. Whittington, *The Canadian Political System: Environment, Structure and Process*, 3rd ed. (Toronto: McGraw-Hill Ryerson, 1984), 266–7.

31 See Anwar Shah, "Introduction: Principles of Fiscal Federalism," in *The Practice of Fiscal Federalism: Comparative Perspectives*, ed. Anwar Shah (Montreal: McGill-Queen's University Press, 2007), 3–42. Public finance theory is more complicated and distinguishes between fiscal gaps and imbalances, for instance. For the purpose of this introduction, I am using *imbalance* in a more general political sense.

federal government, which always seems to have more money that it needs for its own programs. There are reasons for this. One is that some of today's largest sources of revenue, income and corporate tax, typically were first introduced at the federal or national level, and federal governments thus took control of the lion's share of overall revenue. Another and complementary reason is that with the rise of the modern welfare state in the second half of the twentieth century, the social programs that had been left under subnational jurisdiction became the most expensive of all government programs.

In principle, there should be a number of equally simple remedies for this imbalance. One option is to formally transfer jurisdiction for expensive social programs to the federal government. Short of that, the two orders of government can reversely agree to readjust tax powers so that each ends up raising revenue in proportion to its program needs. Or everything can be left as is, and the federal government will simply fork over a chunk of what is presumably national surplus revenue to the subnational governments. And finally, both orders of government can enter into cost-sharing agreements. In this instance, social program jurisdiction remains with the subnational governments, but the federal government, by co-financing it (possibly in return for compliance with certain national standards), will get some political mileage out of it for itself.

In practice, all of these options affect the real distribution of power in federal systems, which is why fiscal federalism is so problematic and contentious to begin with. One would think it is less so in Canada, which has been called a "textbook best-practice system of fiscal federalism."[32] Canada is one of the few federations where the federal government collects less than half of all revenue and federal transfers on average amount to less than a fifth of provincial budgets.[33] Yet the basic fact of vertical imbalance has not gone away, and neither have provincial complaints about the federal government's use of its superior spending powers.

As famously defined by Canadian Prime Minister Pierre Elliott Trudeau, the federal spending power is the "power of Parliament to make payments to people or institutions or governments for purposes on which it (Parliament) does not necessarily have the power to legislate."[34] This is by no means as unproblematic as

32 Robin Boadway, "Canada," in Shah, *Practice of Fiscal Federalism*, 99.

33 Daniel Béland and André Lecours, "Canada's Equalization Policy in Comparative Perspective," *IRPP Insight* 9 (2016): 3.

34 Pierre Elliot Trudeau, *Federal-Provincial Grants and the Spending Power of Parliament* (Ottawa: Government of Canada Working Paper on the Constitution, 1969), 4.

it sounds because such payments can also be made in areas of exclusive provincial jurisdiction. The unconstrained power to spend, in other words, is considered to be different from the constitutionally constrained powers to legislate.

By far the most important use of the federal spending power is for cost sharing of expensive programs under provincial jurisdiction, such as healthcare and social assistance. But apart from these intergovernmental fiscal transfers, the federal government also makes regular payments to individuals, businesses, organizations, and institutions. Trudeau's working paper from 1969 listed close to 100 spending programs of this kind, such as for hospital construction, student loans, flood control, urban renewal, regional development, and assistance to industry.[35]

The complaints are mainly twofold. From a perspective of constitutional federalism, federal government spending in areas of provincial jurisdiction violates the principle of subnational autonomy. By spending in these areas, the federal government creates a presence for itself that blurs lines of responsibility and accountability. If transfers come with conditional strings attached, the federal government can even influence public policy in a way that may undermine whatever plans the provinces might have had themselves in terms of policy development and delivery. Cash strapped and in a bind for the delivery of social programs and services, provinces will have little choice but to enter into cost-sharing agreements.

From a perspective of procedural federalism, the complaint is federal unilateralism. Unless they are enshrined in the constitution, fiscal transfers, even if they are based on formal agreements, are not justiciable. This means that federal governments can renege on promises or commitments. An infamous example occurred on 1995, when the Liberal government of Jean Chrétien made unilateral and "dramatic" cuts to transfer payments. The purpose of these cuts was federal budget deficit reduction, but the successful achievement of this reduction arguably came "on the backs of the provinces," which began to incur growing deficits as their social policy costs continued to increase.[36]

In one way, then, the federal spending power makes a mockery of federalism as an "unconstitutional" practice meant to "adjust the division of powers" to the federal government's advantage.[37] In another way, however, it is the inevitable

35 Ibid., 52–5.

36 See Alain Noël, "Balance and Imbalance in the Division of Financial Resources," in Gagnon, *Contemporary Canadian Federalism*, 284–5.

37 Andrée Lajoie, "Federalism in Canada: Provinces and Minorities – Same Fight," in Gagnon, *Contemporary Canadian Federalism*, 168–9.

corollary of overlapping powers in modern federal systems. Social program cost sharing, for instance, can be seen as an expression of joint responsibilities in a policy field that is no longer a particular concern of provincial governments but has taken on a universal dimension. With regard to the payments federal governments make directly to individuals or organizations, the federal government will argue that its use of the spending power is necessary in the general public interest. Obviously, it is also meant to boost its electoral chances.

Horizontal fiscal imbalance denotes unequal revenue-raising capacities across subnational jurisdictions. These may result from differences of natural resource endowment as well as uneven economic development, remoteness, and the play of market forces in the common economic union. This is a normative problem insofar as the federal idea is based on membership equality requiring social solidarity in the equitable sharing of resources. It is also a practical economic problem insofar as regional inequality weakens the common market.

Federal transfers to governments, people, and institutions can help maintain or restore at least some level of equality.[38] The problem of unequal revenue-raising capacities remains, however. Consider, for example, a classic cost-sharing program such as healthcare in Canada, which was initially established in such a way that the federal government would pay half of the cost by matching whatever the provinces spent on it. While this obviously increased revenue in poorer provinces, the problem of inequality remained, because poorer provinces had less of their own revenue to begin with and therefore received fewer matching funds.

Even before these cost-sharing programs came into existence, therefore, a fiscal equalization program was set up whereby the federal government would top up the revenue available to the poorer provinces to a certain national average. With the exception of the United States, all modern federal systems have such fiscal equalization schemes. In Canada, the federal government's obligation to equalize the provinces' fiscal disparities has been enshrined in the Constitution Act, 1982. As Section 36(2) stipulates, the objective is "to ensure that provincial governments have sufficient revenues to provide reasonably comparable levels of public services at reasonably comparable levels of taxation."

As part of the federal spending power, equalization is obviously less contentious in principle. In practice, however, conflict persists over the formula calculating what is deemed to be the per capita average revenue capacity. As with the other exercises of the federal spending power, federal governments can

38 See Michael M. Atkinson et al., *Governance and Public Policy in Canada: A View from the Provinces* (Toronto: University of Toronto Press, 2013), 89.

manipulate and adjust the formula at their discretion. By comparison, the subnational *Länder* co-determine the equalization scheme in Germany, and in Australia equalization calculations are in the hands of a semi-independent governmental commission.

Overall, as I will argue, a certain degree of vertical fiscal imbalance is a necessary component of federal systems. The imbalance makes it possible to use the federal spending power as a fiscal tool for the purpose of recycling some of the economic gains and profits that in a common economic union inevitably lead to regional inequities and asymmetries. If excessive, such inequities violate the commitment to membership equality on which the stability of a federal union rests. In practice, however, if it is not either tightly circumscribed in constitutional terms or, if this is not the case, embedded in binding intergovernmental cooperation and agreement, the federal spending power obviously can be abused for selfish political gain.

Federal systems deal with the federal spending power differently. The German constitution, for instance, under Article 104a-c, strictly regulates federal spending on matters under *Länder* jurisdiction. Moreover, such spending must be based on federal legislation, for which majority approval of the *Länder* delegates in Germany's second legislative chamber, the *Bundesrat*, is required. Federal unilateralism is all but impossible. Australia, in turn, has gone the opposite way. Section 96 of its constitution flatly states that "the Parliament may grant financial assistance to any State on such terms and conditions as the Parliament thinks fit." Federal unilateralism in the form of conditional grants is a regular occurrence.

From this comparative perspective, the main problem with the federal spending power in Canada is its lack of regulation one way or the other. In the absence of explicit constitutional intent, the courts have abstained from getting involved. As Katherine Swinton has put it: "With an unlimited power of taxation and no legal constraints placed on the spending power to date by the courts, the federal government has been able to influence public policy through tax design and, more importantly, through extensive spending in areas of provincial jurisdiction."[39]

Those who see Canada as a textbook case of fiscal federalism (see above), in other words, will focus on the revenue-raising side of the equation. Those who see it as an overly centralized mockery of federalism will point to the spending side, even though federal government spending in Canada has typically come

39 Katherine Swinton, "Federalism under Fire: The Role of the Supreme Court of Canada," *Law and Contemporary Problems* 55, no. 1 (1992): 124.

with few conditional strings attached. The main general point remains that federal systems are different from unitary ones in that the administration of public finance is embedded in an intergovernmental relationship prone to tensions and conflicts.

Executive Dominance

The previous sections were all about governments rather than parliaments or people. The dominant role that the executive branch plays in federal systems, or, as we shall see, at least in the so-called parliamentary federations, is another characteristic that distinguishes these federations from unitary states. This dominance of what is called *executive federalism* in the Canadian context is often criticized as a democratic deficit because important political decisions are based on intergovernmental deals that government leaders (the prime minister and provincial premiers in the Canadian case) make behind closed doors, and only afterwards are pushed through the legislative process by means of the majorities these leaders command in their respective parliaments. In a unitary parliamentary system, by comparison, such decisions are introduced for debate directly from the parliamentary floor. Executive federalism, in other words, raises the issue of accountability.

Let's put the issue in some historical context again. At the beginning of the nineteenth century, the colonies of British North America each had their own elected parliament, but they were governed by a lieutenant governor and his legislative council, accountable to the British Crown rather than parliament. This meant that if parliament voted down a legislative initiative, the governor and council were not bound by it. In 1837–8, rebellions broke out in the two largest colonies, Upper Canada (Ontario) and Lower Canada (Quebec), at least in part over the issue of "responsible government" – that is, the accountability of the lieutenant governor and the appointed members of his legislative and executive councils to parliament rather than the Crown. This would mean that if a legislative initiative were voted down, it died.

While the 1837–8 rebellion in Ontario was somewhat farcical, it was seriously bloody in Quebec, which is why Lord Durham was dispatched from Britain to the colonies to investigate the situation. The already mentioned Durham Report of 1839 essentially made three recommendations: fusion of the two colonies into one, assimilation of the French, and granting of responsible government. The United Province of Canada was duly created by imperial fiat with a parliament composed of an equal number of members from Ontario and Quebec, even though the Quebec population was considerably larger at the time (that was part of the assimilation plan). Responsible government had to wait another eight years.

The province limped along with a succession of unstable and short-lived coalition governments, not least occasioned by the internal factions that existed in what was now officially called Canada West (Ontario) and Canada East (Quebec). The main dividing lines ran between John A. Macdonald's conservatives and George Brown's reformers in Ontario, and between George-Étienne Cartier's conservatives (Parti Bleu) and Antoine-Aimé Dorion's radical liberals (Parti Rouge) in Quebec.

For these factions, the common parliamentary assembly of the united province was seen as frustrating rather than enabling responsible government. For their leaders, accountability meant serving the particular interests in their respective home provinces, not some compromised general will numerically computed from variable and unstable majority configurations in the united assembly. Under such circumstances, the idea of federalism offered the promise of disentanglement. George Brown, for instance, made no bones about why he joined the pro-Confederation coalition of Ontario and Quebec conservatives. Under the proposed division of powers scheme, as he stated quite unabashedly during the Confederation debates, "local patronage will be under local control."[40]

Federalism, in other words, was seen as a road to disentangled accountability. National governance would be accountable to a national parliament, and provincial governance would be accountable to provincial parliaments. It is for this reason that the rise of executive federalism came to be regarded with suspicion, not only as a re-entangling of governance with blurred lines of accountability, but also as a betrayal of the principle of responsible government, putting the powers taken away from imperial authority back into the hands of domestic executives. Unforeseen by the designers of the classical federations, this turn to executive federalism mainly happened later, during the twentieth century, when the balance between autonomy and interdependence shifted decidedly toward the latter. It also happened significantly only in the so-called parliamentary federations.

The government leaders in these parliamentary federations sit as members in parliament where they usually command a governing majority. The legislative and executive branches of government are fused. This is why prime minister and provincial premiers in Canada can conclude agreements. Under normal circumstances, there is no fear that they cannot deliver on the agreement. By comparison, in so-called presidential federations such as the United States, where the legislative and executive branches of government are strictly separated with mutual veto power, executive federalism in the form of intergovernmental

40 Ajzenstat et al., *Canada's Founding Debates*, 288.

agreements cannot really develop because the president or the state governors would not be able to assure automatically the passage of such agreements in their respective legislatures.

So what about the alleged democratic deficit? In a classical parliamentary democracy like Britain, the prime minister introduces a bill and, after some debate in parliament, maybe a little fine-tuning in committees, the bill gets passed by the prime minister's majority. Apparently, that's democratic. In a parliamentary federation, the first ministers make some policy agreement, then take it home where it gets some debate in their respective parliaments before being passed by the majorities in these parliaments. Apparently, that is a democratic problem. But what is it? The fact that the intergovernmental deal was forged behind closed doors? But all the other bills these first ministers put before their respective parliaments may also have been cooked up behind closed doors, in cabinet meetings or in the prime minister's office. One might argue with more justification that intergovernmental agreements come before parliaments as done deals – no fine-tuning, only take it or leave it. But as I would argue, the discomfort with executive federalism for the most part stems from a rather naive faith in the democratic virtues of parliamentary majority rule.[41]

That discomfort comes in various guises. Most famously in Canada, Alan Cairns once asked whether this form of federalism was not some sort of poker game in which intergovernmental political elites mould society for their purposes rather than execute the will of the people.[42] Peter Russell, in turn, likened it to a form of elite accommodation known as *consociational democracy*, a "top-down form of democracy" in which political leaders make deals with one another to paper over the deep divisions that would otherwise rip the country apart.[43] Of course, for a Quebec nationalist insisting on a relationship with the rest of the country as nation to nation, there is nothing wrong with such elite accommodation, since "negotiations between sovereign partners … should be carried out by representatives of the respective national groups."[44]

41 See Thomas O. Hueglin, "Federalism and Democracy: A Critical Reassessment," in *The Global Promise of Federalism*, eds. Grace Skogstad et al. (Toronto: University of Toronto Press, 2013).

42 Alan C. Cairns, "The Governments and Societies of Canadian Federalism," *Canadian Political Science Review* 10, no. 4 (1977).

43 Peter H. Russell, *Constitutional Odyssey: Can Canadians Become a Sovereign People?* (Toronto: University of Toronto Press, 2012), 5.

44 Alain-G. Gagnon and Raffaele Iacovino, *Federalism, Citizenship, and Quebec* (Toronto: University of Toronto Press, 2007), 177.

As I would argue again, the truth lies somewhere in the middle. On the one hand, I believe that poker games of elite accommodation can only go so far. In a representative democracy, even the most manipulative political leaders cannot govern lastingly against the will of the people. On the other hand, executive federalism is indeed a bit like international relations, where political leaders of sovereign states conclude agreements on behalf of the citizens who elected them. In federal systems, the political leaders of the partially sovereign orders of government negotiate agreements on behalf of the citizens who elected them. The analogy carries only so far, though: In a federal system, the central government negotiates on behalf of all citizens. In international relations as yet, there is no central government.

Imperfection

If one were to distill a common denominator from all the books and articles written about shared sovereignty, judicial decisionism, intergovernmental haggling, fiscal imbalance, and executive dominance in federal systems, it would likely turn out to be a generally perceived sense of systemic deficiency. More than in the case of unitary democratic systems, it seems, "performance, effectiveness, and legitimacy" of federal systems are probed and critically evaluated,[45] or even subjected to a "democratic audit."[46] Maybe only some would go as far as to see federalism as an inevitably "tragic compromise" because it brings together reluctant partners, none of which ever get exactly what they want to begin with.[47] But even when the shortcomings of federalism are not quite cast in such disillusioned fashion, there remains a lingering suspicion that decision making in federal systems cannot ever be efficient, and that to the extent it requires cooperation or even joint decision making, efficiency becomes the victim of a "joint-decision trap."[48] Measured against the ideal of the modern democratic state, at least, federalism is the political form of imperfection.

Unitary and other political systems get scrutinized and criticized as well, of course. But when it comes to federal systems, a generally negative predisposition

---

45 Bakvis and Skogstad, *Canadian Federalism*.

46 Jennifer Smith, *Federalism* (Vancouver: University of British Columbia Press, 2005).

47 Malcom Feeley and Edward L. Rubin, *Federalism: Political Identity and Tragic Compromise* (Ann Arbor: University of Michigan Press, 2008).

48 Fritz W. Scharpf, "The Joint-Decision Trap: Lessons from German Federalism and European Integration," *Public Administration* 66, no. 3 (1988).

prevails that in the case of Canada goes all the way back to John A. Macdonald, who obviously thought that federalism could not ever be more than a second-best solution to the problem of a stable and efficient political order. Before we turn to the story and history of federalism in Canada, I want to suggest that it is indeed compromise – so much a key characteristic of the intergovernmental dynamic in federal systems and so different from straightforward majority rule in unitary parliamentary systems – that accounts for the discomfort with federalism because it offends modern rationality. In order to understand this, we need to take a brief detour to the history of political thought once more.

Modern rationality aims at explaining the entire world in terms of scientific certainty. It was the French philosopher René Descartes who pre-formulated what would become the mantra for the modern rational age of certainty by declaring flat out that "there is only one truth concerning any matter."[49] Thomas Hobbes, who met Descartes in Paris, was one of the first to apply scientific rationality to human affairs and politics. Just as there would be a single general law of gravity, so there had to be a single general law of human behaviour. In a state of nature – that is, before the establishment of a civil society – Hobbes famously postulated there is "warre, as is of every man, against every man." And because of that general human disposition, there was only one solution for the organization of a peaceful civil society: a "common power to keep them all in awe."[50] Any sort of compromise between competing powers was impossible. Sovereignty had to be undivided and absolute.

Taking the cue from Hobbes, then, we might wonder whether the negative perception of federalism stems from discomfort with a form of political order that somehow does not appear civil quite yet because it is still in search of the one optimal solution to the problem of governance. To put it differently: Federalism does not satisfy the modern yearning for rational certainty. And if federalism is inevitable, then at least it should be based on "well-established constitutional rules" and not depend on informal compromises and agreements working around these rules.[51]

With its messy arrangements of shared powers, conflict, and compromise, federalism is somehow pre-modern. Taking the cue from Friedrich Nietzsche rather than Hobbes, we might reach a different conclusion: Federalism is a

---

49 René Descartes, "Discourse on the Method," in *The Philosophical Writings of Descartes*, vol. I (1637; Cambridge: Cambridge University Press, 1985), part II [21].

50 Hobbes, *Leviathan*, chapter 13 [62].

51 Gagnon and Iacovino, *Federalism, Citizenship, and Quebec*, 157.

postmodern form of political organization. Nietzsche became a postmodern icon because to him the modern obsession with certainty based on a logic of universal truths appeared as an illusion. It was this illusion that was the real cause of discomfort because it commanded us to strive for something that could never be achieved. "The fanatics of logic are unbearable, like wasps," Nietzsche proclaimed in his second public lecture at the University of Basle.[52]

Nietzsche did not really offer an acceptable alternative to a world governed by universal truths such as "any number of men living in one state under one authority." His deconstruction of all established forms would only end up in chaos. For postmodern thinkers like Iris Marion Young, however, the deconstruction of universality leads to a newfound respect for diversity.[53] Such diversity inevitably comes with different rationalities. Insofar as federal systems have as their objective to accommodate such diversity, they imply cooperation and compromise as attributes of human nature, which is different from the Hobbesian assumption of that nature as perpetual war.

Canada came into existence as a federation because that was the only way of creating a country. As we shall see, different rationalities never quite succumbed to an overriding sense of national identity, and the dynamic of federalism in Canada has remained caught in a tension of contested concepts about how to apply, interpret, and evaluate the principal institutions, mechanisms, and procedures that make federal systems different from unitary states.

52 Friedrich Nietzsche, "Socrates und die Tragoedie," in *Kritische Studienausgabe*, vol. 1 (1871; Berlin: de Gruyter, 1999), 541 (own translation).

53 Iris Marion Young, *Justice and the Politics of Difference* (Princeton: Princeton University Press, 1990), 239.

Chapter Two
Confederation

All federal systems result from compromise. In the Canadian case, it took a whole series of compromises to bring about Confederation. The main compromise was, of course, that the desired goal – tying all the colonies of British North America into one continental economic union – was not to be had without granting some degree of cultural and linguistic autonomy to Quebec. Another compromise was to create two orders of government with sovereign legislative powers without jeopardizing continued loyalty to the British Empire and its laws. A third compromise, finally, was to combine a core principle of federalism (regional participation in federal decision making in a second legislative chamber) with the core principle of British governance (parliamentary sovereignty). Beneath these compromises, however, lingered a foundational question that would in due time fuel the emergence of deeply contested concepts about the character and operation of the federation: whether Confederation had come about as a compact among equal provinces or as a compact among two nations.

Prior to Confederation, British North America consisted of six separate colonies: Nova Scotia, New Brunswick, Prince Edward Island, and Newfoundland along the Atlantic seaboard in the east; the United Province of Canada along the St. Lawrence River in the centre, comprising Canada East (Quebec) and Canada West (Ontario); and British Columbia on the Pacific coast in the far west. In between Canada and British Columbia, there was a vast space, in large part owned by the Hudson's Bay Company, mostly inhabited by

Indigenous peoples and promising future wealth from settlement, agriculture, and the exploitation of resources.

Confederation was the idea to create a continental economic union by connecting these different and distant parts of British North America with a railway and to protect the new country from American expansionism. What would become the Dominion of Canada in 1867, however, initially consisted only of four provinces: Ontario, Quebec, Nova Scotia, and New Brunswick. Prince Edward Island needed a few more years to make up its mind, British Columbia waited for railway plans to concretize, and Newfoundland preferred to carry on by itself.

In one way, the story of why and how Canada became a federal union rather than a unitary state is very simple: It was a compromise between economic modernizers (English merchant elites in Montreal and Toronto who were seeking new economic fortunes in a continental economic union) and cultural traditionalists (French seigneurial elites who were adamant about preserving their traditional way of life, language, and culture rooted in French civil law and Catholicism).

The unitary state that the merchants favoured thus was not to be had. Therefore, a constitutional compromise was adopted in 1867, giving the English what they wanted (national powers over trade and commerce) and giving the French what they wanted ("property and civil rights," which apart from language and culture most importantly included the continued exploitation of land and tenants). The result was a federal state, which soon enough took on a political dynamic of its own, unforeseen and in many ways unforeseeable by its founders.

In another way, the story of federalism in Canada is a lot more complicated. It is probably quite accurate to say that without the French factor Canada would have become a unitary "legislative union." After all, John A. Macdonald had said so himself.[1] But while the French factor may have been the main reason for taking the federal path, it was by no means the only reason. The idea of a centralized unitary form of government for a territory stretching from the Atlantic to the Pacific with lots of nothing as yet in between was not realistic even with the prospects of a transcontinental railway yet to be built. The desire to remain British did not make for much of a national vision, and the new capital city of Ottawa, a remote lumber town with unpaved streets and new parliamentary buildings not yet finished, certainly did not inspire such a vision.

1 Janet Ajzenstat et al., eds., *Canada's Founding Debates* (Toronto: Stoddart, 1999), 279.

Macdonald may have been a "nation maker."[2] Most of the other participants in the Confederation enterprise were supportive only to the extent that they thought it served their particular interests. In fact, a major motivation for Confederation in Ontario and Quebec was to get out of a legislative union that already existed. There was no self-righteousness of the American kind, only an agreement cobbled together by what has been called "one of the most curious alliances ever forged in Canadian politics."[3] Unsurprisingly, the interests of "Indians," Canada's Indigenous peoples and first occupants of the land, did not find any recognition or accommodation.

Coming Together Lately

Modern states were not created by "any number of men," as Locke claimed. They came into existence when one group of power-hungry men triumphed over all others by successfully monopolizing control of capital and coercion.[4] In some instances, however, no group of power-hungry men was strong enough to impose their will upon the rest. While England and France became unitary nation-states early on, a plurality of German territories lived on side by side until, in the late nineteenth century, a need for combined military and economic strength arose in competition with the unitary nation-states. As none of the territorial rulers was willing to cede powers entirely, the German nation-state took the form of a federation.

The settler colonies of North America, first the United States in 1789 and then Canada in 1867, entered into federation for similar reasons. The American colonies had been formed separately, had developed their own self-governing institutions separately, and therefore would not now yield powers to a distant national government without assurance of continued autonomy at least in local matters. In the case of Canada, not only were there separate colonies across a vast continent, there was among these colonies Quebec, which had been turned from a French settler colony into a British conquest colony on the Plains of Abraham

2 Richard Gwyn, *Nation Maker, Sir John A. Macdonald: His Life, Our Times*, vol. 2, *1867–1891* (Toronto: Random House, 2011).

3 Robert C. Vipond, *Liberty and Community: Canadian Federalism and the Failure of the Constitution* (Albany: State University of New York Press, 1991), 16.

4 Charles Tilly, "Western State-Making and Theories of Political Transformation," in *The Formation of National States in Western Europe*, ed. Charles Tilly (Princeton: Princeton University Press, 1975), 635.

in 1759, and which had no intention of losing to national considerations of coercion and capital the few assurances of cultural autonomy granted by the Quebec Act of 1774.

Federations, then, typically are cases of late state formation.[5] In the case of Canada, the remaining colonies loyal to Britain after American independence in 1776 were thrown onto a trajectory toward what they would call Confederation when they realized that their loyalty to the mother country might no longer be rewarded by military protection and economic privilege. By the 1860s, Canadians were alarmed by American talk of northward expansion in the name of manifest destiny. With a formidable American military force assembled during the Civil War, it had become doubtful that the British would be willing – or capable – to defend their colonial borders as they had done in the War of 1812. Already in 1847, when Britain repealed the so-called Corn Laws that had given Canadian wheat privileged access to British markets, it had dawned on Canadians that their economic well-being would not count for much in the grand scheme of British self-interest. A reciprocity (free trade) treaty with the United States in 1854 had brought some relief, but in 1866 the Americans abrogated that treaty. Late state formation in the form of a federation that would bring together what was left of British North America and would be capable of formulating its own economic and security policies became a paramount task. By then, Confederation plans were already in their final stage.

So, what or who was it that put together one of the most curious alliances in Canadian political history for the purpose of forming a federal union? The three main protagonists were the liberal reformer George Brown in Toronto, his conservative opponent and arch-enemy John A. Macdonald, and George-Étienne Cartier, Macdonald's conservative ally in Quebec.

Virulently anti-Catholic, Brown not least became a champion of representation by population (rep-by-pop) because in the legislative union of 1840, with its parity of members from Ontario and Quebec, his majority of Protestant Ontario reformers could easily be frustrated by a minority of Ontario conservatives ganging up with a majority of Catholic Quebec conservatives. Confederation would bring twofold relief: a new Canadian parliament based on rep-by-pop with a permanent majority of English and Protestant members already on the horizon, and an autonomous Ontario looking after its own affairs without Francophone

5 Frederick K. Lister, *The Early Security Confederations: From the Ancient Greeks to the United Colonies of New England* (Westport: Greenwood, 1999).

interference altogether. But behind all the rep-by-pop posturing loomed more mundane material considerations.

The English merchant elites along the St. Lawrence had long sought to turn Upper and Lower Canada into one commercial state capable of competing with the rapidly modernizing Americans south of the border.[6] What stood in the way were the French Canadians occupying the lower part of the St. Lawrence, who were more interested in living off the land and collecting transportation charges along the river than building canals and ports. Already in 1822, English Canadians had tried, behind Quebec's back, to talk Britain into transforming the two provinces into one legislative union in which they would have had a numerical advantage. The plan was abandoned over Quebec's protestations. When legislative union came in 1840, parity requirements in the assembly made it dysfunctional. Confederation now would solve the problem. By removing Quebec's geographical and ideological stranglehold on trade and commerce, modernization would come, and it would make Toronto, where Brown's *Globe* newspaper all but dominated public opinion, an economic and power hub in the new federation.

If Brown delivered liberal Ontario, Cartier brought conservative Quebec into the fold by his eloquent assurances that Confederation would be the best if not the only path of survival for the French "race." But while Cartier represented seigneurial interests in his Montreal law firm, he was also closely associated with English merchant and railway interests. It was Cartier who lured the Maritime provinces into Confederation with promises of connecting them to an interprovincial railway system, and it was Cartier who would push for the acquisition of Rupert's Land, the vast northwest of the continent, from the Hudson's Bay Company two years after Confederation, not least in order to make possible the construction of a transcontinental railway system.

During the 1837 rebellion, Cartier had been on the side of the rebels fighting for responsible government in Quebec. During the Confederation debates in 1865, however, he did not just give assurances for French cultural survival; he also assured his English merchant clients that "our commercial matters" would be protected – if need be by power of disallowance that the federal government would have over provincial legislation.[7]

And John A. Macdonald? Desmond Morton has called him a "bibulous opportunist,"[8] which I find unfair on both counts. Macdonald's binge-drinking

6 See Donald Creighton, *The Empire of the St. Lawrence* (Toronto: Macmillan, 1970), 214–23.

7 Ajzenstat et al., *Canada's Founding Debates*, 335.

8 Desmond Morton, *A Short History of Canada* (Edmonton: Hurtig Publishers, 1983), 73.

habits are well known, of course, but as Wilfrid Laurier later reminisced, half of the members of parliament were usually drunk by midnight, as the basement saloon of the new parliament building was conveniently exempted from all licensing regulations.[9] Macdonald himself made no bones about what drove him: "I don't care for office for the sake of money, but for the sake of power and for the sake of carrying out my own views of what is best for the country."[10] He never got rich from politics, and the one time he mixed politics with business, when he, quite likely led on by Cartier, accepted election funds in return for the promise of a contract to build the Canadian Pacific Railway, he had to resign as prime minister in 1873. He would be back in office five years later and for another 13 years.

What Macdonald thought was good for the country was that it should remain British and never become American. This, he reasoned, required bringing the rest of British North America under the roof of one government, and to achieve this end he arranged himself with the socioeconomic powers of the day. If that was opportunism, then it was opportunism guided by political instinct for the art of the possible.

From a political economy perspective, then, the curious alliance that engineered Confederation was a triumvirate of interests that were not so curious at all. The Fathers of Confederation met three times to discuss and negotiate federal union. First, in September 1864, they took their plan to Charlottetown, where the three Maritime colonies, Prince Edward Island, Nova Scotia, and New Brunswick, had been contemplating a union among themselves. During the Quebec conference a month later, the delegates, now also joined by a contingent from Newfoundland, hammered out a provisional set of 72 constitutional resolutions, which set the tone for a federal union with a strong central government. At the London conference two years later, with Prince Edward Island and Newfoundland no longer participating, the leading British parliamentary "draughtsman," Sir Francis Reilly, then put into final wording what would be a statute of British parliament.[11] After assent by Queen Victoria, the Dominion of Canada was created with the British North America Act (BNA Act) coming into force on July 1, 1867.

In comparison to the iconic clarity of the American constitution a century earlier, the BNA Act came to be a rather more ambiguous and even contradictory

9 Gwyn, *Nation Maker*, 40.

10 Ibid., 36.

11 See John T. Saywell, *The Lawmakers: Judicial Power and the Shaping of Canadian Federalism* (Toronto: University of Toronto Press, 2002), 9–12.

document.[12] It is easy to see why. The Americans broke with the British tradition and boldly crafted a parsimonious constitutional document of seven articles only, the vision of a new form of government in principle and providing clarity mainly by avoiding detail. The Canadians had in some ways a harder task because they wanted to combine something old, loyalty to Britain and its parliamentary form of responsible government, with something new, a federal union with divided powers. Such an effort needed more attention to detail. The outcome, 147 sections in all, created "the world's first parliamentary federation."[13] But the nagging suspicion never went away entirely that the "inadequacies" of the BNA Act laid the groundwork for a union still "unfulfilled."[14]

The BNA Act indeed begins with a set of contradictory pledges. It first expresses the desire of the three founding provinces, (the United Province of) Canada, Nova Scotia, and New Brunswick, to be "federally united." It then declares that this shall be accomplished under a "constitution similar in principle to that of the United Kingdom." The unwritten constitution of the United Kingdom was firmly grounded on the principle of unitary and undivided parliamentary sovereignty. The constitution of what would henceforth be called the Dominion of Canada, however, was to be parliamentary yet at the same time federal with divided powers. And Canadian parliamentary sovereignty was further toned down by unwavering loyalty to the British Empire. Imperial, unitary, federal, parliamentary: These were the complex, sometimes contradictory, characteristics that came to define BNA Act federalism.

Relics of Empire

For a twenty-first century reader not familiar with the relics of British imperialism, the language of the BNA Act, now the Constitution Act, 1867, is somewhat bewildering. All executive power is vested in the queen (Victoria at the time) we read; in lieu of king or queen, governor generals at the federal level and lieutenant governors at the provincial level exercise all powers with or without the advice and consent of the respective executive councils (that would be prime ministers and provincial premiers, respectively, and their cabinets). Parliament may deal with

12 See ibid., 3.

13 David E. Smith, *Federalism and the Constitution of Canada* (Toronto: University of Toronto Press, 2010), 40.

14 Garth Stevenson, *Unfulfilled Union: Canadian Federalism and National Unity*, 5th ed. (Montreal: McGill-Queen's University Press, 2009), 36–7.

money bills (revenue, taxation, imposts) only upon recommendation by the governor general. Parliamentary legislation must not contravene British law, and if it does, it can be disallowed by the governor general.

Fortunately, we can (almost) forget about all that. Some of these provisions have been formally repealed. Most importantly, the Westminster Statute of 1931 removed the requirement of Canadian legislation to conform with British law, and governor generals were appointed upon recommendation of the Canadian rather than British government. More generally, change has come by means of so-called constitutional conventions, principles of political conduct developed over time without formally changing the constitution itself.[15] A whole set of these conventions has to do with the so-called reserve power of the Crown. This power implies that in principle the British monarch's representatives in Canada may refuse to sign into law a government bill or act contrary to how the prime minister wants them to act in a number of other ways. In practice, however, according to the constitutional conventions developed in Canada as a mature democratic state, this reserve power can no longer be legitimately invoked.

Most of what governor generals or their provincial counterparts do has become merely symbolic and is of no political consequence to the functioning of Canadian politics and federalism. Yes, they sign all the bills into law, and they formally open and close parliamentary sessions, but they sign whatever prime ministers and provincial premiers put before them. As in Britain itself, then, the queen (Elizabeth at this time) no longer wields any real power in Canadian politics and federalism.

Other imperial relics in the BNA Act, though, had and still have a rather profound impact on Canadian politics, and on federalism in particular. The act said nothing about judicial interpretation and review, nor about its amendment should that become necessary with the passing of time. The general assumption simply was that these tasks would fall to the British government. The issue of judicial review did come up during the Confederation debates in 1865. "In case of difference between the federal power and the local governments, what authority will intervene for its settlement," a worried Antoine-Aimé Dorion asked. The laconic answer came from conservative fellow Quebecer George-Étienne Cartier: "It will be the imperial government."[16]

15 Andrew Heard, *Canadian Constitutional Conventions: The Marriage of Law and Politics* (Toronto: Oxford University Press, 2014).

16 Ajzenstat et al., *Canada's Founding Debates*, 311.

The BNA Act only provided for the possibility of establishing a General Court of Appeal for Canada (Section 101), and a Supreme Court of Canada duly was established in 1875. But the final court of appeal for constitutional disputes until 1949 would be a committee of British Law Lords, the Judicial Committee of the Privy Council (JCPC). As we shall see in Chapter 3, the JCPC played a significant and often controversial role in shaping Canadian federalism. Suffice to say for now, it would thoroughly frustrate those who thought it "devoutly to be desired" that the federal union eventually could be transformed into a centralized legislative union after all.[17]

Constitutional amendment was an altogether different matter yet again. Constitutions are foundational agreements. Changing them should in principle require renewed agreement by all constituent members. The Americans had in practice adopted a very high threshold for amendment: a two-thirds majority in both houses of Congress and ratification by the legislatures of three-fourths of the states. The British government, responsible for the approval of BNA Act amendments until constitutional patriation in 1982, would routinely grant amendment requests by the Canadians. For amendments "directly affecting provincial powers," however, it did so only if the request came with unanimous approval by the federal government and all provinces.[18] At least for such cases, then, unanimity took on the status of a constitutional convention.

This in turn became an issue when a protracted search for a domestic amendment formula began in the second half of the twentieth century, now inextricably intertwined with the rising tides of Quebec nationalism. Anything short of unanimity would appear to the lone Francophone province as a potential assault upon its autonomies, just as Dorion had worried. In the end, patriation – the eventual entrenchment of a domestic amendment formula in the Constitution Act, 1982 – did not bring closure because the British government, based on a controversial Supreme Court of Canada ruling that only substantive provincial approval was needed, in its last colonial act granted passage of the act without the approval of Quebec (see Chapter 7).

Unitary Impositions

In order to understand what is meant by "unitary impositions" we need to recall the essence of the federal principle in its classical or coordinate form, according

17 Ibid., 313.

18 Peter W. Hogg, *Constitutional Law of Canada* (Toronto: Carswell, 1998), 61.

to which each order of government should operate separately and autonomously in its respective sphere of jurisdiction. In practice, as the JCPC already established in one of its first important rulings (see Chapter 3), the assignment of powers under the BNA Act would turn out to be more overlapping than strictly separate. What we mean by unitary impositions, however, is something else: deliberate and intended violations of the federal principle in the constitution itself. The intended objective was to make the provinces subordinate to, rather than coordinate with, the federal government.[19]

The most egregious such violations of the federal principle were the provisions for reservation and disallowance of provincial statutes under Section 90. *Reservation* meant that the provincial lieutenant governor could, instead of giving royal assent to a provincial bill, "reserve" it for consideration by the governor general or, rather, the federal cabinet. *Disallowance* meant that the federal cabinet could then simply declare a provincial act null and void.

The federal powers of reservation and disallowance were never formally repealed.[20] However, as in the case of the formal powers of governor generals or the queen, it is of no consequence any more. As already mentioned, the possibility of disallowing Canadian laws by the British government was officially ended by the Westminster Statute of 1931. Reservation and disallowance of provincial legislation by the federal government was a relatively frequent occurrence during the first 50 years of Confederation, but it became rather infrequent during the second 50 years, and it entirely fell out of use during the last 50 years. Constitutional scholars speak of these sections of the constitution as dormant or obsolete by convention.[21]

Another unitary imposition has to do with judicial appointments. Apart from the no longer consequential appointment of provincial lieutenant governors, the BNA Act determines that the federal government will also appoint provincial superior court and appellate court judges. In addition, the federal government also appoints Supreme Court judges. In a judicial system consisting of four tiers, provincial courts, provincial superior courts, provincial appellate courts, and the Supreme Court of Canada (SCC), then, the judges of three levels are appointed by the federal government. Although there is in fact little hard evidence, and notwithstanding the assumed political neutrality of the judiciary, the suspicion

19 See Hogg, *Constitutional Law of Canada*, 115–16.

20 The failed Charlottetown Accord of 1992 would have done so.

21 Heard, *Canadian Constitutional Conventions*, 156–9.

remains that the federal appointment process may also produce a bias in favour of the federal point of view.[22]

The appointment of provincial superior and appellate court judges is regulated in the constitution.[23] The only firm requirement is that judges must be selected from the respective bars in the provinces where the appointment will be made. Provinces have rarely if ever questioned this process of federal selection and appointment, and one may be allowed to wonder whether that is so because the constitution also determines that the federal government pays for the salaries for these judges.

Appointments to the SCC are a different matter. Since the BNA Act only stipulated that the parliament of Canada may provide for the establishment and organization of a final appellate court, the Supreme Court of Canada was established by an act of parliament. The Supreme Court Act of 1875 again has only few firm requirements: appointments are effectively made by the prime minister, and two (now three) of the judges have to be from Quebec so that the court can function properly when dealing with Quebec civil law. In addition, and by convention again, a practice was established to appoint the remaining six judges according to a regional formula: two or three from Ontario, two or three from the west, and one from Atlantic Canada.

The appointment process has been criticized persistently by the provinces as conducive to a centralist bias of judges who determine power disputes between the two orders of government. After coming to power in 2015, the Liberal government of Justin Trudeau attempted to dispel these criticisms by redesigning the appointment process without, however, granting the provinces a co-deciding role. An independent advisory board now conducts a nationwide search for the best candidates. The prime minister then makes appointments from a shortlist provided by the board.[24]

There is another issue related to courts and judges that is not usually mentioned as a unitary imposition on the concept and practice of dual federalism but which gained some notoriety in recent years. The BNA Act gave exclusive legislative authority over criminal law to the federal government.[25] This was obviously

22 See André Bzdera, "Comparative Analysis of Federal High Courts: A Political Theory of Judicial Review," *Canadian Journal of Political Science* 26, no. 1 (1993).

23 Sections 96–100, Constitution Act, 1867.

24 See the announcement by Justin Trudeau, "New Process for Judicial Appointments to the Supreme Court of Canada," August 2, 2016.

25 Section 91(27), Constitution Act, 1867.

done to achieve "uniformity of justice over the whole land," as George Brown declared in reference to the federal appointment of judges.[26] As a member in the House of Assembly of Prince Edward Island put it at the time: "A multiplicity of laws ... tended to the promotion of crime."[27]

At the same time, however, the BNA Act left the provinces with the administration of criminal justice,[28] which effectively meant that the provinces have to comply with whichever way the federal government wants to craft the federal Criminal Code and see it administered. It ultimately comes down to dollars and cents. Thus, when the Conservative government of Stephen Harper enacted a series of so-called "tough on crime" bills during its 2006–15 tenure, which included extended mandatory minimum sentencing requirements, tightened parole rules, and the disallowance of credit for time spent in pre-sentencing custody, a large portion of increased criminal justice costs had to be absorbed by the provinces without their governments being consulted or having a say.[29]

A final unitary imposition upon the principle of federal duality is the declaratory power of Section 92(10c) whereby the Canadian parliament can take power and regulate public works deemed to be "for the general advantage of Canada or for the advantage of two or more of the provinces" even when such work would be undertaken wholly within one province and therefore otherwise be under provincial jurisdiction as "local works and undertakings." One may well think that the primary purpose of this clause was to override further resistance to commercial modernization within Quebec. What John A. Macdonald cited as an example, however, was the Welland Canal in Ontario.[30] And what he surely had in mind as well was federal control over what at the time was still a localized railway system for the most part.

For better or worse, and in rather marked contrast to the other unitary impositions discussed thus far, Section 92(10c) had a huge impact on the development of Canadian federalism. It was invoked 470 times, although the last time was in 1961.[31] Federal control over public works and undertakings would eventually

26 Ajzenstat et al., *Canada's Founding Debates*, 289.

27 Ibid., 326.

28 Section 92(14), Constitution Act, 1867.

29 Rod Story and Tolga R. Yalkin, *Expenditure Analysis of Criminal Justice in Canada* (Ottawa: Office of the Parliamentary Budget Officer, 2013).

30 Stevenson, *Unfulfilled Union*, 31.

31 Standing Senate Committee on Legal and Constitutional Affairs, "The Extraordinary Federal Powers and a Genuine Federation," in *Report to the Senate of Canada*, Part I (Ottawa, 1980).

extend not only to canals and railways but to uranium mining and nuclear energy production, as well as radio, television, and telecommunications networks, including the internet. One of the reasons for the strengthened affirmation of provincial ownership of natural resources in Section 92A of the Constitution Act, 1982, was provincial fear that the federal government would otherwise find ways to take control of oil and gas by means of its declaratory power as well.[32]

Unitary impositions such as the powers of reservation and disallowance in particular led K.C. Wheare, author of one of the first landmark studies on comparative federalism, to conclude that the BNA Act of 1867 only was a "quasi-federal constitution."[33] Wheare overstated his case. By the time he came to his conclusion about the defects of Canadian federalism, in 1946, reservation and disallowance had all but fallen into disuse.

The federal process for the appointment of judges, in turn, while remaining an irritant with regard to the Supreme Court, can hardly be construed as part of a centralizing federal conspiracy. There is in Canada, and has always been, a culture of legal professionalism that has largely remained independent of whoever made the appointment. Case in point: Prime Minister Stephen Harper had the opportunity to appoint six Supreme Court judges during his nine years of tenure, which did not prevent him from suffering several serious defeats on matters dear to his conservative cause, from senate reform to mandatory sentencing.

And in the big picture of federal–provincial finances, the burden of administering criminal justice is not first and foremost on the minds of provincial premiers. What is much more on their minds is the federal spending power, which is not expressly regulated in the BNA Act at all, and which indeed allows the federal government to take unitary action in areas of provincial jurisdiction (see Chapter 5).

Finally, few will dispute that the federal government's declaratory power of assuming control of local public works has been to the general advantage of Canada at least with regard to the creation of a national public infrastructure. As we shall see in the next section, all these provisions primarily were concessions to time and circumstance ancillary to a general division of powers scheme primarily meant to accommodate the complementary interests of economic modernizers

32 See J. Peter Meekison, Roy J. Romanow, and William D. Moull, *Origins and Meaning of 92A: The 1982 Constitutional Amendment on Resources* (Montreal: The Institute for Research on Public Policy, 1985).

33 K.C. Wheare, *Federal Government* (1946; repr., New York: Oxford University Press, 1963), 19.

and cultural traditionalists and as such, at least for the time being, "well-suited to achieve the purposes for which it was designed."[34]

Federal Accommodations

The most defining characteristic of federal systems is how powers are divided among the two orders of government. As the Americans before them, the Canadian founders had to address two basic questions: First, which tasks should be assigned to what order? And second, when in doubt, which order would prevail over the other? While the Canadians more or less followed the American lead with regard to the first question, they deliberately and emphatically intended to go the opposite way with regard to the second.

In hindsight, it is almost amusing how little time the Canadians took debating a division of powers that would arouse so much tension and conflict in years to come when they spent what would seem to be an inordinate amount of time on the question of regional representation in a senate that was never meant to become an institution of powerful significance to begin with. Yet at the time, as we shall see in the next section, regional representation was an issue explosive enough to make or break Confederation. The division of powers in turn, while of course at the heart of the federal compromise, was not particularly controversial in and of itself. With the American precedent before them, and an acute understanding of what needed to be disentangled from joint governance in the United Province of Canada to make the side-by-side existence of French and English manageable within the union, there was "no mystery" to it.[35]

As in the American case, the federal government would have to have the powers necessary for "nation-building and nation-maintaining."[36] Under Section 91 of the BNA Act, it was thus first and foremost given powers over the regulation of trade and commerce, fiscal and monetary policy, and defence. Included also were powers over matters particularly important for a country yet to be put together and with western expansion in mind: transportation and communication, including railways, canals, shipping, and telegraphs. These latter powers were not listed directly in Section 91 but as exemptions from the

34 Stevenson, *Unfulfilled Union*, 36.

35 Saywell, *The Lawmakers*, 12.

36 Donald V. Smiley, *Canada in Question: Federalism in the Eighties* (Toronto: McGraw-Hill Ryerson, 1980), 21.

provincial powers over "Local Works and Undertakings" in Section 92, together with the aforementioned provision of the federal government's declaratory power over intra-provincial public works in the general interest of Canada. In order to accomplish all this, the federal government was empowered to raise revenue by any mode of taxation.

As in the American case, the provinces would end up with whatever was at the time considered and generally accepted as being local. The enumeration in Section 92 broadly covered what at the time went for social policy as well as municipal institutions and the regulation of local business. In addition, the provinces shared jurisdiction over agriculture and immigration with the federal government. Nobody at the time thought that all this would amount to much when the provinces' revenue-raising capacities were limited to "direct taxation," which in an age before the introduction of personal and corporate income taxation did not amount to much either. In fact, own revenues did not even cover whatever limited tasks the provinces were meant to carry out, and from the very beginning they came to depend on federal transfers as first stipulated in Sections 118–20.

There were some peculiar provisions with regard to provincial powers deemed necessary to address specific Canadian issues. Education was listed as a provincial power in a lengthy separate Section 93, when one would have assumed that it simply should have been added to the list of social responsibilities under Section 92. The reason was that Confederation was not to be had without guarantees to protect the divided denominational school system, Protestant and Catholic. Section 93 therefore contained the provision later repeated in the Manitoba Act whereby the federal government could resort to "remedial action" if a province violated those guarantees. As we already know from Chapter 1, however, the Manitoba school crisis was resolved when Wilfrid Laurier won the 1896 federal election and took to the "sunnier way" of negotiating a compromise with Manitoba rather than imposing remedial federal legislation.

The most obvious Canada-specific provision of the entire BNA Act doubtlessly was Section 92(13), provincial jurisdiction over "Property and Civil Rights in the Province." There was no mystery about it, though – it had been taken from the Quebec Act of 1774, where it had assured Quebec's seigneurial system of land tenure and its civil rather than common law regime. Without a similar assurance, as everyone understood full well, Confederation was not to be had. While most in Canada might not have thought much of letting Quebec have what George Brown referred to as its "peculiar institutions,"[37] the British were

37 Cited in Saywell, *The Lawmakers*, 14.

in fact mildly alarmed when the constitutional draft was put before them, even summoning the leading members of the French Canadian delegation in London to the Colonial Office in a futile attempt at dissuading them from their insistence on the formula.[38] Possibly the English understood and anticipated the far-reaching interpretation "property and civil rights" could be given, encompassing the regulation of just about all private and commercial life not just in Quebec but in every province. In fact, as we shall see in Chapter 3, the first and decisive push for such an extensive interpretation of provincial rights would come from Ontario rather than Quebec.

A final provision of some Canada-specific peculiarity was the explicit assignment of the ownership of natural resources to the provinces in Section 109.[39] Yet there was nothing mysterious about that either, and it has become peculiar only in hindsight. The Confederation project was driven by merchant elites primarily interested in the wheels of commerce and transportation. Natural resources at the time played only a minor role in the colonial economy and therefore could be left in the hands of the provinces along with the declining timber industry. If all that was indeed part of John A. Macdonald's centralist machinations, as Stevenson suggests,[40] starving the provinces into financial oblivion as it were, Canada's first prime minister probably would roll in his grave if he knew about the reversal of fortunes that began at Leduc in 1947.[41]

All in all, when it came to the question of who should do what in the new federation, Canadians and Americans were not all that far apart. The other question, however – which order of government should ultimately prevail over the other – was a different matter altogether. To the extent that the historical federalist compromise was one between economic modernizers and cultural traditionalists, it also was one between those seeking to establish a strong central government and those opposed to it. Inevitably, to achieve the required compromise, ambiguities were built into federal constitutions that ultimately would have to be sorted out by means of judicial interpretation (see Chapter 3).

The American constitution assigned to Congress a limited number of explicitly listed powers including, obviously, trade and commerce, as well as, in Section 1.8, a general empowerment to raise revenue for the "general welfare of

38 See ibid., 9.

39 Now reinforced by Section 92A of the Constitution Act, 1982.

40 Stevenson, *Unfulfilled Union*, 32.

41 The first discovery of a major oil field at Leduc in Alberta started the western oil boom; see Chapter 6.

the United States" and to "make all laws … necessary and proper for carrying into execution" its powers as listed. Everything not explicitly listed was assumed to remain in the domain of state powers and was so affirmed as residual states' rights by the 10th Amendment added to the constitution immediately after ratification. In addition, since none of the powers was assigned to Congress exclusively, Article VI gave to the federal government what is known as *paramountcy*: In case of conflicting or contradictory laws, federal law would be "the supreme law of the land."

In the twentieth century, judicial interpretation of the "general welfare … necessary and proper" and supremacy clauses would lead to a significant erosion of states' rights. From the Canadian perspective at the time, however, and not least under the impact of the American Civil War that had been raging for five years, the American constitution had created a federal government not nearly powerful enough. For John A. Macdonald in particular, the states' rights clause together with the lack of a more general legislative empowerment of the federal government was a recipe for disaster.

In a speech emulating Mark Anthony's funeral oration with reverse Shakespearean flourish,[42] Macdonald first called the American constitution "one of the most skillful works which human intelligence ever created," only then to take it apart piece by piece: "State Rights" were the cause for the Civil War, and the lack of a general empowerment to legislate in the national interest was "the point where the American constitution breaks down." Writing their constitution, the Americans had "commenced, in fact, at the wrong end."[43]

Beginning at the right end meant assigning to the federal government a general empowerment "to make Laws for the Peace, Order, and good government," the famous POGG clause of Section 91, and then, in Section 92, enumerate a limiting catalogue of "exclusive" powers where the provinces could legislate on their own. "For greater Certainty," Section 91 also enumerated a list of "exclusive" federal powers, which were, however, not to be mistaken as a restriction upon the "Generality" of the POGG formula. The only major concession to the provinces was the "property and civil rights" clause under Section 92.

What the Canadians meant to achieve by all this was indeed the opposite of what the Americans had done: the federal government would have both a general power to legislate in the national interest and residual powers over everything not specifically assigned to the provinces. What they did achieve was considerable

42 "I come to bury Caesar, not to praise him."

43 Ajzenstat et al., *Canada's Founding Debates*, 282–4.

ambiguity, as in the American case. Apart from blatantly contradictory stipulations, such as the federal government's exclusive right to any mode of taxation and the provinces' exclusive right to direct taxation, it was property and civil rights that would pose limits to whatever the centralist intentions of POGG might have been. Since almost anything can be interpreted as pertaining to property and civil rights as long as it does not fall under criminal law, and since the general legislative powers of the federal government are explicitly limited to those "not coming within the Classes of Subjects by this Act assigned exclusively to the Legislatures of the Provinces," judicial interpretation would not be able to go the way of eroding provincial rights. Moreover, these rights were further protected by the lack of a paramountcy clause. Assuming that with their exclusive lists of divided powers and the generality of POGG they had outsmarted American skills and intelligence, the Canadians did not bother to add a federal supremacy clause to their construction except for the two policy areas, agriculture and immigration, that they had made explicitly concurrent (Section 95).

Finally, there is another section in the BNA Act worth mentioning. While it has not played a role in the evolution of Canadian federalism, it allows a glimpse of how the founders might have anticipated this evolution to unfold. Section 94 empowers the federal government to "make Provision for the Uniformity for all or any of the Laws relative to Property and Civil Rights" in the three English founding provinces. Moreover, on the basis of such provisions all further legislation thereunder will then be under the "unrestricted" jurisdiction of the federal government. However, such provisions will "not have effect in any Province" without approval of that province's government.

At first sight, Section 94 seems innocuous enough: In juxtaposition to the statutory civil law regime in Quebec, why not harmonize civil law in the three provinces based on English common law? There seemed to be initial agreement among the three provinces, and John A. Macdonald was keen to make it the federal government's first priority after Confederation. Yet nothing came of it despite various initiatives.[44]

Upon second thought, however, Section 94 is outright perplexing. We remember that the BNA Act, as a statutory British act, did not contain a constitutional amendment formula because this task was considered to rightfully belong to the imperial authorities in London. Yet in Section 94 there is not only a provision for constitutional change, but at that one allowing for a change in the division of powers. And what is more, the founders not only gave implicit

44 See Saywell, *The Lawmakers*, 14–15.

recognition to Quebec's perpetual distinctiveness, but also did not appear to be troubled by the possibility that the provincial consent formula of Section 94 could result in what is today known as "variable geometry" in the context of European integration: differentiated levels of integration and harmonization as some common law provinces might opt into uniformity while others might not.

Section 94 has remained dormant but it has on occasion aroused some academic interest. For some it sets the precedent for a constitutional amendment formula based on unanimity that should have been heeded when push came to shove during the patriation drama in 1981. For others it proves that Confederation essentially was a binational compact between the French and the English. For others yet again, it invites a debate as to whether the BNA Act was from the very beginning imbued with a notion of constitutional asymmetry insulating a distinct Quebec from the kind of property and civil rights uniformity that Section 94 suggests, or whether the intention of the provincial consent formula was exactly the opposite: an opting-out provision that put all provinces on the same page of constitutional symmetry.[45]

These are all issues that will have to be addressed in later chapters of this book. For now, I would suggest to take Section 94 of the BNA Act as an indication that the Canadian founders had a constitutional vision different from that of the American framers. While the Americans were confident they had written perfection into constitutional stone, the Canadians were both more modest and more pedestrian, aiming at constitutional certainty only – as the saying goes, "as much as possible under the circumstances." As we shall see later, this kind of flexibility in outlook and dynamic is not necessarily a bad thing.

Parliamentary Concessions

At the Quebec conference in October 1864, in depressingly bad weather conditions that were lightened up by all kinds of festivities, balls, and dinners, the delegates took more than a week to settle the question of the Canadian senate. In comparison to this debate, carried on "with considerable warmth," the one on the division of powers went much more smoothly, "scarcely producing a

45 See Samuel V. LaSelva, *The Moral Foundations of Canadian Federalism: Paradoxes, Achievements, and Tragedies of Nationhood* (Montreal: McGill-Queen's University Press, 1996), 49–63; and Kathy L. Brock, "Open Federalism, Section 94, and Principled Federalism: Contradictions in Vision" (paper presented at the Annual Meeting of the Canadian Political Science Association, Saskatoon, May 2007).

ripple.'[46] Why was the question of a second legislative chamber so protracted and contested?

Two possible answers come to mind: The first one is perhaps a bit disrespectful. Regional representation in the second chamber turned into a numbers game that was much easier to understand and pounce on than were the intricacies of divided powers with yet unknown consequences. The second answer is more complicated. The issue was not that a second legislative chamber was seen as violating loyal aspirations to write a "constitution similar in principle to that of the United Kingdom." After all, the parliamentary Westminster system itself had two legislative chambers with formally equal voting powers, the House of Commons and the House of Lords. Instead, it was that a second legislative chamber posed a challenge to the Canadian understanding of responsible government. This was the hard-fought concession wrested from the imperial authorities only a few decades earlier, according to which the executive was accountable to parliament and could not govern against the will of the parliamentary majority. So the question was: How could the executive, prime minister and cabinet, be accountable to two and possibly competing majorities, one in the house and one in the senate?

It may be difficult to understand the intensity of the second chamber debate from today's perspective of a largely discredited Canadian senate that nobody knows how to reform and some would like to see abolished altogether. At the time, however, regional representation in a second legislative chamber at the national level was considered the very embodiment of the federal principle. It is the one consideration the Canadians unquestioningly took from the American precedent. At the Philadelphia convention in 1787, the large states had wanted representation by population, and the small states had insisted on equal representation per state. What came to be known as the great compromise was a Congress with a directly elected House of Representatives representing the people by population and a senate in which two senators from each state were elected indirectly by the state legislatures. Ever since, the perception has prevailed that shared rule in a federal system not only means that central legislation will "apply to the residents of the federation as a whole,"[47] but also that there has to be "some representation of the provinces as provinces in the central legislature."[48]

46 For the full story, see P.B. Waite, *The Life and Times of Confederation 1864–1867: Politics, Newspapers, and the Union of British North America* (Toronto: University of Toronto Press, 1962), 89–94.

47 Smith, *Federalism and the Constitution*, 12.

48 Edwin R. Black, *Divided Loyalties: Canadian Concepts of Federalism* (Montreal: McGill-Queen's University Press, 1975), 10.

The Canadian founders settled on rep-by-pop for the parliamentary assembly. The small Maritime provinces were not happy. Prince Edward Island would only get five parliamentary seats. More in an attempt to save face than for any real change in representative weight, it made a futile demand for six.[49] In the end, the island did not join Confederation. When it did, in 1873, it got its six members of parliament. Due to a declining population in proportion to population growth elsewhere, this number had dribbled down to three by 1914. A constitutional amendment a year later then saved Confederation's smallest province from parliamentary attrition by adding a so-called senatorial clause whereby no province may have fewer seats in parliament than the fixed number of seats it has in the senate. Since then, Prince Edward Island has had four members of parliament.

For Upper Canadians like George Brown, rep-by-pop was not only a matter of principle, it meant bringing "injustice to an end." In the assembly of the United Province of Canada, Brown never got tired of pointing out that Upper and Lower Canada (Ontario and Quebec) had an equal number of representatives even though Upper Canada "numbered four hundred thousand souls more than the population of Lower Canada" and even though it "contributed three or four pounds to the general revenue for every pound contributed by the sister province."[50] In turn, Quebec would have to be compensated for the loss of equality in the assembly by equality in the senate. As Brown conceded: "Our Lower Canada friends have agreed to give us representation by population in the lower house, on the express condition that they shall have equality in the upper house."[51]

What Quebec really meant was senate representation equal to Ontario. Yet what to do with the three much smaller Maritime provinces? While senate representation equal to Ontario and Quebec would have been a gross overrepresentation, anything but a substantive number of senate seats in compensation for near-marginalization in the parliamentary assembly was as vital for the success of Confederation as equality with Ontario was for Quebec. This is when the delegates at the Charlottetown conference came up with a regional formula: 20 seats each for what was declared to be the three "regions" of Canada – Ontario, Quebec, and the Maritimes.[52]

---

49 Waite, *The Life and Times*, 94–5.

50 Ajzenstat et al., *Canada's Founding Debates*, 115.

51 Ibid., 286.

52 Waite, *The Life and Times*, 82.

It wasn't over yet, though. The numbers game heated up a month later at the Quebec conference when Newfoundland entered into the proceedings.[53] Led by John A. Macdonald, the Canadians suggested that the three "regions" (Ontario, Quebec, and the Maritimes, the latter now comprising four provinces) each should have 24 senate seats. The Maritime delegates countered by insisting it should be 24 seats for Ontario and Quebec, but 32 for the four Maritime provinces. It took four full days to break the deadlock: 24 senators for the three regional "divisions" as under the previous formula but four extra senatorial seats for Newfoundland.

Of course, Newfoundland did not join Confederation in 1867. Joseph Little, one of the members of the colony's legislative assembly, later gave blunt expression of what he thought the "contemptible" apportionment of seats in house and senate would have meant for Newfoundland: "powerless for good."[54] For the time being, Nova Scotia and New Brunswick would split the 24 senate seats. Premier Charles Tupper of Nova Scotia offered a different assessment of what that entailed for the province by pointing out that 600,000 people in the Maritimes in the end had been apportioned as much senate representation as 1,100,000 people in Upper Canada, and regardless of how much the population of that province might increase. "The security of the people of the Maritime provinces," he exclaimed, would be safe "for all time to come."[55]

In hindsight, Tupper's exhortation of optimism must appear strange in consideration of the fact that Canada's second or upper legislative chamber was never meant to be co-equal to the lower and first. It is here that the Canadian founders waffled considerably.

On the one hand, the senate primarily was part of what they considered to be a mixed government in which the senate would provide a measure of restraint upon cabinet and the commons. This was a conservative view not any different from what the American federalists had had in mind with their proposition of multiple checks and balances,[56] a "nucleus of resistance" against democracy in the words of John Stuart Mill, cited as a Crown witness during the Confederation debates.[57] To make this resistance effective, the senate had to have formal powers

53 See ibid., 89–94.

54 Ajzenstat et al., *Canada's Founding Debates*, 99.

55 Ibid., 264.

56 See Alexander Hamilton, John Jay, and James Madison, *The Federalist* (Indianapolis, IN: Liberty Fund, 2001), No. 51.

57 Ajzenstat, et al., *Canada's Founding Debates*, 93.

equal to that of the parliamentary assembly. For the same reason, to avoid merely a duplication of majoritarian democracy and partisanship, senators also were to be appointed by the Crown (i.e., by the prime minister) rather than elected. And just to make sure that the appointees were of the desired quality, there would be a qualification requiring senators to have $4,000 worth of net property, which at the time was an insurmountable hurdle for most.

On the other hand, the Canadians could not renege on what they considered to be their proudest political achievement up to that point: responsible government. The very idea that the prime minister and cabinet should be accountable to parliament and depend on the support of its majority ultimately was incompatible with the idea of the senate as a nucleus of resistance. That the senate would not use its formal powers against the will of the majority was part of the choice to make it an appointed rather than elected body, thus depriving it of democratic legitimacy in its own right. Ultimately, however, there was only hope that senators would not unduly interfere with the will of parliamentary majorities. As John A. Macdonald put it categorically: "They will not do it."[58]

Macdonald's point of reference was a precedent that had occurred in the mother country a few decades earlier. In 1831 and 1832, the British House of Commons had twice passed a bill reforming an electoral system still privileging wealthy landowners in small boroughs at the expense of boroughs with large industrial city populations. When the House of Lords twice rejected the bill, the Whig Prime Minister Earl Grey urged the king, William IV, to appoint an additional 50 Whig peers to the House of Lords so that the bill could get passed. Before that happened, though, and in the wake of public rioting, the Lords relented by passing the bill with those opposed to it abstaining.

This was the incident that gave Macdonald the conviction that the Canadian senate would not "oppose what they know to be the settled opinions and wishes of the people."[59] The Canadians did not, however, want to follow the precedent by a provision that would have allowed the government of the day to stack the senate with whatever number of like-minded senators might be necessary to ensure compliance with the will of the parliamentary majority. The reason was that such a provision would have upset the regional formula of senate appointments that, in the words of George Brown, lay "at the base of the whole compact on which this scheme rests."[60]

58 Ibid., 82.

59 Ibid., 82.

60 Ibid., 87.

The numbers game flared up one last time at the final London conference in 1866 when the British insisted that the BNA Act should have a provision for additional senatorial appointments after all. With indefatigable ingenuity, Macdonald came up with a solution that would allow for additional appointments without violating the formula of regional apportionment: Section 26 of the BNA Act provided for the appointment of three or six additional senators, one or two for each of the three regions; later, when the west was designated as a fourth region, the formula would be extended to four or eight.

By and large, the Canadian senate has lived up to the founders' expectations by not standing in the way of the parliamentary will of the majority. It has, however, on occasion delayed or rejected bills when it thought that these were not supported by the will of the Canadian people at large. Two famous recent incidents of this kind occurred during the tenure of Progressive Conservative Prime Minister Brian Mulroney. In 1988, the Liberal majority in the senate delayed passage of the Free Trade Agreement that Mulroney had concluded with the United States. Sensing that a political upset was possible, Liberal senators argued that a decision of such importance should first be put to the people. Mulroney called an election, won re-election, and the senate then duly passed the agreement. A few years later, in 1990, the senate blocked the controversial and widely unloved introduction of a general sales tax (the Goods and Services Tax, GST). In this instance, in order to get the GST passed, Mulroney, claiming that the Liberal senators were "undermining the principle of responsible government," took the hitherto unprecedented step of invoking Section 26 and stacking the senate with eight additional conservative senators.[61] In both instances, however, the idea of the senate as a regional chamber upholding the federal principle did not play any significant role.

"Indians"

Only one terse stipulation in the BNA Act, Section 91(24), made mention of the majority of the people living on the territory comprising the new Dominion of Canada: "Indians, and Lands reserved for the Indians" would be placed under exclusive federal jurisdiction. In the absence of any discussion of the matter during the Confederation debates, the most plausible explanation must be precedent: The British had, at least in principle, conducted their interactions with what were

61 See C.E.S. Franks, "The Senate in Modern Times," in *Protecting Canadian Democracy: The Senate You Never Knew*, ed. Serge Joyal (Montreal: McGill-Queen's University Press, 2003).

then uniformly called "Indians" as a – however lopsided – nation-to-nation relationship.[62] In a way, dealing with Indians was part of foreign affairs and, in light of past military alliances such as during the War of 1812, of defence. Another and more practical reason, however, was also surely that the new Canadian state was already gearing up for western expansion where Indian affairs would obviously be beyond the reach of the already existing provinces.

The Indian Act of 1876, then, would not only lay out how do deal with the "Indians" but also define who they were: essentially, only those people of Indigenous descent pushed off to reserve lands where, as so-called status Indians under a series of treaties, they would receive some subsistence-level government services and benefits in return for the surrender of their traditional land. The same level of government services and benefits would not be extended to off-reserve or non-status Indians. In fact, it was government policy to minimize its financial obligations by excluding as many Indians from legal status as possible.[63] As Duncan Campbell Scott put it, head of the Department of Indian Affairs from 1913 to 1932: "I want to get rid of the Indian problem."[64]

Non-status Indians would essentially become a provincial or even local responsibility. They were, therefore, often caught between a rock and a hard place, as provincial governments routinely insisted that under Section 91(24) the federal government was generally and financially responsible for all Indigenous peoples. Such was also the fate of the Métis people, French-speaking descendants of fur traders and Indigenous women, who thought they had formed a "New Nation" along the Red River Valley in what would later become Manitoba,[65] but who were being displaced by white settlement and railway construction and many of whom, betrayed by unfulfilled government promises, ended up in destitution as itinerant farmers.[66]

Not that status Indians as "wards"[67] of the Crown under the direct supervision of federal government policy fared any better. Indian policy as understood

62 See John Bird, Lorraine Land, and Murray Macadam, eds., *Nation to Nation: Aboriginal Sovereignty and the Future of Canada* (Toronto: Irwin, 2001).

63 See James Daschuk, *Clearing the Plains: Disease, Politics of Starvation and the Loss of Indigenous Life* (Regina: University of Regina Press, 2019), 163.

64 Cited in Thomas King, *The Inconvenient Indian: A Curious Account of Native People in North America* (Toronto: Anchor Canada, 2013).

65 See Desmond Morton, *A Short History of Canada* (Edmonton: Hurtig Publishers, 1983), 65.

66 Daschuk, *Clearing the Plains*, 163.

67 Officially so designated by a 1950 Supreme Court judgment, *St. Ann's Island Shooting and Fishing Club v. The King*, [1950] SCR 211.

and practised by the Fathers of Confederation and subsequent federal governments was not policy for Indians but Canadian policy in the national interest and therefore detrimental to Indian interests.[68] Essentially, that meant to make room for white settlement. The sordid saga of the federal government's Indian policy of betrayal, displacement, and starvation will be picked up again in Chapter 6.

Pushed off the land, Indigenous peoples were told to become civilized by turning to agriculture on what was mostly poor soil within the confines of their reserves. When they did that, often competing successfully with the white settler communities around them, government policy would deprive them of modern agricultural tools because they were deemed not yet civilized enough to use these; a pass system kept them locked up on their reserves; and, contrary to perceptions of what makes a good white citizen, a permit system stifled their ability to engage in any kind of commercial transactions. Or, of course, they could be told to pack up for resettlement on even more remote and infertile reserve land where they simply and safely could be neglected.[69] All the while and despite their status as subjects of federal law, reserve Indians nevertheless had to comply with provincial regulations for fishing and hunting, which often curtailed even further what they were allowed to do on the remaining land left to them.[70]

Apart from systematic socioeconomic marginalization, Indigenous peoples in Canada were also subjected to two other forms of coercive "civilization." The Indian Act decreed that traditional forms of governance had to be replaced by western-style band council elections. At a time when responsible government in the new Confederation meant that only a propertied fraction of male Canadians were allowed to vote for members of parliament, the decree aimed at extinguishing traditional forms of governance that, while not elective or democratic in a western sense, often were more complex and inclusive than what amounted to Canadian governance at the time, even according a significant degree of authority to women.[71] Such was the case, for instance, with the Haudenosaunee or Iroquois Confederacy in southern Ontario, which held on to

68 Menno Boldt, *Surviving as Indians: The Challenge of Self-Government* (Toronto: University of Toronto Press, 1993), 68–9.

69 On that whole sad story, see Sarah Carter, *Lost Harvests: Prairie Indian Reserve Farmers and Government Policy* (Montreal: McGill-Queen's University Press, 1990), especially 66.

70 See Donald Purich, *Our Land: Native Rights in Canada* (Toronto, Lorimer, 1986), 66.

71 See Donald S. Lutz, "The Iroquois Confederation Constitution: An Analysis," *Publius: The Journal of Federalism* 28, no. 2 (1998).

its elaborate system of confederate governance[72] until 1924, when it was forced into band council elections at RCMP gunpoint.[73]

Yet the ultimate form of coercive "civilization" came in the form of re-education. Indian children would be taken away from their parents, eventually by the tens of thousands, to have their Indigenous culture brainwashed off their memories in punitive and often abusive residential schools run by the churches on behalf of the government. The residential school system was officially ended only in 1996 with the closure of the last of these schools in Saskatchewan.[74]

We might ask: What has all this got to do with federalism? There are a number of more than obvious answers. To begin with, Canada's federal system was constructed without any inclusion and consideration of, or even respect for, the peoples that had occupied the land from times immemorial. That federal system was constructed to satisfy conflicting interests of nation-building and regional autonomy among white settler colonies. The two orders of government, then, would jealously protect their powers in order to be seen as the primary service providers for their respective citizenries. For Indigenous peoples, however, federalism often meant the opposite, "constitutional wrangling" to evade responsibilities[75] (see Chapter 5).

The belated formal recognition of "existing aboriginal and treaty rights" under Section 35 of the Constitution Act, 1982, has for the most part resulted in an increased practice of "inviting" the representatives of Indigenous groups and peoples to participate in policymaking processes at the federal and provincial levels as well as in intergovernmental forums. This kind of participation, however, does not mean principled inclusion in the institutions and procedures of Canadian federalism. It has been characterized correctly as an informally "emerging mosaic of aboriginal multilevel governance."[76] The difference between federalism and multilevel governance is that the former includes a normative

72 See A.C. Parker, *The Constitution of the Five Nations or the Iroquois Book of the Great Law* (1916; repr., Ohsweken: Iroqrafts, 2006).

73 See Shin Imai, "The Structure of the Indian Act: Accountability in Governance," Comparative Research in Law & Political Economy Research Paper No. 35 (2012), 4.

74 See Truth and Reconciliation Commission of Canada, *Final Report of the Truth and Reconciliation Commission of Canada*, vol. 1, *Summary* (Toronto: James Lorimer, 2015), 37–133.

75 Purich, *Our Land*, 67.

76 Martin Papillon, "Canadian Federalism and the Emerging Mosaic of Aboriginal Multilevel Governance," in *Canadian Federalism: Performance, Effectiveness, and Legitimacy*, eds. Herman Bakvis and Grace Skogstad (Toronto: Oxford University Press, 2012).

commitment to equal membership for all participants, whereas the latter merely describes a process driven by inequalities of power and influence. Moreover, Indigenous peoples themselves had a very different concept of their federal relationship with Canada to begin with.

An Incomplete Contract

So what should we make of what happened in 1867? Was it the appropriate beginning for a new country called Canada, or was it a foul compromise concocted among competing elites for their respective economic gain? To put it differently: When competent observers and analysts of Canadian federalism speak of the "failure of the constitution,"[77] "tragedies of nationhood,"[78] an "unfulfilled union,"[79] or a "constitutional odyssey" without a "common vision,"[80] is it just business as usual, part of the discomfort that accompanies federalism as an imperfect form of political rationality? Or is it expression of something more fundamental, the fear that 1867 was a wrong turn taken, throwing Canadians onto a path-dependent trajectory of institutionalized failure?

To be fair, most of the gloomy assessments cited above stem from a time when Canadians really did find themselves enmeshed in constitutional crisis and uncertainty: the inability to bring the constitutional odyssey to an end that was acceptable for all; the ongoing threat of Quebec's secession; the rise of the western Reform Party and the Bloc Québécois signalling the demise of a national party system; and mounting confrontations with Indigenous peoples leading to the shooting deaths of a soldier at Oka in 1990 and an Indigenous protester at Ipperwash in 1995.

In the meantime, the dust seemed to have settled on most of these issues. Indeed, if the pollsters have gotten it right, turning the page on gloom and doom helped a new Liberal prime minister, Justin Trudeau, get elected in 2015, who promised "sunnier ways" of governance. At a time when right-wing populism with ugly overtones of racism and xenophobia appeared on the rise in many countries, *The Economist* was praising Canada as a beacon of inclusive liberal openness.[81]

77 Vipond, *Liberty and Community.*

78 LaSelva, *The Moral Foundations.*

79 Stevenson, *Unfulfilled Union.*

80 Russell, *Constitutional Odyssey: Can Canadians Become a Sovereign People* (Toronto: University of Toronto Press), 273.

81 *The Economist,* "Canada's Example to the World: Liberty Moves North," October 29, 2016.

As it turns out, the sun did not shine for long. In 2019, the Coalition Avenir Québec government of Premier François Legault passed Bill 21, which restricts the wearing of religious symbols in public service. Largely supported in Quebec, the bill is widely seen as an attack on liberal inclusiveness in the rest of Canada. Renewed confrontations between Royal Canadian Mounted Police (RCMP) and Indigenous protesters have resumed at the beginning of 2020 over a controversial liquid natural gas pipeline in British Columbia. And intergovernmental relations have become frosty over the Trudeau government's approach to combating climate change, which particularly in Alberta and Saskatchewan is seen as an attack on the energy sector.

In the federal election of 2019, the Trudeau Liberals lost 20 seats and were reduced to a minority government. In Alberta and Saskatchewan, they were wiped off the electoral map entirely. In Quebec, the separatist and previously moribund Bloc Québécois rebounded from 10 to 32 seats. And, as of January 2020, a new separatist Wexit party has been granted ballot eligibility for the next federal election. Named in analogy to Brexit (the recently completed exodus of Britain from the European Union), Wexit Canada plans to run federal and provincial candidates across all four western provinces.

The religious symbols disagreement with English Canada is not likely to lead to a new separatist surge in Quebec. Neither is it likely that Indigenous protesters will be able to seriously threaten powerful economic interests in the long run. And it is probably safe to predict that western separatist sentiments, mostly confined to Alberta and Saskatchewan to begin with, will be as short lived as they were the last time when conflict with the federal government erupted over energy policy (see Chapter 6). The hard question remains, however: What do we make of a Confederation settlement expediently put together "for immediate purposes,"[82] with deliberate alacrity to conceal its contradictory stipulations – "especially those concerning federalism"[83] – and brought about by "undemocratic procedures"[84] without popular involvement?

Let's talk about democracy first. A lot has been made of the fact that the Americans had their constitution ratified by the people in the several states, whereas the Canadians left it to the provincial legislatures – or not even that: The legislatures of New Brunswick and Nova Scotia never voted in favour of the Quebec Resolutions. They voted only to send delegates to London for further

82 Saywell, *The Lawmakers*, 12.

83 Vipond, *Liberty and Community*, 20–2.

84 Stevenson, *Unfulfilled Union*, 40.

exploration of a constitutional deal, which was then finalized right there and then without further involvement of the provincial legislatures.[85]

It is true that the American constitution was ratified by elected conventions in all of the 13 original states even though the last holdout, Rhode Island, did so only after the already constituted US government threatened them with economic sanctions. What is not so true is that the process was any more democratic than in Canada. Here as there, the entire process was driven and controlled by those who were enfranchised, which represented only a fraction of the population due to property qualifications. The difference, then, is only that the propertied classes got to vote twice in America in comparison to only once in Canada. The Americans were only better at creating a myth of popular consent.[86]

A persistent Canadian myth, in turn, has been that the general empowerment of the federal government for "Peace, Order, and good Government," the POGG clause, signalled a less liberal predisposition of Canada's founders than the equivalent "general welfare" clause adopted by the American framers. As Garth Stevenson has pointed out, it was the Colonial Office in London that at the last moment switched the formula from "peace, welfare, and good government," as originally drafted at the Quebec conference.[87] The point is that every federal constitution contains such a formula to make sure that the powers given to the central government can be used fully to legislate on matters common to all. The difference in comparison to the American welfare clause is that it came in the guise of a residual powers clause. As we shall see in Chapter 3, that did not amount to much in the opinion of those who had to give practical meaning to abstract formulations of constitutional intent.

The main question to be answered, then, is whether the BNA Act intentionally or unintentionally betrayed the federal principle. I think it did not. As just about every commentator and analyst of the constitutional settlement in 1867 rightly points out, John A. Macdonald had centralist intentions and, as the future first prime minister freely admitted himself, would have preferred a "legislative union," which is to say a unitary state. George Brown also wanted a strong central legislature in which rep-by-pop would prevent Quebec from standing in the way of economic progress. Both men may have deliberately downplayed the ambiguities built into the division of powers to rally the troops necessary for adoption, but they also understood that economic union without federalism was not to be had.

85 Jennifer Smith, *Federalism* (Vancouver, BC: University of British Columbia Press, 2005).

86 Russell, *Constitutional Odyssey*, 8.

87 Stevenson, *Unfulfilled Union*, 31.

The price of nationhood was shared sovereignty. As indicated by Section 94 with its peculiar suggestion of harmonizing the law in the common law provinces, Macdonald, Brown, and others probably thought that common Britishness would eventually whittle away differences among these provinces, thus unwittingly contributing to a view, fully developed in Quebec only later, of Confederation as a compact between two nations. Yet most of the Canadian founders were lawyers, knowing full well that constitutional guarantees of provincial powers over property and civil rights could not be ignored or undone.

In terms of federalism, I believe that the BNA Act was a constitutional contract as good as the American one before it. Imperial relics and unitary impositions would not seriously or lastingly stand in the way of the federal order, and many of the most conflictual issues later on, such as finding a commonly acceptable domestic constitutional amendment formula and the overbearing presence of the federal spending power, simply could not be anticipated at the time. Colonialism rather than federalism is to blame for the gravest shortcoming in hindsight, the casual and callous subjugation of Indigenous peoples to the nation-building project, wherein the adopted federal–provincial structure of the Canadian state would provide convenient excuses for inaction and neglect. The senate, finally, at the time considered the centrepiece of the federal bargain, was set up for failure if the idea was to allow for a significant regional input in the shared rule of federal legislation. But that was not really different from the American senate, nor any other senate-type second chamber later on.

The division of powers was reasonable and, except for a few peculiarities such as provincial ownership of resources, not much different from the American constitutional contract. The Americans had balanced a residual powers clause in favour of the states with three general provisions in favour of the central government: the general welfare clause, the necessary and proper clause, and the supremacy clause. The Canadians balanced a residual powers clause in favour of the central government with exclusive provincial powers of what the provinces, including Quebec, thought at the time as appropriate for the management of local affairs. In both instances, the essential nation-building powers went to the central government.

If there was a problem with Canada's federal constitution, then, it was one shared with all others: "The basic contracts that create and maintain federations, no matter how well specified, are fundamentally incomplete."[88] Even the most

88 Jonathan Rodden, *Hamilton's Paradox: The Promise and Peril of Fiscal Federalism* (Cambridge: Cambridge University Press, 2006), 37.

circumspect analysis of political need at the time could not possibly foresee what the future would hold. Governments were small in the nineteenth century, and government functions were limited. Canadian founders, as the American framers did, would anticipate future needs for additional powers, and as per the general clauses they inserted into the division of powers scheme they indicated where new powers should go.

Even as intended, though, the precision of the law only goes so far in determining power boundaries in a political process driven by ambition and expediency. When conflicts arise, as they inevitably do, the different orders of government in federal systems can either negotiate intergovernmental agreement or they can refer the matter to the courts. The Canadian founders at the time did not anticipate the crucial role intergovernmental and especially fiscal relations would play in the federal system under much more complex twentieth-century governance conditions (see Chapter 5). They also did not anticipate the central role the courts would play in guiding the federal system through changing times. This is the subject matter of Chapter 3.

Chapter Three
Judicial Interpretations

All federal systems have a court of final appeal for power disputes between the two orders of government. Over the course of its history, the Canadian federation has had two. Although the Supreme Court of Canada (SCC) was established early on, final appeal remained with the British Judicial Committee of the Privy Council (JCPC) until 1949. The JCPC recognized early on that the powers allocated to the two orders of government under the British North America (BNA) Act were often overlapping rather than mutually exclusive. Taking federalism seriously, it denied the federal government any kind of paramountcy in the name of national interest – as Macdonald might have wanted – and therefore has been accused of a decentralist bias. After 1949, the SCC began to allow broader interpretations of the national interest. It has therefore been accused reversely of a centralist bias in favour of the federal government. More recently, in light of the overlapping nature of powers in the Canadian federal system, the SCC has also emphasized the need for intergovernmental cooperation. Judicial interpretation in this way has reflected deep-seated conceptual disagreements about Canadian federalism: between a centrist concept emphasizing national unity and a decentralist concept prioritizing regional diversity; and between a classical concept of federalism demanding as much autonomy as possible between the two orders of government and a cooperative concept accepting interdependence as the inevitable consequence of overlapping powers.

The SCC was established in 1875. Until 1878, when it decided its first constitutional case, *Severn v. The Queen*, the burden of sorting out power disputes fell to the already existing provincial courts. The provincial judges quickly realized, if they had not already known, that John A. Macdonald's assertion during the Confederation debates that all "conflict of jurisdiction and authority" had been avoided[1] had been nothing more than an expedient lie.

In the constitutional cases coming before them, the judges had to decide whether such mundane issues as insolvency and insurance or the licensing and regulation of liquor would fall under federal jurisdiction of trade and commerce or had to be considered part of the provincial power over property and civil rights. It is here that the judges in the various provinces, while generally understanding trade and commerce as an expansive nation-building power, nevertheless developed a doctrine of so-called mutual modification that would become an essential part of Canadian constitutional jurisprudence: In the case of overlapping ambiguity, federal and provincial powers "both had to be limited to allow room for the other."[2]

When the SCC took over as the final court of appeal in Canada, tone and tenor shifted more decisively to a nation-building direction. The constitutional question in *Severn v. The Queen* was whether the province of Ontario had a right to issue liquor licences. The court denied this right by declaring that the federal trade and commerce power, "being full and complete, cannot be restricted." Moreover, the court more generally hinted at a general predisposition toward federal paramountcy by declaring that the BNA Act had been designed intentionally so as to avoid the "evils" that had resulted from "the question of State rights" in the United States.[3] It looked as if John A. Macdonald's vision of a highly centralized union would find the support of constitutional jurisprudence.

However, the SCC only was the final *Canadian* court of appeal. As the founders had freely admitted during the Confederation debates, the last word of constitutional interpretation of the BNA Act would remain with the imperial authorities, and more precisely with the Law Lords sitting on the JCPC in London. When the SCC was created in 1875, the Liberal government of Alexander Mackenzie[4] and his justice minister, Edward Blake, intended to abolish appeals to the JCPC, but the authorities in London opposed the move as a serious

1 Janet Ajzenstat et al., eds., *Canada's Founding Debates* (Toronto: Stoddart, 1999), 283.

2 John T. Saywell, *The Lawmakers: Judicial Power and the Making of Canadian Federalism* (Toronto: University of Toronto Press, 2002), 25.

3 *Severn v. The Queen*, [1878] 2 SCR 70.

4 The Liberals came to power in 1873 when John A. Macdonald's Conservative government was brought down by the Pacific Scandal. Macdonald then defeated the Liberals again in 1878.

threat to Canada's loyal connection with the mother country. The arguments against abolition by Henry Reeves, which were somewhat self-serving since he was the JCPC's long-serving clerk and registrar, deserve to be quoted at some length because they provide an early hint of the direction the JCPC intended to take Canadian federalism:

> The Dominion of Canada has recently been erected on a federal basis, including several provinces. Questions of great nicety must arise under such a constitution between the federal and provincial legislatures and judicatures. These are precisely questions upon which the decision of a Court of Final Appeal, not included within the Confederation, would be most impartial and valuable ... Laws passed by a strong political majority, and administered by Judges and Courts appointed by the representatives of the same majority, are less likely to ensure an entire respect for the rights of all classes ...[5]

And so it would be, by imperial fiat, and so it would remain until 1949. The Canadians had their federal constitution, but the JCPC would tell them what it meant – and what they meant it to be was not exactly what John A. Macdonald had had in mind. In this chapter, I will focus only on division of power disputes, which lie at the heart of the constitutional federal compact. The discussion of the judicial interpretation of Charter and Indigenous rights, both entrenched in the Constitution Act, 1982, will follow in Chapter 7, and the role the Supreme Court of Canada played in the question of Quebec separatism will be examined in Chapter 8.

Pith and Substance

In much of the English Canadian literature on federalism, the JCPC has received a bad rap for turning the founders' intention of creating a highly centralized federal system on its head.[6] Instead of following the path begun by the SCC's home-grown early decisions giving the peace, order, and good government (POGG) clause as well as the federal trade and commerce power a meaning of almost

5 Cited in Saywell, *The Lawmakers*, 59.

6 See Garth Stevenson, *Unfulfilled Union*, 4th ed. (Toronto: Oxford University Press, 2009), 57–8; Gerald Baier, "The Courts, the Constitution, and Dispute Resolution," in *Canadian Federalism*, eds. Herman Bakvis and Grace Skogstad (Toronto: Oxford University Press, 2012), 81.

ubiquitous applicability, the JCPC would insist on a much more limited meaning of trade and commerce, and it would eventually deny the paramountcy of the POGG clause as a general legislative empowerment in the national interest. Following their own rationale and not really interested in the Canadian founders' intentions, the British Law Lords thus would sow the seeds for the kind of provincialism threatening to tear the nation apart a century later. Only the fully sovereign SCC after 1949 would restore some balance by a "cautious run of centralization."[7]

Unsurprisingly, the JCPC gets a better rap in some of the French Canadian literature. Instead of being criticized for whittling away federal power in favour of unbridled provincialism, the British Law Lords are praised for shielding the provinces from "the abuses of power by the central government."[8] French Canadian scholars also would more likely side with Henry Reeve and his suspicion that the cozy vicinity of politics and law in Ottawa, with the judges of the SCC all appointed by the federal government, may indeed give cause for concern.[9]

What gets lost in between these dichotomizing centralization–decentralization perspectives is the genuine effort of the JCPC to understand the legal nature of the BNA Act beyond whatever the founders may have thought or intended. By extension, the JCPC's decisions also contributed to a remarkably principled approach to judicial interpretation that would ultimately define Canadian federalism as a political enterprise requiring cooperation and compromise rather than taking place in separate and watertight compartments. What the Law Lords discovered, and what Canada's provincial courts had already earlier established for themselves, was that the attempt of assigning exclusive powers to each order of government was an exercise in futility. Judicial interpretation instead had to determine not so much who was allowed under the constitution to do what, but instead who should be allowed to do how much of what so that a balance of power between the two orders of government was maintained. In this way, the Law Lords also gave sharper contours to the federal principles, which the founders had left deliberately undecided.

7 Baier, ibid.

8 Alain-G. Gagnon, "Taking Stock of Asymmetrical Federalism in an Era of Exacerbated Centralization," in *Contemporary Canadian Federalism: Foundations, Traditions, Institutions*, ed. Alain-G. Gagnon (Toronto: University of Toronto Press, 2012), 257.

9 Jean-François Caron, Guy Laforest, and Catherine Vallières-Rolland, "Canada's Federative Deficit," in Gagnon, *Contemporary Canadian Federalism*, 143–4.

The first major case related to the division of powers was the precedent-setting *Parsons* case of 1881.[10] The constitutionally relevant question was whether jurisdiction over property and civil rights would allow Ontario to regulate the provincial fire insurance business, or whether such regulation fell under the federal power of regulating trade and commerce. As delivered by Sir Montague Smith, the judgment departed from the SCC's earlier understanding of trade and commerce as a power with near-unlimited reach, and thus made room for the provincial regulation of intra-provincial business.

It did so in four consecutive steps. First came an acknowledgement of the obvious: The "very general language" of Sections 91 and 92 made it difficult if not impossible to draw legislative boundaries with final certainty. Second, even though the gist of the BNA Act obviously was to accord "pre-eminence to the dominion parliament," this could not possibly mean that "in the case of a conflict of powers" provincial powers simply "should be absorbed in those given to the dominion parliament." Third, the task then was "to ascertain in what degree and to what extent" the action undertaken in the case at hand might fall under either section of the BNA Act. And finally, fourth, a decision would have to be reached by determining which of the two sections in question should receive a more limited reading "by necessary implication or reasonable intendment." Following this reasoning, the Law Lords decided that regulating a provincial insurance business was more a matter of contractual – and hence civil – law than an activity broadly falling under trade and commerce.

This reasoning, I would contend, neither gives credence to the accusation that the JCPC opened the gates to unbridled provincialism, nor does it appear to be imbued by an urgent sense of shielding the provinces from federal abuse. Instead, it marks the beginning of what would become a uniquely Canadian contribution the judicial interpretation of federal constitutions: the doctrine of "pith and substance." This doctrine provides a principled two-step process of deciding the validity of laws or regulations by either order of government in case of conflict with the powers of the other order.[11]

The court first has to determine the essential character (pith and substance) of the law with regard to its intended objective and effects on public policy. Once the pith and substance of a law is thus established, the court must then decide to which of the contending powers, federal or provincial, it properly belongs and to

10 *The Citizens Insurance Company of Canada and The Queen Insurance Company v Parsons (Canada)* [1881] UKPC 50 (26 November 1881).

11 See Patrick Monahan, *Constitutional Law* (Toronto: Irwin Law, 2002), 117–21.

which it is merely incidental. The law is valid if its pith and substance is considered to be falling under the powers of the enacting government. In the *Parsons* case, then, the JCPC found Ontario's regulation of the provincial fire insurance business valid by judging that its essential character had to do more with contract law falling under the provincial power of property and civil rights than with the federal trade and commerce power, to which it was found to be merely incidental.

The doctrine of pith and substance arises and derives its validity from the acknowledgement that the powers in the Canadian federal system can be, and often will be, overlapping rather than mutually exclusive as constitutionally intended. Overlapping powers mean that both orders of government can, in principle, legislate on the same subject matter. In the case of conflict, the courts cannot settle once and for all which order has jurisdiction over a particular matter. Instead, judicial interpretation is held, as the JCPC first suggested in *Parsons*, "to decide each case which arises" on its own merit, and without "entering more largely upon an interpretation than is necessary for the particular question in hand." In other words, the courts must determine the pith and substance of every piece of contested legislation and then decide whether this legislation rightfully belongs to the power arsenal of the enacting government.

This mode of judicial interpretation obviously runs counter to what might be the most iconic question in Canadian federalism: Is whatever matter at hand a federal or provincial responsibility? In reality, as the JCPC first understood, most matters are more complicated, and this understanding has guided Canadian judicial interpretation to this day. Thus, in a recent reference case,[12] the SCC had to decide whether the federal government of Conservative Prime Minister Stephen Harper could replace the provincial regulation of securities with a single national securities regulator. The SCC denied this and declared the proposed Securities Act invalid. In doing so, however, the court first acknowledged that both orders of government can legitimately regulate the trade of financial assets. The provinces may do so under the property and civil rights clause and for purposes of "local concerns protecting investors and ensuring the fairness of the markets through regulation of participants." The federal government in turn may do so under its trade and commerce power for "matters of undoubted national interest and concern." The court then found that the act as proposed aimed at a "wholesale takeover" of all aspects of securities regulation, and it thus declared the act

12 Canadian superior courts, including the SCC as the final court of appeal, not only decide cases of litigation but also hear so-called *reference cases* involving constitutional questions brought before them for advisory opinion by either order of government.

invalid because the "main thrust of the legislation – its pith and substance" thus was not "qualitatively different" from "local concerns."[13]

Strangely, since the proposed Securities Act was a reaction to the 2008 world financial crisis, the federal government and the province of Ontario did not try to bolster their case by making reference to that other clause in the BNA Act that the founders had intended as an override for all local stirrings of resistance against the national interest: peace, order, and good government. Perhaps they did not think they would get a lot of mileage out of a clause the JCPC once had downgraded to the status of an emergency clause only, thus giving rise to what has been widely denounced ever since as a deplorable "constitutional imbalance" that even the SCC in its later decisions could remedy only in part.[14]

As I want to argue in the next section, however, the JCPC's emergency doctrine, just as the one on pith and substance, made a significant contribution to an appropriate understanding of Canadian federalism. While surely disproportionate in its early pronouncements, it held later courts to restrictive caution in defining the national interest so that a balance of federal and provincial powers would be maintained.

From Need to Necessity

Not everybody back in Canada was happy about how the JCPC set out to shape Confederation. John A. Macdonald probably wondered what he had been thinking when he opposed Edward Blake's move to have JCPC appeals abolished. And the Supreme Court judges certainly did not feel very "supreme" when their understanding of Canadian federalism was routinely second-guessed by the British Law Lords or when, as was increasingly the case, they were bypassed altogether when Canadian litigants took their cases to London directly.

Among those generally happy with the JCPC's rulings was Oliver Mowat, once a clerk in John A. Macdonald's Kingston law office, then one of the Fathers of Confederation alongside Macdonald, and finally the Liberal Premier of Ontario for a whopping 24 years. As premier, he became the champion of a provincial rights movement that made him Macdonald's main constitutional foe.[15] Originating in Ontario under Mowat's powerful leadership, this provincial rights movement aimed at correcting Macdonald's lopsided vision of a highly

13 *Reference re Securities Act*, 2011 SCC 66.

14 Monahan, *Constitutional Law*, 246.

15 See Richard Gwyn, *Nation Maker* (Toronto: Random House Canada, 2011), 347–73.

centralized federation. Federalism, the provincialists argued, first of all meant that "each level of government is supreme or sovereign within its sphere"; it meant secondly "a balanced division of power" in which neither level overwhelms the other; and finally it meant "contractualism," the (ultimately untenable) view that the federation had been "created as a compact among the provinces."[16]

It is impossible, at this point, to resist quickly fast-forwarding a century when another epochal rivalry about Canadian federalism would play out between a prime minister, Pierre Elliott Trudeau, and René Lévesque, the combative premier of Quebec. As in the case of Macdonald and Mowat, Trudeau and Lévesque had once been reluctant allies for a common cause, in this instance the modernization of Quebec during what would later be dubbed the Quiet Revolution.[17] And also as in the case of Macdonald and Mowat, crucial parts of the drama would be played out in the courts. We shall return to this in Chapter 7.

More than anything else, it probably was the legal eloquence of Mowat and others that swayed the JCPC to adopt a more federally balanced reading of the BNA Act. Mowat argued the *Parsons* case himself, and he appeared before the JCPC several times more in person, as did Edward Blake, who was sent to London on behalf of Ontario several times. On balance, even latter-day critics of the JCPC agree that the Law Lords got it about right when it came to judicial interpretation of the division of powers as laid out in the enumerated powers of Sections 91 and 92.[18] Their take on the general POGG clause, however, was something else altogether.

POGG was indeed the trap Macdonald had meant to create, luring the provinces into a constitutional scheme that satisfied their local instincts at the time while creating, for all time to come, a wide open gate for the federal government not only to take exclusive hold of everything else by means of a residual clause, but moreover to overrule even local autonomy when this was deemed necessary in the national interest. This juxtaposition of federal and provincial powers was intended as the exact opposite of what the Americans had done (or had at least pretended to do), which was a slim list of federal powers kept in check by residual states' powers covering everything else. Just in case, or "for greater certainty," as Section 91 put it, the Canadians added a list of exclusive federal powers.

16 Robert C. Vipond, *Liberty and Community: Canadian Federalism and the Failure of the Constitution* (Albany: State University of New York Press, 1991), 5.

17 See John English, *Citizen of the World* (Toronto: Knopf Canada, 2006), 376–81.

18 Saywell, *The Lawmakers*, 114.

It was this constitutional oddity, first declaring that the federal government exclusively possessed all powers not explicitly given to the provinces and then adding a list of such federal powers nevertheless, that the British Law Lords pounced on. To their legal minds, these parallel pronouncements of federal powers could not simply be there "just in case." There had to be a reason, and that reason obviously had to be some sort of differentiation between explicit and implicit or residual jurisdiction. As delivered by Lord Watson, the judgment in the 1896 *Local Prohibition* reference first made this distinction. In essence, the JCPC argued as follows: There was some overlap between the specifically enumerated federal and provincial powers listed in Sections 91 and 92, respectively. As established earlier and beginning with *Parsons*, conflicts could be decided case by case according to the pith and substance doctrine. Applying the same doctrine in the case of provincial powers and POGG, however, would "practically destroy the autonomy of the provinces" because this clause had such a wide and general meaning that "there is hardly a subject enumerated in s. 92" upon which the federal government might not be able to legislate "to the exclusion of the provincial legislatures."[19] Except in the most exceptional of circumstances, therefore, POGG should not be invoked to the detriment of provincial powers. POGG, in other words, was relegated to the status of a residual clause only.

The final *coup de grâce* to whatever may have been John A. Macdonald's vision of a faux federation was then delivered in the 1922 *Board of Commerce* decision. As delivered by Lord Haldane, the JCPC ruling effectively reduced POGG to an emergency clause. It could only be invoked under circumstances dictated by necessity "beyond anything provided for by the enumerated heads in either s. 92 or s. 91." The Law Lords cited "war or famine" as examples and found that in the matter at hand, concerning the protection of society against commercial hoarding and price gouging during the socially unstable aftermath of World War I, such a "standard of necessity" was not evident.[20]

It was this case more than any other that gave the JCPC its bad reputation. It opened the door to a string of subsequent decisions that effectively turned the constitutional intention of 1867 upside down by anointing the provincial property and civil rights clause with the kind of ubiquitous meaning and reach that it just had denied to the federal POGG clause in the earlier *Local Prohibition* case.[21] Most

19 *The Attorney General for Ontario v. The Attorney General for the Dominion of Canada* (Canada) [1896] UKPC 20 (9 May 1896).

20 *The Attorney General of Canada (Appeal No. 103 of 1920) v. The Attorney General of Alberta and others* (Canada) [1921] UKPC 107 (8 November 1921).

21 See Stevenson, *Unfulfilled Union*, 53–7.

notorious among these decisions was the one rendered in the 1937 Employment and Social Insurance Act reference that invalidated the centrepiece of the so-called New Deal legislation introduced by the Conservative federal government of Prime Minister R.B. Bennett as a response to the devastating social effects of the Great Depression. Echoing the SCC's earlier verdict on the matter, the JCPC's key arguments were that unemployment insurance clearly fell under the provincial jurisdiction of property and civil rights, that POGG did not apply because it was intended to be permanent, and that the act therefore could not be seen as dealing with "any special emergency."[22]

The JCPC's bad reputation is a bad reputation mostly in hindsight. At the time, the Law Lords could not possibly get the impression that federal welfare legislation requiring a radical reversal of its BNA Act interpretation was an ardent desire of the Canadian political class. Bennett had introduced the legislation in 1935 not least as a last-minute effort to stave off looming electoral defeat. He nevertheless lost the federal election to Mackenzie King in that same year. As Liberal opposition leader, Mackenzie King basically had avoided taking a firm stand either way by hiding behind the assumption that the legislation would be deemed unconstitutional. And once prime minister, by referring the issue to the courts, he did not convey any sense of urgency for Bennett's New Deal either. King was not opposed to social legislation in principle, though, but he was opposed to act on matters for which he lacked formal powers. In 1940, he introduced a federal unemployment insurance plan after the provinces had agreed to transfer this power to the federal government by means of constitutional amendment.

The entire process delayed urgently needed welfare relief to suffering Canadians by five years. The JCPC probably is least to blame. To be sure, the Law Lords could not see the necessity for permanent unemployment relief, but the "jurisdictional hide-and-seek" up to this point[23] probably did not convey to them the impression that Canada's political classes thought much otherwise. The real problem was that the devastating social consequences of the Great Depression required a political response that went far beyond whatever Canadian modernizers and traditionalists had a century earlier imagined as a reasonable compromise in dividing federal and provincial powers. Canadian federalism needed a whole

22 *The Attorney General of Canada (Appeal No. 101 of 1936) v. The Attorney General of Ontario and others* (Canada) [1937] UKPC 7 (28 January 1937).

23 Keith Banting, "Canada: Nation-Building in a Federal Welfare State," in *Federalism and the Welfare State: New World and European Experiences*, eds. Herbert Obinger, Stephan Leibfried, and Francis G. Castles (Cambridge: Cambridge University Press, 2005), 99.

new compromise about who should reasonably do what, and the intergovernmental agreement on unemployment insurance in 1940 was the first step toward such a compromise. The eventual outcome was a welfare state in which the federal government would play a much larger role than either the JCPC or the provinces anticipated or wanted.

It is once more impossible to resist quickly fast-forwarding half a century to the 2008 world financial crisis, which had all the trappings of turning into another Great Depression. The worst social consequences were avoided, however, precisely because, contrary to the 1930s, the main instruments of fiscal stabilization, social insurance, and fiscal equalization were already in place. We shall return to the rise of the Canadian welfare state in Chapter 5.

In the meantime, however, I want to offer my own evaluation of the JCPC's role in the evolution of Canadian federalism. The historical compromise leading to Confederation in 1867 can still be appreciated, albeit in somewhat simplified fashion, as one between feudalism and capitalism – local privileges versus a national market economy. By the 1930s, when the JCPC rendered its most infamous decisions, however, the great ideological divide had become one between capitalism and socialism. And while socialism was associated with a strong centralized state, federalism had come to be seen as a free market remedy.

On the left, for instance, Harold Laski warned that federalism was becoming obsolete because its fragmented powers proved helpless against the rise of giant capitalism.[24] On the right, Friedrich Hayek hopefully suggested that federalism would lead to deregulation all around because neither the individual members of a federation nor the federation as a whole would be in a position to implement strong social policies. Competing with one another in a single market, individual members would not be able to afford social regulation, and the central union government would be prevented from doing so in light of socioeconomic diversity: "such legislation ... will be viewed in a different light in poor and rich regions."[25]

As has been observed by others,[26] the JCPC would not have been immune to these kinds of arguments, and it is quite unlikely that their lordships even intended to make common cause with socialist centralism. However,

---

24 Harold J. Laski, "The Obsolescence of Federalism," *The New Republic* 98, no. 1274 (1939).

25 Friedrich Hayek, "The Economic Conditions of Interstate Federalism," in *Individualism and Economic Order,* ed. Friedrich Hayek (1939; repr., Chicago: Chicago University Press, 1980), 263. Hayek's article was about a European federation. See also Wolfgang Streeck, *Buying Time: The Delayed Crisis of Democratic Capitalism* (London: Verso, 2014), 97–103.

26 See Stevenson, *Unfulfilled Union,* 51.

I nevertheless want to suggest that the JCPC by and large remained faithful to the principle of federalism as a balanced system of power sharing. It did so most poignantly in the *Board of Commerce* decision when it tied the potentially ubiquitous reach of the POGG clause to a "condition of necessity" for its successful invocation as an emergency clause.[27]

The Law Lords were wrong in denying such necessity for social legislation in their decisions during the 1930s. But what they were wrong about was not the necessity limitation they placed on POGG. It was that they could not see that permanent welfare relief such as unemployment insurance had become a necessity. Canada's own Supreme Court had not seen it either, and at least some would argue that the King government also pursued the matter only reluctantly.[28] Necessity became fully obvious only after the catastrophe of World War II. Then, the general clauses empowering central governments in the name of national interest and stability almost unhinged many federal systems from the opposite end, but thanks to the JCPC's earlier restrictive reading of the POGG clause, not so in Canada.

In what was then West Germany, for instance, the designers of the 1949 constitution were mindful of the fact that Nazi dictatorship and world war had in large part been a consequence of social destabilization during the 1920s. Consequently, they wrote into that constitution, the Basic Law, as they called it, that in the case of concurrent jurisdiction, the federal government could preempt *Länder* (provincial) legislation if it declared that there was a need to maintain equitable living conditions for all Germans. This clause, Article 72(2) of the Basic Law, was used so excessively that many observers began to speak of a creeping "unitarization" of German federalism.

In 1994, a constitutional reform effort aiming at rebalancing the federal system after reunification somewhat tightened the clause: The federal government could no longer simply declare that there was a need for equitability but had to demonstrate that federal legislation was necessary to maintain it. And finally, in 2004, the Federal Constitutional Court of Germany spelled out what that "condition of necessity" meant: Federal legislation could only correct already existing inequality but no longer claim a need for proactively preventing it.[29] This interpretation came close to seeing Article 72(2) as an emergency clause.

27 *The Attorney General of Canada (Appeal No. 103 of 1920) v. The Attorney General of Alberta and others* (Canada) [1921] UKPC 107 (8 November 1921).

28 See Richard Simeon and Ian Robinson, *State, Society, and the Development of Canadian Federalism* (Toronto: University of Toronto Press, 1990), 78–86.

29 Fritz W. Scharpf, *Föderalismusreform* (Frankfurt: Campus, 2009), 95.

At least from this comparative vantage point, the JCPC's restrictive rulings on the reach of the POGG clause appear in a somewhat more benign light. In order to maintain the intended balance of the federal system, POGG could not be invoked by declaring that there was a need to do so. There had to be a demonstrable necessity.

Beyond Provincial Concern

In one of the last cases before them, the *Canada Temperance Federation* case of 1946, the Law Lords of the JCPC loosened the emergency noose that had strangled the POGG clause. Booze once again was at the forefront of Canadian constitutional wrangling.

Apart from the Northwest Territories, Ontario was the last temperance holdout in Canada. Keen on much-needed sales revenue, the Ontario government had in 1927 introduced a public sales monopoly overseen by what is still known to Ontarians today as the Liquor Control Board of Ontario (LCBO), even though the last in a whole series of referendums on the question had still yielded a slim majority in favour of prohibition. The Canada Temperance Act in its 1927 version, however, allowed municipalities to prevent the sale of liquor by means of locally held referendums. In 1939, asked by the provincial government to rule on the validity of the act, the court of appeal of Ontario did so in the affirmative. The appeal was then heard before the JCPC in 1946. The federal government, supported only by a number of temperance leagues, stood against the united phalanx of almost all the provinces. To everyone's surprise, the Law Lords upheld the act. As a consequence, some local areas, such as in west Toronto, would stay dry into the twenty-first century.

The Law Lords were in somewhat of a bind. On the one hand, they did not want to disavow one of the JCPC's earlier rulings in which the regulation of alcohol-related matters had been declared to be a residuary federal power under the POGG clause.[30] On the other hand, they were no longer prepared to argue, as the JCPC had done in one of its more twisted decisions, that "the evil of intemperance" was such a "menace to the national life of Canada" that it warranted to call upon federal emergency powers in the name of peace, order, and good government so as to prevent "the nation from disaster."[31] Instead, they now opined that legislative authority will "fall within the competence of the

30 *Charles Russell v. The Queen* (New Brunswick) [1882] UKPC 33 (23 June 1882).

31 *The Toronto Electric Commissioners (Appeal No. 99 of 1924) v. Colin G. Snider and others* (Ontario) [1925] UKPC 2 (20 January 1925).

Dominion Parliament as a matter affecting the peace, order, and good government of Canada" when its real subject matter (pith and substance again!) "goes beyond local or provincial concern and interests and must from its inherent nature be concern of the Dominion as a whole."[32]

The Law Lords not so much had a belated change of heart as they acknowledged that the times had changed. At the end of World War II, much of the industrialized western world had come to accept that democratic stability required social policy intervention and that national governments had to play a central role in it. After all, the Canadian provinces themselves had unanimously consented only six years earlier to a constitutional amendment that established unemployment insurance as a new national responsibility. While the JCPC's 1946 ruling surely did not cover any new social policy ground, its reasoning nevertheless opened the door for a more generous interpretation of the POGG clause when the SCC took over as final court of appeal in 1949.[33]

Just how much the SCC opened that door toward a centralist interpretation of Canadian federalism has been a question as controversial as the one about how provincialist the JCPC's interpretation of it had been before. And unsurprisingly, while the provinces had obviously welcomed the JCPC's rulings favourable to them, they would now berate the SCC for its centralist bias as being in collusion with the federal government. Before delving into this question, however, two clarifications are in order.

First, some of the harshest criticisms of the SCC's performance have come over its rulings on two controversial constitutional questions that went far beyond anything the JCPC ever had to deal with. One was the question of the degree of provincial approval required for the 1982 constitutional amendment package that included a domestic amendment formula and the Charter of Rights and Freedoms. The other question was about the constitutionality of secession in the aftermath of the 1995 Quebec referendum. These questions, while obviously speaking to the core of a federation's foundational agreement, fall outside the normal range of judicial interpretations of the division of powers. We shall return to them in Chapters 7 and 8, respectively.

Second, the view, particularly prevalent in Quebec, according to which Canadian federalism has entered an "era of exacerbated centralization"[34] for the

32 *The Attorney-General of Ontario and others (Appeal No. 2 of 1940) v. The Canada Temperance Federation* (Ontario) [1946] UKPC 2 (21 January 1946).

33 See Baier, "The Courts," 81.

34 See Gagnon, "Taking Stock of Asymmetrical Federalism."

most part pertains to federal spending power intrusions into areas of provincial jurisdiction such as healthcare. The SCC hardly had a hand in this de facto circumvention of the constitutional division of powers because it was mostly based on intergovernmental agreement. This story will be picked up again in Chapter 5.

The story we shall follow in this chapter is about how the SCC continued to interpret – or reinterpret – the division of powers in the operation of Canadian federalism. In essence, as I will argue, the SCC remained faithful to the tradition of constitutional interpretation begun by the JCPC a century earlier, and it did so by continuing to examine and uncover the pith and substance of each case at hand. If that looked like strengthening the federal government at the expense of provincial jurisdiction, then this was so mainly because the court had to deal with a whole range of issues that were now more widely perceived as cross-jurisdictional and therefore beyond provincial concern.[35]

In *Crown v. Zellerbach*, for instance, the court effectively accorded to the federal government exclusive jurisdiction over oceanic environmental protection as a national concern under the POGG clause even though pollution might occur in coastal waters owned by the province.[36] In *General Motors of Canada*, it upheld a federal act forbidding price discrimination as a valid exercise of the federal government's trade and commerce power in the interest of national economic union.[37] And in the *Firearms* reference, it decided that in consideration of its pith and substance, gun registration fell under the federal criminal law power rather than provincial regulation of private property, as the government of Alberta contended.[38]

Far more contentious were a number of earlier decisions that appeared to meddle with what the provinces thought to be their constitutional home turf. The cases in question foreshadowed in legally constrained language what would soon amount to open political warfare with Ottawa on two fronts: separatism in Quebec and energy policy in the west (see Chapter 7).

Even before the sovereigntist Parti Québécois under the leadership of René Lévesque came to power in 1976, Quebec governments had embarked on an aggressive path of asserting constitutional rights they thought were theirs. Thus, the government's Public Service Board had begun to issue licences for

35 See Baier, "The Courts," 81; also Peter W. Hogg, "Is the Supreme Court of Canada Biased in Constitutional Cases?" *The Canadian Bar Review* 57, no. 4 (1979): 730–1.

36 *R. v. Crown Zellerbach Canada Ltd.*, [1988] 1 SCR 401.

37 *General Motors of Canada Ltd. v. City National Leasing*, [1989] 1 SCR 641.

38 *Reference re Firearms Act* [2000] 1 SCR 783.

the distribution of cable television even though the federal Canadian Radio-television and Telecommunications Commission (CRTC) would do the same. Push came to shove in 1975 when the CRTC issued a licence for operation in a region already covered by a provincial licence:[39] The RCMP seized the transmission equipment of the provincial operator; the province replaced it; Ottawa charged the provincial operator with operating without a federal licence; the province followed suit by charging the federal operator with operating without a provincial licence; and the federal operator, François Dionne, went to court.

The legal process ended three years later when the *Cable Television* case was heard by the SCC in 1978.[40] Quebec's Public Service Board argued that cable television should remain under provincial jurisdiction since access to cable – contrary to airwaves – could be locally controlled. The SCC nevertheless held that the already existing federal jurisdiction over broadcasting should also include cable television along with all other forms of telecommunication. The decision meant that cable television would be regulated by Canadian content rules rather than fall under Quebec's language and culture policy regime. In a rare instance of cultural divisiveness spilling into the court, six English Canadian judges carried the decision while three Quebec judges dissented.[41]

The Lévesque government's reaction was markedly restrained. It had abstained from direct intervention in the case to begin with, leaving it to the Public Service Board to make the case. One can only speculate that Lévesque calculated that provincial control of cable television was a lost cause anyway, and the decision as expected would instead strengthen the separatist argument according to which Canadian federalism would never offer Quebec a fair deal.

Another pair of SCC decisions in 1978 and 1979, however, concerning the ownership and management of natural resources, triggered unrestrained hostility in the western provinces. In the *CIGOL* case of 1978,[42] the SCC disallowed as indirect taxation a "royalty surcharge" the province of Saskatchewan had intended to cash in with on the oil and gas industry's windfall profits in the aftermath of the 1973 OPEC crisis. A year later, it ruled in the *Potash* case[43] that pro-rationing potash production destined for external markets according

39 Following Ian Bushnell, *The Captive Court: A Study of the Supreme Court of Canada* (Montreal: McGill-Queen's University Press, 1992), 426.

40 *Public Service Board et al. v. Dionne et al.*, [1978] 2 SCR 191.

41 Bushnell, *The Captive Court*, 427.

42 *CIGOL v. Saskatchewan*, [1978] 2 SCR 545.

43 *Central Canada Potash Co. Ltd. et al. v. Government of Saskatchewan*, [1979] 1 SCR 42.

to demand amounted to price fixing and therefore unduly infringed upon the federal trade and commerce powers. These decisions were all the more galling because the federal government had itself reacted to the explosion of oil prices in the aftermath of the OPEC crisis by imposing an oil price freeze as well as a new federal oil export tax while threatening similar measures with regard to natural gas.[44]

Did these cases really prove that the SCC had gone over to the dark side of exacerbated centralism, as at least some provincialist voices have alleged? There is no doubt that the SCC interpreted federal jurisdiction more widely than had the JCPC in some of its most notorious rulings during the 1920s and 1930s. But the court handed wins and losses to provinces as well as to the federal government, and the overall record of balance has in fact not been much different from that of the JCPC.[45] One might observe with considerable justification that the main reason for the SCC's centralist reputation was that the provinces complained more loudly than the federal government when they "found its decisions inconvenient."[46]

One of the provincial victories worth mentioning was the *Labatt Breweries* case of 1980,[47] not so much because Canada's highest court was preoccupied with booze yet again but because the decision showed – as many other decisions would show just as well – how close Canadian constitutional jurisprudence has remained faithful to the path and tradition the JCPC began a century earlier. The case was about the regulation and marketing of beer. Under its Food and Drugs Act, the federal government had regulated the alcoholic content of "light beer" within a range from 1.2 to 2.5 per cent. Labatt had begun to market a new 4 per cent beer that it labelled "Labatt's Special Lite." When the case reached the SCC, the main question no longer was whether Labatt had successfully circumvented federal regulations by calling its beer "lite" instead of "light." The question asked by Labatt, with supportive intervention by the government of Quebec, was whether

44 John F. Conway, *The West: The History of a Region in Confederation* (Toronto: Lorimer, 1983), 195.

45 See Peter H. Russell, *Leading Constitutional Decisions* (Ottawa: Carleton University Press, 1982), 7–8; Gerald Baier, "The Law of Federalism: Judicial Review and the Division of Powers," in *New Trends in Canadian Federalism*, 2nd ed., eds. François Rocher and Miriam Smith (Toronto: University of Toronto Press, 2012), 122–3.

46 Stevenson, *Unfulfilled Union*, 63.

47 *Labatt Breweries of Canada Ltd. v. Attorney General of Canada*, [1980] 1 SCR 914.

the federal regulation of alcohol content was unconstitutional to begin with. In a 6:3 decision, but this time with Quebec judges on either side of the divide, the court held that it was.

The case stands out also because the judgment rendered by the court begins with a strong opinion of dissent by Chief Justice Bora Laskin, the most well-known critic of the JCPC's alleged provincialist bias. Reaching all the back to the 1881 *Parsons* case, Laskin began by emphasizing that the question at hand in his regard was "a highly important issue" in need of "extended considerations." He then argued, as the JCPC had in *Parsons*, that federal legislation was a valid exercise of the trade and commerce power if the essence of such legislation was "general regulation of trade affecting the whole Dominion." While the JCPC had denied this in *Parsons*, Laskin came to the opposite conclusion in *Labatt Breweries*, arguing that the regulation of alcoholic content was in line with other "uniform prescriptions" for foods, drugs, cosmetics, and so on.

The majority decision also relied on the *Parsons* case but reached a different conclusion. Once again, the judges reiterated that it was impossible to rely on "anything approaching a constitutional formula." It all came down to the pith and substance of the case at hand. As first established in *Parsons*, the valid exercise of the federal trade and commerce power has to have as its objective legislation that affects "industry and commerce at large or in a sweeping, general sense." It is not valid when that objective is "regulation of a single trade, even though it be on a national basis" – such as in the case at hand, the regulation of alcoholic content for beer. Moreover, the decision added for good measure that the general peace, order, and good government clause could not be invoked to uphold the impugned federal regulation. "The brewing and labelling of beer and light beer," the judges declared, did not live up to either of the "two branches" that *Parsons* had first established as valid meanings of POGG. Neither did it give rise to a "national emergency," nor did it amount to a matter of "national concern transcending the local authorities' power to meet and solve it by legislation."

Overall, the SCC has taken seriously the promise of provincial autonomy on which the success of Confederation rested. The claim that the SCC "failed … to meet the high standards of objective neutrality"[48] in adjudicating Canadian federalism is, in my view, untenable. As first developed by the JCPC, the Canadian doctrine of pith and substance precisely aims at maintaining neutrality, one case at a time. One can disagree with the outcome, but one cannot deny the genuine intent and effort.

48 Caron, Laforest, and Vallières-Roland, "Canada's Federative Deficit," 143–4.

A major turning point in Canadian constitutional jurisprudence came with the New Deal legislation of the 1930s when urgent national programs of social relief were impeded or at least delayed by the courts. The Supreme Court in the United States subsequently abandoned federalism altogether by allowing the trade and commerce clause in particular to be abused for unrestrained Congressional supremacy.[49] By comparison, the Supreme Court of Canada, while cautiously correcting some of the JCPC's most extreme provincialist exaggerations, found its own way of maintaining a Canadian version of federal balance.

That version, I would submit, much more resembles a European rather than American tradition of federalism. Four hundred years ago, the German political theorist Johannes Althusius first pre-formulated what would become the quintessential question of modern federalism: the distinction between matters that concern all members of a federation alike and matters that concern them separately.[50] The pith and substance doctrine has in mind the very same distinction, between that which "goes beyond local or provincial concern," as the JCPC had put it in the *Canada Temperance Federation* case of 1946, and that which does not transcend "local authorities' power to meet and solve it by legislation," as the SCC ruled in the *Labatt Breweries* case of 1980.

In the same year when the SCC heard that case, the European Court of Justice issued one of its most famous decisions in the *Cassis de Dijon* case.[51] It was about alcohol content as well. The Germans tried to discriminate against a French liquor, *Cassis*, by arguing that it should not be allowed to be called a liquor because its 16 per cent alcohol content did not meet the German standard of 25 per cent. The court effectively ruled that if the alcohol content was good enough for France, it had to be good enough for Germany. Henceforth, the mutual recognition of different standards became a general rule for the single market of the European Union. What connects the *Cassis* ruling with the *Labatt* ruling is the same consideration that lies at the heart of the federal division of powers: whether uniform regulations are necessary for the overall well-being of the union or whether diversity can be safely accepted.

Overall, I want to argue, Canadian constitutional jurisprudence in the twentieth century has remained faithful to the federal principle understood as a

---

49 For evidence, see Thomas O. Hueglin and Alan Fenna, *Comparative Federalism: A Systematic Inquiry* (Toronto: University of Toronto Press, 2015), 319.

50 Johannes Althusius, *Politica Methodice Digesta* (1614; repr., Aalen: Scientia, 1981), 70.

51 *Rewe-Zentral AG v. Bundesmonopolverwaltung für Branntwein* (Germany), 120/78 [1979] 20 February 1979.

balanced exercise of divided and shared rule in this sense. It has done so, however, in marked departure both from the Canadian founders' centralist intentions and from the centralist evolution that federalism took in the United States. In the twenty-first century, it may have expanded this understanding in a new direction.

Federalism Demands Nothing Less

In a series of four decisions beginning in 2001, the SCC began to employ a concept that had until then rarely, if ever, found its way into Canadian constitutional jurisprudence: subsidiarity.[52] It is a European concept, and it has played a central role in European Union governance since the Maastricht Treaty of 1993.

As the Treaty on European Union stipulates, the principle of subsidiarity amounts to three interrelated guidelines for the allocation of powers in federal systems: Article 1 generally declares that all decisions should be taken "as closely as possible to the citizen," which effectively means at the lowest level of government possible; Article 5(3) then specifies that in cases of concurrent (or overlapping) jurisdiction, the higher level of government shall only decide or legislate if "the objective of the proposed action cannot be sufficiently achieved" by the governments of the lower levels themselves; Article 5(4) finally determines that whatever action taken at the higher level "shall not exceed what is necessary to achieve the objectives" of the intended legislation.

Subsidiarity in this European understanding, then, contains both a preference or bias for decentralized jurisdiction and a limitation on centralized action even when it is considered legitimate. Legislation shall not go further than necessary, thus leaving room for complementary legislation at the lower levels of government. In two decisions, the 2001 *Spraytech* decision[53] and the 2007 *Canadian Western Bank* decision,[54] the SCC appeared to endorse the full meaning of subsidiarity in this sense.

The *Spraytech* case in itself was hardly earth-shattering. Neither federal nor provincial governments intervened in the case. The court upheld a local bylaw restricting the use of pesticides even though these pesticides were approved by federal law and the companies using them operated in accordance with provincial (Quebec) law. The court's reasoning was extraordinary nevertheless: "The case

52 Erika Arban, "La Subsidiarité en Droit Européen et Canadien: Une Comparaison," *Canadian Public Administration* 56, no. 2 (2013).

53 *Canada Ltée (Spraytech, Société d'arrosage) v. Hudson (Town)*, 2001 SCC 40.

54 *Canadian Western Bank v. Alberta*, 2007 SCC 22.

arises in an era in which matters of governance are often examined through the lens of the principle of subsidiarity. This is the proposition that law making and implementation are often best achieved at a level of government that is not only effective, but also closest to the citizens affected and thus most responsive to their needs, to local distinctiveness, and to population diversity."

In the *Canadian Western Bank* case six years later, the SCC had to deal with a much weightier matter of overlapping federal–provincial jurisdiction. Banks in Alberta selling insurance objected to provincial licensing with the argument that this was invalid interference with the federal Bank Act, which allowed them to do so. The court held that it was not. It argued that the regulation of insurance, essentially under provincial jurisdiction over property and civil rights since *Parsons*, did not interfere substantively enough with the "core" of the federal power over banking so that both could not be considered valid in a complementary way. A more expansive understanding of provincial interjurisdictional interference with a federal power, the court then added, might not only lead to "an unintentional centralizing tendency in constitutional interpretation," but also undermine "principles of subsidiarity" as established in the earlier *Spraytech* decision.

As Chief Justice Beverley McLachlin made clear in one of the later decisions, the principle of subsidiarity could never be used to "override the division of powers." It could only be employed to ensure "adequate space for provincial regulation" in instances of overlapping jurisdiction.[55] And this, finding complementary space for federal and provincial regulation, became the centrepiece of the court's ruling in the 2011 *Securities* reference,[56] a ruling considered so extraordinary by Richard Simeon, Canada's most seasoned federalism expert at the time, that he wanted to convene an entire conference about it.[57] The principle of subsidiarity did not play an explicit role in the ruling, but the argument of a cooperative approach to complementary legislation as first raised in the court's subsidiarity deliberations did.

In the aftermath of the 2008 world financial crisis, the Conservative federal government of Stephen Harper had sought to replace the existing provincial systems of securities regulation with a single national securities regulator. Supported by the province of Ontario, the federal government asked the SCC for an advisory opinion whether the proposed Securities Act was a valid exercise of the federal trade and commerce power in that it addressed a national concern.

55 *Reference re Assisted Human Reproduction Act*, 2010 SCC 61.

56 *Reference re Securities Act*, 2011 SCC 66.

57 Personal communication; Simeon passed away prior to following through with his plan.

Opposition came from the provinces of Alberta, Quebec, Manitoba, and New Brunswick. Their argument was that the proposed act infringed upon the provinces' powers over property and civil rights. The court unanimously held that the proposed act was unconstitutional because it aimed at a "wholesale takeover" of securities regulation going way beyond what was necessary to satisfy what might have constituted a new national concern.

The bombshell surprise came at the end of the judgment. After noting the obvious, namely that regulating securities in Canada is a matter containing "both central and local aspects," the court admonished the litigants to find "common ground" and suggested "a cooperative approach that permits a scheme that recognizes the essentially provincial nature of securities regulation while allowing Parliament to deal with genuinely national concerns." Such a cooperative approach, the court continued, would reflect the "growing practice of resolving complex governance problems that arise in federations." Finally, the judgment ended with what almost amounts to an exhortation of the virtues of cooperative federalism: "Cooperation is the animating force. The federalism principle upon which Canada's constitutional framework rests demands nothing less."

Why would this decision be considered so extraordinary? In many ways, it only followed a path begun with the pith and substance doctrine in the *Parsons* case 130 years earlier: Divided powers are in reality overlapping, and the role of the courts is to sort out who should be allowed to do what. And obviously, if both orders of government can legislate in the same policy field, intergovernmental cooperation is required. However, the *Securities* decision marked a departure from long-standing traditions of Canadian constitutional jurisprudence in two ways.

First, the court acknowledged much more clearly than before a shift from a classical or dualist understanding of federalism whereby each order of government is supposed to operate separately in its own sphere of jurisdiction, to a more flexible and cooperative form of federalism wherein overlapping powers become the norm rather than the exception. As indicated by the references to subsidiarity in the preceding cases, this form of federalism also includes a more dynamic dimension in that the adjudication of the legitimate exercise of powers becomes more readily tied to time and circumstance. It is for this reason that defenders of provincial rights regard the SCC's new preoccupation with subsidiarity with suspicion because they fear it might tilt the federal balance even more toward centralization in the name of national concern and efficiency.[58]

58 See Eugénie Brouillet, "Canadian Federalism and the Principle of Subsidiarity: Should We Open Pandora's Box?" *Supreme Court Law Review* 54, no. 2 (2011).

Second, by admonishing the intergovernmental combatants that federalism demands to find a cooperative solution to the problem of overlapping powers, the court acknowledged what had already for some time become a prominent characteristic of Canadian federalism: "a trend ... to settle intergovernmental disputes away from the courts" by means of intergovernmental cooperation and agreement, effectively working around the constitution.[59] Yet while one can welcome this trend as a victory for democracy because decision-making power is moved from the judicial branch back to the political process, one can also conversely see it as a betrayal of federalism precisely because the power guarantees of the constitution are in danger of becoming diluted in political gamesmanship. The relationship of law and politics is a tenuous one.

Law and Politics

In their draft of the first modern federal constitution, the American framers had made provision for a "Supreme Court" as the judicial guardian of that constitution.[60] As Alexander Hamilton made clear in Federalist Paper No. 80, this guardianship would also include the final arbitration of power disputes between the two levels of government.[61] Hamilton also tried to deflect the suspicion and criticism of those who argued that in this way the judiciary might become superior to the legislative power: "The power of the people is superior to both," he argued in Federalist Paper No. 78, and "where the will of the legislature declared in its statutes stands in opposition to that of the people declared in the constitution, the judges ought to be governed by the latter, rather than the former."[62] This was an argument for constitutional, not popular, supremacy. And it did not at all close the door to judicial superiority. As one prominent American Supreme Court judge confidently put it at the beginning of the twentieth century: "We are under a Constitution, but the Constitution is what the judges say it is."[63]

59 See Baier, "The Courts," 80.

60 Article III.

61 Alexander Hamilton, John Jay, and James Madison, *The Federalist* (1787–8; Indianapolis: Liberty Fund, 2001), 412.

62 Ibid., 404.

63 Charles Evans Hughes, then (1907) governor of New York, but associate justice of the US Supreme Court from 1910–16, and chief justice from 1930–41; cited in Merlo J. Pusey, *Charles Evans Hughes* (New York: Macmillan, 1951), 204.

Although they already knew and had before their eyes almost a century of powerful constitutional jurisprudence by the US Supreme Court, the Canadians did not give much thought to the role the judiciary would play in Canadian constitutional matters. Next to the provincial courts, the Supreme Court of Canada would provide not much more than "a second, another appeal."[64] Final arbitration would be left to the JCPC.

Until 1949, that is, which is why Canada's long-serving Chief Justice Beverley McLachlin has suggested distinguishing three phases in the evolution of Canadian constitutional jurisprudence: a post-colonial period, 1867–1949, during which "Canada's judges applied English law" under the watchful eye of the JCPC; a transitional period, 1949–82, during which "dependence on British sources" weakened and Canadian judges "began to articulate Canadian perspectives on the old principles"; and "the modern era" since 1982, when a new balance had to be found between the three branches of government – legislative, executive, and judicial – because "traditional judicial tasks" such as "adjudicating the division of powers" were supplemented by entirely new tasks of interpreting "the guarantees of the Charter and of aboriginal and treaty rights."[65]

Respectfully, I beg to differ. There is no denying, of course, that the introduction of Charter rights as well as the belated recognition of Indigenous rights has posed additional challenges to the judicial interpretation of the powers that Canada's two orders of government possess under the constitution; we shall return to this issue in Chapter 7. I would argue, however, that the JCPC from the very beginning developed a judicial perspective that was very much Canadian rather than English.

At the core of English (unwritten) constitutionalism lies the principle of parliamentary supremacy, which means that no court can question or overturn parliamentary acts. The role of the JCPC was an imperial one, to make sure that colonial administrations complied with English law. That the BNA Act as a British statutory act did so was not in question. That statute, however, contained a federal division of powers. The exercise of parliamentary supremacy was apportioned between two orders of government.[66] The Law Lords therefore were confronted with something new that had no precedent in English law. They had

64 Bushnell, *The Captive Court,* 39.

65 Beverley McLachlin, "Canada's Legal System at 150: Democracy and the Judiciary" (speech, Empire Club of Canada, Toronto, ON, June 3, 2016).

66 See Monahan, *Constitutional Law,* 84–5.

to render judgment on the meaning of that apportionment as written down in the act. For purposes of interpretation and illustration, they could avail themselves of precedent in English law, but they could not ignore the constitutional federal intent. And that ultimately meant that what the JCPC delivered was a concept of constitutional rather than parliamentary supremacy no different from that in the United States.

In this respect, Section 52(1) of the Constitution Act, 1982, according to which "the Constitution of Canada is the supreme law of Canada," has only affirmed the obvious. One can of course quibble with the way in which that supreme law has been read and interpreted over the years. But I do not believe that the JCPC's reading was particularly English. If it was overly decentralist from a pan-Canadian nationalist perspective in hindsight, then that was so because such a perspective at the time was nowhere in sight. As Alan Cairns has argued, the JCPC's rulings for the most part were "harmonious" with Canada's underlying territorial and regional pluralism.[67]

Of course, the decisions that shut down the federal government's New Deal legislation during the 1930s were misguided. But that happened in the United States as well, and it happened because the Great Depression had ushered in national policy needs that only few understood quite yet. And if the SCC after 1949 embarked on a path of recalibrating federal–provincial balance in a more centralizing fashion, then this was so because it was in turn harmonious again with a new understanding of time and circumstance born out of war and depression.

That understanding in particular came to be expressed politically by new left-wing parties such as the Co-operative Commonwealth Federation (see Chapter 4) and its successor, the New Democratic Party, pushing for social policy initiatives requiring "concerted central government action supported through regular and stable financing."[68] But it was the SCC that gave principled expression to a new sense of balance, and herein lies the importance of judicial review and constitutional interpretation more generally.

67 Alan C. Cairns, "The Judicial Committee and Its Critics," *Canadian Journal of Political Science* 4, no. 3 (1971).

68 Luc Turgeon and Jennifer Wallner, "Adaptability and Change in Federations: Centralization, Political Parties, and Taxation Authority in Australia and Canada," in *The Global Promise of Federalism*, eds. Grace Skogstad, David Cameron, Martin Papillon, and Keith Banting (Toronto: University of Toronto Press, 2013), 203.

The court's more recent references to the principle of subsidiarity, finally, do not signal anything radically new. They only put into more contemporary language what has been a specifically Canadian approach to the constitutional interpretation of federalism all along. It is based on the recognition, alien to American as well as German constitutional jurisprudence, of what François Rocher has identified as one of the core principles of Canadian federalism: the realization that "the federal order, which encompasses a multiplicity of powers that are both autonomous and interdependent, cannot be definitive."[69]

The question remains, however: If it is the constitution itself that reigns supreme in the Canadian system of federalism, and if it is the judges who have the last word over what this constitution says or means, is it not then the judiciary that ultimately triumphs over the will of the people as expressed by their elected representatives? Not so, says Katherine Swinton. "One should not overestimate the role of the Court in the management of the federal system," she argues. Its decisions are "important to the federal-provincial negotiating process," but they are "not the final word."[70] In other words, the SCC's decisions and references provide constitutional clarifications on the basis of which conflict and compromise can unfold in the political arena. As we shall see in the next two chapters, the conflicts and compromises are mostly about money.

---

69 François Rocher, "The Quebec-Canada Dynamic or the Negation of the Ideal of Federalism," in *Contemporary Canadian Federalism: Foundations, Traditions, Institutions,* ed. Alain-G. Gagnon (Toronto: University of Toronto Press, 2012), 95.

70 Katherine Swinton, "Federalism under Fire: The Role of the Supreme Court of Canada," *Law and Contemporary Problems* 55, no. 1 (1992): 139.

CHAPTER FOUR

FROM A CRISIS OF CAPITALISM TO A CRISIS OF FEDERALISM

If one had to identify the one moment that triggered the most critical turning point in Canadian federalism, it would have to be the crash of the New York Stock Exchange in October 1929. Mass unemployment and poverty during the Great Depression that followed threw into question the wisdom of the division of powers that the founding fathers had enshrined in the British North America (BNA) Act. To put it in a nutshell: While the provinces had been assigned the constitutional powers to provide relief, they did not have the necessary revenue to do so; and while the federal government had the revenue, it lacked both formal powers and the political will to act. The crisis of capitalism turned into a crisis of federalism.

Initially, hiding behind the formal constraints of the BNA Act, the federal government refused to provide financial assistance to the near-bankrupt provinces. Challenge then came from particularly hard-hit Prairie provinces when right-wing populism in Alberta began to defy the established constitutional order and left-wing populism in Saskatchewan posed a more fundamental challenge to the established political and economic order. When the federal government finally decided to act, not least pushed by the "enlightened reactionaries" among business leaders fearing social destabilization of the entire capitalist system, its efforts were thwarted by the Judicial Committee of the Privy Council (JCPC) on constitutional grounds, as expected.

With the federal government insisting that it would not commit to more than temporary poor relief unless it was given formal powers, the provinces eventually agreed to a constitutional amendment transferring the responsibility for unemployment insurance to the federal government. The provinces remained deeply divided, however, with regard to further centralization, as suggested by the Rowell-Sirois Commission.

The eventual and belated construction of a modern Keynesian welfare state with significant involvement of the federal government had to wait until after the end of World War II (see Chapter 5). It was the crisis of the 1930s, however, that threw into question the Confederation settlement of 1867. As the thorough investigations of the Rowell-Sirois Commission made abundantly clear, the division of powers under the BNA Act no longer worked. Social stability had to become a national concern. In time, this would lead to a reversal of functions in the Canadian federal system. The federal government would get more involved in social policy issues once thought to be the property and civil rights domain of the provinces. The provinces in turn would take on a more active role in economic activities, which the BNA Act had assigned to the nation-building powers of the federal government.

Dramatic Crisis and BNA Act Federalism at a Loss

Before 1929, as Richard Simeon and Ian Robinson put it, "a decentralized version of the classical model of federalism was firmly in place."[1] This meant that the division of powers as prescribed by the BNA Act worked, if not exactly as Macdonald had imagined then at least as the JCPC had reimagined it. The Great Depression dramatically changed this harmonious picture. Mass unemployment and staggering provincial debt required a wholesale rethinking of fiscal relations and the division of powers with it.

When the federal and provincial first ministers finally sat down to discuss the findings of the Rowell-Sirois report on Dominion–provincial relations in January 1941, the atmosphere had become anything but harmonious. One observer at the conference described it as "the god damnedest exhibition and circus you can imagine."[2] Canada had become caught in a crisis of federalism, and to understand this, we first need to look at the crisis of capitalism that caused it.

For our present purposes, we can understand capitalism as a system of economic reproduction relying on supply and demand in a largely unregulated free

1 Richard Simeon and Ian Robinson, *State, Society, and the Development of Canadian Federalism* (Toronto: University of Toronto Press, 1990), 56

2 Robert Bothwell, Ian Drummond, and John English, *Canada, 1900–1945* (Toronto: University of Toronto Press, 1987), 274.

market, in which the means of production are owned by private individuals and enterprises, and in which the stock market plays a crucial role by allowing investors to buy shares in enterprises expected to yield the most profitable return. The Great Depression was a worldwide systemic breakdown of this system. There is no general consensus on what exactly triggered the breakdown. The most plausible explanation points to a combination of massive capital concentration resulting in overproduction and excessive inequality leading to underconsumption.[3] When the mismatch between supply and demand became obvious, a chain reaction set in: panic sales at the stock market; a drastic decline in world trade, economic demand, and credit; the collapse of commodity prices; and, as the inevitable consequence of it all, mass unemployment.

For several reasons, the Great Depression was nowhere more severe than in Canada. The Canadian boom years of the 1920s had led to overproduction and overcapacity in a country where most working people, men and women, still lived on less than the $1,200 a year the Department of Labour had identified as the threshold for a decent living.[4] As a resource-exporting country, Canada was hit particularly hard by the collapse of world market commodity prices: By 1932, the prices of Canada's main exports had fallen by 53 per cent and farm products by 70 per cent, industrial production fell 48 per cent, employment 33 per cent, and per capita income 48 per cent.[5]

The unemployment numbers did not even include the masses of underemployed who were precariously surviving at the margins of subsistence, women in particular, nor the thousands of mostly young men who became "hobos," crisscrossing the country on freight trains in search of work and eventually rounded up in military-style labour camps. It also did not include farmers who were hit hardest, at least in the Prairie west, not only by collapsing world market prices and crushing debt, but also, compounding the misery, by years of drought, grasshoppers, and soil erosion.

The crisis was further compounded by the ever-larger presence of American capital in the Canadian economy.[6] American direct investment

3 See Robert L. Heilbroner, *The Nature and Logic of Capitalism* (New York: Norton, 1985), 164.

4 Desmond Morton, *A Short History of Canada* (Edmonton: Hurtig Publishers, 1983), 173.

5 John F. Conway, *The West: The History of a Region in Confederation* (Toronto: Lorimer, 1983), 98.

6 See Donald Creighton, *Canada's First Century* (1970; repr., Toronto: Oxford University Press, 2012), 176–81; Janine Brodie, *The Political Economy of Canadian Regionalism* (Toronto: Harcourt Brace Jovanovich, 1990), 136–41; Glen Williams, *Not for Export*, 3rd ed. (Toronto: McClelland & Stewart, 1994), 88–92; Kari Levitt, *Silent Surrender: The Multinational Corporation in Canada* (Toronto: Macmillan of Canada, 1970), 58–70.

quadrupled during the 1920s, taking aim at the resource industries the provinces had begun to develop in the north and at manufacturing in the south by means of so-called branch plants. These subsidiaries of American companies operating in Canada served the double purpose of invading the Canadian market, which was protected from foreign imports by a shield of protective tariffs, and of benefiting from the preferential treatment that Canadian-made exports might receive in Britain and the Commonwealth. When the Depression struck, however, the flow of American money came to a grinding halt, and with it vanished much of the prosperity and the jobs it had created. What is more, Canadian exports to the United States, which had surpassed those to Britain at the beginning of the decade, entirely dried up as the Americans surrounded themselves with impenetrable tariff walls as well.

For several reasons, Canadian governments had no answer to the crisis. First, few at the time understood, as the Rowell-Sirois Commission would only years later, that this was a massive structural crisis that could not be fixed with the usual efforts of poor relief. Second, the scope of social intervention needed went entirely beyond the fiscal capacities of the provinces to whom social policy responsibilities such as poor relief had been assigned in exclusivity under the BNA Act. Third, stubbornly following the rationale of classical federalism with strictly divided powers, the federal government of Liberal Prime Minister Mackenzie King had no intention of alienating provincial premiers by spending money on what he thought were local affairs to begin with.

The provinces did provide relief as best as they could, but they ran out of money and went into debt very quickly. And when they asked King for assistance in April 1930, he famously declared in parliament that he "would not give them a five cent piece" for "alleged unemployment purposes."[7]

King's remark probably cost him the election that year. The new Conservative Prime Minister, R.B. Bennett, had promised action. During a special session, still in 1930, parliament passed an Unemployment Relief Bill that provided grants to the provinces, of which he himself thought they were, even though substantial, "palliative" at best. They were not even that. Municipalities, generally in charge of providing relief, had to match whatever money was passed on to them by the provinces with the result that those who needed it the most often got the least.[8] These relief payments nevertheless were the first significant

7 Cited in J.L. Granatstein et al., *Nation: Canada Since Confederation* (Toronto: McGraw-Hill Ryerson, 1990), 310.

8 John Herd Thompson with Allen Seager, *Canada 1922–1939* (Toronto: McClelland and Stewart, 1985), 210.

instance of the federal government financing responsibilities under provincial jurisdiction.[9]

Bennett's main answer to the Depression was to sharply increase tariffs for all goods manufactured in Canada. Protecting the fledgling manufacturing industry in central Canada from foreign competition, tariffs had become one of the two main prongs of the so-called National Policy[10] ever since Macdonald had introduced them in 1879. The other prong was the transcontinental railway, transporting settlers and domestically manufactured goods to the expanding west and shipping cheap resources eastward in what was to be a continental domestic market. Under the circumstances of the Depression, however, Bennett's tariff protectionism, in part designed as misguided retaliation against the American tariffs already in place, only slowed the economy even more.

Overall, the established political classes of the 1930s firmly believed that balancing the budget by cutting government expenditures was the most appropriate remedy. Austerity, as we would call it today, was like medicine: It had to be bitter to work. To the extent that this sounded like a deliberate politics of misery, it was so intended. As John David Eaton of the now-defunct Eaton's company later reminisced, while the price collapse during the Depression provided him and his ilk with a grand old time as he could "spend an entire evening dining and dancing at a posh restaurant for less than ten dollars," he thought that the Depression generally was a good thing because it "taught men the value of a job."[11] New ideas had to come from elsewhere.

Prairie Populism

Farmers in the west hated the tariff and the entire National Policy with it. The tariff meant higher costs for the farm equipment and other manufactured goods they needed. "National Policy" stood for high freight rates and high interest rates on the credits they needed for seed and equipment and, particularly in Alberta, for farm mortgages not yet paid off. The villains were the politicians in cahoots with eastern bankers and the Canadian Pacific Railway. Agrarian

9 H. Blair Neatby, *The Politics of Chaos: Canada in the Thirties* (1972; repr., Ottawa: The Golden Dog Press, 2003), 56–7.

10 See classically, V.C. Fowke, "The National Policy – Old and New," *Canadian Journal of Economics and Political Science* 18, no. 3 (1952), reprinted in *Approaches to Canadian Economic History*, eds. W.T. Easterbrook and M.H. Watkins (Toronto: Gage Publishing, 1980).

11 Granatstein et al., *Nation*, 307.

radicalism directed against the Liberal and Conservative party establishment had been brewing for some time. While unionism, socialism, and communism had been weakened if not muted when the RCMP ended the Winnipeg General Strike of 1919 with baseball bats and guns, farmers' movements had a more lasting impact. They sprang up everywhere, formed parties, won elections in several provinces, and even managed to establish a presence in the national parliament. With the onset of the Depression, two western political party formations began to challenge the established order.

In 1932, William ("Bible Bill") Aberhart, a high school principal and part-time Baptist preacher in Calgary, began to intersperse his evangelist radio broadcasts with a so-called social credit theory.[12] This theory essentially held that the Depression's main problem was that people didn't have enough money to spend even though plenty of it was available. Aberhart declared that this was the fault of the profiteering machinations of eastern finance capital and the politics in support of it. He announced that his new Social Credit Party would simply pump new money into circulation, socialize credit, and pay every man and woman a social credit dividend of 25 dollars per month. The message fell on receptive ears of both debt-ridden farmers and cash-strapped urbanites, and Social Credit won the 1935 provincial election, sweeping away the hapless United Farmers of Alberta government that had been in power since 1921.

Once in power, the Aberhart government "embarked on a course of sustained constitutional defiance of the federal government's exclusive monetary power, complemented by a frontal assault on finance capital."[13] It defaulted by refusing to pay off the holders of a 1916 series of bonds falling due; it unilaterally cut the interest on government debt by half; it passed a law making farm foreclosure next to impossible; it levied punitive taxes on banks and corporations; and it even began to issue its own currency. Nearly all these measures were clearly unconstitutional, and Aberhart has been often portrayed as a whacko populist driven by missionary hubris who wouldn't even stop at trying to force newspapers to print his point of view. The $25 dividend was never paid. But, as John F. Conway has pointed out, for a precious number of years, until the courts put a final end to it, Aberhart successfully provided debt protection and helped Alberta farmers keep their farms. The relentlessness as well as popularity of his approach eventually led to more generous voluntary debt adjustment by banks and other financial institutions afterwards.[14]

12 Neatby, *The Politics of Chaos,* 143–61.

13 Conway, *The West,* 119–23.

14 Ibid., 124–5.

Aberhart's approach to battling the Depression also introduced Canadians to the idea of monetary policy and its importance for socioeconomic stability, and it even foreshadowed the kind of Keynesian economic management that would take hold as part of the so-called post-war consensus in Britain and other western democracies after World War II. And, lest we forget, unlike US President Barack Obama during the 2008 crisis, Aberhart bailed out people, not banks and corporations. In any case, the federal government's move to establish the Bank of Canada as a private corporation a year before Social Credit swept to power, and its transformation into a Crown corporation three years later, probably was not a coincidence.

The other western party formation was of a very different kind. Farmers were not the only inhabitants of the west. There were also growing numbers of workers on the farms, in the mines, and in the manufacturing and construction industries. They shared in common "dangerous work in uncertain industries at unsatisfactory wages."[15] Working-class demands were mostly ignored by governments, and strikes were routinely clubbed down. The Winnipeg General Strike had been only one of many similar acts of repressing what politicians and the business community alike denounced as the spectre of socialism if not communism. This situation changed when western labour parties were joined by farmer organizations and a new national party was founded called the Co-operative Commonwealth Federation (CCF).[16] At its first convention at Regina in 1933, the CCF anointed as its leader James S. Woodsworth, a Methodist minister turned politician who had been in Ottawa as a member of parliament from Winnipeg since 1921. Woodsworth's conciliatory genius is widely credited with bringing workers, farmers, and left-leaning intellectuals together for a common cause.

At Regina, the CCF also adopted the so-called Regina Manifesto, which called for public ownership of financial institutions, public utilities, and transportation companies, the Canadian Pacific Railway in particular. It also put collective bargaining, unemployment insurance, and social insurance on the agenda. This was socialism in that it meant to replace the existing regime of capitalism, but it fell way short of communism. In order to keep farmers on board, it did not call for farm collectivization, instead guaranteeing security of land tenure.

The CCF would not sweep any elections until 1944, when it formed the provincial government in Saskatchewan under the leadership of Tommy Douglas. But its potentially wide appeal to poverty-stricken Canadians of all stripes could

15 Ibid., 97.

16 Granatstein et al., *Nation*, 320–1; Neatby, *The Politics of Chaos*, 98–100.

not go unnoticed. Two years after the Regina convention, the prime minister, R.B. Bennett, faced with looming electoral defeat for years of inaction, had what Woodsworth called his "deathbed conversion."[17] In a series of radio broadcasts, he announced a social policy package that would include unemployment insurance, minimum wages, maximum work hours, and agricultural support programs. It came too late to save his government. Bennett lost the 1935 election and Mackenzie King was back in power, referring Bennett's "New Deal" legislation to the courts where, as we already know from Chapter 3, it ultimately was judged unconstitutional.

Enlightened Reactionaries

There have been a number of explanations of why Bennett would try to change course so radically at the last minute. Obviously, he sought to stem the rising tides of populism and radicalism, and in fact King's lopsided 1935 victory owed more to the Conservatives losing support to the Social Credit, the CCF, and a new Reconstruction Party that had broken away from them than to any kind of convincing alternative platform King's Liberals might have put forward.[18] Obviously, Bennett also emulated if not copied Roosevelt's New Deal approach south of the border, which, if nothing else for now, certainly appeared to be a formula for political success.[19]

An important push, however, came from neither radicals nor from political opportunists but from concerned business leaders in manufacturing and finance who realized that capitalism needed some form of social stabilization to survive.[20] In our story of Canadian federalism, this conservative push for what eventually and belatedly would give way to the establishment of a Keynesian welfare state in Canada – against the instincts of political leaders reluctant to meddle with the traditional division of powers under the BNA Act and against the judgments of the JCPC – must give us pause for thought. Under the impact of the Great Depression, did Canada's business classes push for centralization? Not exactly.

17 Neatby, *The Politics of Chaos*, 96–7.

18 Granatstein et al., *Nation*, 328–9; Morton, *A Short History*, 185.

19 Neatby, *The Politics of Chaos*, 66–8.

20 Alvin Finkel, "Origins of the Welfare State in Canada," in *The Canadian State: Political Economy and Political Power*, ed. Leo Panitch (Toronto: University of Toronto Press, 1977), 352–4.

The general response to the crisis of capitalism was a call for regulatory state intervention, or "statification."[21] The eventual outcome was the Keynesian welfare state, which sought to regulate capitalism with a combination of redistributive monetary and social policies. This outcome was not the result of socialist opposition to capitalism but, as Karl Polanyi famously put it, it was largely owed to "enlightened reactionaries" who understood that unregulated market capitalism is self-destructive.[22] In federal systems, such policies were not feasible at the subnational level and thus overturned the traditional division of powers that had assigned social policy to the constituent units. Canada's capitalist classes, in other words, supported statification, and statification inevitably meant centralization.

Once back in power, King still believed that balancing the budget by cutting government expenditure was the best course of action. Yet almost all provinces were by now on the brink of bankruptcy. Faced with overall Canadian creditworthiness at stake (what if nobody would lend the country money any more at all?), the federal government "bailed away with guarantees and emergency payments as successive provincial loans fell due."[23] However, if the King of 1930 would not give a five cent piece, he now would not give a penny more. Unless, that is, he got control over provincial borrowing. Thus, he proposed to the provinces the establishment of a central loan council of the kind already existing in Australia. Aberhart balked at the idea of having Ottawa control future provincial borrowings. King refused to advance any further funds, and this is how Alberta defaulted on its bond obligations.[24]

When John Bracken, the premier of Manitoba, was about to follow Aberhart's example and unilaterally slash interest rates on government debt, King, very much against his instincts, had to extend additional emergency payments to the province. Something had to be done, and King did what Canadian politicians always do when they are at wit's end: They call for commissions to study the matter. In 1936, King appointed a National Employment Commission, to be followed a year later by the Royal Commission on Dominion–Provincial Relations. As is often the case with commissions, however, and as King would learn soon enough, the findings turned out to be unexpected or even unwelcome.

The National Employment Commission found that unemployment was a national problem, and the federal government should therefore bear the entire

21 Heilbroner, *Nature and Logic of Capitalism*, 116–17.

22 Karl Polanyi, *The Great Transformation* (1944; repr., Boston: Beacon Press, 1957), 164.

23 Bothwell, Drummond, and English, *Canada, 1900–1945*, 270.

24 Ibid., 271.

cost of relief. It also recommended that deficit spending should make up for the lack of private investment during the Depression. Keynesianism was knocking at Canadian doors. The thrifty prime minister was horrified, but his minister of labour, Norman Rogers, apparently was not, and he had considerable support in cabinet. King relented, and the 1938 federal budget became the first instance of a federal government taking active steps to stimulate the economy.[25] A federal system of unemployment insurance, which would require provincial consent, still had to wait.

King was at heart not only a fiscal conservative, as we would say today, he was also a traditional (or classical) federalist in that he strongly objected to the federal government spending money on matters not under its control and jurisdiction. And an enormous amount of money had been spent that way – some 40 per cent of all relief expenditure during the Depression years.[26] Conversely, of course, if there was consensus that the federal government should entirely foot the bill for social programs such as unemployment insurance, it also ought to have the formal powers to do so – and hence get the political credit for doing it. But any overt attempt to centralize powers would put King's other federalist mission, national unity, into jeopardy and possibly his party's political future with it. Most of the Liberal seats in the 1935 election had come from Ontario and Quebec, and in both provinces he was met with fierce opposition by strong and popular premiers, Mitch Hepburn in Ontario and Maurice Duplessis in Quebec – not to mention the populist maverick Aberhart in Alberta.

Rowell-Sirois Commission

Finding a way out of all these conundrums was the purpose of setting up the Royal Commission on Dominion–Provincial Relations, better known as the Rowell-Sirois Commission (named after its two consecutive chairs), with a mandate "to provide for a re-examination of the economic and financial basis of Confederation and of the distribution of legislative powers in the light of the economic and social developments of the last seventy years."[27] It came to be one of the most thorough investigations of a country's governance system and performance – then or since. It brought into sharp socioeconomic focus what

25 Neatby, *The Politics of Chaos*, 83–5.

26 Creighton, *Canada's First Century*, 208.

27 Joseph Sirois and Newton Wesley Rowell, *Report of the Royal Commission on Dominion–Provincial Relations: Book I* (Ottawa: Privy Council Office, 1940), 9.

the JCPC had already expressed in judicial terms in the 1881 *Parsons* case (see Chapter 3): The division of exclusive powers set up in the BNA Act as a matter of principle was simply not sustainable in practice.

These were the commission's main findings:

- The original setup of Confederation had "brought to fruition" the creation of economic union.[28]
- It had done so, however, as the Depression showed in particular, by distributing losses "very disproportionately" upon certain regions.[29]
- In the wake of the Depression, the distinction between "poor relief" and "cyclical mass unemployment" had gone unrecognized.[30]
- The federal government, while shouldering nearly half of the relief burden, "did not have adequate control" over where and how the money was to be spent.[31]
- Instead of decentralized borrowing and debt accumulation by the provinces, a centralized regime of national borrowing could have resulted in "considerably lower interest rates."[32]
- The division of powers was under "heavy strain" because the tax powers as originally assigned no longer yielded nearly enough revenue since both orders of government had begun to competitively occupy the same new tax fields, mainly income and corporate tax.[33]

Hardly anyone would have seriously disagreed with these findings. The conclusions the commission drew from them in terms of recommendations, however, were a different matter altogether.

The commissioners recommended a double pack of far-reaching changes.[34] On the one hand, they wanted the provinces to leave the collection of income,

28 Donald V. Smiley, ed., *The Rowell-Sirois Report* (Toronto: Macmillan, 1978), 150.

29 Ibid., 170.

30 Ibid., 175.

31 Ibid., 178.

32 Ibid., 180.

33 Ibid., 188.

34 Simeon and Robinson, *State, Society, and the Development of Canadian Federalism*, 106.

corporate, and succession taxes entirely to the federal government. In return, the federal government would take over all provincial debt and pay the provinces so-called National Adjustment Grants, calculated province by province in such a way as to "safeguard the autonomy of every province by ensuring to it the revenue necessary to provide services in accordance with the Canadian standard."[35] On the other hand, the commissioners wanted the federal government to become wholly responsible for contributory old age pensions, if such a system were to be implemented in the future, and for unemployment insurance as "one onerous function of government which cannot, under modern conditions, be equitably or efficiently performed at a regional or provincial basis."[36]

These recommendations, in other words, suggested a recalibration of the Canadian federation in a way meant to bring socioeconomic stability and a measure of equality to regions and provinces by reassigning to the federal government the powers to do so. In essence, it meant to strengthen the federal government at the expense of the provinces. It also meant that the Canadian state should take on an active redistributive role in the capitalist system.

It should be easy by now to see why and how Canada had stumbled from a "crisis of capitalism"[37] to a "crisis of federalism."[38] While much of the business community was strongly supportive of such a recalibration, since it feared labour unrest or even a wholesale attack on capitalism, the resource industries, which were intimately intertwined with the resource-owning provinces, were opposed.[39] Provincial responses were varied and divided. In general, the more cash strapped and debt ridden a provincial government, the more inclined it would be to go along with a loss of power in return for equalizing federal handouts[40] – hence the "god damnedest exhibition and circus" that characterized the 1941 Dominion–provincial conference.

The conference was overshadowed by World War II, which had been raging for over a year already. The war also muted provincial opposition to strong federal leadership. Already in 1940, a happy political configuration had allowed

35 Sirois and Rowell, *Report of the Royal Commission on Dominion–Provincial Relations*, Section G, 272.

36 Ibid., 270.

37 Thompson with Saeger, *Canada 1922–1939*, 193.

38 Bothwell, Drummond, and English, *Canada, 1900–1945*, 269.

39 Finkel, "Origins of the Welfare State," 357.

40 Bothwell, Drummond, and English, *Canada 1900–1945*, 276.

King to secure provincial consent for a constitutional amendment adding unemployment insurance to the federal government's exclusive powers.[41] First, Maurice Duplessis, staunchly conservative-nationalist and anti-war, was replaced by the liberal Adélard Godbout in the October 1939 Quebec election. Then King himself was triumphantly re-elected in March 1940, which silenced Ontario's Mitch Hepburn, his most vociferous critic. And finally, the Rowell-Sirois report, which was tabled two months later in May, gave King incentive and reason to make a move.

To have the federal government pay for a new and expensive program was one thing – not even Aberhart in Alberta disagreed. The permanent cessation of tax powers to the federal government, however, was quite another. The 1941 conference ended in disarray. Afterwards, however, the war effort argument allowed King and his finance minister, James Lorimer Ilsley, to coax the provinces one by one into at least a temporary arrangement that later came to be known as *tax rental*. As suggested by the Rowell-Sirois report, the federal government would collect all personal income, corporate income, and other corporate taxes and in return pay stipends or rents to the provinces, either equivalent to what they had collected from these taxes in 1940 or equivalent to their ongoing debt payments.[42] The provinces really did not have much choice but to agree to these arrangements, since the federal government under wartime emergency conditions could have imposed them unilaterally just as well.[43] But the provincial lack of resistance probably also had to do with the fact that under the circumstances, and at least for the time being, exchanging powers over uncertain revenue for a fixed income of sorts did not seem like such a bad idea.

Reversal of Functions

In medical terms, a crisis is a moment leading to either life or death. It is ultimately impossible to know whether largely unregulated market capitalism really was at the point of self-destruction during the 1930s, but massive state intervention certainly was required for its eventual recovery. Unable to respond in a timely fashion, the federal system in Canada was in disarray, but it would be an exaggeration to say that it was outright moribund at any given time. Writing

41 Ibid., 273–4; Finkel, "Origins of the Welfare State," 359.

42 Bothwell, Drummond, and English, *Canada 1900–1945*, 275.

43 Richard J. Van Loon and Michael S. Whittington, *The Canadian Political System: Environment, Structure, and Process* (Toronto: McGraw-Hill Ryerson, 1984), 284.

at the time in an Italian prison cell, the great Italian Marxist Antonio Gramsci provided a more befitting crisis definition for the epoch, which he saw as much a crisis of authority and leadership as a crisis of material conditions. The crisis, he wrote, was the crisis of a transitional period during which "the old is dying and the new cannot be born."[44]

The transitional nature of the epoch has been the subject matter of this chapter, a dramatic and temporarily debilitating turning point for Canadian federalism with recovery not yet in sight when World War II brought the intergovernmental conflict over authority and leadership to a forced standstill. Recovery, although never uncontested, only came after the war, when the Canadian government took on a significant social policy role in the construction of a modern Keynesian welfare state.

In order to appreciate the transformative impact of the crisis of the 1930s upon federalism in Canada, we need to compare the original blueprint for Confederation to the eventual post-crisis outcome, even though the details of this outcome will be discussed in full only in Chapter 5. As planned by the founders, most revenue up to the crisis had gone to the federal government for the single purpose of economic development, transportation, infrastructure, and public works.[45] The provinces, in turn, with limited access to revenue, had been left in charge of social policy, which in terms of welfare at the time amounted to little more than temporary poor relief. Less than half a century after the crisis, according to estimates for the 1970s, about three-fifths of general welfare-related expenditures were now undertaken by the federal government, and the provinces had assumed a similarly dominant position in all areas of economic development.[46]

While the double crisis of capitalism and federalism during the 1930s surely was the decisive trigger, the extent of this astounding reversal of functions in the Canadian federal system cannot be explained by the crisis alone. To begin with, signs of change had already become visible before the onset of the crisis during the 1920s, when the provinces had taken a more active role in economic development and the federal government had first become involved in social policy with the

44 Antonio Gramsci, *Prison Notebooks*, vol. II, ed. and trans. Joseph A. Buttigieg (New York: Columbia University Press, 2011), 33.

45 See Smiley, *The Rowell-Sirois Report*, Book 1, 84–6.

46 Garth Stevenson, "Federalism and the Political Economy of the Canadian State," in Panitch, *The Canadian State*, 86; as Stevenson's estimates stem from the 1970s, numbers would be different today in light of the current escalation of healthcare costs in particular.

Old Age Pensions Act of 1927. Moreover, Canada's involvement in World War II effectively ended the crisis. By 1942, the booming war economy had eradicated unemployment.[47] The immediate pressure for dramatic change was gone. And finally, the federal government's growing involvement in social policy after the war has remained contested to this day, particularly so in Quebec, as an attack on provincial autonomy. What, then, explains this reversal of functions more fully?

Political history is often told in terms of agency: Great leaders powerfully shape their countries and the lives of the people living in them. Telling the political history of federal countries in this way requires two modifications to the agency approach. On the one hand there is leadership at two different levels of government, and on the other hand the constitutional division of powers constrains the full exercise of leadership power. Thus, the story of Canadian federalism is often told in terms of political rivalries: John A. Macdonald and Oliver Mowat in the nineteenth century; Mackenzie King, Mitch Hepburn, and Maurice Duplessis in the first half of the twentieth century; or, as we shall explore in Chapters 6 and 7, Pierre Trudeau and René Lévesque in the second half of the twentieth century.

There is no doubt that the trajectory of Canadian federalism was strongly influenced by these interpersonal rivalries and competing visions. Agency, however (notwithstanding Bennett's deathbed conversion), is of little help in explaining the transformation that first began with the federalization of unemployment insurance. Most of the political leaders at the time were reluctant to touch the division of powers. If anything, the rivalry between King, Hepburn, and Duplessis slowed down the transformation. And while Roosevelt in the United States had aggressively taken on the Supreme Court's opposition to the New Deal,[48] King had deferred to the JCPC.

A more persuasive explanation points to political expediency: the federal government's search for a new and second national policy after the first national policy, the creation of a continental economic union, had more or less been accomplished, and initiatives for further economic development increasingly came from the provinces. According to this explanation, the federal government eventually realized that "a government without functions would be a government

47 Simeon and Robinson, *State, Society, and the Development of Canadian Federalism*, 89.

48 In 1937, Roosevelt threatened to appoint five additional Supreme Court judges to halt the invalidation of New Deal legislation by the court. The court eventually sanctioned most of the legislation.

without respect" and therefore, reluctantly and against obvious constitutional obstacles, took on public welfare as a new national concern.[49]

In this way, the reversal of functions in Canada's federal system was "politically constructed" as a substitute nation-building tool with the federal government's ultimate objective of reaching "every single citizen."[50] If the Old Age Pensions Act of 1927 marked the modest beginning of this calculated process of transformation, then healthcare after the war became its successful endpoint (see Chapter 5): Even though it is delivered by provincial health insurance plans, Canadians think of healthcare as an iconic national achievement. And if the crisis of the 1930s showed the disarray of the Canadian federal system over how to circumvent constitutional constraints, the Rowell-Sirois Commission provided a blueprint that emboldened federal governments after the war to redefine national concerns.

While this explanation is compelling to a point, it still leaves out an important part of the story. In almost all historical accounts of Confederation, the process is described as one in which "the interests of business and government elites were coterminous."[51] Not surprisingly, the new federal state was given all the powers necessary to carry out what Marxist political economists have called the *accumulation* function of the state:[52] It was to provide for an infrastructural environment, particularly with regard to transportation, without which private profit making would have been impossible or at least more difficult.

In light of the support of business and finance for Bennett's New Deal legislation already mentioned, one would expect a similarly cozy relationship of economic and political elites as the driving force behind Canadian federalism's great transformation. And indeed studies have shown that this relationship hardly changed over time. Bennett had been a director of Imperial Oil as well as the

---

49 Fowke, "National Policy," 245–51.

50 Gerard W. Boychuk, *National Health Insurance in the United States and Canada* (Washington: Georgetown University Press, 2008), 193.

51 See classically H.G.H. Aitken, "Defensive Expansionism: The State and Economic Growth in Canada," in *Approaches to Canadian Economic History*, eds. W.T. Easterbrook and M. H. Watkins (Toronto: Gage Publishing, 1980); Gregory Albo and Jane Jensen, "A Contested Concept: The Relative Autonomy of the State," in *The New Canadian Political Economy*, eds. Wallace Clement and Glen Williams (Toronto: Gage Publishing, 1980), 187.

52 See James O'Connor, *The Fiscal Crisis of the State* (New York: St. Martin's Press, 1973), 6; on this and the following, I am indebted to Stevenson, "Federalism and the Political Economy."

Royal Bank before and after his prime ministership. King had worked for John D. Rockefeller before entering politics. Seventy per cent of Bennett's cabinet and 64 per cent of King's had close business connections.[53]

Confronted with what had amounted to an existential crisis of capitalism, Canada's enlightened reactionaries in business, finance, and government now supported a transformation that assigned to the federal state what Marxist political economists have called the *legitimation* function of the state:[54] It had to provide for social security, not only to prevent class conflict but also to balance economic growth with income stability. As the Rowell-Sirois report had pointed out, this reversal of functions was necessary because the survival of the capitalist system required redistributive efforts that went way beyond what the provinces could accomplish.

In a unitary state, the competing political forces and parties will battle over the balance between accumulation and legitimation within the arena of one governmental system. In a federal state like Canada, this battle is not only duplicated by the existence of two governmental arenas, federal and provincial, it is also tied into a structure of intergovernmental relations, cooperation, and conflict as pre-figured by the constitutional division of powers.[55] It was because of these constrictions of federalism that King was reluctant about taking on unemployment insurance. When it finally became a federal responsibility in 1941, King noted that this was perhaps a good thing because the contributions of employers and employees could be invested directly in the war effort and might cushion an economic downturn in the wake of demobilization after the war.[56]

The provinces in turn, cash strapped as they were, did not have much of a choice at the time. Under no circumstances, however, would they relinquish the legitimation function in its entirety. With the exception of unemployment insurance and pensions, therefore, cost sharing became the default option of social policymaking. Intergovernmental relations essentially became fiscal relations.

53 Wallace Clement, "The Corporate Elite, the Capitalist Class, and the Canadian State," in Panitch, *The Canadian State*, 229–31.

54 See again O'Connor, *Fiscal Crisis*, 6.

55 Stevenson, "Federalism and the Political Economy," 71.

56 Leslie A. Pal, *State, Class, and Bureaucracy: Canadian Unemployment Insurance and Public Policy* (Montreal: McGill-Queen's University Press, 1988), 150.

CHAPTER FIVE

MOSTLY FISCAL RELATIONS

World War II had resolved the crisis of capitalism. Wars, while devastating for people, are usually good for the economy. The crisis of federalism, however, had not been resolved. While social policy was still for the most part under provincial jurisdiction, the federal government collected most of the tax revenue. During the post-war years of growth and prosperity, however, the conflict over how to address this obvious imbalance was no longer driven by the urgency to address immediate social need. Instead, it became a matter of principle among competing governments.

There were two options in principle: Either significant social policy responsibilities were to be aligned with tax powers in a centralized federal state, as the Rowell-Sirois Commission had recommended in 1940, or significant tax powers had to be handed back to the provinces so they could deliver social policy programs under their jurisdiction, as Quebec's Tremblay Commission would suggest in 1956. While both are logical in principle, neither option was acceptable to the other side.

As they had at the Dominion–provincial conference in 1941, the richer provinces in particular fiercely opposed tax centralization, which would not only deprive them of using tax incentives for the purpose of economic province-building but would moreover make them dependent on federal money transfers in the form of conditional grants. Quebec in particular also objected to national social policy leadership, which it saw as an attack on cultural autonomy. The federal government in turn did not want to let go of the lion's share of revenue that it thought it needed to achieve socioeconomic stabilization as a new national objective. As a consequence, Canadian federalism entered a new era of intensified intergovernmental conflict and compromise, centred on the questions that the Rowell-Sirois Commission had identified as essential for a modernized version of Canadian federalism: How should revenue be reassigned in a fiscally sound and efficient way? Who should pay for the expensive new policies that were recognized as essential for socioeconomic stabilization? To what extent should there be equitability in the provision of public services across provinces?

The outcome was a series of compromises. Instead of abandoning any tax fields in their entirety, the federal government entered into tax-sharing agreements whereby the provinces would eventually collect more than half of all revenue. In addition, the federal government committed to unconditional fiscal equalization payments whereby the per capita fiscal capacity of provinces below the national average was raised to that average. And instead of insisting on exclusive jurisdiction over major new social programs, the provinces acceded to cost-sharing agreements whereby the federal government would (initially) pay half of all outlays. Only in the case of healthcare would the transfers be conditional, ensuring portability and common service delivery standards across all provinces.

Even two constitutional amendments regarding pensions contained compromise. The federal government received jurisdiction to set up the Canada Pension Plan (CPP), but the provinces insisted on retaining paramountcy, which meant that the plan could be changed only with substantive provincial support. Allowing Quebec to establish its own parallel Quebec Pension Plan also set a precedent for what perhaps would become the quintessential form of compromise in Canadian federalism: opting-out provisions for shared-cost programs allowing Quebec to receive funding or tax room for setting up comparable programs of its own.

Step by step, a stable post-war order of public welfare was constructed for the citizens of Canada on whom the electoral success of their governments depended. It was a different story for Indigenous peoples, who continued to suffer discriminatory levels of welfare neglect under the Indian Act. The recognition of Indigenous rights in the Constitution Act, 1982, has made such neglect more difficult. Betterment, however, despite the more sincere efforts of recent governments, appears to move at a glacial pace. From an Indigenous perspective, Canadian federalism is far from a success story of intergovernmentally managed fiscal relations for the benefit of all citizens.

Neither is it seen as much of a success story from a provincialist perspective. No matter how many compromises struck and intergovernmental agreements concluded, a fiscal imbalance has always remained, providing federal governments with superior spending power beyond the fiscal needs of their own programs. And this federal spending power has always been contested as a convenient tool of meddling in matters under provincial jurisdiction. Arguably, however, it is not the fiscal imbalance as such that is the main bone of contention – it is the unilateralism of federal governments seen as manipulating fiscal relations for their own benefit.

Tax Sharing

As we saw in Chapter 4, tax rental was meant to be a temporary arrangement for the duration of World War II. Yet when the war was over, tax rental agreements would be renewed three times and continue, with some modifications, into the 1960s. Most provinces simply could not afford to set up costly tax collection systems parallel to the federal one already in existence. Only Ontario and Quebec refused to sign the new and second tax rental agreement for the 1947–52 period, and while Ontario would rejoin the tax rental fold in 1952, Quebec would permanently remain outside of it, thus setting the precedent for the general contracting-out strategy in its conduct of fiscal relations with the federal government ever since.

By the 1950s, Quebec had begun to resent more than just tax rental. Back in power since 1944, the conservative-nationalist government of Maurice Duplessis regarded with suspicion how the federal relief efforts during the Depression and World War II now turned into permanent social policy activism, with the federal government unilaterally introducing family allowances in 1944 and broadening its 1927 old age pension scheme in 1951. The continued federal control of what by now were the most important sources of revenue, personal and corporate income taxes, only added to the suspicion that what was going on was a wholesale attack on Quebec's traditional values, which included leaving social policy to church and private charity. As the 1956 Tremblay report put it, the federal provision of family allowances and pensions smacked of "state-controlled and socialistic forms of social security."[1]

The Tremblay report was Quebec's belated response to the Rowell-Sirois report. If the Rowell-Sirois Commission had suggested permanent tax centralization and federal social policy involvement, the Tremblay Commission now

1 Cited in David Kwavnick, ed., *The Tremblay Report* (Toronto: McClelland and Stewart, 1973), xvii.

suggested the opposite: Direct taxes on personal and corporate income "should be reserved to the provinces." In this way, nothing would then stand in the way of the provinces "assuming full responsibility" in all matters of social security.[2] And if the Rowell-Sirois Commission had argued that the original division of powers under the British North America (BNA) Act had outlived its purpose and needed to be adjusted based on time and circumstance, the Tremblay Commission now insisted that all that was needed was a return to the original intentions of the BNA Act.

In order to make their case, the Tremblay commissioners resorted to a peculiar kind of reasoning. The BNA Act, as all would agree, was unclear or even contradictory about the division of tax powers because in Section 91(3) it had given to the federal government exclusive powers to "any mode or system of taxation" while in Section 92(9) it left to the provinces a "particular" power to "direct taxation within the province," which also was declared to be exclusive. The intention could only have been, the commissioners argued, that "the particular would seem to be excluded and withdrawn from the general," from which the logical conclusion should be drawn that direct taxes were meant to be assigned to the provinces "in exclusivity."[3]

From a literalist reading of the BNA Act, this conclusion must appear "entirely unconstitutional."[4] The Tremblay commissioners obviously based their argument on a claim of original constitutional intent.[5] In order to appreciate what this original intent might have been, however, we need to return to Confederation, and even before that, we need to clarify the difference between direct and indirect taxes, which is by no means as straightforward as it sounds. *Direct taxes* are collected "directly" from taxpayers, whether persons or corporations. *Indirect taxes* are consumption taxes levied on goods and services, and therefore hit taxpayers "indirectly."

The most obvious examples of direct taxes are personal and corporate income taxes as well as property taxes. Historically the most obvious examples of indirect taxes are customs duties on foreign imports and excise imposts on domestic goods. With regard to consumption taxes, a distinction has been made by the courts between "indirect" value-added or turnover taxes, such as the GST

2 Kwavnick, *Tremblay Report*, 216.

3 Ibid., 172–3.

4 Garth Stevenson, *Unfulfilled Union* (Montreal: McGill-Queen's University Press, 2009), 129.

5 On the difference, see Thomas O. Hueglin and Alan Fenna, *Comparative Federalism: A Systematic Inquiry* (Toronto: University of Toronto Press, 2015), 314–15.

in Canada, and sales taxes, which are deemed "direct" as long as they are charged separately under the pretense that the retailer acts as a sort of government agent directly collecting it from the customer.[6]

The distinction between direct and indirect taxes is nearly irrelevant today as both the federal and provincial governments avail themselves of the three major sources of revenue: income, corporate, and, with the exception of Alberta, sales taxes. But the distinction is essential for the understanding of constitutional intent. A year prior to Confederation, customs duties made up 80 per cent or more of all revenue in the Maritime provinces. In the United Province of Canada, 66 per cent of all revenue came from customs duties and another 17 per cent from excise duties. The only direct taxes of some significance were municipal property taxes.[7] The practice of levying personal and corporate income taxes as well as sales taxes was still some time off in the future, and the Fathers of Confederation did not expect that they would ever become significant sources of revenue because they were deemed unpopular.

Since it was clear that the big-ticket items of public expenditure would be in the national domain (economic nation-building, western expansion, the transcontinental railway, and defence), it was uncontroversial that power over the major sources of revenue at the time, customs and excise duties, would be assigned to the federal level of government. The provinces, in other words, lost these most important sources of revenue at the point of Confederation.

The powers given to the provinces over social matters, in turn, were not expected to cost much. Most of it was still in the hands of private or church charity or downloaded to municipalities, to the extent that they already existed, and paid for by municipal property taxes, licences, and permits. What remained for provincial expenditure were minor contributions to education and public welfare.[8] Going by constitutional intention, then, the provinces were neither meant to assume any responsibilities of paramount national importance nor were they expected to ever be in command of a significant portion of public revenue. One can of course argue, as was the Tremblay report's main intention, that this was wrong and contrary to true federalism as a system of balanced autonomy, but one cannot pretend the BNA Act intended to do otherwise.

---

6 Joseph Eliot Magnet, "The Constitutional Distribution of Taxation Powers," *Ottawa Law Review* 10 (1978): 493–6.

7 Joseph Sirois and Newton Wesley Rowell, *Report of the Royal Commission on Dominion–Provincial Relations* (Ottawa: Privy Council Office, 1940), 49.

8 Ibid., 49–50.

Since the provinces were deprived of any significant source of revenue, the federal government would take over provincial debt and, in return, gain control over provincial borrowing by means of so-called debt allowances. In order to compensate the provinces for lost revenue-raising capacity, they would further be paid subsidies, annual grants of 80 cents per capita, fixed on the basis of the 1861 census for the two large provinces and growing on the basis of subsequent census figures for the two small provinces until each of them reached a population of 400,000. In addition, and after last-minute wrangling, these subsidies were topped up by a fixed annual lump sum ranging from $50,000 for New Brunswick to $80,000 for Ontario. Similar arrangements would be made when new provinces were admitted to the federation.

The Fathers of Confederation made no bones about what the underlying purpose and rationale of these arrangements were meant to be. As the Quebec Resolutions of 1864 had stated flat out, the provinces, "in consideration of the transfer to the General Government of the powers of Taxation," would live on "grants," and the fiscal Confederation settlement would be "considered in full settlement of all future demands upon the General Government for local purposes."[9] While these "statutory subsidies" continue to this day,[10] they are no longer of importance in the overall picture of Canadian fiscal relations. They are significant, however, in that they were precedent setting for the way in which Canadian fiscal relations would unfold over time.[11]

First of all, they established a pattern of provincial dependency on federal handouts that continues to this day. Second, because they proved inadequate from the onset, they established a pattern of intergovernmental haggling over fiscal resources in which the federal government, endowed with superior taxing powers, generally had the upper hand. Third, they established, as the Tremblay report noted approvingly, a pattern of "not only different but even preferential financial treatment" of some provinces over others.[12] That could be interpreted, as the Tremblay commissioners did, as an early form of fiscal equalization. But it also could be taken more ominously as a federal divide-and-rule strategy of striking deals with individual provinces at the cost of others – "beggar thy neighbour

9 Government of Canada, *The Quebec Resolutions (The 72 Resolutions)*, Resolution No. 64 (Ottawa: Library and Archives Canada, 1864).

10 Peter W. Hogg, *Constitutional Law of Canada* (Toronto: Carswell, 1998), 142.

11 See also Garth Stevenson, "Fiscal Federalism and the Burden of History," Institute of Intergovernmental Relations working paper, 1–16.

12 Kwavnick, *Tremblay Report*, 121.

federalism," as Kathy Brock would describe it when a similar strategy resurfaced during the late 1990s.[13] Finally, these subsidy provisions established a pattern of what Robert Bourassa much later would call *federalisme rentable*, whereby the federal government would buy loyalty by granting "better terms"[14] to individual provinces as political expediency might dictate: "Of the twenty-six concessions made since 1867 to individual provinces, only five have gone to governments definitively of the opposite political faith. Moreover, all the important concessions have been made immediately before or immediately after a federal election."[15]

Even "better terms," alongside income from licences and fees as well as from the public domain (the provincial ownership of land and resources), did not come close to covering provincial expenditures. Debt allowances had to be raised in some instances, and the provinces had no choice but to do what nobody had expected them to do: resort to direct taxation. British Columbia was first in levying an income tax in 1873, and Quebec pioneered a corporation tax in 1883. By the end of the century, "corporation taxes, succession duties, property and income taxes were already providing about 10 per cent of total provincial revenues."[16]

Decisive change came during the 1920s. With the federal government cash strapped by war debt and hamstrung by its convictions about fiscal thrift, the initiative for modernization and economic growth largely fell to the provinces. During the boom years, provincial revenue nearly doubled. By 1930, more than two-thirds of this increase came from three new sources of provincial revenue: liquor control, motor vehicle licences, and gasoline taxes. Subsidies and income from the public domain, on which the provinces had been expected to rely in perpetuity, fell to under 10 per cent of overall provincial revenue.[17]

We can now appreciate how the provincial rights movement of the late nineteenth century and its post–World War I continuation into the twentieth century was not just about lofty principles of rectifying "the impurities of the constitution" in light of true federalism,[18] and how the frequent intergovernmental

13 Kathy Brock, "Executive Federalism: Beggar Thy Neighbour?" in *New Trends in Canadian Federalism*, 2nd ed., eds. François Rocher and Miriam Smith (Toronto: University of Toronto Press, 2012), 78.

14 Stevenson, *Unfulfilled Union*, 128.

15 J.A. Maxwell, cited ibid.

16 Sirois and Rowell, *Report*, 89.

17 Ibid., 146–7.

18 Robert C. Vipond, *Liberty and Community: Canadian Federalism and the Failure of the Constitution* (Albany: State University of New York Press, 1991), 5.

disputes about the distribution and sale of liquor in particular were not just about "the evil of intemperance," as the JCPC Law Lords had put it in their 1925 *Snider* decision.[19] At least for the provinces, at stake were fiscal or even existential interests and needs.

As we saw in Chapter 3, many of the constitutional cases coming before the JCPC had to do with the regulation and licensing of local business. Even the righteous Law Lords in Westminster acknowledged that their decisions "might interfere with provincial revenues."[20] Or with monopolized income: Ontario had established the LCBO in 1927, and by the end of the decade liquor control had become one of the most important and fastest-growing sources of provincial revenue.[21] It is for this reason that the province sought in 1939 to invalidate the Canada Temperance Act, which permitted municipalities to stay dry.[22]

Fast-forward to the present: At the time when the Tremblay report suggested a wholesale reassignment of Canada's tax powers in the 1950s, the federal government collected around 70 per cent of all revenue. Since then, the percentage has steadily declined to about 40 per cent at the present time.[23] What happened in between is a story of tax sharing in which the federal government eventually ceded more tax room to the provinces.

Right at the war's end, the federal government sought to perpetuate its grip on major revenue sources as the Rowell-Sirois Commission had suggested. Under the impact of Britain's 1942 Beveridge report, a new generation of politicians and senior civil servants, soon dubbed the Ottawa mandarins, convinced the King government that post-war economic reconstruction and social stabilization needed a new approach, known as Keynesian macroeconomic management, to stave off both economic crisis and, in its wake, socialism. This not only meant unemployment insurance and other forms of social security, but also proactive state intervention aimed at preventing unemployment to begin with. Control of the main fiscal levers, taxing and spending, was seen as essential for Keynesian demand management.

---

19 *The Toronto Electric Commissioners (Appeal No. 99 of 1924) v. Colin G. Snider and others* (Ontario) [1925] UKPC 2 (20 January 1925).

20 John T. Saywell, *The Lawmakers: Judicial Power and the Shaping of Canadian Federalism* (Toronto: University of Toronto Press, 2003), 91.

21 Sirois and Rowell, *Report*, 147.

22 *The Attorney-General of Ontario and others (Appeal No. 2 of 1940) v. The Canada Temperance Federation* (Ontario) [1946] UKPC 2 (21 January 1946); see Chapter 3.

23 Livio di Matteo, *A Federal Fiscal History: Canada, 1867–2017* (Toronto: Fraser Institute, 2017), 22.

In return, the provinces would be compensated by relatively generous per capita stipends. The provinces were confronted with these so-called Green Book proposals at the 1945–6 Reconstruction Conference, the first of many such intergovernmental conferences on fiscal matters to come.[24] The provinces did not outright reject what effectively meant a continuation of the war tax rental regime. But they complained that compensation wasn't nearly enough, and in the end, all attempts at compromise came to naught. While Quebec was opposed in principle, it was Ontario that was not interested in what ultimately would have meant sharing its own fiscal riches with others.[25] So in the absence of a common accord, tax rental, now negotiated province by province, continued. But it continued on borrowed time.

For the 1947–52 period, neither Ontario nor Quebec participated. In the absence of agreement, the federal government continued to occupy the income tax field in full. In order to avoid their electorates' wrath over what effectively would have amounted to double taxation, neither provincial government dared to impose a personal income tax of its own. For the next period, 1952–7, Ontario rejoined the tax rental agreements with regard to the most important source of revenue, personal income tax. Quebec did not, but two years later, cornered by a looming fiscal crisis and emboldened by "the arguments of several Tremblay commissioners," Maurice Duplessis, in one of his last major acts as premier, resorted to double taxation by introducing a provincial personal and corporate income tax amounting to 15 per cent of the federal tax.[26]

The tremors of double taxation were felt in Ottawa. The prime minister of the day, Louis St. Laurent, who had replaced Mackenzie King in 1947, felt obliged to reach some sort of accommodation with Quebec without, however, offering Duplessis special treatment and thus alienating the other provinces.[27] What resulted were the 1957–62 tax-sharing agreements whereby all provinces could opt for either a tax rental payment as before or for a so-called tax abatement. The tax rental payment was now calculated on the basis of 10 per cent of intra-provincial federal personal income tax collection, 9 per cent of federal corporation taxes, and 50 per cent of federal estate taxes (succession duties). Alternatively, tax

24 R.M. Burns, *The Acceptable Mean: The Tax Rental Agreements, 1941–1962* (Toronto: Canadian Tax Foundation, 1980).

25 Richard Simeon and Ian Robinson, *State, Society, and the Development of Canadian Federalism* (Toronto: University of Toronto Press, 1990), 107–13.

26 Ibid., 146–7.

27 Ibid., 147.

abatement meant that if a province wished to levy its own taxes in any of these fields the federal government would grant tax room in the same three tax fields and in the same percentage amounts. Ontario chose abatement over rental only in the corporation income tax field.[28] The abatement for Quebec in all three tax fields was applied unilaterally by the federal government because an agreement could not be reached. As the Tremblay report did not fail to point out, Ottawa's offer only amounted to retreating from 10 per cent of the federal personal income tax collected in the province, thus falling short of the 15 per cent the province was already collecting on its own.[29]

The decisive step from tax rental to tax sharing came with the Federal-Provincial Fiscal Arrangements Act of 1961, a step "different in form from anything that had existed before."[30] Partial withdrawal from the three main revenue sources now became the default arrangement. The act also contained a dynamic element. In the personal income tax field, for instance, the federal government's withdrawal would progress from 16 per cent in 1962 to 20 per cent in 1966. After renegotiations with the ever-demanding provinces, the withdrawal by 1966 actually amounted to 24 per cent. For the 1967–72 period it would be 28 per cent.[31] As a consequence, the federal government began collecting less revenue than the provinces for the first time since the 1930s.[32]

Tax collection agreements also started in 1961, whereby what is now known as the Canada Revenue Agency would continue to collect provincial tax shares. Under this regime, the provinces must use the tax base (i.e., the definition of what is taxable income) set by the federal government but can set their own tax rates and brackets. In 1962, only Quebec chose to stick entirely to its own tax collection system. Ontario opted out of joint collection of corporate taxes at that point, and Alberta followed suit in 1981. The quest for corporate tax autonomy in Canada's three richest provincial political economies had nothing to do with a desire to raise more revenue. The objective was to escape the straightjacket of a federally determined tax base to do the opposite: grant exemptions and incentives to business, so much so that in Alberta, for example, corporate taxes have become a "negligible" revenue source.[33]

---

28 Richard Van Loon and Michael Whittington, *The Canadian Political System: Environment, Structure, and Process* (Toronto: McGraw-Hill Ryerson, 1984), 286–7.

29 Kwavnick, *Tremblay Report*, 151.

30 Van Loon and Whittington, *Canadian Political System*, 289–90.

31 Ibid., 293.

32 Di Matteo, *Federal Fiscal History*, 22.

33 Stevenson, *Unfulfilled Union*, 146.

A somewhat similar story unfolded more recently with regard to consumption taxes, which have by now become the third largest source of revenue after personal and corporate taxes. By the 1960s, all provinces had a retail sales tax with the exception of Alberta. The federal government had since 1925 levied a so-called manufacturers' sales tax, which was a hidden tax levied on wholesale goods, but not on services. In 1991, then, the conservative federal government of Brian Mulroney replaced this manufacturers' sales tax with a Goods and Services Tax (GST). This is a value-added tax which is levied at every purchase of goods or services but it ultimately works like a sales tax because consumers pay in the end whereas manufacturers or service providers can reclaim the GST paid on intermediate purchases. It is also the consumption tax used by most industrialized nations, and particularly so in Europe.

As already mentioned in Chapter 2, the introduction of the GST was so unpopular with Canadians that the senate took it upon itself to block passage of the bill in a rare act of legislative defiance, and Mulroney had to resort to the unprecedented step of stacking the second chamber with eight additional and obviously conservative senators. The entire episode doubtlessly contributed to the disastrous defeat of the Conservatives in the federal election two years later when their majority of 151 seats was reduced to rubble – the remaining two seats did not even qualify for official caucus status. Anticipating defeat, Mulroney had retired shortly before that election, leaving it to Kim Campbell to take the fall as Canada's shortest lived and only female prime minister. The Liberal winner of the 1993 election, Jean Chrétien, had campaigned on promising to rescind the GST. Once in office, however, he would not think of it.

With the GST there to stay, the provinces were faced with the question of tax coordination yet again. The federal government offered a scheme of tax sharing similar to that adopted in the income tax field earlier: provincial sales taxes and federal GST would be converted into a Harmonized Sales Tax (HST) with a common tax base and some flexibility as to the apportionment of provincial shares.[34] Three of the four Atlantic provinces signed on in 1997, Ontario did so in 2010, and the fourth Atlantic province, Prince Edward Island, followed suit in 2013. Quebec, of course, begged to differ, replacing the provincial sales tax with a Quebec Sales Tax (QST) in 2012. The QST is equivalent to the HST elsewhere, but instead of the federal government as the collector, it is the province that collects both portions of the tax.[35]

34 Robin Boadway, "Canada," in *The Practice of Fiscal Federalism: Comparative Perspectives*, ed. Anwar Shah (Montreal: McGill-Queen's University Press, 2007), 114.

35 Ibid.

In British Columbia, the 2010 replacement of the provincial sales tax with the HST caused political havoc. Liberal Premier Gordon Campbell had concealed already existing plans during the 2009 election campaign. With the provincial finances in bad shape, the premier's eyes had also been on a $1.6 billion transition payment from the federal government. Campbell resigned, and his successor, Christy Clark, had to repeal the HST in 2013 in compliance with the outcome of a referendum on the question triggered by more than 700,000 signatures of angry voters. Apart from the costs incurred by reverting to a provincial sales tax, the province also had to repay the $1.6 billion it had received from the federal government.

One might think that the issue of tax assignment and revenue sharing in the Canadian federation ought to be settled by now. The provinces in particular should have little to complain about. By the 1990s if not earlier, Canada (along with Switzerland) had become one of only two federations where the subnational governments collect more revenue than the federation itself.[36] Canadian provincial and local governments overall also depend less on federal government handouts than do their counterparts in all other federations; federal transfers comprise only about 20 per cent of provincial and local revenue. Invariably, comparable figures for most other federations are significantly higher.[37]

In terms of tax sharing, then, the Canadian federation appears well balanced even though a 20 per cent provincial dependency on federal transfers is by no means insignificant. This is, however, only half of the story. The other half is about the nature of those transfers – the degree to which, as Quebec contended at the Reconstruction Conference in 1945, they establish "a system of grants that would allow the Dominion to exercise over [the provinces] a financial tutelage control."[38]

Cost Sharing

The most basic principle of public finance in federal systems is proportionality. Each order of government should have control over the financial means necessary

36 Ronald L. Watts, *The Spending Power in Federal Systems: A Comparative Study* (Kingston: Institute of Intergovernmental Relations, 1999), 52; for recent comparative numbers see Paolo Dardanelli and John Kincaid, eds., *Dynamic De/Centralization in Federations*, special issue, *Publius: The Journal of Federalism* 49 (2019).

37 Harvey Lazar, "Trust in Intergovernmental Fiscal Relations," in *Canadian Fiscal Relations: What Works, What Might Work Better*, ed. Harvey Lazar (Montreal: McGill-Queen's University Press, 2005), 15; numbers from various years from 1993–2001.

38 Kwavnich, *Tremblay Report*, 146.

to carry out its constitutionally assigned responsibilities. While this sounds right in principle, it is almost impossible to establish or maintain in practice. As we just saw in the previous section, even though the Canadian federation is almost exceptionally well balanced in terms to tax sharing, the provinces significantly depend on federal fiscal transfers.

There was some disproportionality already built into the BNA Act of 1867. Even though their social policy responsibilities were thought to be modest, the provinces (at least some of them), depending on federal subsidies to begin with, never quite had enough revenue. When the Great Depression struck almost a century later, however, disproportionality became catastrophic. Unemployment and poor relief consumed enormous amounts of revenue, which the provinces did not have and which the federal government was reluctant to give. Already during World War II it dawned on the "enlightened reactionaries" among economists and political planners that this mismatch between social policy responsibility and revenue-raising capacity was not an emergency owed to a one-time capitalist malfunction but a permanent assignment problem for ongoing socioeconomic stabilization.

There were, in principle again, two solutions to the problem. The Rowell-Sirois Commission clearly thought the situation was entirely new in that social security had become a national concern. Consequently, it suggested to re-establish proportionality by centralizing both revenue-raising and social policy powers. The Tremblay Commission, on the other hand, clearly thought that social policy should be left with the provinces as the BNA Act had intended, and that therefore proportionality had to be re-established by decentralizing revenue-raising powers.

In practice, a compromise was struck between the provinces' constitutional and the federal government's superior fiscal powers. The provinces would continue to be responsible for and administer social policy, but they would do so with the help of federal cost-sharing agreements in return for compliance with "minimal nationwide standards."[39] A quick glance beyond borders can easily establish just how uniquely Canadian that compromise was – and still is. In Germany, the constitution expressly prohibits so-called "mixed financing."[40] And in the United States, cost sharing typically amounts to a "coercive" regime

39 Boadway, "Canada," 99.

40 Article 104a(1) Basic Law; exceptions do exist, however, and the "joint tasks" entered into the constitution in 1969 have watered down the concept of keeping expenditures separate.

of federally imposed conditionality[41] whereby Congress can interfere with state jurisdiction almost at whim.[42]

Cost-sharing regimes in Canada extend to everything from agriculture, industry, and the environment, to healthcare and social assistance. The only major exceptions are unemployment insurance, which the constitutional amendment of 1940 assigned to exclusive federal fiscal responsibility, and pensions, which after a 1951 constitutional amendment became a formally concurrent power with provincial paramountcy to the effect that the federal government cannot make changes to the (federally financed) CPP without substantive provincial approval (two-thirds of the provinces representing two-thirds of the population).

Following Keith Banting's seminal distinction, then, there are three different "federalisms" at work in Canada: classical or divided federalism, as in the case of unemployment insurance; joint-decision federalism, as in the case of the CPP; and shared-cost federalism, which in more ways than one has become the central preoccupation in Canadian fiscal relations.[43] In sheer quantitative terms, federal fiscal transfers to the provinces and territories for shared-cost programs (healthcare and social assistance in particular) amount to more than half of all transfers,[44] and healthcare spending alone amounts to some 40 per cent of overall provincial spending.[45]

In qualitative terms, cost-sharing agreements typically are the result of lengthy and periodically repeated negotiations. It is for this reason that intergovernmental relations in Canadian federalism are for the most part fiscal relations, squaring off provincial jurisdiction against the federal government's spending power. Because of this spending power, the federal government usually has the

41 John Kincaid, "The Rise of Coercive Federalism in the United States," in *The Future of Australian Federalism: Comparative and Interdisciplinary Perspectives*, eds. Gabrielle Appleby, Nicholas Aroney and Thomas John (Cambridge: Cambridge University Press, 2012), 173–5.

42 Tim Conlan, "From Cooperative to Opportunistic Federalism: Reflections in the Half-Century Anniversary of the Commission on Intergovernmental Relations," *Public Administration Review* 66, no. 5 (2006); see also Hueglin and Fenna, *Comparative Federalism*, 176–7.

43 See Keith Banting, "The Three Federalisms Revisited: Social Policy and Intergovernmental Decision-Making," in *Canadian Federalism*, eds. Herman Bakvis and Grace Skogstad (Toronto: Oxford University Press, 2012).

44 Government of Canada, *2008 December Report of the Auditor General of Canada* (Ottawa: Office of the Auditor General of Canada, 2008).

45 Canadian Institute for Health Information, "National Health Expenditure Trends, 1975 to 2016," 2016.

upper hand. The informality of the process also allows the federal government to adopt a take-it-or-leave-it approach or even resort to unilateralism in the absence of agreement.

Accounts of the wrangling over ever-more-complex cost-sharing formulae every five years, in tandem with the tax-sharing negotiations already discussed, can be read not just as a barometer of the periodic atmospheric disturbances in federal–provincial relations,[46] but more generally of climate change in the international political economy and the Canadian position within it.[47] With that broader political economy framework in mind, the history of social cost sharing in Canada after World War II can be divided into two major phases: a first phase of open-ended fiscal largesse lasting until the mid-1970s, and a second phase of fiscal crisis that is still ongoing.

The first phase coincided with exponential economic growth largely owed to post-war reconstruction and international trade facilitated by currency stability under the Bretton Woods system. Prosperity in what a leading American political scientist called an "age of affluence"[48] led to a generous regime of social spending in which the federal government did not want to be seen as leaving the initiative to the provinces.

Thus in 1957 the federal government introduced the first in a series of major social cost-sharing programs: hospital insurance (officially the Hospital Insurance and Diagnostic Services Act [HIDS]). Similar plans had been discussed before, and credit goes to Saskatchewan under the CCF leadership of Tommy Douglas for having followed through with its own plan a decade earlier even though an expected cost-sharing arrangement with the federal government had fallen through.[49] A decade later, much of the cost-sharing initiative came from Ontario, which like other provinces wanted hospital insurance but argued that it

---

46 Van Loon and Whittington, *Canadian Political System*, 284–98; Herman Bakvis, Gerald Baier, and Douglas Brown, *Contested Federalism: Certainty and Ambiguity in the Canadian Federation* (Toronto: Oxford University Press, 2009), 148–9.

47 See Sarah Fortin, "From the Canadian Social Union to the Federal Social Union of Canada," in *Contemporary Canadian Federalism: Foundation, Traditions, Institutions*, ed. Alain-G. Gagnon (Toronto: University of Toronto Press, 2012), 309–14.

48 Robert E. Lane, "The Politics of Consensus in an Age of Affluence," *American Political Science Review* 59 (1965).

49 Gerard W. Boychuk, *National Health Insurance in the United States and Canada* (Washington: Georgetown University Press, 2008), 93–4.

could not afford it without federal assistance. By 1963, when Quebec joined the plan, close to 99 per cent of Canadians were covered.[50]

Then in 1966 came the Canada Assistance Plan (CAP). It combined into one several earlier cost-shared social programs for old age, disability, and unemployment assistance. Mainly because of Quebec's objections, the CAP came to be the first cost-sharing program that included a "contracting-out" provision whereby provinces could declare that they preferred to run their own programs in return for further personal income tax abatements.[51] Only Quebec opted out from major programs such as the CAP, and as a consequence ended up with tax abatements totaling 44 per cent of personal income tax, 10 per cent of corporate tax, and 75 per cent of succession duties.[52]

A year later, in 1967, the federal government converted its earlier grants for post-secondary education offered directly to universities into a federal–provincial shared-cost program. Quebec, which had forbidden its universities to accept the earlier grants, now as per usual opted for additional tax room and would provide similar grants to its universities directly.[53]

Finally, 1968 saw the introduction of the last of the major cost-sharing programs, the Medical Care Act, which was meant to cover the cost of most (but not all) physicians' services. Ontario was dead opposed this time around, and so were a number of other provinces. The bitter doctors' strike was not forgotten when Saskatchewan had gone ahead with a similar plan a few years earlier. In the end, the federal government outmanoeuvred provincial opposition by announcing a 2 per cent increase of the federal personal income tax, which it called a social development tax even though it was clearly meant to pay for the federal share of healthcare. The message was clear: All taxpayers would be paying for medical insurance regardless of whether their provincial governments adopted a plan or not. By 1971, all provinces had signed on with medicare plans in place.[54]

These major cost-sharing programs are conditional grants because the federal money comes with strings attached. For healthcare, the original four strings or conditions were "public administration," mainly in order to disallow private for-profit services; "comprehensiveness," so that provinces would

50 Simeon and Robinson, *State, Society, and the Development of Canadian Federalism*, 149.

51 Kenneth McRoberts, *Misconceiving Canada* (Toronto: Oxford University Press, 1997), 41.

52 Van Loon and Whittington, *Canadian Political System*, 291–2.

53 Daniel Béland et al., *Fiscal Federalism and Equalization Policy in Canada* (Toronto: University of Toronto Press, 2017), 94.

54 Boychuk, *National Health Insurance*, 130.

not arbitrarily limit coverage of standard services to save money; "universality," to ensure "100 per cent" coverage of all provincial inhabitants; and "portability," which disallowed "any minimum period of residence in the province" so that all Canadians would remain insured at all times, even when moving from one province to another. The Canada Health Act (CHA) of 1984 then added a fifth condition: "accessibility," which was aimed at prohibiting the widespread practice of "extra-billing" in the form of charging patients more for a procedure than the healthcare plan will reimburse.[55] Overall, these conditions are meant to ensure a reasonable degree of uniformity in the delivery of healthcare while still leaving considerable room for the provinces to design and administer their individual healthcare plans.[56]

A particular and at the time by no means unusual feature of cost sharing during this earlier phase was its financial open-endedness. The federal government would match provincial expenditure dollar for dollar regardless of what provinces decided to spend, which effectively meant it had no control over the final amount of its own expenditure. The only explanation for this fiscal largesse is to be found in the economic boom of the first post-war decades, which led governments (and most economists) to believe that control of the capitalist system had been mastered and never-ending growth and prosperity were in sight. A rude awakening, however, was only a few years away.

In 1971, international trade was reintroduced to the instabilities of floating currencies when President Nixon effectively pulled the rug out from under the Bretton Woods Agreement by ending the gold convertibility of the US dollar. In 1973–4, the OPEC crisis and the following stock market crash led to stagflation (simultaneous price inflation and economic stagnation), rising unemployment, and growing budget deficits that would not go away for more than 20 years. At least some political economists diagnosed a systemic fiscal crisis of the capitalist state resulting from a structural gap between revenue and expenditure that would deepen as economic growth slowed, profits remained privatized, and the need for social expenses expanded.[57]

The crucial turn in Canadian fiscal relations came at an intergovernmental conference in 1976, when Prime Minister Pierre Elliott Trudeau confronted his provincial colleagues with a new approach to cost sharing according to which,

55 Government of Canada, Canada Health Act (RSC 1985, c. C-6).

56 Bakvis, Baier, and Brown, *Contested Federalism*, 144–5.

57 James O'Connor, *The Fiscal Crisis of the State* (New York: St. Martin's Press, 1973); Fred Block, "The Fiscal Crisis of the Capitalist State," *Annual Review of Sociology* 7 (1981).

in his words, "federal payments should be calculated independently of provincial program expenditures."[58] The reason for this change, as Trudeau pointed out, were systemic deficiencies of the open-ended 50–50 approach: mainly a lack of cost control at both levels of government; inequality as poorer provinces might not tap into matching funds because of a lack of their own resources; and a provincial policy process driven by the availability of federal funds rather than their own priorities.[59]

The negotiated and mutually agreed-upon outcome was Established Programs Financing (EPF), which combined the previous transfers for medical and hospital insurance as well as post-secondary education into one block funding transfer that was no longer tied to actual provincial expenditure. Instead, based on the 1975–6 payments, annual increases would be calculated on the basis of population and gross national product (GNP) growth. Moreover, the transfer would consist of a combination of near-equal amounts of cash payment and tax abatement, the latter equalized on a per capita basis for the benefit of the poorer provinces. And finally, there would be transition payments amounting to a revenue guarantee.[60] For the time being, the 50–50 funding formula stayed in place for the only other major cost-sharing program, the CAP.

EPF as first established for the 1977–82 period was not yet the end of federal fiscal largesse. In fact, because inflation pushed up the nominal GNP, the federal government was by the end of the decade financing 60 per cent of cost sharing rather than 50 per cent under the old formula.[61] But fiscal relations in Canadian federalism entered a new phase that was overshadowed by fiscal crisis. And that meant that a succession of federal governments would nibble away at their commitment of cost sharing one round of negotiations at a time.

In 1982, the federal government and the provinces for the first time did not reach agreement on how to proceed with EPF.[62] Trudeau, back in power after a nine-month hiatus during the short-lived Conservative prime ministership of Joe Clark (1979–80), now appeared more adamant than ever in forcing his vision of federalism upon the country. That vision entailed that it was the federal

58 Pierre Elliot Trudeau, "Established Program Financing: A Proposal Regarding the Major Shared-Cost Programs in the Fields of Health and Post-Secondary Education," in *Canadian Federalism: Myth or Reality*, ed. J. Peter Meekison (Toronto: Methuen, 1977), 250.

59 Ibid., 248.

60 Van Loon and Whittington, *Canadian Political System*, 295–6.

61 Ibid., 296.

62 Simeon and Robinson, *State, Society, and the Development of Canadian Federalism*, 289–95.

government's role to determine the country's future. In the midst of a constitutional crisis (see Chapter 7) as well as Quebec separatism and western alienation (see Chapter 6), Trudeau sought to tighten the screws of what he thought was a social policy system that was falling apart.

There was indeed some evidence that the provinces, plagued by their own fiscal deficit problems, abused the EPF system. Because federal cash transfers only paid for about one-quarter of the programs to which national standard conditions were supposed to be attached, most provinces had allowed extra-billing and other fees. Because the transfers came as block funding, there was no accountability as to whether the provinces actually used the funds for the purposes intended. And because of the transitional revenue guarantee, the provinces could cut their own costs with impunity. As Trudeau saw it, and as confirmed to a considerable extent by a parliamentary task force established to this effect (the Breau Task Force), the provinces were underfunding the programs for which Ottawa paid dearly.[63] Still in 1985, as it turned out, five provinces would spend less on post-secondary education than the amount transferred to them for this purpose by the federal government.[64]

The task force did not say that Ottawa should cut spending. However, Trudeau wanted both – spending cuts and tightened conditions – and since he could not get agreement, he proceeded unilaterally. The revenue guarantee was ended. In 1983, while EPF continued as a block transfer, the federal government re-divided the payment portions for health and post-secondary education and then put a cap on the latter.[65] In 1984, the CHA added the fifth of the national standard conditions for the delivery of healthcare (see above), and it threatened sanctions (withholding of funds) in the case of violations. Then, deciding during a walk in a blizzard on February 29, 1984, that he would retire, Trudeau was gone. But the provincial hope for improvement in fiscal relations in a post-Liberal Ottawa was short lived. As it turned out, the fiscal crisis had become the independent variable in fiscal relations regardless of who was prime minister or which party was in power.

The first budget of the Conservative government of Brian Mulroney de-indexed EPF transfers from the rate of inflation. They would henceforth grow

63 Ibid., 293.

64 Ibid., 329.

65 The federal government had imposed an anti-inflationary "six and five" per cent for public-sector salary and wage increases for two years beginning in 1982, and the education transfer was capped accordingly.

only in tandem with the GNP growth rate minus 2 per cent.[66] In 1990, the federal government put a cap on CAP. This was particularly hard on provincial finances because the 1990s also saw major cuts and eligibility restrictions to unemployment insurance. These began during the last years of the Mulroney government and continued unabated after the Liberals of Jean Chrétien took federal power in 1993. Provinces were faced with less CAP money but increasing social assistance needs as the social blanket of federal unemployment insurance became thinner and thinner.

Then, in 1995, Liberal Finance Minister Paul Martin unilaterally announced the most draconian cuts to social transfers yet. For the 1995–6 fiscal year, EPF would be calculated at GNP percentage growth minus 3 per cent, and CAP would be frozen at the 1994–5 level. Beginning with the 1996–7 fiscal year, EPF and CAP would be merged into one block transfer now called the Canada Health and Social Transfer (CHST), with its overall amount set in absolute terms at $26.9 billion and $25.1 billion for the next two fiscal years. After that, the CHST would increase again, albeit beginning from a much lower platform, at a rate of GDP – 2, GDP – 1.5, and GDP – 1 per cent for the remaining three years of the five-year fiscal period.[67] What this meant was an overall reduction of federal transfers by 34 per cent.[68] What it also meant was that the federal government would soon return to a balanced budget for the first time since the early 1970s, thus sanitizing its finances "on the back of the provinces."[69]

With the world by now firmly in the grip of neoliberal social deregulation ideology, some governments even welcomed this form of downloaded austerity. In Ontario, for instance, where the Conservative government of Mike Harris was boasting to carry out what it grandly proclaimed to be a "common sense revolution," welfare was cut by more than 20 per cent in 1995.[70] Infamously, David Tsubouchi, the minister of communications and social services, told

66 Simeon and Robinson, *State, Society, and the Development of Canadian Federalism*, 328.

67 Government of Canada, "A Brief History of the Canada Health and Social Transfer" (Ottawa: Department of Finance, 2004).

68 Fortin, "From the Canadian Social Union," 312.

69 Alain Noël, "Balance and Imbalance in the Division of Financial Resources," in *Contemporary Canadian Federalism: Foundations, Traditions, Institutions*, ed. Alain-G. Gagnon (Toronto: University of Toronto Press, 2012), 285, citing Thomas Courchene.

70 Janice MacKinnon, *Minding the Public Purse: The Fiscal Crisis, Political Trade-offs, and Canada's Future* (Montreal: McGill-Queen's University Press, 2003), 144.

poverty-stricken welfare mothers to haggle for dented cans of tuna which, as he insisted without providing any evidence, could be had for as little as 69 cents.

All the while, the federal government, by slashing unemployment benefits even though continuing to collect workers' forced savings, availed itself of a nice little nest egg, ameliorating its budget situation even further. Unemployment insurance, now euphemistically called employment insurance, which had contributed $6 billion to the federal deficit in the early 1990s, would now begin to rake in an accumulated surplus reaching $36 billion by 2001.[71]

This was federalism at its worst. Canada's most vulnerable were in danger of falling victim to intergovernmental fiscal finger pointing and buck-passing with the ultimate effect of returning to nineteenth-century welfare conditions: Survival increasingly depended on private charity. The number of Canadian food bank users almost doubled during the 1990s.[72] To be sure, the systemic fiscal crisis of the Canadian federal state was very real. Social programs had begun to consume the largest chunks of revenue in federal as well as provincial budgets. But the alternative to cutting social expenditure (raising taxes for those who could afford to pay more) was never an option at either level of government. Entering into a free trade agreement with the United States had seen to that, as competition with the world's most deregulated capitalist economy required corporate privilege, bonuses, and stock options, not social responsibility.

The wealthier provinces in particular had always expressed reservations about federal spending power intrusions into provincial jurisdiction. What sent them into combative overdrive in 1995, however, was Ottawa's decision "not to spend."[73] As that decision had come with nice words about future cooperation on principles and objectives, the provinces took action. At their annual meeting in 1996, the premiers established a Provincial–Territorial Council on Social Policy Renewal aimed at how the provinces might regain social policymaking – and financing – initiative. A few months later, the federal government joined the council, which now became the Federal–Provincial–Territorial Council on Social Policy Renewal. Two years later, negotiations began for a Social Union Framework Agreement (SUFA). It was eventually signed in 1999 with the main objective of putting fiscal relations on more predictable and common ground.

71 Fortin, "From the Canadian Social Union," 311.

72 Beth Wilson with Carly Steinman, *Hunger Count 2000: A Surplus of Hunger* (Toronto: Canadian Association of Food Banks, 2000).

73 Fortin, "From the Canadian Social Union," 316–18.

In essence, the SUFA was an intergovernmental compromise of mutual goodwill. The provinces accepted the legitimacy of the federal spending power and with it the federal government's leadership role in social policy. The federal government in turn committed to "stable and sustainable funding." It would also abstain from introducing new social programs "without the agreement of a majority of provincial governments." Transparency and accountability would be strengthened through collaboration, public information sharing, and outcome monitoring.[74] Quebec did not sign on in the end, and mainly so because of the lack of a formal opting-out clause covering not only major cost-sharing programs but federal transfers to individuals and organizations as well.[75]

By most accounts, the SUFA neither brought to an end federal unilateralism nor had a significant impact on the conduct of intergovernmental relations or on public involvement.[76] If some change did come, it was probably owed more to sanitized federal finances than to any serious thoughts about recalibrating the intergovernmental mechanism of social policy delivery. A contributing factor were the findings of the 2002 Romanow Commission on the future of healthcare in Canada, which had left no doubt about the existence of funding gaps.[77]

The 2003 First Ministers' Meeting on Health Care Renewal was a turning point.[78] For purposes of transparency and accountability, the CHST would be divided again into a separate a Canada Health Transfer (CHT) and a Canada Social Transfer (CST).[79] The federal government committed to increased health funding levels meant to address the gaps left by the 1995 cuts. Canada's first ministers also agreed on federal funding for specially targeted initiatives meant to reduce notoriously long waiting times for diagnostic services, improve availability of primary healthcare, and provide catastrophic drug coverage.

---

74 Canadian Intergovernmental Conference Secretariat, "Agreement: A Framework to Improve the Social Union for Canadians," First Ministers' Meeting, Ottawa, February 4, 1999.

75 Harvey Lazar, "The Social Union Framework Agreement and the Future of Fiscal Federalism," in *Toward a New Mission Statement for Canadian Fiscal Federalism*, ed. Harvey Lazar (Montreal: McGill-Queen's University Press, 2000), 111.

76 See Sarah Fortin, Alain Nöel, and France St-Hilaire, eds., *Forging the Canadian Social Union: SUFA and Beyond* (Montreal: Institute for Research on Public Policy, 2003).

77 Roy J. Romanow, "Building on Values: The Future of Health Care in Canada," Commission on the Future of Health Care in Canada, November 2002.

78 Government of Canada, "The 2003 Accord on Health Care Renewal," 2004.

79 A good overview of the entire post-war development can be found in Government of Canada, "History of Health and Social Transfers," 2014.

Clearly, the federal government's strategy was to enhance public recognition of its leadership role in addressing these particular health policy concerns. It was a strategy that soon would come to be resented by the provinces as "boutique federalism." In 2016, Liberal Prime Minister Justin Trudeau's efforts at striking a new common health accord came to naught precisely because the provinces objected to targeted special funds for home care and mental health in lieu of what they considered adequate overall funding for the health systems under provincial jurisdiction and administration.[80]

Only a year later, in a "historic agreement" at the First Minister's Meeting in 2004,[81] the federal government then committed to an unprecedented 10-year plan (instead of the usual five) for increased healthcare transfers, which included a 6 per cent annual escalator and thus effectively restored pre-1995 funding levels without, however, as the provinces grumbled, covering dramatically increasing provincial expenditures. The Liberal federal government, with Paul Martin now at the helm as prime minister, also sought to appease Quebec by concluding separate agreements on healthcare, childcare, and parental insurance in 2005. As it stands today, health spending amounts to about 40 per cent of provincial and territorial program spending,[82] and the share of federal funding, which had fallen to 14 per cent by the end of the 1990s, now stands at about 23 per cent.[83]

From Quebec also came a more general political initiative of addressing the political fallout from the 1995 transfer cuts, which in the view of many had led to "a major revival of political controversy within Canada about the main elements of our system of fiscal federalism."[84] In 2003 the Liberal government of Jean Charest invited the other provincial governments to form the interprovincial Council of the Federation (CoF) as a strategic tool to recalibrate the Canadian federation so that the provinces once again become "veritable partners" rather

80 Ian Peach, "Prime Minister Trudeau Needs to Have a Serious Discussion with the Provinces about the Substance and the Process of Making Good National Policies in a Federal State," *Policy Options*, July 2016.

81 Antonia Maioni, "Health Care," in Bakvis and Skogstad, *Canadian Federalism*, 170–1.

82 Barua Bacchus, Milagros Palacios, and Joel Emes, "The Sustainability of Health Care Spending in Canada 2017" (Vancouver: Fraser Institute, March 2017), 5.

83 Government of Québec, "For a Fair Share of Federal Health Funding" (Quebec City: Budget 2017–2018).

84 Harvey Lazar, "Foreword," in *Canadian Fiscal Arrangements: What Works, What Might Work Better*, ed. Harvey Lazar (Montreal: McGill-Queen's University Press, 2005), vii.

than remain the recipients of unilateral federal action.[85] In many ways echoing SUFA language, the CoF founding agreement emphasized the provincial need for "adequate financial resources," "respect" for the constitutional division of powers, and "exercising leadership on national issues of importance to provinces."[86] In other words, a prime objective of the CoF, jointly funded with its own secretariat and regularized biannual meetings, was to reach common positions that would prevent the federal government from playing a divide-and-rule game.

Yet while the CoF has become a well-established institution of interprovincial cooperation, it has not prevented the federal government from divide-and-rule business as usual. As already discussed in Chapter 2, the newly anointed federal government of Justin Trudeau went to work in 2015 with the promise of "sunnier ways," which essentially meant a more cooperative approach to intergovernmental relations. Yet when a common agreement on healthcare funding was not forthcoming because of the aforementioned objections to boutique federalism, the government proceeded to strike bilateral agreements with individual provinces on a take-it-or-leave-it basis, which proved successful not least because the process began by first getting on board the poorest provinces who needed the money the most.

Fiscal Equalization

As we saw in Chapter 4, the crisis of capitalism during the 1930s had pushed the fiscal arrangements of Canadian federalism into disarray. In 1940, the Rowell-Sirois Commission responded to this fiscal crisis by recommending tax centralization at the federal level in return for annual federal grants, foreshadowing fiscal equalization in such a way as to enable all provinces to provide equitable public services as measured by a Canadian average standard. What the commission likely had recommended simply as a practical response to social instability resulting from fiscal imbalance nevertheless gave expression, at a deeper level, of what amounts to a foundational commitment to social solidarity among the members of a federal union.

Ultimately, social solidarity in federal systems means some form of revenue redistribution from richer to poorer provinces. Such redistributive solidarity can

85 François Rocher, "The Quebec-Canada Dynamic or the Negation of the Ideal of Federalism," in Gagnon, *Contemporary Canadian Federalism*, 107–8.

86 Council of the Federation, "Council of the Federation Founding Agreement," Charlottetown, Prince Edward Island, December 5, 2003.

come in many forms, from federal payments to individual citizens in the form of unemployment insurance, for instance, which disproportionately benefits provinces with lower rates of employment, to regional development policies offering a variety of fiscal and funding incentives aimed at diminishing regional economic disparity, to the aforementioned CHST, which draw per capita funding from federal revenue regardless of how much of that revenue is collected from each province (and which actually make up a larger portion of federal transfer payments than do the equalization payments themselves).[87]

But the quintessential expression of redistributive solidarity in federal systems is fiscal equalization. Its iconic status is probably owed to the fact that, whereas other forms of transfers are at least in name linked to specific programs for the benefit of citizens rather than governments, fiscal equalization gives unconditional expression to the principle of membership equality. Unsurprisingly, then, while tax centralization in the form of tax rental agreements remained a temporary feature in Canadian federalism, unconditional fiscal equalization became one of its permanent features, eventually enshrined in Section 36(2) of the Constitution Act of 1982, stipulating that the federal government is committed to equalization payments so that all provinces can provide "reasonably comparable levels of public services at reasonably comparable levels of taxation."

With varying thoroughness, all modern federal systems except the United States are committed to fiscal equalization.[88] Some federations, at least in part, rely on a form of horizontal equalization whereby revenue from the richer jurisdictions is directly redistributed to the poorer ones. In the Canadian case, the task of equalization is exclusively assigned to the federal government, which means that fiscal support for poorer provinces has to come entirely out of the federal government's budget. The redistributive effect is indirect in that some of the general revenue collected by the federal government in the richer provinces will be transferred to the poorer ones.

A particular Canadian problem pertaining to fiscal equalization is the provincial ownership of natural resources. The particularly lucrative oil and gas industries are concentrated in the three westernmost provinces, with Alberta the wealthiest resource province by far. The royalties accruing from the exploitation of these resources disproportionally add to the fiscal wealth in these provinces. Royalties also cannot be taxed by the federal government and are therefore out of reach for federal

87 Béland et al., *Fiscal Federalism*, 87–8.

88 See Hansjörg Blöchlinger and Claire Charbit, "Fiscal Equalization," *OECD Economic Studies* 44 (2008).

redistributive purposes. The problem is further compounded by the price volatility in the world's commodity markets, which create notorious boom and bust cycles that cause periodically fluctuating fiscal capacities in the resource-exporting provinces. The federal government's fiscal capacity may come under considerable strain if boom cycle royalties are included in the equalization formula, as they should be if equalization is supposed to mean equitable fiscal means for all provinces.

The first incidence of unconditional equalization occurred in conjunction with the 1952–7 tax rental agreements. The principle underlying these agreements was that the federal government would collect all the revenue in the vacated tax fields and then pay back to each province a rent proportional to the revenue yield collected. For the 1952–7 period, however, the federal government committed to disproportionate minimum payments for the poorer provinces, further adjusted upward by a formula derived from per capita GNP and population size. This meant that for the first time the poorer or "have-not" provinces could count on guaranteed payment levels regardless of the actual revenue yield.[89]

From this initial commitment to equalize fiscal capacities developed a formula-driven system of fiscal equalization that has been a permanent part of Canadian federalism since it was first adopted in 1957. While the formula has changed over time, no doubt to the delight of the mathematically inclined aficionados of public finance,[90] the basic underlying principles have remained the same. A national per capita fiscal capacity standard is calculated and compared to the actual per capita fiscal capacity in each province.[91] To avoid situations where provinces choose to keep taxes low in order to maximize equalization, per capita provincial fiscal capacity is calculated as its fiscal ability to raise taxes as determined by average taxation rates across all provinces.[92] If that provincial capacity is below the national standard, the province receives the difference as its equalization payment. If it is above, no payment will be made, which means that above-average fiscal capacity will not be punished by taking away money, as has been the case in Germany's horizontal system of equalization.

89 Van Loon and Whittington, *Canadian Political System*, 286; see also Béland et al., *Fiscal Federalism*, 7.

90 See Jim Feehan, "Canada's Equalization Formula: Peering Inside the Black Box ... and Beyond," *School of Public Policy Research Papers* 7, no. 24 (2014).

91 The territories are not included in the equalization scheme and receive special cost-based transfers; see ibid., 119.

92 François Boucher and Jocelyn Maclure, "The Equalization Program Does Not Subsidize Quebec's Welfare State," *In Due Course* (Canadian Public Affairs blog), September 4, 2014.

What changed over the years and created occasional intergovernmental friction were the two main variables of the formula: the number of tax sources used and the number of provinces included in the calculation. Based on only three tax sources, personal income, corporate income, and succession duties on inheritance, the 1957 formula set out to adjust provincial fiscal capacities to an average calculated from the two provinces with the highest per capita revenues. This not only meant that all provinces except Ontario would receive equalization payments,[93] it also meant that the Atlantic provinces would have to receive additional adjustment grants because the narrowly chosen tax base would not sufficiently address fiscal disparities in these provinces.[94]

Based on three tax sources only, the calculations of provincial fiscal capacity were hypothetical,[95] and the intent of upward adjustments to the average of the two richest provinces was overly ambitious. Already in 1962 revisions to the formula were made that marked the beginning of a balancing act that has continued to this day.[96] In 1962, 50 per cent of natural resource revenues were added to the formula, which was now calculated on the basis of all 10 provinces. In 1967, 16 tax sources were included, and by the 1980s the number had grown to 33. In 1982, under the impact of the OPEC crisis and exploding oil prices, the formula was changed yet again to include only five provinces, excluding the four poorest Atlantic provinces along with Alberta, which had become the richest. Keeping the oil-rich province in the formula at that time would have meant that even Ontario qualified for equalization payments. In 1995, under the impact of the fiscal deficit crisis, Liberal Finance Minister Paul Martin placed a GNP-linked cap on the growth of equalization payments.

In 2004, with Paul Martin as prime minister, the formula was changed more substantively. All payments would come out of a pool fixed at $10 billion and growing by 3.5 per cent annually.[97] Provincial allotments would still be calculated on the basis of fiscal capacity as measured by all tax sources, including

93 At the time, Ontario and British Columbia had the highest per capita revenue yield. Averaging the two, however, would make British Columbia a receiver of equalization payments.

94 David B. Perry, *Financing the Canadian Federation 1867 to 1995: Setting the Stage for Change* (Toronto: Canadian Tax Foundation, 1997), 120.

95 Ibid.

96 Ibid., 120–72; Béland et al., *Fiscal Federalism*, 21–52.

97 Wade Locke, "Cutting through the Gordian Knot: An Objective Assessment of the Equalization Implications for Newfoundland and Labrador of the 2007 Federal Budget," *Newfoundland Quarterly* 100, no. 2 (2007): 49.

natural resource revenue. But, as Béland and colleagues note, under the fixed pool scheme, equalization was turned into a zero-sum game: More money for one province would inevitably mean less for others.[98] Provincial outrage was swift, and nowhere more so than in Newfoundland, where Premier Danny Willliams ordered all Canadian flags to be lowered on public buildings.[99]

After three years and as recommended by a panel of experts, the newly elected Conservative government of Stephen Harper returned the equalization formula to its current and more traditional form. This essentially meant a formula based on a 10-province average based on 33 tax sources, now grouped into five broader categories, and the inclusion of 50 per cent of resource revenue. Harper had campaigned with a promise of excluding resource revenue. Non-inclusion was a particular issue for Newfoundland. The province, which has been dependent on equalization payments for a long time (at times up to 50 per cent of every public dollar spent), had only recently begun to benefit from offshore oil discovery. Inclusion of oil revenues in the equalization formula meant that whatever the province had gained in oil wealth might be wiped out again by a reduction in equalization payments.

The Harper government's compromise was to give the resource-rich provinces a choice of having their fiscal capacity calculated with either 0 or 50 per cent resource revenues included. The federal government would pay whichever amount turned out to be higher under the two formulae, but there would be a cap. A province's fiscal capacity would not be allowed to exceed the lowest level of fiscal capacity in a non-receiving province.

This time, Danny Williams took out a full-page advertisement in the *Globe and Mail* denouncing Harper for breaking his pre-election promise of excluding resource revenue altogether. Saskatchewan's premier, Lorne Calvert, even threatened to take the federal government to court. The tempest effectively ended in 2008 when the world financial crisis led to a thorough re-shuffling of "have" (recipient) and "have-not" (non-recipient) provinces, with the effect of escalating equalization costs for the federal government. On the one hand Ontario, with the largest population of all provinces, for the first time became a have-not province. On the other hand British Columbia became the non-receiving province with the lowest fiscal capacity level, which meant that the equalization cap moved upward because of British Columbia's higher fiscal capacity. After fiddling with the formula for a while to contain costs, the Harper government in 2011 imposed

98 Béland et al., *Fiscal Federalism*, 36.

99 This and the following is based on ibid., 36–40.

a new cap, limiting the growth of equalization payments to gross domestic product (GDP) growth.

As soon as Ontario became a have-not province it started complaining about the unfairness of the formula. The complaints were justified in part because equalization entitlements are calculated on a rolling three-year average, which meant that Ontario did not receive payments for a number of years when its fiscal capacity was already below average but the three-year calculation kept it above. By the same token, however, Ontario would continue to receive payments for a number of years even after re-entering the club of "have" provinces, which in 2016 seemed imminent, mainly because of Alberta's faltering economy and weakening fiscal position.[100]

For the 2020–1 fiscal year, the "have" provinces include Newfoundland and Labrador, Ontario, Saskatchewan, Alberta, and British Columbia. The remaining provinces, Prince Edward Island, Nova Scotia, New Brunswick, Quebec, and Manitoba, collectively are projected to receive some $20 billion in equalization payments, of which about $13 billion will go to Quebec.[101] For the territories, there is a Territorial Formula Financing (TFF) program that reflects the higher cost of public service delivery in the north. In Nunavut, for example, TFF transfers amount to over 80 per cent of revenues.[102]

Fiscal equalization, it has been said, is "the glue that holds the federation together" and as such is "one of the most tangible manifestations of Canadian solidarity."[103] It is not surprising that this statement would come from one of the premiers of Atlantic Canada's provinces. During the early years of equalization, 50 cents of every dollar that Newfoundland spent came from Ottawa,[104] and still today equalization payments make up between 25 and 30 per cent of revenue in the Maritime provinces.[105] Comparable public services at comparable rates of

100 Karen Howlett and Jane Taber, "Ontario to Lose Equalization Payments as Alberta's Economic Fortunes Fall," *The Globe and Mail*, December 17, 2016.

101 Government of Canada, "Major Federal Transfers, 2017," Department of Finance.

102 Government of Nunavut, "Main Estimates 2017–2018" (Iqaluit, NU: Department of Finance, February 2017).

103 Nova Scotia Premier John Hamm, cited in P.E. Bryden, "The Obligations of Federalism: Ontario and the Origins of Equalization," in *Framing Canadian Federalism: Essays in Honour of John T. Saywell*, eds. Dimitri Anastakis and P.E. Bryden (Toronto: University of Toronto Press, 2009), 76.

104 Perry, *Financing the Canadian Federation*, 122.

105 Béland et al., *Fiscal Federalism*, 90.

taxation would be way out of reach if fiscal equalization did not exist as a "commitment to sharing and social solidarity."[106]

As at least some economists and public finance experts argue, however, this commitment also has a potentially counterproductive effect in the form of "welfare dependency": The recipient provinces will simply rely on the cash instead of finding ways of improving their own productivity and, therefore, fiscal capacity.[107] However, this "transfer dependency" argument not only bears striking similarity to neoconservative misrepresentations of poverty as a self-inflicted condition resulting from laziness and a lack of initiative,[108] it also tends to ignore Atlantic Canada's historical predicament as "the only region which secured no economic benefits ... from Confederation."[109]

Enshrined in the constitution, of course, fiscal equalization is no longer up for debate in principle. Yet in practice it often appears as a microcosm of all that fuels intergovernmental conflict and wrangling in Canadian federalism more generally.[110] Fiscal equalization is always difficult in the face of highly uneven fiscal capacities. In Germany, for instance, one of the most generous equalization schemes of any federation became problematic only after reunification in 1990 added six mostly poor eastern German *Länder* (provinces) to the equation. One of the main problems in Canada is the provincial ownership of natural resources, which adds significant royalties to the fiscal coffers of only a few provinces. Including them in the equation can become excessively expensive for a federal government that has to foot the entire bill. To leave them out entirely may make it virtually impossible to provide for comparable public services at comparable rates of taxation for everyone.

Newfoundland[111] had become the epicentre of intergovernmental conflict about resource revenue and equalization at about the same time that exploding

106 Errol Black and Jim Silver, *Equalization: Financing Canadians' Commitment to Sharing and Social Solidarity* (Winnipeg: Canadian Centre for Policy Alternatives, 2004).

107 Ibid., 21.

108 Ralph Matthews, *The Creation of Regional Dependency* (Toronto: University of Toronto Press, 1983), 59.

109 David G. Alexander, *Atlantic Canada and Confederation: Essays in Canadian Political Economy* (Toronto: University of Toronto Press, 1983), 46.

110 See Janice MacKinnon, "Equalization: Its Problems and the 2007 Federal Budget," in *Transitions: Fiscal and Political Federalism in an Era of Change*, eds. John R. Allan, Thomas J. Courchene, and Christina Leuprecht (Kingston: Institute of Intergovernmental Relations, 2009); Béland et al., *Fiscal Federalism*, 40–8.

111 Newfoundland officially became Newfoundland and Labrador only in 2001.

oil prices during the first OPEC crisis made the inclusion of resource revenue in the equalization formula problematic. The offshore discovery of the Hibernia oil field in 1979 led to a dispute first over whose oil it was, and then, after the province had been granted access to oil revenue, over how this revenue should be counted against the massive equalization payments Canada's poorest province was receiving ever since entry into Confederation in 1949. As already discussed, the inclusion of even 50 per cent of the province's oil revenue in its fiscal capacity calculation might wipe out qualification for equalization payments and, since these revenues were by no means similar to those in oil-rich Alberta, leave the provincial finances in the same dire situation as before. However, Newfoundland, together with Nova Scotia, eventually managed to have all its resource revenue exempted from equalization clawbacks. These so-called "side deals" added fuel to the fire of general discontent over the imagined or real unfairness of equalization.

First came the constitutional dispute over whose oil it was.[112] The federal government of Liberal Prime Minister Pierre Trudeau argued that offshore resources did not fall under the provincial ownership clause of Section 92, and he could point to a 1967 Supreme Court ruling to that effect in the case of British Columbia. Newfoundland's Conservative government led by Premier Brian Peckford countered that the province had owned offshore resources under international law prior to entering Confederation in 1949, and that this ownership had not been transferred to the federal government. In 1984, the Supreme Court ruled in the federal government's favour.

Before winning the 1984 federal election, however, the leader of the Conservative opposition, Brian Mulroney, had promised Peckford that, if elected, the federal government would share resource management with the province and let it collect taxes and royalties as if it owned the oil. The outcome then was the 1985 Canada–Newfoundland Atlantic Accord.[113]

A key component of the accord was that the improvement of the province's fiscal capacity by means of oil revenue would be offset by reductions in equalization transfers only in part. The province, in other words, would get a chance to get out of its "have-not" status by a form of temporary double-dipping. For the first five years, the province would keep 90 per cent of the amount of equalization otherwise counted against oil revenue. During subsequent years that percentage would be reduced by 10 per cent annually. The problem was that

---

112 See Jenny Higgins, "The 1985 Canada–Newfoundland Atlantic Accord," Newfoundland and Labrador Heritage Site, 2012.

113 A similar accord was struck a year later with Nova Scotia.

this arrangement did not really benefit Newfoundland all that much because oil revenues grew slowly at the beginning, and when they became more significant, so did the equalization deductions.

Push came to shove in 2004. Danny Williams, Conservative premier of Newfoundland and Labrador since the previous year, sought to negotiate a new accord granting the province 100 per cent exemption from equalization deductions. When the Liberal government of Paul Martin introduced the fixed pool equalization scheme that included natural resource revenue, Williams resorted to the first of the aforementioned publicity stunts of having the Canadian flags in the province lowered. Martin, in a fragile minority government situation and worried about Liberal ridings in Newfoundland, signed a new accord, both with Newfoundland and with Nova Scotia, that included 100 per cent protection from equalization clawbacks.[114] This considerably soured the federal government's relationship with other resource-rich provinces. As Janice MacKinnon, a former finance minister of Saskatchewan, pointed out, the Atlantic accords were "side deals" that undermined any sense of fairness among provinces. While Newfoundland and Nova Scotia received equalization in full regardless of resource revenue, the clawback for Saskatchewan at times exceeded 100 per cent.[115]

Conflict over how to deal with the asymmetrical allocation of lucrative natural resources such as oil and gas in a federation committed to the equalization of fiscal capacities is not confined to the federal government's side deals with Newfoundland and Nova Scotia. It is also indirectly embedded in one of the perennial irritants about fiscal equalization: the fact that Quebec routinely receives more than half of all funds.[116] A myth persists, particularly in Canada's west, according to which the equalization formula helps to subsidize a regime of lower taxes and costlier social services in Quebec. In quantitative terms, the reality is more prosaic: Quebec has the largest population of all equalization-receiving provinces, discounting of course Ontario's brief appearance in this category. On a per capita basis, Quebec ranks fifth out of six recipient provinces.[117] Moreover, however, Quebecers persistently pay the highest taxes in Canada overall. The fact that under a more progressive tax regime low-income Quebecers and those with

114 Béland et al., *Fiscal Federalism*, 37.

115 MacKinnon, "Equalization," 76.

116 Béland et al., *Fiscal Federalism*, 67.

117 Boucher and Maclure, "The Equalization Program."

children pay less taxes than elsewhere[118] may contribute to myth building in more conservative parts of the federation.

MacKinnon begs to differ by pointing out that the Quebec government did resort to tax cuts when the revised 2007 equalization formula provided it with a windfall of additional funds. And she echoes western resentment by suggesting that Quebec's perpetual "have-not" status may have something to do with a political unwillingness to take on "problems with its economic structures and social programming."[119] Here is where resources come into the picture again. The complaint is that Quebec wants to spend lavishly on social programs while at the same time neglecting to develop its own resource industries. As Todd McKay, Prairie director of the Canadian Taxpayers Federation, alleges more generally, provinces "with significant non-renewable resources … pay for equalization and provinces that haven't developed non-renewable resources collect from equalization."[120] The complaint is misguided in part because, as we just saw, Quebecers pay dearly for their social programs.

Another complaint, however, with regard to renewable resources has some validity. The equalization formula does not adequately take into account provincially owned hydro companies, such as Hydro-Québec, which sells electricity to Quebecers far below market prices. Higher prices would increase the province's fiscal capacity and thus reduce its equalization payments.[121]

Rather off the mark, however, are the most recent complaints about the unfairness of equalization that have come from the current conservative premier of Alberta, Jason Kenney. The context for these complaints is Alberta's ailing economy. Oil prices have collapsed to the point that new projects of oil sands exploration may no longer be profitable for the mostly foreign oil companies from which Alberta collects its royalties. In addition, the landlocked province desperately seeks to expand pipeline capacities to get the oil it does produce to ports from which it can be shipped to international markets. Several provinces, including Quebec, are opposed to pipeline expansion across their territory for environmental reasons (see Chapter 6).

118 *Montreal Gazette*, "Quebec Remained the Most-Taxed Province in 2017, Report Shows," January 11, 2019.

119 MacKinnon, "Equalization," 85–6.

120 Todd McKay, "Are You a Province that Doesn't Want to Develop Its Resources? Equalization Has a Nice, Juicy Payout Just for You," *Financial Post*, January 12, 2017.

121 Béland et al., *Fiscal Federalism*, 42–3.

In what amounts in particular to a case of "Quebec envy,"[122] Kenney alleges that Alberta, which currently has a serious budget deficit, nevertheless pays for Quebec's lavish equalization at a time when Quebec enjoys a budget surplus. This is so, he alleges, echoing a common western grievance (see above), because the formula unfairly penalizes Alberta for its resource wealth, much of which it redistributes to other provinces even when these choose not to develop their own resources. Kenney moreover asserts that since Alberta contributes so much to equalization, Quebec as the main beneficiary of equalization should not be allowed to oppose pipelines. And he finally threatens to hold a provincial referendum for a mandate to initiate a constitutional amendment that would abolish equalization altogether.[123]

Few if any of these allegations and assertions hold up to fact. Nor is there any way, if that is what the accusation of unfairness implies, to come up with an equalization formula that would make Alberta a beneficiary.

First of all, it is of course the federal government that makes equalization payments entirely out of its own revenue, and it collects this revenue from all provinces according to income and wealth. Equalization therefore does have an intended redistributive effect in the name of social solidarity. In the case of Alberta, despite the current economic downturn and considerable unemployment, per capita income and wealth have remained the highest in the country. Even if resources were taken entirely out of the equation, the province would not see a penny of equalization.

Second, Alberta's deficit is mainly owed to the fact that it has the lowest level of taxation in the country. Equalization, however, as we saw earlier, is calculated by a province's ability to raise revenue based on average taxation rates across the country, not by how much revenue it chooses to raise. Alberta's deficit, therefore, does not bring it one inch closer to any equalization entitlement.

And third, if the commitment to equalization was indeed removed from the constitution (a remote possibility at best since a constitutional amendment to this effect would require approval of seven provinces representing at least 50 per cent of the Canadian population; see Chapter 7), Albertans would still pay exactly the same amount of taxes into federal coffers as before. The threat to hold a referendum on equalization therefore is nothing more than a publicity

122 See Daniel Béland and Melanee Thomas, "Jason Kenney's Case of Quebec Envy," *Policy Options*, November 2019.

123 See Kieran Leavitt, "Alberta's Equalization Referendum 'Political Science Fiction,' Experts Say," *Star Edmonton*, August 20, 2019.

stunt meant to increase pressure on other governments not to stand in the way of pipeline expansion.

Together with the CHT and the CST, equalization is one of the federal government's three major transfer programs. Equalization currently amounts to about one-quarter of federal expenditure for these three programs. All three have a significant redistributive effect on provincial finances. Yet while the CHT and CST are calculated on a per capita basis, equalization not only follows a more complicated rationale, but is also more open to criticism.

Overall, there can be no doubt that the organization of fiscal relations in the Canadian federation reflects a serious commitment to social solidarity across provincial boundaries. It also appears that the legitimacy of the federal government's role in this organization of fiscal relations is no longer contested, even when this role significantly touches on matters under provincial jurisdiction. What remains contested is the degree to which the doubtlessly existing vertical fiscal imbalance may empower federal governments to use their superior spending power at their own discretion and for their own political purposes.

Before we give some concluding thoughts to this perennial source of conflict in Canadian fiscal relations, however, we must at least briefly acknowledge that a similar level of social solidarity and fiscal circumspection is sorely lacking when it comes to Canada's Indigenous peoples, who have been treated as second-class citizens under the Indian Act. The finding of Canada's auditor general in 2018, according to which the federal government's inability to provide comparable social equality for Indigenous peoples in the country amounts to an "incomprehensible failure,"[124] certainly puts more than just a damper on any assessment celebrating Canada as a success story of social solidarity.

Under the Indian Act

Indigenous peoples today comprise some 1.4 million individuals making up about 3 per cent of the Canadian population. Of these, roughly half are recognized as members of Canada's First Nations, although only a little more than half of these actually live on the reserves assigned to them.[125] The financial

124 Cited in Lucy Scholey, "'Incomprehensible Failure:' Auditor General Says Federal Government Not Improving Life for Indigenous People," *APTN News*, May 29, 2018.

125 Emmanuel Brunet-Jailly, "The Governance and Fiscal Environment of First Nations' Fiscal Intergovernmental Relations in Comparative Perspectives" (Victoria: National Centre for First Nations Governance, 2008), 7.

predicament these more than 600 bands of First Nations find themselves in can be best understood by a comparison with municipalities: Both are dependent political entities.

While Section 92(8) of the BNA Act assigned to the provinces the exclusive right over "municipal Institutions in the province," Section 92(24) listed "Indians, and Lands reserved for the Indians" among the exclusive federal responsibilities (subsection 25). As the saying goes, municipalities became "creatures of the provinces" and Indians became "wards of the Crown."[126] Yet while municipalities can rely on some 80 per cent own-source financing, mostly from property taxes and user fees such as for municipal water services,[127] First Nation governments for the most part continue to depend on federal government handouts that come annually and with strict conditions about their use. It was meant that way.

The Indian Act of 1876 first spelled out what the responsibility for "Indians, and Lands reserved for the Indians" would mean, and its basic principles are still in force:[128]

- To be an "Indian" under the act means to be registered or to be entitled to be registered as a status Indian (2(1)).
- "Indian moneys" are all "moneys collected, received or held" by the Crown (2(1)).
- Reserves are "held" by the Crown, and the government "determines" its use (18(1)).
- "No Indian is lawfully in possession of land in a reserve" unless the band council makes such an allotment with the "approval of the Minister" (20(1)).
- The government determines how "Indian moneys shall be expended" (61(1)).
- The government regulates all socioeconomic activities on reserves, including medical treatment, housing, and sanitary conditions (73(1, a–m)).

126 See critically Warren Magnusson, "Are Municipalities Creatures of the Provinces?" *Journal of Canadian Studies* 39, no. 2 (2005).

127 Andrew Sancton, *Canadian Local Government: An Urban Perspective* (Toronto: Oxford University Press, 2011); Harry Kitchen, "Canadian Municipalities: Fiscal Trends and Sustainability," *Canadian Tax Journal* 50, no. 1 (2002): 161.

128 The Indian Act in its current form is available at http://laws-lois.justice.gc.ca/eng/acts/i-5.

One of the main purposes of these stipulations was to minimize the number of status Indians for which the federal government would be responsible, and thus to minimize the financial burden on the federal purse.[129] Still in 2019, the federal government carefully pointed out that the Supreme Court's 2016 *Daniels* decision[130] extending the federal government's law-making responsibilities under Section 91(24) of the Constitution Act, 1867, to Métis and non-status Indians does not change "who is an 'Indian' in the Indian Act."[131]

In its original version, the Indian Act also contained provisions about "enfranchisement."[132] These provisions essentially circumscribed various conditions under which Indians could become Canadian citizens, which by the same token meant that they would lose any protection and benefits accorded to them under the Indian Act. As David Laird, the minister in charge of Indian affairs at the time, put it rather bluntly when he introduced the act in the House of Commons: Indians would be given a stark choice, "either be treated as minors or as white men."[133]

Canadians like to grumble that "Indians do not pay taxes." And indeed, under Section 87 of the Indian Act, property and employment income of status Indians is exempted from taxation, as is employment income, but only if and when property or income are "situated on a reserve." Likewise, business income is tax exempt only if it is derived from on-reserve activities. There is also a rather bewildering array of regulations regarding exemption from goods and services and harmonized sales taxes, one of which being that goods bought off-reserve are only exempt so long as they are "delivered to a reserve by the vendor or the vendor's agent."[134]

Under these regulations, tax exemption is essentially tied to reserve-related activities and transactions. Yet reserve life generally provides few opportunities

129 See Michael J. Prince and Frances Abele, "Funding an Aboriginal Order of Government in Canada: Recent Developments in Self-Government and Fiscal Relation," in *Toward a New Mission Statement for Canadian Fiscal Federalism*, ed. Harvey Lazar (Montreal: McGill-Queen's University Press, 2000).

130 *Daniels v. Canada (Indian Affairs and Northern Development)*, 2016 SCC 12.

131 Government of Canada, "Information on the Tax Exemption Under Section 87 of the Indian Act," 2019.

132 Government of Canada, The Indian Act, RSC 1985, c. I-5.

133 Cited in John Leslie and Ron Maguire, eds., *The Historical Development of the Indian Act* (Ottawa: Indian and Northern Affairs, 1978), 60.

134 Government of Canada, "Information on the Tax Exemption."

for taxable economic activities. It was meant that way. The Indian Act deliberately prevented status Indians from participating in the socioeconomic benefits that Confederation was meant to bestow on all other Canadians.[135] Instead, following the pattern of earlier treaty agreements (which were essentially treaties of massive land cessation in return for vague promises of welfare), First Nations financing for the most part consists of federal government transfers that are "highly discretionary and specific to particular uses, such as schools, health care, housing, and welfare." And even when, as is increasingly the case, First Nations "assume some administrative responsibility for delivering the programs," they nevertheless "remain accountable to the federal government for how the funds are spent."[136]

According to the 2007 calculations of the Assembly of First Nations, this kind of funding is outright discriminatory: "The average per capita expenditure of all Canadian governments on non-indigenous Canadians stands at about $15,000/$16,000, while it is only about $9,000 for Aboriginal Peoples." Not only does a 2 per cent cap on annual funding increases imposed in 1996 remain below both the inflation rate and Indigenous population growth, it also compares unfavourably with the annual 6.6 per cent increases in CHT and CST transfers to the provinces.[137]

Even if some of the numbers may be disputed with regard to all Indigenous peoples,[138] the overall picture for reserves is not in question. According to a 2011 report of the auditor general of Canada, it is "not always evident whether the federal government is committed to providing services on reserves of the same range and quality as those provided to other communities across Canada."[139] In the words of Harold Calla, chair of the First Nations Financial Management Board established in 2006, there is no "linking of funding levels to national standards for services such as in the equalization program for provinces."[140]

Why isn't there? Two explanations come to mind. One is path dependency. Once the Indian Act was put in place, it became increasingly difficult over time to

135 For more recent developments, see Prince and Abele, "Funding an Aboriginal Order."

136 Boadway, "Canada," 115.

137 Brunet-Jailly, "The Governance and Fiscal Environment of First Nations," 7.

138 See Mark Milke, "Facts about Aboriginal Funding in Canada" (Calgary: Fraser Institute, 2016).

139 Office of the Auditor General of Canada, "2011 June Status Report of the Auditor General of Canada," 2011, Chapter 4.

140 Cited in David Schwartz, "How Does Native Funding Work?" *CBC News*, February 8, 2013.

look for what obviously would have to be a radical alternative. Even Indigenous peoples themselves have appeared reluctant at times to do away with an act that, while clearly relegating them to second-class-citizen status nevertheless seemed better than nothing at all. The other explanation even more depressingly brings us back to the two functions of the capitalist state: accumulation and legitimation. In the nineteenth century, Indian policy was part of the federal government's accumulation strategy, clearing the land of Indians standing in the way of economic development. In the second half of the twentieth century, then, when the Canadian federal state took over important parts of the legitimation function, there was no political reward for including Indigenous peoples.

The recognition of "existing aboriginal and treaty rights" in Section 35(1) of the Constitution Act of 1982 has made systemic financial neglect of Indigenous peoples more difficult. The 10-year $5.1 billion funding pledge of the 2005 Kelowna Accord, for instance, negotiated with provincial and territorial premiers as well as the leaders of various Indigenous organizations by then Liberal Prime Minister Paul Martin, was meant to close the financial gap. It was not implemented by the Conservative government of Stephen Harper that took over from Paul Martin only four days after the accord was struck. A so-called First Nations Governance Initiative by the federal government around the same period failed as well.[141] As Canada's provinces would readily attest, good governance is not to be had without stable and sufficient funding.

In 2016, Justin Trudeau's newest Liberal government announced that it would commit to Indigenous funding that was "more significant" than what was on offer under the Kelowna Accord.[142] Honest efforts at improving Indigenous living conditions in recent years cannot be disputed. Yet, as evidenced by the auditor general's verdict of "incomprehensible failure still as of 2018,"[143] the general impression over time must be that these efforts deserve to be characterized more as the government dragging its feet than as swift and decisive action.

The constitutional recognition of Indigenous rights in particular has not ended jurisdictional squabbles over which order of government has to pay for the social well-being of Indigenous peoples. A most disheartening demonstration of Canadian federalism's inability to adequately accommodate the needs of

141 Kathy L. Brock, "Striving for Fairness: First Nations, Current Reforms and Provincial Intereests," in *Canadian Fiscal Relations: What Works, What Might Work Better*, ed. Harvey Lazar (Montreal: McGill-Queen's University Press, 2005).

142 Martin Papillon, "Why We Need a New Kelowna Accord," *Ottawa Citizen*, April 4, 2016.

143 Scholey, "Incomprehensible Failure."

Indigenous peoples in its regime of divided responsibility and governance was the death of Jordan River Anderson, a 5-year-old Cree boy in 2005. Jordan died 800 kilometres away from his family in a Winnipeg hospital because the government of Manitoba and the federal government, for a period of two years until his death, argued over who should pay for home care. The Manitoba government argued that Health Canada was responsible under its general responsibility for Indians in Section 91(24) of the Constitution Act, 1867. The federal government argued, with reference to Section 92(7), which assigns exclusive powers over hospitals to the provinces, that the provincial healthcare system should pay.[144]

To be caught between a rock and hard place in the Canadian federal system is an all-too-common experience for Indigenous peoples. A perhaps less egregious yet nevertheless indicative case is that of the Manitoba Métis Federation's Health and Social Directorate.[145] As soon as the Supreme Court's 2016 *Daniels* decision came down, obliging the federal government to include Métis and non-status Indians as "Indians" under Section 91(24) of the Constitution Act, 1867, the Manitoba government ended funding for this nationally renowned institution for Métis health research. Instead of acknowledging right away that it now had a constitutional obligation to replace this funding, the Liberal Trudeau government increased general funding for the Métis Nation in the name of reconciliation.[146]

Fiscal Imbalance and the Spending Power

As we have seen so far in this chapter, public finance in a federal system like Canada's almost inevitably comes down to a numbers game, and what is considered "fair" more often than not is in the eye of the beholder. Ideally, of course, each order of government should have revenue proportional to the costs for the programs and services under its constitutional responsibility. In practice, that is next to impossible in a complex political economy with rapidly shifting variables such as commodity prices and the business cycle more generally.

Therefore, as in all federal systems, there will be a twofold fiscal imbalance: horizontally among the provinces because of differences in resource endowment,

144 See Maya Gunnarson, "Jurisdictional Disputes and Indigenous Health: The Emergence of Jordan's Principle," *McGill Journal of Law and Health*, November 2018.

145 See Josée G. Lavoie, "Medicare and the Care of First Nations, Métis and Inuit," *Health Economics, Policy and Law* 13 (2018): 293.

146 Manitoba Métis Federation, "Budget Continues Trudeau's Commitment to Reconciliation with the Métis Nation," news release, March 2019.

infrastructural capacity, market performance, and how these factors impact their own fiscal capacity as well as federal transfer calculations; and vertically between the two orders of government, not only because federal governments naturally will want to limit the drain on their own finances with regard to the transfers they commit to, but also because it is impossible to determine the exact amount of justifiable transfer revenue needed by each province at any given moment.

Only by ignoring Indigenous financial relations with the rest of Canada can it be said that "the Canadian federal system represents the textbook best-practice system of fiscal federalism."[147] With regard to the rest of Canada, however, equalization and social transfers result in the delivery of comparable public services at comparable levels of taxation to all citizens. The level of conditionality is the lowest among established federations.[148] The provinces, in other words, are largely autonomous in making important decisions about the delivery of public services under their jurisdiction. Moreover, at least by comparison, the overall dependency of provincial governments on transfer payments is modest. Canadian provinces have access to all major sources of taxation, and they collect more than half of all revenue, which is a rarity among federations.

By no means, however, does this mean that all is well in Canadian fiscal relations. The distribution and sharing of revenue in a federal system under conditions of rapidly changing socioeconomic and political conditions is always a contentious matter, but three issues stand out in particular.

The first one is federal unilateralism. Even though decisions about transfers are typically accompanied by intergovernmental negotiations preceding the beginning of a new five-year fiscal period, the federal government ultimately has the power to act alone. This is particularly so in the case of equalization, which is in principle entirely in the federal government's purview even though in practice provincial leaders will try to exert political pressure to achieve more favourable outcomes in design and calculation of the formula.[149] Shared-cost programs on the other hand, including the major social transfers, are in principle based on intergovernmental agreement because these programs fall under provincial jurisdiction. The provincial outrage over the drastic cuts to social transfers in the 1995 federal budget of then Finance Minister Paul Martin was as much over the fiscal hole they created for the provinces as over the unilateralism with which they

147 Boadway, "Canada," 99.

148 Watts, *The Spending Power in Federal Systems*, 56–7.

149 See Daniel Béland and André Lecours, "Equalization at Arm's Length," Mowat Centre, University of Toronto, March 2012, 12.

were administered. And even though Prime Minister Paul Martin's 2004 budget restored some confidence in the predictability of federal fiscal behaviour in accordance with SUFA guidelines, the issue did not go away. As the most recent 2017 round of healthcare agreements demonstrate, the federal government can resort to a take-it-or-leave-it approach that falls only a little short of unilateralism.

The second issue, systemic fiscal imbalance, also became a matter of heated intergovernmental dispute after the 1995 cuts. The government of Quebec in particular established a Commission on Fiscal Imbalance, the Séguin Commission, which in 2002 duly reported the obvious: The Canadian federal system throughout its history had been characterized by "a situation in which, in light of effective occupation of tax fields, Québec and the other provinces have insufficient revenues to exercise their fields of jurisdiction while, to the contrary, the federal government has revenues in excess of what is necessary to fund its fields of jurisdiction."[150] The 1995 cuts constituted a particularly egregious incidence of federal fiscal misconduct. Paul Martin obviously thought he could appease the provinces by returning the federal government's funding commitments to pre-1995 levels in his government's 2004 budget. Not good enough, argued Alain Noël, who had been one of the Séguin commissioners: Federal funding levels remained out of synch with the increase in the provinces' social spending expenditures.[151]

The third and final issue is the federal spending power. As in all federal systems, the federal government has at its disposal more revenue than is necessary for the programs under its own jurisdiction, and it will use this surplus spending power to pursue national policy objectives even in areas of exclusive provincial jurisdiction. Especially from a strongly autonomist Quebec perspective, this is the most contentious issue in Canadian federalism. It has never been settled by the courts,[152] although the opinion prevails, at least in English Canada, that federal spending in areas of exclusive jurisdiction is constitutional as long as it does not amount to regulatory intrusion into that jurisdiction.[153] The federal

150 Government of Québec, "Fiscal Imbalance in Canada: Historical Background," Commission on Fiscal Imbalance, Supporting Document 1 (2002).

151 Noël, "Balance and Imbalance," 289.

152 See Andrée Lajoie, "The Federal Spending Power and Fiscal Imbalance in Canada," in *Dilemmas of Solidarity: Rethinking Redistribution in the Canadian Federation*, eds. Sujit Choudhry, Jean-François Gaudreault-DesBiens, and Lorne Sossin (Toronto: University of Toronto Press, 2006), 154–9.

153 Katherine Swinton, "Federalism, the Charter, and the Courts; Rethinking Constitutional Dialogue in Canada," in *Rethinking Federalism: Citizens, Markets, and Governments in a Changing World*, eds. Karen Knop et al. (Vancouver: University of British Columbia Press, 1995), 297–8.

government thus makes program payments to provincial governments, such as the social transfers; to individuals, such as family allowances; or to institutions, such as research grants.

Unilateralism, fiscal imbalance, and the spending power are linked since fiscal imbalance is what supplies the federal government with the means to spend in areas outside its own programs to begin with. The recipients of federal money can refuse to accept it, particularly if it comes with conditions about its use attached. But being deprived of sufficient fiscal means themselves, provincial governments can rarely afford to say no to shared-cost programs, unless, that is, they can opt out of them with compensation, a possibility routinely used by Quebec since the 1960s. And even then, at least as seen through the lens of Quebec nationalism, the province will be deprived of receiving full political credit for program delivery in what are supposed to be their own policy fields because they will have to compete with perceived or real federal leadership in those same fields.

Does this mean that rather than being a "textbook best-practice system" Canada's fiscal federalism is so deeply flawed that it should be radically changed by eliminating fiscal imbalance? That would require a recalibration of tax powers aimed at the abolishment of shared-cost programs altogether along with other federal spending power intrusions into provincial jurisdiction, as Quebec governments have demanded again and again.[154] Two arguments suggest otherwise.

The first argument is about dual citizenship in a federal system. When the BNA Act was drafted in the nineteenth century, social policy was assigned to the provinces because it was not expected to ever become an important part of politics – hence the limited assignment of tax powers that came with it. This changed dramatically only after the impact of the Great Depression in the twentieth century. Of course, one might argue that tax powers should have been adjusted when social policy became the largest part of provincial expenditure. The problem is, however, that something else changed as well.

As the Rowell-Sirois Commission had put it in 1940, social policy had changed from providing "poor relief" to finding answers to "cyclical mass

154 See Government of Québec, "Québec's Historical Position on the Federal Spending Power 1944–1998," Secrétariat aux Affaires intergouvernementales canadiennes, Direction des politiques institutionnelles et constitutionnelles, Ministère du Conseil exécutif (July 1998).

unemployment."[155] Social policy, in other words, had become part of macroeconomic management and thus had taken on a significant national dimension. The rise of the welfare state that began with the 1940 constitutional amendment assigning unemployment insurance to the list of exclusive federal powers also created a dualized form of social citizenship,[156] provincial as well as national. And with it, like it or not, social policy came to be recognized by governments as well as societies as a joint responsibility.

The second argument is about the federal government's responsibility for redistributive social solidarity. Without some financial means in excess of its own program requirements, the only option to bring about such solidarity would be voluntary interprovincial equalization of some sort, which is an unlikely option since provincial governments have nothing to gain by redistributing scarce financial resources to citizens outside their own electoral orbit. It is instead the federal government that gains legitimacy by providing equitable socioeconomic conditions for a national citizenship to which it is accountable. The question then boils down to the amount of fiscal imbalance that would be considered acceptable. A reasonable answer would be that it must be large enough to be effective but contained enough not to undermine provincial fiscal capacities. Ultimately, this balance of "solidarity and autonomy"[157] can only be determined through intergovernmental dialogue.

In the Canadian federal system, such dialogue is embedded in almost permanently ongoing processes of intergovernmental relations. And since these processes and interactions almost routinely revolve around, or at least significantly include, finances, intergovernmental relations have been described in this chapter as mostly fiscal relations. A particular problem in Canada is that in comparison to other federations, these relations developed and have remained "outside any formal legal, or even written, framework."[158] The SUFA is a case in point. Its

155 Donald V. Smiley, ed., *The Rowell-Sirois Report, Book I* (Toronto: Macmillan, 1978), 175.

156 See Jean-François Gaudreault-DesBiens, "The Irreducible Federal Necessity of Jurisdictional Autonomy, and the Irreducibility of Federalism to Jurisdictional Autonomy," in Choudhry, Gaudreault-DesBiens, and Sossin, *Dilemmas of Solidarity*, 194–9.

157 Alain Noël, "Social Justice in Overlapping Sharing Communities," in Choudhry, Gaudreault-DesBiens, and Sossin, *Dilemmas of Solidarity*, 66.

158 Johanne Poirier and Cheryl Saunders, "Conclusion: Comparative Experiences of Intergovernmental Relations in Federal Systems," in *Intergovernmental Relations in Federal Systems*, eds. Johanne Poirier, Cheryl Saunders, and John Kincaid (Toronto: Oxford University Press, 2015), 463.

well-intended framework for cooperation, transparency, and conflict resolution is based on voluntary action and therefore has remained ineffective. We shall return to the problems associated with this mostly informal nature of Canadian intergovernmental relations or, as it is sometimes called in Canada, interstate federalism, in Chapter 8.

CHAPTER SIX

DIFFERENCE, DEPENDENCY, AND DISPLACEMENT

Obviously not everything driving Canadian federalism revolves around finances. At about the same time that Canada's major cost-sharing programs were being established, social and political changes known as the Quiet Revolution swept through the province of Quebec. Demands for more fiscal autonomy did come with these changes, but the Quiet Revolution was about much more than finances – it was a nationalist awakening that ultimately threatened separation unless Quebec's distinct status in Confederation was recognized. Also at about the same time, the search for a domestic constitutional amendment formula reopened a divisive debate about liberty and community: whether, as Canada's Liberal prime minister through much of the time, Pierre Trudeau, believed, a modern Canada was to be a liberal country of equal citizens regardless of where they lived or what language they spoke, or, in the words of Trudeau's Conservative opponent, Joe Clark, whether the true character of Canada was that of a community of communities with distinct collective identities.

This debate over regional and cultural difference was by no means confined to Quebec, and it came to a head when Canada's first ministers finally sat down to negotiate a constitutional settlement that would not only "patriate" the constitution by adding a domestic amendment formula but would also include a charter of individual rights and freedoms. Before turning to the tumultuous events surrounding patriation in 1982 in Chapter 7, we first have to identify in this chapter the deep-seated cultural and socioeconomic differences that have accompanied and shaped the dynamic of Canadian federalism more generally.

For obvious reasons, the account of these differences, the conflicts they created, and the compromises resulting from them begins with Quebec nationalism as it emerged powerfully in the wake of the Quiet Revolution during the 1960s, eventually pushing Canada precariously close to a breakup in 1995. Conflicts and compromise over difference, however, have by no means been confined to the question of Quebec's distinct status in Confederation. What was later called western alienation had its beginning in the very conditions under which the Prairie provinces were created and became part of Confederation. Also, from the very beginning Confederation contained the seeds of eastern dependencies on central handouts under an inward-looking National Policy, with the result that the Maritime provinces lost their traditional role as the hub of overseas trade. And finally, at least prior to the constitutional recognition of their inherent and treaty rights in 1982, the main role assigned to Canada's Indigenous peoples was to get out of the way.

Quebec Nationalism

The history of Quebec nationalism begins with the defeat of Nouvelle France by the English on the Plains of Abraham on September 13, 1759. Not much changed in the lives of ordinary French Canadians since the Quebec Act of 1774 granted religious freedom to the Roman Catholic majority, sanctioned the seigneurial system of landownership, and permitted the continued use of French civil law. The situation changed dramatically when some 50,000 English-speaking Loyalists streamed into the colony after the end of the American War of Independence in 1783 and began to complain about what they saw as French privileges under the Quebec Act. The result was the Constitution Act of 1791, which first divided the colony into two separate provinces, Upper Canada (Ontario) and Lower Canada (Quebec).

The two newly created provinces were given elected assemblies with very limited legislative powers. Real power remained in the hands of a provincial governor appointed by the Crown. That governor in turn appointed executive and legislative councils accountable to him. In both Upper and Lower Canada this state of affairs led to increasingly louder demands for responsible government – that is, accountability of councils and the governor to the assembly – and eventually resulted in the Rebellions of 1837–8. In Lower Canada, the calls for responsible government had nationalist overtones. While the mostly French Canadian Parti Patriote led by Louis-Joseph Papineau dominated the legislative assembly, the unaccountable councils represented and supported the interests of Anglophone merchants.

Because of the Rebellions, Lord Durham was dispatched to British North America as governor general with a mandate to report on governance problems in the unruly provinces. Durham arrived in Quebec in May 1838 but resigned only five months later in November when he saw his authority undermined by political opponents on the home front. Back in England, he finished what came to be known as the Durham Report a couple of months later at the end of January 1839.[1] As we shall see, the brevity of time devoted to a highly complex political problem resulted in a catastrophic misjudgment of the situation, led to obvious as well as misguided recommendations, and crucially prepared the grounds for the inevitability of a future federation in which Quebec would figure as an always uncomfortable and often isolated partner.

The obvious recommendation was responsible government. After all, had not America been lost only a short while ago when demands of "no taxation without representation" remained unheard? The misguided recommendation was to put the two Canadas back together in one legislative union. It was misguided because of Durham's catastrophic misjudgment of French Canadian resilience. Durham thought that "it is obvious that the process of assimilation to English habits is already commencing"[2] and therefore assumed that assimilation could be completed easily "by a popular government, in which an English majority shall permanently predominate."[3]

As recommended, the 1840 Act of Union conjoined the two provinces, now called Canada West and Canada East, in one legislative union with one government. The Act of Union did its part to ensure "the political superiority of the Anglophone population"[4] by stipulating that the two parts of the new union would be "represented by an equal Number of Representatives"[5] even though at the time Canada West had a much smaller population than (overwhelmingly but not exclusively Francophone) Canada East. Adding insult to injury, the act also

1 Gerald M. Craig, ed., *Lord Durham's Report* (1839; repr., Toronto: McClelland and Stewart 1963), iii–iv.

2 Ibid., 151.

3 Ibid., 157.

4 John Dickinson and Brian Young, *A Short History of Quebec* (Montreal: McGill-Queen's University Press, 2008), 183.

5 "The Union Act: An Act to Reunite the Provinces of Upper and Lower Canada, and for the Government of Canada," 3 & 4 Vict., c. 35 (U.K.), July 23, 1840.

ordained that all public business henceforth would be conducted "in the English Language only."[6]

Responsible government would have to wait another eight years, and when it finally came it ironically contributed to undermining the intended scheme of French Canadian subordination. Governance now required majority approval in the legislature, which was not to be had without French Canadian support. Sustaining majority support effectively required co-governance by a double ministry representing the two Canadas. Thus, continuing a practice already established since inception of the union, the first responsible government of the United Province of Canada in 1848 was the double ministry of liberal reformers Louis-Hippolyte LaFontaine (premier, Canada East) and Robert Baldwin (co-premier, Canada West), and the last one prior to Confederation would be that of the conservatives John A. Macdonald (Canada West) and George-Étienne Cartier (Canada East). Instead of diminishing the duality of English and French Canada, then, political practice confirmed and even deepened it.

Ironically as well, the imposition of equal representation for both parts of the union further strengthened rather than undermined the continued political presence of French Canada. By the 1850s, the population of Canada West had well surpassed that of Canada East. This meant that it was now French Canadians who were overrepresented in the legislature, which in turn caused frustration on the English Canadian side because French Canadians could "block any legislation" contrary to their interests.[7] This was one of the main reasons why the reformer George Brown would in the end join the conservative coalition of Macdonald and Cartier, thus bringing about Confederation (see Chapter 2).

Providing reasonable assurances of cultural survival by means of the property and civil rights clause in Section 92(13) of the British North America (BNA) Act, Confederation seemed an acceptable compromise to what was now the province of Quebec.[8] Moreover, the provincial rights movement spearheaded by Ontario and the mostly province-friendly rulings by the Judicial Committee of the Privy Council (JCPC) in London (see Chapter 3), appeared putting to rest Parti Rouge leader Antoine-Aimé Dorion's fears that Macdonald's centralist inclinations would triumph over provincial autonomy in the end.[9]

6 Ibid., Section XLI.

7 Kenneth McRoberts, *Quebec: Social Change and Political Crisis* (Toronto: McClelland and Stewart, 1988), 52.

8 See more critically Garth Stevenson, *Unfulfilled Union* (Montreal: McGill-Queen's University Press, 2009), 36–7.

9 See Janet Ajzenstat et al., eds., *Canada's Founding Debates* (Toronto: Stoddart, 1999), 311.

For the remainder of the nineteenth century, nationalist sentiments were mainly stirred up by events outside the province, such as the 1869–70 Red River and 1885 North-West Rebellions of the French-speaking Métis people against their land displacement by government and railway interests, as well as the legislative attacks on French-Catholic schools in New Brunswick (1871) and Manitoba (1890). Although more directed against virulently anti-Catholic condemnation of the Rebellions in Ontario than concerned with the plight of French-speaking minorities in the remote Canadian west,[10] a growing conviction fermented among Quebecers that their province was the only safe place for French language, culture, and Catholic religion, and that it therefore had to be defended at all costs. As one commentator put it emphatically as well as prophetically after the execution of Métis leader Louis Riel in 1885:

> The province of Quebec is ours; it is our property, and let's tell the English we intend to keep it. No concessions: absolute power in our own house, French governments throughout. No more English mayors in Montreal, and let's have the French flag on the city hall. No more English MPs where our nationality is in the majority ... Reading in French of the minutes of municipal councils and the legislative assembly ...[11]

Two fatefully interrelated events early in the twentieth century further strengthened these defensive nationalist instincts. In 1912, the government of Ontario issued Regulation 17, which meant to limit French language education in separate (Catholic) schools.[12] In fact, while Ontario avoided abolishing French-Catholic instruction altogether as Manitoba had intended in the 1890s, Regulation 17 had overt assimilationist intentions. As Section 2(3) reads, French instruction would be available for "pupils unable to speak and understand the English language," yet "as soon as the pupil enters the school" English instruction would begin and "as soon as the pupil has acquired sufficient facility in the use of the English language he shall take up in that language the course of study."[13]

10 A.I. Silver, *The French Canadian Idea of Confederation 1864–1900* (Toronto: University of Toronto Press, 1982), 67–110.

11 Jules Deriares, cited in ibid., 171–2.

12 See Robert Bothwell, Ian Drummond, and John English, *Canada, 1900–1945* (Toronto: University of Toronto Press, 1987), 124.

13 Cited in Sara Z. Burke and Patrice Milewski, eds., *Schooling in Transition: Readings in Canadian History of Education* (Toronto: University of Toronto Press, 2012), Appendix E, 318.

Anger over yet another attack upon French language and culture lingered on throughout World War I and put oil on the flames of what came to be known as the 1917 conscription crisis, often portrayed as the pivotal moment in the history of Quebec's estrangement from the rest of Canada. Since the turn of the century, a novel brand of anti-imperialist nationalism had taken root in Quebec. Taking its cue from Henri Bourassa, grandson of Louis-Joseph Papineau and founder of one of Quebec's and indeed Canada's most important newspapers, *Le Devoir*, a new and younger generation of Quebecers not only demanded "widest possible autonomy" for the province within Canada, but also "widest possible political, commercial and military autonomy" regarding Canada's colonial link to the British mother country.[14]

Anti-imperialism combined with extending the idea of responsible government to foreign policy. In 1899, as a young Liberal member of parliament, Bourassa had resigned his seat when Prime Minister Wilfrid Laurier committed Canadian troops to participating in the British Empire's war against the Boers in South Africa without consulting parliament.[15] When World War I broke out in 1914, Quebec nationalists were not opposed to voluntary Canadian participation. Yet with Regulation 17 in Ontario on their minds, the point was not lost on them that the Canadian government was quick "to defend civilization and justice on European soil" whereas a "fair place for French-speaking Canadians" at home apparently was not a political priority. Thus, when conscription came under Laurier's Conservative successor Robert Borden, riots broke out, first in Montreal and later in Quebec City where soldiers fired into the crowd, killing five civilians.[16]

Along with growing alienation came a change in intergovernmental strategy. Quebec governments switched from traditional demands for increased statutory subsidies before World War I, which the BNA Act obliged the federal government to pay to the provinces, to calls for greater financial autonomy afterwards.[17] Louis-Alexandre Taschereau, Quebec's long-reigning Liberal premier (1920–36), not only resented the constraining level of tax centralization that had been brought on by the war effort but also continued policy interference with provincial jurisdiction when the war was over. In particular, he objected to the

14 See Paul-André Linteau, René Durocher, and Jean-Claude Robert, *Quebec: A History 1867–1929* (Toronto: James Lorimer, 1983), 491.

15 Ibid., 490.

16 Ibid., 525–6.

17 See ibid., 515–20.

1927 pension scheme, the first federal intrusion into social policy. When the Great Depression struck, Taschereau's Liberal counterpart at the federal level, Mackenzie King, remained reluctant about taking on a stronger social leadership role for good reason: He owed his own longevity as prime minister, at least in part, to the support he received in Quebec ever since he had opposed conscription in 1917.

As we saw in Chapter 4, the social crisis during the 1930s triggered a crisis of BNA Act federalism, which had assigned to the federal government the tools of constructing an economic union (accumulation function) and had left the provinces with the responsibility for social stability (legitimation function). The provinces did not have the financial means of responding to the social crisis, and the federal government did not have the authority to do so. The result was that what we call today a modern welfare state was delayed by more than a decade. After the end of World War II, then, it was the federal government that pushed for a significant share of the legitimation function.

The general formula of federal cost sharing in return for compliance with a rather loose set of national standards appeared fair to most English-speaking provinces and reflected the new reality of a dualized social citizenship.[18] It was considerably more problematic in Quebec, where it not only was seen as a serious incursion into provincial affairs but moreover clashed with ultramontanist Catholic doctrine. In 1931, Pope Pius XI had enounced in his *Quadragesimo Anno* encyclical that self-organized "social governance" was in danger of being destroyed by a new statism that only recognized individuals and didn't leave room for "Catholic principles and their application."[19]

At the time when the modern welfare state took shape, social governance in Quebec was still firmly in the hands of the Catholic Church, which was in charge of education, hospitals, and other social institutions. That church, wrote the archbishop of Montreal, Joseph Charbonneau, in 1941, is "a powerful, disciplined, conquering army, where all are on active service."[20] Between 1940 and

18 Jean-François Gaudreault-DesBiens, "The Irreducible Federal Necessity of Jurisdictional Autonomy, and the Irreducibility of Federalism to Jurisdictional Autonomy," in *Dilemmas of Solidarity: Rethinking Redistribution in the Canadian Federation*, eds. Sujit Choudhry, Jean-François Gaudreault-DesBiens, and Lorne Sossin (Toronto: University of Toronto Press, 2006), esp. 194–9.

19 Pius XI, *Quadragesimo Anno*, Papal Encyclical (May 15, 1931).

20 Cited in Michael Gauvreau, "From Rechristianization to Contestation: Catholic Values and Quebec Society, 1931–1970," in *Contemporary Quebec: Selected Readings & Commentaries*, eds. Michael D. Behiels and Matthew Hayday (Montreal: McGill-Queen's University Press, 2011), 133.

1960, the number of priests in Quebec increased from 5,000 to 8,400; around 1950, there was "one religious (father, brother or sister) for every eighty-nine Catholics" in the province.[21]

This was also the era of Quebec Premier Maurice Duplessis and his Union Nationale, sometimes portrayed as Quebec's great darkness (*la grande noirceur*).[22] The Union Nationale was a coalition of conservatives and nationalists formed in 1935. With Duplessis at the helm, it had already held power from 1936 to 1939, when it was defeated by the Liberals who, in alliance with their federal colleagues, seemed to offer better assurance against conscription, which yet again became a defining issue at the beginning of World War II. The federal Liberals, however, broke their promise not to introduce conscription, and the provincial Liberals agreed to the 1940 constitutional amendment transferring to the federal government exclusive power over unemployment insurance. Denouncing both, Duplessis regained power in 1944 and would remain premier until his death in 1959.

The success of Duplessis, winning four consecutive provincial elections, was based on party loyalty, patronage, and an "outdated electoral map" that disadvantaged the Liberal opposition.[23] His darkness was anti-modernism. In fact, it was traditionalism clinging to the nineteenth-century Confederation formula. While Francophone Quebec would remain a rural place in which property and civil rights remained in the domain of traditional elites and the clergy, trade and commerce would be left to Anglophone and, increasingly, American capitalists. The modern welfare state was an aberration, and anyone working for social change was a "communist."[24]

From 1948–57, Canada had a Liberal prime minister, Louis St. Laurent, who took the Depression experience and subsequent recommendations of the Rowell-Sirois Commission as a mandate to reform the federal system so that the federal government would gain control over socioeconomic stability. That included co-responsibility for welfare and education as well as Keynesian management of the economy. This, as the Rowell-Sirois commissioners had argued, would require fiscal centralization. Quebec was more adamantly opposed to

21 Paul-André Linteau, René Durocher, and Jean-Claude Robert, *Quebec since 1930* (Toronto: James Lorimer, 1991), 240.

22 Jocelyn Létourneau, *A History for the Future: Rewriting Memory and Identity in Quebec* (Montreal: McGill-Queen's University Press, 2004), 129.

23 Linteau, Durocher, and Robert, *Quebec since 1930*, 149.

24 See ibid.

this incursion into provincial autonomy and jurisdiction than were most other provinces, and in the end, while the federal government indeed became co-responsible for social policy, tax centralization, as we saw in Chapter 5, was halted and even reversed.

Quebec's answer to the Rowell-Sirois report was the Tremblay report. Commissioned by Duplessis, its mandate was to examine "the encroachments by the central power in the field of direct taxation" and their effect on "the provinces, municipalities and school corporations."[25] The commissioners delivered much more than the expected condemnation of fiscal centralism. Based on a thorough examination of French Canadian culture and history, they declared that Quebec was "not a province like the others"[26] and that, therefore, provincial autonomy was essential for survival.

The nationalism of Duplessis was not just a battle for provincial autonomy, though. It was steeped in social conservatism, which meant "clerical *anti-étatisme*."[27] A symptomatic moment came in 1953. Following recommendations of the 1949 Massey Commission on National Development in the Arts, Letters and Sciences,[28] the St. Laurent government had begun in 1951 to give financial aid to universities. Two years later, Duplessis ordered Quebec universities to refuse this aid.[29] The move had not so much to do with a defence of provincial jurisdiction as it was motivated by anti-statism in general and by efforts to restrict academic funding for a new and growing generation of secular intellectuals opposed to social conservatism in particular.[30]

The term *Quiet Revolution* is usually associated with the Liberal premiership of Jean Lesage (1960–6). But it was during the Duplessis years that change was quietly fermenting all along. Even though the number of priests was still increasing during the 1950s, it was increasing at a lower rate and could not keep pace with the "rapid growth of schools, hospitals and social services."[31] The Catholic Church, in other words, was beginning to lose control over social institutions to a new generation of secular professionals.

---

25 David Kwavnick, ed., *The Tremblay Report* (Toronto: McClelland and Stewart, 1973), 2.

26 Ibid., 45.

27 McRoberts, *Quebec*, 88.

28 The commission report is available at https://www.collectionscanada.gc.ca/massey/h5-400-e.html.

29 Linteau, Durocher, and Robert, *Quebec since 1930*, 281.

30 See McRoberts, *Quebec*, 92–5.

31 Linteau, Durocher, and Robert, *Quebec since 1930*, 240.

The argument according to which French Canadian "national survival" depended on "agriculture and rural modes of organization and life," still conjured up by the Tremblay report,[32] rapidly lost its appeal in a Quebec "where the forces of urbanization and industrialization were clearly irreversible."[33] Television opened up new perspectives of modern life.[34] It was these inevitable forces of modernization that produced a new generation of intellectuals who challenged the status quo and whom Duplessis therefore feared with good reason.

Foreshadowing battles to come, these intellectuals can be grouped into two competing camps. Both were opposed to the nationalism of old, but both had very different views of the place that a new Quebec should occupy in the federation.[35] One was the view of a liberal and social democratic state with equal opportunity for all citizens regardless of language, culture, or religion. The other view championed a more Quebec-centred neo-nationalist view. French language and culture would only survive in a modernized Quebec in which French Canadians held majority control. While Pierre Elliott Trudeau already occupied a prominent place in the liberal camp, René Lévesque, a popular TV commentator and labour activist at the time, would emerge as the combative champion of Quebec sovereignty only a decade later.

The Lesage government pursued an aggressive neo-nationalist agenda of making Francophone Quebecers, as its 1962 electoral slogan went, "masters in their own – provincial – home" (*maîtres chez nous*). All but eliminating the influence of the church, it established for the first time a Quebec Ministry of Education in charge of the entire school system as well as curriculum matters. With René Lévesque as minister of natural resources, it nationalized private hydroelectric utility companies owned and managed by English Canadians and incorporated them into one gigantic public enterprise, Hydro-Québec. As we already know from Chapter 5, the Lesage government insisted on a separate Quebec Pension Plan. Not the least purpose of it was to promote Francophone business through the Quebec Deposit and Investment Fund (*Caisse de dépôt et placement du Québec*), which managed the pension plan money as well as other insurance programs.[36] Through it all, Lesage sought to establish French as the

32 Cited in McRoberts, *Quebec*, 85.

33 Ibid., 84.

34 Linteau, Durocher, and Robert, *Quebec since 1930*, 287–8.

35 See Michael D. Behiels, *Prelude to Quebec's Quiet Revolution: Liberalism versus Neo-Nationalism, 1945–1960* (Montreal: McGill-Queen's University Press, 1985).

36 See Stephen Brooks and A. Brian Tanguay, "Quebec's *Caisse de dépôt et placement*: Tool of nationalism?" *Canadian Public Administration* 28, no. 1 (1985).

dominant working language in the province. English-speaking hydro executives either had to learn French or leave.[37]

Separatism was not quite yet on the agenda, but the plot began to thicken. In 1965, Pierre Elliott Trudeau entered federal politics to combat what he perceived as a retrograde form of provincial nationalism. The Lesage government lost the 1966 provincial election, handing power back to the Union Nationale for another four years. In 1967, Lévesque left the provincial Liberals and founded the Movement for Sovereignty-Association (*Mouvement Souveraineté-Association*), which a year later, in 1968, became the first openly separatist provincial party, the Parti Québécois (PQ). In that same year Trudeau became Liberal prime minister of Canada. The stage was set for a showdown of epic proportions.

First, though, it was the provincial Liberals returning to power in 1970 with Robert Bourassa having replaced Jean Lesage as leader. Hardly in office, Bourassa had to deal with an unprecedented challenge known as the October crisis. The *Front de libération du Québec* (FLQ), a loosely organized group of Marxist–Leninist revolutionaries operating in Quebec, had carried out violent acts of terrorism in the name of liberating Quebec from its alleged colonial status throughout the 1960s. In October 1970, different cells of the FLQ kidnapped, within the span of a few days, first British Trade Commissioner James Cross and then Bourassa's minister of labour, Pierre Laporte. Bourassa called for federal help. Trudeau sent the army, 10,000 soldiers in riot gear, and then invoked the War Measures Act, which, suspending civil rights, allowed the army to arrest and detain some 500 suspects. While Cross was eventually released, Laporte was murdered the day after invocation of the War Measures Act.[38]

Bourassa was blamed in some quarters for having invited what many saw as Trudeau's disproportionate response to the crisis, if not an outright witch hunt of suspected separatists. Campaigning against the "separatist threat," Bourassa was nevertheless re-elected in a 1973 landslide election, winning 102 out of 110 seats. Ominously, the PQ by then won almost one-third of the provincial vote, which only translated into six seats but made it the official opposition nonetheless. Three years later, having promised to hold a referendum before going ahead with separation, Lévesque led the PQ to victory, winning 71 seats with over 40 per cent of the popular vote.[39]

---

37 On the whole, see McRoberts, *Quebec*, 131–8.

38 See Linteau, Durocher, and Robert, *Quebec since 1930*, 526–7.

39 Ibid., 535–7.

English Canada was not so much shocked as it was confused. What was it that Quebec wanted and didn't have? In his book-length answer, specifically written for an English-speaking readership as requested by his publishers, André Bernard identified three demands or objectives that he claimed united all Francophone Quebecers: national survival, economic well-being, and the idea of a homeland.[40]

National survival meant for Francophone Quebecers the ability to continue to function in their own language and culture. Industrialization and urbanization had begun to threaten this survival. By 1971, 37 per cent of French-speaking Quebecers lived and worked in the Montreal area. Almost half of these could get their first jobs only if they spoke English.[41]

By economic well-being, Francophone Quebecers meant catching up to the rest of the country and to the English-speaking minority within the province. By the mid-1970s, Ontarians enjoyed a per capita income of 19 per cent above the Canadian average. The per capita income of Quebecers was 14 per cent below that average, and it was only at that level because of the high income of the English-speaking economic elite within the province: Of the 20 per cent of families, households, or individuals with a real income of $4,000 or less, 95 per cent were French speaking; of the 12 per cent earning $20,000 to $100,000, 90 per cent were English speaking or bilingual; of the 3 per cent with a real income above $100,000, 90 per cent were English speaking.[42] The numbers were not surprising: While French Canadian businesses provided for 47 per cent of private-sector employment in Quebec, they only accounted for 15 per cent of the added value in the provincial economy.[43]

Justifying the quest for a homeland is hardest to quantify. At Confederation, Quebec had been faced with three mainly English-speaking provinces in federal politics. Now there were nine. Also at Confederation, parliamentary representation had still provided some semblance of balance between the two language groups. Now French Canadians were hopelessly outnumbered at the federal level. Due to a declining birth rate and the influx of allophone immigrants of which only 1.5 per cent came with French as their mother tongue,[44] the proportion of

40 André Bernard, *What Does Quebec Want?* (Toronto: James Lorimer, 1978).

41 Ibid., 38–9.

42 Ibid., 49, 61.

43 Ibid., 63.

44 Ibid., 86.

the French-speaking population in Canada had fallen to 23 per cent. The number for unilingual French-speaking Quebecers was 17 per cent.[45]

Finally, Quebec neo-nationalists argued that policy decisions were made in Ottawa by mostly English-speaking senior civil servants, with the consequence that they either did not suit Quebec's priorities or that English-speaking Canadians heard about program and funding opportunities long before information filtered down to the French-speaking community.[46] The survival of the French language and culture in Canada as a whole was no longer guaranteed. It could only be secured in Quebec. Nationalism had gone territorial.

Trudeau had gone to Ottawa to stem the tide of that territorial nationalism. The introduction of official bilingualism in 1969 was aimed at ending linguistic minorization at the federal level, which in turn would make shoring up Quebec as a closed Francophone fortress unnecessary. But change would come slowly, and Quebec nationalists were not convinced. The introduction of bilingual air traffic control at Quebec's airports, for instance, took an entire decade, was confronted with a pilots' and air traffic controllers' strike in the name of air safety disguised as English-speaking job protection, and required the surprised findings of a commission that bilingual air traffic control operations at airports elsewhere in the world actually worked.[47]

Better, then, to ensure undisputed French language domination at home. Already Bourassa's 1974 Official Language Act, Bill 22, contained the main elements of what would in 1971 become the PQ's Charter of the French Language, Bill 101: the francization of public administration, the workplace, and education. French was declared the sole official language in the political and judicial system. English language instruction from kindergarten to secondary education would be available only for children with a parent having previously received substantive English instruction in Quebec. In particular, this would exclude the children of Anglophone parents moving to Quebec from other parts of Canada after 1977 and the children of allophone parents, of which in Montreal over 90 per cent attended English schools at the time. Businesses with more than 50 employees had to hold a francization certificate and, most controversially, all commercial advertising and public signs had to be in French.[48]

45 Ibid., 80.

46 Ibid., 85–6.

47 Sandford F. Borins, *The Language of the Skies: The Bilingual Air Traffic Control Conflict in Canada* (Montreal: McGill-Queen's University Press, 1983).

48 Marcel Martel and Martin Pâquet, *Speaking Up: A History of Language and Politics in Canada and Quebec* (Toronto: Between the Lines, 2012), 166–9.

Then, in 1980 and as promised, came the referendum. Lévesque had developed the concept of sovereignty-association because he knew that Quebecers would not support a plan of outright separation.[49] Sovereignty-association meant that Quebec would become sovereign politically – raise its own taxes, make its own laws, and conduct its own foreign relations – but would remain in an economic and currency union with the rest of Canada. Trudeau, who had just gained a new lease on political life after the defeat of the short-lived Conservative Clark government, vigorously intervened in the referendum campaign by making a "solemn commitment" of constitutional renewal.[50] In other words, he promised Quebec a new and more accommodating federalism.

The PQ lost the referendum by a 60/40 margin. Trudeau's promise of a new federalism would turn out to be constitutional patriation in the form of a domestic constitutional amendment formula and a charter of rights and freedoms. The amendment formula fell way short of the veto Quebec had (almost) always had insisted on, and the charter of (individual) rights challenged Quebec's (collective) language laws. We shall continue with the patriation saga in Chapter 7. The remainder of this chapter, however, must first turn to differences and grievances in other parts of the country.

Western Alienation

At the very same time when the political battle over the first referendum on sovereignty-association was fought in Quebec, separatist sentiments were welling up in western Canada as well. Both were, in fact, closely related.

On December 13, 1979, the minority government of Joe Clark, conservative and from Alberta, was defeated in Ottawa. On February 18, 1980, Pierre Trudeau, liberal and from Quebec, returned to power. Seventy-four out of 147 members of the new Liberal caucus were from Quebec, where Trudeau had won all but one seat. Not a single Liberal member had been elected west of Winnipeg. Four days after the election, Elmer Knutson, an Alberta tractor-parts-dealer-millionaire, wrote in the *Edmonton Journal* that Trudeau's victory had reversed the outcome of the battle at the Plains of Abraham: The Francophones had finally defeated the Anglophones. Quebec should be forced out of Confederation.[51]

---

49 Létourneau, *A History for the Future*, 138.

50 Cited in McRoberts, *Quebec*, 326.

51 Knutson's letter is cited in Denise Harrington, "Who Are the Separatists?" in *Western Separatism: The Myths, Realities & Dangers*, eds. Larry Pratt and Garth Stevenson (Edmonton: Hurtig Publishers, 1981), 24–5.

Anti-Quebec sentiments turned to calls for western independence when the May 20, 1980, referendum kept the Francophone province in Confederation after all. Three days after the referendum, Knutson emerged as leader of the Western Canada Federation (West-Fed), joining forces with another separatist group already in existence, Western Canada Concept, led by Victoria, BC, lawyer Doug Christie.[52] Separatist rhetoric heated up when news transpired that Trudeau's October 1980 budget would contain a new National Energy Program (NEP) aiming at a greater federal share of Canadian ownership of the oil industry as well as of the revenues derived from it. With his usual dismissive arrogance, calling western separatism "hysterical,"[53] Trudeau went ahead with the budget despite frantic interventions by the Alberta government. This in turn led to the spectacular public conversion to the cause of western separatism of Carl Nickle, a prominent Calgary oil tycoon, former conservative member of parliament, and recipient of the Order of Canada. Knutson and Christie, thus far accompanied only by a modest number of fellow travellers, now got to speak in front of packed houses. A Christie rally in November 1980 filled 2,700 seats of Edmonton's Jubilee Auditorium, with the crowd chanting "Free the West."[54]

Western separatism arose as quickly and spontaneously as it also subsided again. Yet while it was denied political success or even recognition, it nevertheless gave dramatic if momentary expression to the west's more general and ongoing discontent with its place in Confederation, a sense of "western alienation" sustained by "an abiding Western suspicion that Confederation has been, and continues to be, a bad deal for the West."[55]

That deal was one of unequal exchange under a regime of internal colonialization: western Canada would provide (cheap) resources to be sold in domestic and international markets by central Canadian traders and merchants reaping most of the profits; western Canadians would have to buy (expensive) manufactured goods from central Canadian providers sheltered by national tariff policies; economic development in western Canada would generally depend on capital investment and credit decisions made by central Canadian financial institutions;

---

52 Christie would later gain notoriety as legal counsel for Holocaust deniers such as James Keegstra and Ernst Zundel.

53 Harrington, "Who Are the Separatists?" 28.

54 Ibid., 29–30.

55 John F. Conway, *The Rise of the New West: The History of a Region in Confederation* (Toronto: James Lorimer, 2014), 16.

and the inequality of this economic exchange would be exacerbated further by central Canadian control of the means of transportation and communication.[56] As George Brown's *Globe* had marvelled at the prospects of western expansion in an 1862 editorial, "It is an empire we have in view, and its whole export and import trade will be concentrated in the hands of Canadian merchants and manufacturers."[57]

As we saw in Chapter 2, Confederation came about as a compromise. In order to achieve national economic union, concessions had to be made to French Canadians adamant about their retention of language and culture. The quest for economic union very much included territorial expansion to western riches before the Americans got there. And no concessions were necessary at least with regard to the Prairies, "a vast underpopulated hinterland" purchased from the Hudson's Bay Company in 1868 "without consultations with the local people."[58] British Columbia, of course, already an existing British colony in its own right, would enter Confederation in 1871 on negotiated terms similar to those established by the BNA Act.

National economic union required a national economic development strategy. The most compelling explanation for the crucial role the west played in post-Confederation economic development is still the staple theory first developed by Harold Innis.[59] In essence, staple theory wants to provide an explanation of, if not strategy for, economic development in a country like Canada, the primary wealth of which derives from the production and export of natural resources such as fur, fish, lumber, minerals, and wheat. Such staples are not only prone to boom and bust cycles in world commodity markets, they also generate little added value and hence do not contribute much to domestic capital formation.

56 See Donald V. Smiley, "The Political Context of Resource Development in Canada," in *Natural Resource Revenues: A Test of Federalism*, ed. Anthony Scott (Vancouver: University of British Columbia Press, 1976), 65–6; David Leadbeater, "An Outline of Capitalist Development in Alberta," in *Essays on the Political Economy of Alberta*, ed. David Leadbeater (Toronto: New Hogtown Press, 1984); Janine Brodie, *The Political Economy of Canadian Regionalism* (Toronto: Harcourt Brace Jovanovich, 1990), 100–5.

57 Cited in Loleen Berdahl and Roger Gibbins, *Looking West: Regional Transformation and the Future of Canada* (Toronto: University of Toronto Press, 2014), 6.

58 Conway, *The Rise of the New West*, 25.

59 Harold Innis, *The Fur Trade in Canada: An Introduction to Canadian Economic History* (1930, repr., Toronto: University of Toronto Press, 1999).

In order to get out of this "staples trap,"[60] the theory suggests an economic development strategy of so-called backward, forward, and final demand linkage.[61] The basic idea is to develop domestic industries linked to the staples production itself. Backward linkage means investment in the domestic production of equipment, machinery, and means of transportation to intensify the production of staples – backward because they are investments prior to the production of the staple itself. Forward linkage means processing and refining after the staples are harvested or mined, thus adding value to the product before it is exported. Final demand linkage gives expression to the idea that increased income levels will result in the development of a domestic consumer industry.

All that did eventually happen in Canada, but the problem, at least from a western perspective was (and is) that while the west essentially remained stuck with staples production, the profit- and income-generating dynamic of backward, forward, and final demand linkage mainly unfolded in central Canada. Still today, while more than three-fourths of secondary manufacturing is concentrated in central Canada, the west accounts for almost two-thirds of primary production.[62] Even the profits resulting from primary production disproportionately accrued in central rather than western Canada. In 1886, a western farmer might get 53 cents for a bushel of wheat from a middleman who then sold it for a dollar at its final Liverpool destination.[63] By 1931, two central Canadian cities alone, Montreal and Toronto, accounted for almost half of Canada's wholesale trade.[64]

It cannot all be blamed on the machinations of central Canadian "industrial capitalists, landowners, railway and steamship entrepreneurs, and financial adventurers in the growing Canadian banking and insurance system," a new "ruling class" adamant about seeking new fortunes by pushing for John A. Macdonald's Confederation scheme of an "enforced east-west national home market."[65] At least it was not an outright conspiracy. It could hardly be expected that major industries would prefer Prairie conditions of sparse populations and

60 M.H. Watkins, "A Staples Theory of Economic Growth," in *Approaches to Canadian Economic History*, eds. W.T. Easterbrook and M.H. Watkins (Toronto: Gage Publishing, 1980), 63.

61 Ibid., 55.

62 Michael Howlett, Alex Netherton, and M. Ramesh, *The Political Economy of Canada: An Introduction* (Toronto: Oxford University Press, 1999), 113; numbers are from 1996.

63 Conway, *The Rise of the New West*, 45.

64 Kenneth Buckley, "Capital Formation in Canada, 1896–1930," in Easterbrook and Watkins, *Approaches to Canadian Economic History*, 181.

65 Conway, *The Rise of the New West*, 22–3.

long distances over central Canada, with its already much more favourable production and market conditions.

A contributing factor was, however, what essentially came to be known as Macdonald's National Policy.[66] Put in regionally neutral terms, the objective was "to protect Canadian producers from … [mainly American] foreign competition, to create an integrated and largely self-sufficient economy, and to develop an industrial economy."[67] But what the National Policy really amounted to was a "series of asymmetrical regional policies" that would keep the western hinterland "in a subordinate relationship to the rest of the country."[68] The policy had two essential prongs: the transcontinental railway as the crucial link between western resources and central Canadian industry, and a tariff wall not only shielding Canadian producers from unwanted competition but moreover providing much-needed federal revenue, which within a few years would increase by a third.[69]

The railway had, of course, been part of the Confederation scheme all along. But financing problems had delayed construction, and then came the Canadian Pacific Scandal. In 1873, the contract for what was touted to be a quintessentially Canadian project had gone to Sir Hugh Allan, a Montreal shipbuilding and railway magnate. When it transpired that Allan not only had American connections but moreover had massively contributed to Macdonald's electoral campaign the previous year, the embattled prime minister had to resign.[70] The Liberals won the 1874 election, but Macdonald was back in power four years later, by which time he had not only adopted the idea of a national tariff policy but also moved swiftly on the railway.

The Canadian Pacific Railway (CPR) Act of 1881 gave the company and its financiers ownership of 25 million acres of prime western land as well as discretion over the exact course of main and branch lines. The CPR, in other words, could lay the rail tracks in such a way as to maximize their own benefit.[71] Taken together with the large amount of land left in the ownership of the Hudson's Bay

66 See V.C. Fowke, "The National Policy – Old and New," in Easterbrook and Watkins, *Approaches to Canadian Economic History*.

67 J.L. Granatstein et al., *Nation: Canada since Confederation* (Toronto: McGraw-Hill Ryerson, 1990), 35.

68 Brodie, *The Political Economy*, 114.

69 Granatstein et al., *Nation*, 36.

70 For a detailed if somewhat exculpatory account, see Richard Gwyn, *Nation Maker, Sir John A. Macdonald: His Life, Our Times*, vol. 2, *1867–1891* (Toronto: Random House, 2011), 205–58.

71 Conway, *The Rise of the New West*, 34.

Company when the western territories were purchased in 1868, this meant that the lure of the west as a land of free homesteading was false. In order to expand and develop their original holdings, Prairie settlers had to "purchase lands already owned" more often than not, and with expensive credits from eastern banks no less. Between 1905 and 1930, nearly half of all free homesteads failed in Alberta and Saskatchewan.[72]

The CPR's transportation monopoly also allowed price gouging on freight rates, which during the 1880s consumed about half of western farmers' gross income.[73] Only in 1897 did the federal government intervene with the so-called Crow's Nest Pass Agreement.[74] In a classical tit for tat, it would provide financial aid for a new rail line across Crow's Nest Pass into southern British Columbia, and in return the CPR would lower the rates on grain and flour shipments from the Prairies eastward as well as on westward shipments of items crucial for farmers, such as agricultural machinery, materials for house construction, furniture, and fuel.[75]

While the grievances of western farmers were alleviated for the moment, the agreement, which continued to exist with some interruptions and modifications until 1993, only gave further expression to regional asymmetry and uneven exchange. Western farmers could only benefit from the Crow rate by shipping staples. And there was no guarantee, of course, that the producers of manufactured goods in central Canada would pass their reduced freight rates on to them. Why would they, when the other prong of the National Policy, the tariff wall, more or less provided them with a monopoly position?

Along with the railway, the tariff became the most hated object of western discontent. Protecting Canadian markets had not been one of the Confederation objectives. On the contrary, some form of free trade ("reciprocity") had been part of the scheme, the intensification of trade with the Americans after the loss of preferential treatment by Britain. During the 1870s, however, when the Canadian economy was besieged by a "serious depression" as well as "heightened expansionism of US capital," the idea of a protective tariff "for the benefit of central Canadian capital" gained popularity.[76] In fact, it greatly contributed to bringing

72 Ibid., 40.

73 Brodie, *The Political Economy*, 115.

74 Ibid.; see also Conway, *The Rise of the New West*, 53–4.

75 The text of the agreement is available at https://www.collectionscanada.gc.ca/canadian-west/052920/05292083_e.html.

76 Leadbeater, "An Outline of Capitalist Development in Alberta," 18.

Macdonald back to power when he adopted it during the 1878 election campaign and the Liberal government of Alexander Mackenzie refused to even consider it.[77]

For the west, the tariff made a bad situation worse. Wheat farmers and other western commodity producers, already forced to compete in unprotected and volatile world markets, squeezed by freight rates, and dependent on central Canadian banking power determining investment, credit, and mortgage decisions, now also had to buy much more expensive manufactured goods. The tariff on farm equipment, for instance, was raised from the initial 17.5 per cent in 1879 to a whopping 35 per cent by 1883. For central Canada, on the other hand, the tariff worked. Before tariffs first went up in 1879, most farm equipment was supplied by American producers via St. Paul, Minnesota, and the trade hub in Winnipeg. Afterwards, central Canadian firms such as Harris and Massey[78] were able to break into and even dominate the market.[79]

The colonial attitude of the federal government toward the western hinterland had already come to the fore most conspicuously during the 1869–70 Red River Rebellion. When Rupert's Land and the North West Territory came under Dominion control in 1868, the mostly French-speaking Métis people as well as a majority of white settlers feared for their language as well as land rights. In defiance of the new lieutenant governor sent from Ottawa, they set up a provisional government led by Louis Riel. Unable to crush the insurrection outright, fearing that Indigenous peoples would join the rebels, and under the gun from the sympathizing Quebec faction in its own ranks, the Macdonald government in 1870 conceded the formation of a new province, Manitoba.[80]

It did not concede very much. Ridiculed as a "postage stamp province," Manitoba originally comprised only about 10,000 square miles, barely covering the settlement area.[81] In addition, the new province was only granted "inferior constitutional status."[82] Contrary to the founding provinces at Confederation, to British Columbia a year later, and to Prince Edward Island in 1873, Manitoba was denied ownership of natural resources, as were Saskatchewan and Alberta when they became provinces in 1905. The federal government wanted to retain full control over how the west would be settled and for whose main benefit. Only in

77 Granatstein et al., *Nation*, 35.

78 Massey-Harris in 1891, Massey-Harris-Ferguson in 1955, and Massey-Ferguson in 1958.

79 Leadbeater, "An Outline of Capitalist Development in Alberta," 18–19.

80 For the full story, see Conway, *The Rise of the New West*, 25–32.

81 Ibid., 30; Manitoba's current boundaries were only established in 1912.

82 Fowke, "The National Policy," 246.

1930, when the settlement phase was essentially over, did the government agree to transfer resource ownership to the three provinces. The Prairies would not forget how they had been treated any less than Quebecers would keep alive the memory of the conquest.

A wheat boom took the sting out of second-class treatment. It began in 1896 and with interruption during the war years essentially lasted into the 1920s. But when the Depression hit, it became painfully clear what it meant to be kept in a staples trap. The (mostly western) farmers' share of the national income fell from 15 to 7 per cent between 1929 and 1933, while that of (mostly central Canadian) industries rose from 29 to 35 per cent during the same period.[83] No wonder, then, that agrarian protest and populist political realignment had their primary home in the west (see Chapter 4).

Dramatic change came on February 13, 1947, when Imperial Oil struck the first major oil field at Leduc just south of Edmonton. Before Leduc, Canada had produced about 21,000 barrels of crude oil daily. None of it was exported, and an additional 200,000 barrels had to be imported. By 1960, Canadian oil production topped half a million barrels. The development of natural gas production followed a similar pattern. Alberta accounted for about 70 per cent of oil production, with Saskatchewan coming second at 27 per cent. Alberta also produced 71 per cent of natural gas, with British Columbia coming second at 17 per cent.[84]

By that time, a network of pipelines had been built pumping oil and gas across the country and into the United States. In 1961, the Progressive Conservative federal government of John Diefenbaker, a westerner from Saskatchewan, introduced the National Oil Policy, which aimed at aggressive expansion of both oil exports into the United States and shipments to the Canadian east. A core part of the latter strategy was that consumers west of Quebec would be supplied with Canadian oil only. In return for being destined as a captive market for Canadian-produced oil, Ontario in particular would receive financial support for the further development of its refining and petrochemical industries. This expansion policy further reinforced the centre-hinterland model of Canadian economic development: resource extraction in the west, forward linkage processing and refinement in the east. In order to understand why western provincial governments nevertheless welcomed it, we need to take a closer

83 Conway, *The Rise of the New West*, 93.

84 André Plourde, "Oil and Gas in the Canadian Federation," Working Paper No. 2010-01, Department of Economics, University of Alberta, 2010.

look at "power and influence"[85] in what was generally seen as the rising of a "new West."[86]

Both the Social Credit governments in Alberta and the CCF in Saskatchewan took on the role of "classic rentiers."[87] This meant that they auctioned off sections of Crown reserves to the highest bidder, mostly American oil companies, and then simply collected royalties. Particularly in Alberta, resource wealth nevertheless trickled down to a "rising urban bourgeoisie" of local entrepreneurs, managers, and professionals linked to government as well as resource corporations "in a quasi-corporatist alliance of interests."[88]

The alliance was more tenuous in Saskatchewan. The CCF government of Tommy Douglas first entertained and then dropped the idea of public ownership. In order not to completely lose face, it eventually entered into a joint venture with the province's cooperative refineries, which had existed since the 1930s. In doing so, it also bypassed the usual bidding process. Even though the joint venture was "exceedingly modest" in terms of overall exploratory capacity, the oil industry was outraged, and a leading Toronto-based investment firm warned of negative consequences for the province's credit rating.[89]

The stars seemed aligned with what Alberta Premier Peter Lougheed would later call "a fundamental change in the economy of Canada."[90] On August 30, 1971, with crucial support from the new urban bourgeoisie, Lougheed's Progressive Conservatives had ended the 36-year reign of Social Credit in Alberta.[91] At that time, the Western Texas Intermediate (WTI) price for a barrel of crude oil was $21. Three years later, after the first OPEC crisis, it jumped to $54. Six years later, again, after the second OPEC crisis, it peaked at $122.[92] Alberta and the rest of the west finally had a chance of escaping their hinterland predicament – economic diversification in the form of backward as well as forward linkage appeared possible. Yet there were others wanting to cash in on the oil bonanza.

---

85 John Richards and Larry Pratt, *Prairie Capitalism: Power and Influence in the New West* (Toronto: McClelland and Stewart, 1981).

86 Conway, *The Rise of the New West.*

87 Richards and Pratt, *Prairie Capitalism*, 72.

88 Ibid., 167.

89 Ibid., 178–87.

90 Ibid., 173.

91 Ibid., 148.

92 Macrotrends, available at http://www.macrotrends.net/1369/crude-oil-price-history-chart.

The spoils of every barrel of crude oil have to be divided among three competing parties. The oil industry wants to make a profit, the provinces collect royalties, and the federal government imposes taxes on everything except provincial royalties deemed immune because of the provincial ownership of resources. Within a few years, competition turned to confrontation.

In the fall of 1973, the federal government imposed an oil price freeze as well as an energy export tax. It also disallowed resource companies to deduct provincial royalties from their taxable income. The provinces in turn not only increased royalty rates but also came up with all kinds of public ownership schemes in the form of provincial Crown corporations meant to insulate the industry from federal regulation and taxation.[93] Urged on by the NDP on the support of which it depended, the Liberal minority government of Pierre Trudeau also created a federal Crown corporation, Petro-Canada, meant to diminish foreign control of Canada's energy sector.

Then, after the second oil shock in 1979 and the political shock of Joe Clark's defeat and Trudeau's triumphant return to power, came the NEP. As a national energy strategy, it made sense. Trudeau and his energy minister, Marc Lalonde, wanted to keep the domestic oil price below world market prices for the benefit of Canadian manufacturers, encourage Canadianization of the oil and gas industry, push domestic exploration with the objective of self-sufficiency, and capture a larger portion of revenues for all Canadians.[94] From a western perspective, however, it was nothing more than another central Canadian scheme of keeping the hinterland at bay.

An oil war had begun. Premier Lougheed told Albertans to "prepare to suffer and bleed."[95] Twice, in March and in June of 1981, the Alberta government cut the eastward oil flow by 5 per cent.[96] A popular bumper sticker in Alberta read "Let the Eastern Bastards Freeze in the Dark."[97] A common joke in Ontario was that Air Canada had advised its pilots to switch off all lights during night flights across Alberta for safety reasons.[98]

---

93 Conway, *The Rise of the New West*, 166–7.

94 Ibid., 177–8.

95 Cited in ibid., 181.

96 Ibid., 181.

97 Mary Janigan, *Let the Eastern Bastards Freeze in the Dark: The West versus the Rest in Confederation* (Toronto: Vintage Canada 2013), 338.

98 Personal recollection.

Trudeau blinked first. In need of provincial allies in the already ongoing conflict over constitutional patriation (see Chapter 7), he made a conciliatory speech. It was reciprocated by Lougheed, who was worried about the rising tide of western separatism.[99] The oil war ended with a complicated oil pricing agreement signed by Trudeau and Lougheed in September 1981, with similar agreements with British Columbia and Saskatchewan to follow.[100] In essence, Alberta would be granted considerable price hikes but the domestic oil price would still be kept below world market prices. Ottawa would at least abstain from imposing an export tax on natural gas destined for the lucrative American market.[101]

Arguably, the biggest winners were the foreign energy corporations. Several of them had threatened to pack up and leave during the height of the conflict. Under the NEP, the industry's share of oil and gas revenue would have fallen from 39.4 per cent in 1979 to 31.6 per cent. Under the new agreement, the industry would rake in 44.3 per cent. By comparison, the federal government's share would go up from 12.1 per cent in 1979 to 25.5 per cent (but down from the 27.4 per cent imposed under the NEP). And Alberta's share would decrease from 48.5 per cent in 1979 to 30.2 per cent (as compared to 41 per cent under the NEP).[102]

By the time the agreement was signed, the WTI oil price had already fallen below $100. Five years later, it was pegged at $30 and hence almost at the same level as when it all started with the 1973 oil crisis.[103] The boom was over. The ultimate lesson for the western provinces was that they had "only very imperfect and uncertain authority over natural resources."[104] The lesson for the federal government was, as one observer put it at the time: "There are some things we can't have and probably don't need. One of them is a national energy policy."[105]

99 Conway, *The Rise of the New West*, 182–3.

100 See the detailed analysis in John F. Helliwell and Robert N. McRae, "Resolving the Energy Conflict: From the National Energy Program to the Energy Agreements," *Canadian Public Policy* 8, no. 1 (1982).

101 Conway, *The Rise of the New West*, 183–4.

102 Ed Shaffer, "The Political Economy of Oil in Alberta," in Leadbeater, *Essays on the Political Economy of Alberta*, 189.

103 Macrotrends.

104 Conway, *The Rise of the New West*, 167.

105 H.V. Nelles, "Canadian Energy Policy 1945–80: A Federalist Perspective," in *Entering the Eighties: Canada in Crisis*, eds. R. Kenneth Carty and W. Peter Ward (Toronto: Oxford University Press, 1980), 91.

All subsequent federal governments heeded this advice. Even when the WTI oil price shot up again to an unprecedented $160 in 2008,[106] the federal government, then led by a Conservative (and western) prime minister, Stephen Harper, made no attempt at regulation.

Neither was this the intention of Harper's successor, Liberal Prime Minister Justin Trudeau, who came to power in 2015 at a time when oil prices were already falling again. Ironically, however, it fell to Pierre Trudeau's son to get enmeshed in a renewed energy conflict with the west yet again. Justin Trudeau had campaigned with a promise to make a significant contribution to environmental protection and to combat greenhouse gas emission in particular. Once in office, his strategy had two main prongs: enforcing a carbon pricing regime on the provinces unless they had an equivalent policy of their own and tightening impact assessment regulations for environmentally sensitive infrastructure projects, such as pipelines, on the capacity expansion of which the landlocked province of Alberta depended to reach overseas markets.

Both initiatives have rekindled sentiments of western alienation. A Wexit (western exit) movement has even formed, named so in analogy to the Brexit drama unfolding in Europe at the same time. The name certainly is an overstatement, as it has been mainly Alberta, and to a lesser extent Saskatchewan, that see themselves as the target of central Canadian disrespect. When Trudeau was re-elected in 2019 with a minority government, he did not win a single seat in these two provinces.

Eastern Dependencies

When westerners say east, they mean central Canada. When central Canadians say east, they mean Atlantic Canada, comprising Newfoundland (Newfoundland and Labrador since 2001) and the three Maritime provinces of Nova Scotia, New Brunswick, and Prince Edward Island.

Except for a vague Canadian version of manifest destiny according to which some eventual form of union north of the United States appeared inevitable, it remains rather unclear what exactly it was that lured British North America's easternmost colonies into Confederation. Newfoundland, of course, and despite being nearly destitute, would not be swayed to join until 1949 to begin with, and Prince Edward Island held out for better terms of entry until 1873.

106 Macrotrends.

For the Maritimes, Confederation "was the remedy for no particular evils, the solution of no particular difficulties."[107] Earlier contemplations of a Maritime union were mainly grounded in the "yearning of Nova Scotia for restoration of her ancient boundaries," as Prince Edward Island had been established as a separate colony in 1769 and New Brunswick in 1784.[108] The idea had less traction in New Brunswick and hardly any in Prince Edward Island. Maritime union had been the official reason for the first Confederation conference in 1864. It was probably convened in Charlottetown just "to make sure that the Island's leaders showed up."[109]

Some say it was the free-flowing champagne at Charlottetown that overcame reluctance to join the larger union.[110] It probably wasn't the dependence on permanent subsidies agreed to and written into the BNA Act, a poor compensation for the loss of customs duties. The promised railway link to a continental market was of some attraction, since the Atlantic trade was becoming more competitive and the traditional role of the Maritimes as a trade hub between Britain and the New England states was about to become less lucrative when reciprocity with the United States was lost in 1866. Additional inducements for Prince Edward Island in 1873 included the establishment of regular ferry service between the island and the mainland, a federal takeover of the island railway (which had pushed the colony to the brink of bankruptcy), and money to buy out the foreign and mostly absent owners of agricultural land.[111]

Be all that as it may, the Maritimes joined Confederation much like a "foreign colony."[112] As a staples economy relying on the "production and export of timber, lumber products, fish and ships,"[113] it was the economically "least integrated" part of British North America.[114] The prospects of a continental economic

107 P.B. Waite, *The Life and Times of Confederation 1864–1867* (Toronto: University of Toronto Press, 1962), 50.

108 Ibid., 51.

109 Desmond Morton, *A Short History of Canada* (Edmonton: Hurtig Publishers, 1983), 73.

110 Waite, *The Life and Times*, 73; Granatstein et al., *Nation*, 1–3.

111 Francis W.P. Bolger, "Prince Edward Island and Confederation, 1863–1873," *Canadian Catholic Historical Association*, Report 28 (1961), 28–9.

112 T.W. Acheson, "The National Policy and the Industrialization of the Maritimes, 1880–1910," in *Industrialization and Underdevelopment in the Maritimes, 1880–1930*, eds. T.W. Acheson, David Frank, and James D. Frost (Toronto: Garamond Press, 1985), 25.

113 Ibid., 1.

114 Ibid., 25.

union offered "no economic benefits" to a region in need of a "genuinely international orientation."[115] By no means were the Maritimes a hinterland. Shipbuilding in particular had created prosperity. Halifax, Nova Scotia, and St. John, New Brunswick, were cities second only to Montreal, Quebec City, and Toronto at the time. With the advent of the steel-hulled steamship, however, wooden shipbuilding was in unrecoverable decline.[116] The completion of the intercolonial railway in 1876 and the National Policy after 1879 were greeted as a welcome opportunity to re-establish economic stability.

In fact, nowhere else in Canada did the prospects of a national mercantilist haven of entrepreneurial opportunity generate more immediate and impressive results. Yet nowhere else did the National Policy have more devastating consequences. With a new focus on textiles as well as on steel and iron products, Nova Soctia's industrial output increased by 66 per cent during the 1880s as compared to 51 per cent each in Ontario and Quebec; industrial capital investment, average wages, and manufacturing output in St. John, New Brunswick, surpassed that of Canada's classical steel town, Hamilton, Ontario.[117] Soon enough, however, it became clear that Maritime producers could not lastingly compete with those closer to central Canadian markets.

Distance and the freight rate stood in the way yet again. Overinvestment gave way to underinvestment as financial capital was leaving the region. By 1900, when the Bank of Nova Scotia moved its headquarters to Toronto, almost 50 per cent of its overall deposits still came from the Maritimes, but its lending within the region had shrunk to 32.5 per cent. Capital was drained from the Maritimes for more profitable investment elsewhere.[118] As shipbuilding and other Maritime-related activities revived during the two world wars, public procurement remained the region's best hope. During the 1920s St. John boasted the world's largest dry dock. Its last hurrah came with the Canadian Navy's Halifax-class frigate program, which saw nine warships built in the St. John shipyards during the 1990s.[119] Due to a complete lack of orders soon thereafter, the shipyard closed in 2003.[120]

115 David G. Alexander, *Atlantic Canada and Confederation: Essays in Canadian Political Economy* (Toronto: University of Toronto Press, 1983), 46.

116 Steel-hulled shipbuilding in the Maritimes only began during World War I.

117 Acheson, "The National Policy," 1–2, 4.

118 James D. Frost, "The 'Nationalization' of the Bank of Nova Scotia, 1880–1910," in Acheson, Frank, and Frost, *Industrialization and Underdevelopment*, 39, 45.

119 Irving Shipbuilding, "Our History."

120 Kevin Fox, "Canada's Largest Shipyard Closes," *Globe and Mail*, June 27, 2003.

As had the Maritimes more than half a century earlier, so did Newfoundland under its first premier Joseph R. ("Joey") Smallwood chart a course of overly ambitious industrialization. In such a new and industrialized province, Newfoundlanders were told, fishers could "burn their boats."[121] The result were mega-projects dependent on out-of-province capital support and with calamitous results more often than not. Hydroelectric power from Churchill Falls in Labrador, one of the largest projects of its kind in North America, ended up being sold to Hydro-Québec at a long-term and still ongoing flat rate without escalator, which made the Francophone utility corporation the main beneficiary by reselling power at market prices. An oil refinery at Come by Chance on Newfoundland's Avalon Peninsula resulted in one the largest bankruptcies in Canadian history, plunging the province further into debt.[122]

Newfoundlanders did have to burn their boats in the end. The province's darkest day came in 1992 when the federal minister of fisheries, John Crosbie, a Newfoundlander himself, imposed a moratorium on cod fishing, and some 40,000 fishers and fish-processing plant workers lost their livelihood.[123] The cod was gone due to overfishing that had been neglected and mismanaged for far too long by the federal fisheries department during a sparring game over fishing quotas between traditional inshore fishers and the corporate (Canadian and foreign) offshore trawler business.[124]

The greatest layoff in Canada's history happened in Canada's poorest province. Newfoundland had to rely more on federal transfer payments than any other province – at one point, 50 cents out of every public dollar spent (see Chapter 5). Federal unemployment benefit payments to the province saw a 900 per cent increase during the 1970s mega-project period, well before the 1992 cod catastrophe, and second only to Prince Edward Island.[125] And while oil revenue sharing eventually heaved the province out of its have-not predicament, it did

121 Valerie A. Summers, "Newfoundland between a Rock and a Hard Place: Regime Change in Newfoundland," in *The Provincial State in Canada: Politics in the Provinces and Territories*, eds. Keith Brownsey and Michael Howlett (Peterborough: Broadview Press, 2001), 27.

122 Ibid., 29–30.

123 Ibid., 41.

124 See Ralph Matthews, *The Creation of Regional Dependency* (Toronto: University of Toronto Press, 1983), 194–215.

125 Richard Starr, *Equal as Citizens: The Tumultuous and Troubled History of a Great Canadian Idea* (Halifax: Formac Publishing, 2014), 185.

not mitigate its status as the province with the highest unemployment rate, 14 per cent as of January 2018, compared to the Canadian average of 5.9 per cent.[126]

Again, it cannot all be simply blamed on Confederation and the National Policy. Moreover, a distinction must be made between the effect of both on western Canada and on Atlantic Canada. The peripheral status of western Canada as a resource hinterland was clearly part of the design. The Maritimes, in turn, became absorbed into a central Canadian nation-building project of "industrial and financial consolidation"[127] for which they were ill-suited as "initial attempts at industrialization ... all occurred in traditional communities ideally located for the Atlantic market, but in the most disadvantaged positions possible for a continental one."[128] In the case of Newfoundland, the kind of "large-scale 'propulsive' industrialization" led by foreign capital interests and favoured by federal and provincial governments prevented the development of a local economy with local resources for local consumption.[129]

As we saw earlier, the quasi-colonial exploitation of western resources was central to the Confederation project. Atlantic Canada, one might conclude, was not really needed at all for that project. In the context of Canada's regionalized economy, Atlantic Canada did end up providing a valuable resource, however: labour. It has been estimated that about "half of the region's most productive workers" left during the 1920s.[130] Such migrant labour forces, a mobile reserve army of labour of sorts, contribute to keeping wages down in core regions where they find employment during periods of boom. When the boom is over, however, they are laid off and often return home. In this way, the social cost of unemployment is exported to the periphery. The pattern can still be observed today (e.g., with labour migration between Cape Breton, Nova Scotia, and the Athabasca oil sands in Alberta).[131]

---

126 Statistics Canada, "Unemployment Rate by Province," January 2018.

127 R. James Sacouman, "The Differing Origins, Organization, and Impact of Maritime and Prairie Co-Operative Movements to 1940," in *Underdevelopment and Social Movements in Atlantic Canada*, eds. Robert J. Brym and R. James Sacouman (Toronto: New Hogtown Press, 1979), 42.

128 Acheson, "The National Policy," 25.

129 Matthews, *The Creation of Regional Dependency*, 191–2.

130 Henry Veltmeyer, "The Capitalist Underdevelopment of Atlantic Canada," in Brym and Sacouman, *Underdevelopment and Social Movements*, 23.

131 Nelson Ferguson, "From Coal Pits to Tar Sands: Labour Migration between an Atlantic Canadian Region and the Athabasca Oil Sands," *Just Labour: A Canadian Journal of Work and Society* 17&18 (2011).

Notwithstanding Newfoundland's recent outbursts of anger over equalization (see Chapter 5), the historical role of Atlantic Canada in Canadian federalism for the most part has been acquiescence to the federal government's handling of fiscal relations with the provinces. You don't bite the hand that feeds you. And notwithstanding recent access to resource revenues from oil and gas, the region, as compared to the rest of Canada, still finds itself saddled with significantly lower growth and income rates as well as disproportionate levels of unemployment.[132]

It is doubtful whether the usual neoliberal suggestions for remedy coming from a Fraser Institute study – a combination of tax cuts, government austerity, and market deregulation – would bring an end to Atlantic Canada's predicament as a peripheral region dependent on central handouts. The authors of the study point to Ireland and Michigan as neoliberal success stories. Yet Michigan is located in the very centre of the North American economy, and Ireland, while peripheral, is the only member-state of the European Union giving American multinationals access to the Eurozone without having to learn a different language.[133]

This is not to say that Atlantic Canada's dependency predicament simply ought to be accepted as a perpetual given. The removal of interprovincial barriers to trade, as the Fraser Institute study suggests, would probably bring economy-of-scale benefits to the region. And in an age of electronic communication, peripheral location no longer poses an insurmountable obstacle to economic renewal. However, just as the desired transition from a fossil fuel to a renewable energy economy cannot simply be carried out on the backs of one or two provinces such as Alberta and Saskatchewan, neither can social solidarity for Atlantic Canada simply be sacrificed on the altar of what the Fraser Institute deems to be "economic freedom." Federalism, as we see yet again, is always based on compromise, requires often-contested choices, and always results in uneasy balances.

Indigenous Displacement

Compromise is not what comes to mind when we consider the predicament of Canada's Indigenous peoples in the post-Confederation drama of forging a national economic union. Their role was simply to get out of the way. Of course,

132 On this and the following, see Ben Eisen et al., "Catching Up with Canada: A Prosperity Agenda for Atlantic Canada," Fraser Institute, 2019.

133 Before Brexit, the UK was, of course, the European Union's other English-speaking member-state. But it did not join the Eurozone.

the process of "displacement and assimilation" had begun much earlier. As early as 1637, the first "reserve" was established in New France by Jesuits believing that "a settled and secure environment would promote adoption of Christianity."[134] A secure environment for Indigenous peoples was not on the mind of John Cornwallis when Halifax was founded a century later, in 1749. The citadel was built on tribal ground without negotiation, compensation, or even consultation. Long since caught in the crossfire of eighteenth-century English–French turf wars over what was then known as Acadia, the Mi'kmaq of Nova Scotia declared war. Cornwallis countered with the infamous "scalping proclamation," offering a bounty of "ten Guineas for every Indian Micmac taken or killed, to be paid upon producing such Savage or his scalp."[135] There seems to be a general assumption that Indigenous peoples fared worse under the English than under the French.[136]

After the final French surrender, the Royal Proclamation of King George III in 1763 appeared to mend fences.[137] First, to prevent further "Frauds and Abuses," Indian lands henceforth had to be "purchased," and could be purchased only by the Crown. This set into motion a process of Indian land cessations by means of treaties rather than one-sided dispossessions. Some 500 treaties were eventually concluded.[138] Second, outside existing colonial boundaries, Indigenous peoples should not be "molested or disturbed" in their "possessions." This meant effectively a halt to western expansion until "further Pleasure be known." Such pleasure would become known soon enough, however, after the colonies gained control over Indian affairs in 1860 and western expansion became a central objective of Confederation.[139]

The Royal Proclamation did not help the Mi'kmaq, as the British rulers of Nova Scotia simply ignored it under the pretext that all territory had become Crown land when it had been ceded by the French. Accordingly, the Mi'kmaq

134 Government of Canada, "Volume One: Looking Forward, Looking Back," *Report of the Royal Commission on Aboriginal Peoples,* 1996, 130–4.

135 Cited in Daniel N. Paul, *We Were Not the Savages* (Halifax: Nimbus, 1993), 107–8.

136 See James S. Frideres and René R. Gadacz, *Aboriginal Peoples in Canada* (Toronto: Pearson Prentice Hall, 2008), 13–20.

137 The text has been reproduced in many places. A useful and annotated one available at https://www.aadnc-aandc.gc.ca/eng/1370355181092/1370355203645.

138 Patrick Macklem, *Indigenous Difference and the Constitution of Canada* (Toronto: University of Toronto Press, 2001), 133.

139 J.R. Miller, *Compact, Contract, Covenant: Aboriginal Treaty-Making in Canada* (Toronto: University of Toronto Press, 2009), 122.

were "dispossessed by default" and received nothing in return.[140] Elsewhere, however, particularly in Upper Canada, parcels of land were traded in exchange for "benefits that might include reserves, annual payments or other types of payment and certain rights to hunt and fish."[141] By 1827, the Crown had thus acquired most of the arable land in southern Ontario,[142] and by 1862 it was in possession of northwestern Ontario, with its mineral wealth on the Canadian Shield adjacent to the Great Lakes.[143]

Then came Confederation and, with it, the push for rapid western expansion to forge a continental economic union. A railway had to be constructed, and settlers had to be settled. Three obstacles stood in the way. One was Rupert's Land, entirely in the hands of the Hudson's Bay Company (HBC) by means of a Royal Charter, comprising most of the west and northwest all the way to the Rocky Mountains. This obstacle was removed by purchasing the land from the HBC for £300,000 in an agreement ratified by Britain in 1868. Under this agreement, HBC also retained 20 per cent of the west's fertile lands.[144]

The second obstacle in the way was the Red River Colony in what was about to become Manitoba. Not only was it already inhabited by white settlers, it was also home to Catholic and French-speaking Métis people of mixed European and Indigenous ancestry.[145] The colony was under HBC administration. Both groups of inhabitants feared for their rights when Rupert's Land was acquired by Canada. When the new lieutenant governor designate arrived in October 1869, he was refused entry to the colony. This was the beginning of the so-called Red River Rebellion. In December 1869, the Métis and a considerable number of white settlers united to form a provisional government led by Métis leader Louis Riel. Negotiating provincial status for the colony with Canada for the next six months, Riel had three main objectives: making land tenure secure for its inhabitants, protecting French culture, and obtaining political amnesty, particularly since Riel had tried and executed Thomas Scott, a Protestant government

140 Harald E.L. Prins, *The Mi'kmaq: Resistance, Accommodation, and Cultural Survival* (Orlando: Harcourt Brace, 1996), 154.

141 Government of Canada, "Treaties and Agreements," Crown–Indigenous Relations and Northern Affairs Canada.

142 Miller, *Compact*, 95

143 Ibid., 110–18.

144 On the following, see Conway, *The Rise of the New West*, 27–32

145 For a more detailed account, see W.L. Morton, "Introduction," in *Manitoba: The Birth of a Province*, vol. 1, ed. W.L. Morton (Canada: Manitoba Record Society Publications, 1965).

surveyor who had led various attacks against the provisional government, for insurrection in March 1870.

Manitoba became Canada's fifth province in May 1870 – however, as aforementioned, it was postage-stamp sized. As Riel had feared, the new province was denied land and resource rights enjoyed by other provinces. Political amnesty was not granted either. When a military expedition arrived in Manitoba in August 1870, Riel fled to the United States. Eventually cheated out of their land rights with tactics of delay and harassment, many Métis moved northwest to present-day Saskatchewan. There, in 1885, once again led by Riel, who had been called back from exile, they rose in another rebellion. The grievances leading to this so-called North-West Rebellion were the same as before: land and language rights. This time, however, a military confrontation led to bloody defeat of the Métis and their Cree allies. Riel surrendered and was hanged for treason – white Protestant Canada's revenge for the execution of Thomas Scott. Cree chiefs Poundmaker and Big Bear were sent to prison.

Once again we might ask: What has all this got to do with Canadian federalism? The two rebellions certainly sharpened the divide between English and French Canada. While Protestant English-speaking Ontario was outraged by the execution of Thomas Scott, Catholic French-speaking Quebec was outraged by the hanging of Louis Riel. If there was any genuine support for the Métis, it was because they spoke French, not because they were Indigenous. Canadian federalism was still firmly centred on the original compromise, balancing English economic interests with French cultural concerns. If the west was to be a new battlefield even temporarily, its Indigenous population was no more than collateral damage.

It was this Indigenous population, living on the wide land stretching all the way from Ontario to the Rocky Mountains into British Columbia and the Northwest Territories, that formed the third obstacle for western expansion. To get that obstacle out of the way was the purpose of the 11 so-called numbered treaties concluded between 1871 and 1922.[146] These treaties were gigantic "real estate transactions designed to free Indigenous lands for settlement and resource development."[147] Under Treaty 6, for instance, signed in 1876, the Cree, Assiniboine, and Ojibwa surrendered 120,000 square miles of territory in what is now central Saskatchewan and Alberta in return for "one square mile of reserve land per family of five"; a one-time payment of $12 for "each Indian beneficiary";

146 For an overview, see Thomas J. Courchene, *Indigenous Nationals, Canadian Citizens: From First Contact to Canada 150 and Beyond* (Montreal: McGill-Queen's University Press, 2018), 54–6.

147 Government of Canada, "Volume One: Looking Forward, Looking Back," 133.

farm stock, equipment, and seed as well as a flag, medal, horse, harness, and wagon for "each Indian chief"; annual payments of a couple of thousand dollars, presumably for each of the signatories; hunting and fishing rights; the promise of a reserve school; as well as a "medicine chest."[148]

For the Prairie tribes and bands, unaccustomed as they were to think of life in terms of property and possessions, this list of provisions and promises must have sounded impressive. In reality, it condemned them to a marginalized life of subsistence. What is worse, Canadian governments did not think of treaties as binding contracts but as convenient political arrangements valid only until "further Pleasure be known." Already during the 1880s, treaty commitments were broken by cutting payments and sending children to distant residential schools rather than providing the promised on-reserve schools.[149]

Here is not the place for a thorough discussion of the perfidious treatment Indigenous peoples received from often openly racist Indian agents and corrupt contractors, the graphic details of which can be found in James Daschuk's harrowing account.[150] This treatment included policies of forced starvation. The deliberate withholding of rations to Indigenous peoples already on the brink of starvation was administered both to make them move to mostly undesirable reserve land not in the way of railway construction and white settlement and to break any lingering spirit of resistance. The ultimate objective was to relieve the public purse of its obligations by turning Indians into subsistence farmers on reserve lands that nobody else wanted.

What must be noted, however, is that the practice of forced starvation, as evidenced by one of Prime Minister John A. Macdonald's most infamous utterances, was known and sanctioned by the federal government. In the House of Commons debate of April 26, 1882, the honourable members worried about the cost of Canada's treaty obligations to Indigenous peoples. When it came to the appropriation of $294,525.20 for "destitute Indians," they expressed concern that the largesse of this expenditure would turn "a barbarous population like the Indians" into "pensioners upon the Public Treasury," taking away any incentive "to settle down under a system of farming." Consequently, there were calls for "some stringent check upon the appropriation."[151]

148 Macklem, *Indigenous Difference*, 135.

149 Miller, *Compact*, 190–1.

150 James Daschuk, *Clearing the Plains: Disease, Politics of Starvation, and the Loss of Indigenous Life* (Regina: University of Regina Press, 2019), esp. 99–126.

151 *Official Debates of the House of Commons of the Dominion of Canada*, vol. 12 (1882), 1186.

At this point, the prime minister rose, informing the house that stringent checks were already in place. One "cannot allow them to die for want of food," Macdonald declared, "but they have been reduced to one-half and one-quarter rations." Moreover, he assured the honourable members, "the agents as a whole … are doing all they can, by refusing food until the Indians are on the verge of starvation, to reduce the expenses."[152]

Macdonald may have made this last remark about agents conscientiously at work for the good of the public treasury with a measure of sarcasm directed at the members of the house annoying or boring him with their petty insistence on cost when he was much more interested in the big picture of the National Policy, which, after all, had been the main topic of the debate that day. But there can be no doubt that Indians in his mind were not equal partners under the treaties. In the commons debate of July 13, 1885, when asked whether it was not outright fraud to deliver supplies to the Indians that were of substandard quality and quantity, Macdonald answered point blank that Indians could not be defrauded because "they have no right to that food." Indians, he elaborated, "are simply living on the benevolence and the charity of the Canadian Parliament, and, as the old adage says, beggars should not be choosers."[153]

The courts generally concurred. Still in 1929, a decision denied the existence of traditional hunting and fishing rights as treaty rights because "uncivilized people" had no independent power to enter into a treaty to begin with.[154] And while a 1979 decision first acknowledged the existence of such rights, it also affirmed that these could be limited or even extinguished by "such legislative restrictions as may later be passed."[155] Even though each of the two decisions followed a different rationale, they nevertheless had in common the outright denial of what Indigenous peoples themselves would have regarded as the essence of their relationship with the European settler society: a nation-to-nation relationship among equal and equally sovereign partners. In the 1929 decision, they were denied legal standing outright. In the 1979 decision their legal standing was still subjected to the sovereignty of the Canadian state.

---

152 Ibid.

153 *Official Report of the Debates of the House of Commons of the Dominion of Canada*, vol. 20 (1885), 3319.

154 Cited in Macklem, *Indigenous Difference*, 139.

155 Cited in ibid., 141.

Regionalism and Federalism

As other federal state-building projects during the founding years of modern industrial capitalism, Confederation in 1867 essentially was a project aimed at national economic union. In sharp contrast with other federal state-building projects such as Switzerland before (1848) and Germany afterwards (1871), however, Confederation sought to tie together disparate parts that had hardly anything in common and shared no national sentiments of belonging. Its main political union strategy was the promise of a railway yet to be built. The National Policy a decade later made economic union a reality, but it did so by exacerbating uneven regional development with consequences that were in part intended and in part unintended.

There was no doubt that Confederation as an economic project was meant to benefit what westerners would later call central Canada, which at the time meant Upper Canada and Montreal. By century's end, southern Ontario and southwestern Quebec had become Canada's industrial heartland, and "upholding the National Policy became the essential political prerequisite for winning and holding a significant share of the region's motherlode of parliamentary seats."[156] The Conservatives under Macdonald had regained power in 1878 by promising tariff protection to central Canadian manufacturing interests,[157] and a 15-year reign of the Liberals ended in 1911 when these manufacturing interests, firmly in the Liberal camp, smelled betrayal over Wilfrid Laurier's free trade plans and threw their lot in with the Conservatives yet again.[158]

Except for British Columbia, a western settler society did not yet exist in 1867. To create one was part of the national plan. That plan as intended can be explained as one of internal colonialism in two stages. Stage one would push Indigenous peoples off the land to make room for white settlers ("actual settlers," as Macdonald put it in 1873), who he hoped would eventually outnumber and displace the "unruly" Métis in Manitoba, even though the province had ostensibly been created as a concession to the latter.[159] Stage two of the colonial scheme then was to develop a Prairie hinterland economy that would supply cheap resources and become a captive market for central Canadian manufactured goods.

156 James Bickerton, "Regionalism in Canada," in *Canadian Politics*, eds. James Bickerton and Alain-G. Gagnon (Peterborough: Broadview Press, 1999), 219–20.

157 Donald Creighton, *Canada's First Century* (1970; repr., Toronto: Oxford University Press, 2012), 36–40.

158 Ibid., 121–5.

159 D.N. Sprague, *Canada and the Métis, 1869–1885* (Waterloo: Wilfrid Laurier University Press, 1988), 107.

Maybe this is too conspiratorial a view. After all, it was settlers from Ontario who first went out west in droves to find a "better life." The west was supposed to become "the granary of the empire," and hence heartland rather than hinterland of what was then still a largely agricultural economy.[160] Yet the fact remains that the Canadian central state retained resource ownership even after the Prairie provinces were created, and economic development in what Macdonald referred to as Canada's "crown colony" remained tied to central Canadian financial control and interest.[161]

Ironically, the energy conflict during the 1980s, which momentarily turned western alienation into western separatism, no longer can be explained as a case of internal colonialism in this way. As we saw in Chapter 4, the crisis of capitalism during the 1930s had triggered what would eventually become a wholesale rearrangement of power distribution in Canadian federalism, with the federal government taking on a significant share in social policy provision. As Garth Stevenson put it, Canadian federalism emerged as "a system reflecting the fragmented and regionalized nature of the economy, in which clear jurisdictional boundaries are absent."[162] In such a system, the intention of the federal government under Prime Minister Pierre Trudeau to secure a portion of the western energy bonanza for all Canadians was entirely legitimate.

So was western outrage insofar as it was grounded in past grievances. The resulting stalemate meant the abandonment of a national energy policy for the time being. As history would have it, it would fall to Pierre Trudeau's son, Justin, the current prime minister, to reopen the national policy question over carbon pricing and pipelines. The conflict lines are already drawn in the (oil) sand(s). We'll return to the national policy question in Chapter 8.

The eventual marginalization of the Maritimes, and the economic underdevelopment of Newfoundland and Labrador with it, can be seen as an unintended if predictable consequence of Confederation. More than in any other part of Canada, this raises the question about federalism and capitalism. If the price to be paid for national economic union inevitably is that "the unfettered market does not operate in a spatially impartial way,"[163] then that question boils down to whether federalism

160 Doug Owram, "Reluctant Hinterland," in Pratt and Stevenson, *Western Separatism*, 46–7.

161 Ibid., 52.

162 Garth Stevenson, "Federalism and the Political Economy of the Canadian State," in *The Canadian State: Political Economy and Political Power*, ed. Leo Panitch (Toronto: University of Toronto Press, 1977), 93.

163 Bickerton, "Regionalism in Canada," 212.

has provided a significant corrective. The answer is no and yes. On the one hand, as James Bickerton has pointed out, federalism has not protected Atlantic Canada from the negative effects of countercyclical Keynesian macroeconomic management policies first suggested by the Rowell-Sirois Commission and adopted by federal governments after World War II.[164] Fighting inflation with high interest rates, for instance, would have a further depressing effect on a region already plagued by underinvestment. On the other hand, as we saw in Chapter 5, social transfer and equalization payments have significantly contributed to the provision of equitable public services and living conditions.

It is these social transfer payments that aggrieve Quebec because they are seen, at least in nationalist quarters, as undermining provincial autonomy. From a nationalist perspective, it may seem inappropriate to treat Quebec at all under the heading of regionalism and federalism even if it is acknowledged as a region unlike the others. However, the point of this chapter has been that all of Canada's major regions are unique configurations of political economy and social culture in their own right. Quebec is, of course, the only one of these regions in which French is the predominant language. The question then is whether and how Canadian federalism had dealt with this cultural difference.

Confederation, to paraphrase the famous question André Bernard posed for the rest of the country, gave to Quebec what it wanted at the time: property and civil rights in order to remain distinct as of its own choice. For the remainder of the century, the animating force in Canadian intergovernmental conflict was the provincial rights movement spearheaded by Ontario, not Quebec (see Chapter 3). As perhaps first indicated by the demand for more tax autonomy rather than increased subsidies in the aftermath of World War I, Quebec's political and socioeconomic awakening was fully triggered only when the changed nature of Canadian federalism became apparent after the end of World War II. The partial takeover of the social legitimation function by the federal government was first opposed by the remnants of anti-modernism in the province, and then by an evolving modernization movement that transferred the provision of social justice from Catholic charity to the commitment of a strong provincial state. Both had in common what has been called a "counterparadigm" opposed to the hegemonic form of liberalism in English Canada.[165]

---

164 Ibid., 224.

165 Daniel Salée, "Transformative Politics, the State, and the Politics of Social Change in Quebec," in *Changing Canada: Political Economy as Transformation*, eds. Wallace Clement and Leah F. Vosko (Montreal: McGill-Queen's University Press, 2003), 25.

Traditional Francophone Quebec had largely operated and functioned outside the institutions and mechanisms of Canadian federalism. The modern welfare and intervention state no longer permitted such splendid isolation. The Quiet Revolution essentially aimed at providing a remedy for the Francophone exclusion from the commanding heights of modern political, economic, and social life. As we saw previously, there had been two intellectual paths toward inclusion, Pierre Trudeau's bilingual strategy against Francophone minorization at the federal level of government and René Lévesque's strategy of Francophone majorization within the territorial boundaries of the province. I believe both strategies were equally important for the space that Francophone Quebec would eventually occupy in what by all comparative standards must be regarded as "one of the most accommodating federations in the world."[166]

Confederation most certainly has not been accommodating for Indigenous peoples. The reason is simple: Canada's First Nations were never part of the federal bargain. While the earlier or "Georgian" treaties before Confederation still resembled "confederal compacts recognizing mutual rights and autonomies among sovereign signatories," the post-Confederation or "Victorian" treaties "addressed Aboriginal people as 'Her Majesty's Subjects' and enforced English protocol with the ultimate goal of the surrender of most of British North America to Euro-Canadian society."[167] Under the Indian Act of 1876, Indigenous peoples became "wards" of the Crown and were hence deprived even of basic citizen rights.

It has been noted that Indigenous peoples in Canada were "remarkably pacific" in trading most of their land away even after it had become obvious that the federal government would fail to uphold its side of the bargain more often than not.[168] A common explanation points to a catastrophic cultural misunderstanding.[169] What for the Crown meant the cessation of property rights was understood by Indigenous peoples as a sharing of land. I believe that this misunderstanding cannot really explain the later post-Indian Act treaties when any "kin-like relationship of equals" on the part of the federal government gave way to "paternalistic" subordination.[170] Especially in the west and north, Indigenous

166 Létourneau, *A History for the Future*, 139.

167 Thomas O. Hueglin, "Exploring Concepts of Treaty Federalism: A Comparative Perspective," paper prepared for the Royal Commission on Aboriginal Peoples, 1994, 20.

168 Miller, *Compact*, 192.

169 Government of Canada, "Volume One: Looking Forward, Looking Back," 160–2.

170 Miller, *Compact*, 187.

peoples negotiated out of despair as each deal further "worsened their social conditions and made the next one more urgent."[171]

The account of persistent nationalist aspirations in Quebec, of western alienation, and of eastern dependencies does not suggest that Canadian federalism ultimately has been a failure. On the contrary, it goes to show that its institutions and mechanisms were flexible enough to hold an impossible country together. The most serious test of this flexibility since the 1930s came in the early 1980s when the Liberal prime minister, Pierre Trudeau, emboldened by his sudden and unexpected resurrection from retirement, forced a decision on constitutional patriation.

The pieces of a constitutional puzzle were all there to be picked up. Deeply contested was the way in which they would be made fit together. Out of western alienation arose the demand that the equality of all provinces finally had to be secured. Quebec nationalism conversely brought to the table the conviction that the survival of a Francophone province required asymmetry. Atlantic Canada worried about a continued commitment to social solidarity. However different and even antagonistic their positions, all participants had in common deep-seated suspicions about the political motives of a prime minister who had written that "the state has to decide what the nation should remain,"[172] and for whom the provincialist vision of Canada as a community of communities amounted to a "confederation of shopping centres."[173] Only as an afterthought, this moment of constitutional patriation would also become the moment when Canadian federalism could no longer ignore its neglected and abusive relationship with Indigenous peoples.

171 Hueglin, "Exploring Concepts," 24.

172 Pierre Elliott Trudeau, *Federalism and the French Canadians* (1968; repr., Toronto: Macmillan, 1977), 190.

173 Cited in Stephen Clarkson and Christina McCall, *Trudeau and Our Times,* vol. 1, *The Magnificent Obsession* (Toronto: McClelland and Stewart, 1990), 276–7.

Chapter Seven

Patriation and the Constitution Act, 1982

On November 2, 1981, Canada's first ministers assembled at Ottawa's old railway station turned conference centre to negotiate the first comprehensive constitutional change package since Confederation. It was a political spectacle indelibly etched into the memory of those who watched it. In front of television cameras with national and provincial flags on full display, the prime minister and provincial premiers gave the impression that they were out to demonstrate how accurate Richard Simeon's earlier characterization had been of Canadian federalism as "federal–provincial diplomacy."[1]

The eventual outcome was the Constitution Act, 1982. It accomplished what was called "patriation" because it brought the constitution "home" in that it contained a homegrown – that is, domestic – constitutional amendment formula, which finally ended Canada's legal dependency on Britain. It also gave Canadians a Charter of Rights and Freedoms, it strengthened provincial rights and control over natural resources, it made fiscal equalization a federal constitutional obligation, and, as a post-conference add-on, it recognized "existing" Indigenous treaty rights. It would appear to be, in other words, after the critical turning point following the crisis of the 1930s, the second such turning point in Canadian federalism since Confederation.

1 Richard Simeon, *Federal–Provincial Diplomacy: The Making of Recent Policy in Canada* (Toronto: University of Toronto Press, 2006).

Contrary to the earlier and mostly non-constitutional transformation of Canadian federalism in the aftermath of the Great Depression, however, the constitutional settlement of 1982 did not lead to a significant realignment of powers. This was a particular affront to Quebec insofar as promises of a new federalism arguably had contributed to the defeat of the 1980 referendum on sovereignty-association. As Daniel Latouche put it at the time: "Now we know. There will be no 'New Canada.'"[2]

The Long Road to Patriation

The patriation saga properly begins with Confederation in 1867.[3] The British North America (BNA) Act was a British statute. It provided the new Dominion of Canada with a legal template for self-governance, but it did not exactly make it a sovereign country. The final power over amendments as well as interpretation of the BNA Act would remain with the government in Westminster. Propositions to end this colonial state of affairs first surfaced during the 1920s. However, an intergovernmental conference in 1927 ended without agreement on a domestic amendment formula. At that time, it is worth noting, the insistence that Confederation had been a compact among provinces and constitutional amendments therefore required unanimity came from Ontario rather than Quebec. The federal government in turn argued that except for matters of language and religion, a two-thirds majority would suffice. Thus, in the absence of agreement on a domestic constitutional amendment formula, when the British government granted sovereignty to all its Dominions by means of the 1931 Statute of Westminster, a "special Canadian codicil" excluded from this grant the power to amend the BNA Act.[4]

The question of an acceptable domestic amendment formula resurfaced after World War II. By then, Canadian federalism had taken the path of social policy power sharing, and the autonomist aspirations of Quebec would become

2 Daniel Latouche, "The Constitutional Misfire of 1982," in *And No One Cheered: Federalism, Democracy and the Constitution Act*, eds. Keith Banting and Richard Simeon (Toronto: Methuen, 1983), 96.

3 One of the best accounts across time is Peter H. Russell, *Constitutional Odyssey: Can Canadians Become a Sovereign People?* (Toronto: University of Toronto Press, 2004); see also Nadia Verrelli, "Searching for an Amendment Formula: The 115-Year Journey," in *Constitutional Amendment in Canada,* ed. Emmett Macfarlane (Toronto: University of Toronto Press, 2016).

4 See Robert Bothwell, Ian Drummond, and John English, *Canada, 1900–1945* (Toronto: University of Toronto Press, 1987), 242–4.

the most serious stumbling block to successful patriation. Constitutional change of any kind would be acceptable only if it provided Quebec with greater social policy autonomy, which would then be safeguarded by the power to veto all future amendments to the contrary. Twice the governments of Canada reached unanimous agreement on a new and domestic constitutional amendment formula, and twice the government of Quebec reneged.

The first formula was the so-called Fulton–Favreau formula of 1964. Named after two federal ministers of justice who had consecutively developed it, constitutional amendment would require unanimous consent for all matters related to the division of powers as well as to the use of the English and French language. Most other matters would fall under a 7/50 formula whereby a successful amendment required approval by the federal parliament as well as the consent of two-thirds (seven out of ten) of the provinces representing at least 50 per cent of the Canadian population.[5] Under pressure from nationalist quarters as well as the opposition, the Liberal Lesage government in Quebec withdrew its support two years later. Ironically, the main objection was directed at the unanimous consent requirement, which would have given Quebec its veto power in all but name. As Union Nationale opposition leader Daniel Johnson put it, however, the rigid amendment formula would turn out to be a "straightjacket" (*camisole de force*) preventing Quebec from achieving in the future the kind of constitutional changes its nationalist ambitions desired.[6]

The so-called Victoria Charter of 1971 was a much broader and more ambitious project. It was very much the brainchild of Pierre Trudeau, who had descended upon Ottawa in order to put his stamp and vision on Canadian federalism, first as justice minister in 1967, and then as prime minister a year later. Trudeau aimed at what he saw as wholesale constitutional modernization, which apart from a domestic amendment formula first and foremost included a bill of rights. What Canada's first ministers eventually came up with was a complex package of concessions and compromises, 61 articles in 10 parts touching on everything from individual and language rights to parliamentary and electoral procedures to regional equalization to Supreme Court appointments to annual First Ministers' Meetings.[7]

The crucial parts of the agreement, however, pertained to the amendment formula and to social policy. The amendment formula adopted a regional pattern

5 Russell, *Constitutional Odyssey*, 72.

6 Cited in ibid., 74.

7 See Simeon, *Federal–Provincial Diplomacy*, 118–20.

somewhat similar to the distribution of senate seats in the federal legislature: Ontario and Quebec would each have a veto, two Atlantic provinces would have a veto, and so would two of the western provinces representing at least 50 per cent of the region's population. As first suggested by the Liberal Bourassa government of Quebec, modified social policy power provisions would focus on Section 94a of the BNA Act, which had established concurrent pension powers under provincial paramountcy in 1951. The Victoria Charter added family, youth, and occupational allowances to this provincial primacy provision, but it fell short of including other policy fields that had been on Quebec's wish list, unemployment insurance in particular.[8]

Upon departure from Victoria, and aware of the fact that the agreement had gone as far as it possibly could, everyone was given 10 days to either accept or reject the deal without further discussion. This so-called "ultimatum," together with the widely perceived insufficiency of the social policy power provisions, caused outrage in Quebec. Newspaper advertisements proclaimed that "the days of conscription have returned." Opposition parties, labour unions, and the entire spectrum of nationalist groupings all were of one mind: rejection. After seven days, Bourassa complied.[9]

The constitutional debate would heat up again, particularly in English Canada, when the provincial Parti Québécois victory in 1976 seemed to pose the alternative of either successful patriation or separation.[10] After several rounds of intergovernmental negotiations failed to produce an agreement, Trudeau decided to up the ante by declaring on October 2, 1980, and on national television that he would proceed unilaterally, seeking approval from London for a constitutional change package without provincial consent.[11] Four days later, he followed suit with a parliamentary resolution outlining his plans. This set in motion a political drama that would captivate Canada for 13 months until the final showdown in November of the following year.[12]

8 Ibid., 116, 119.

9 Ibid., 120–1.

10 See Russell, *Constitutional Odyssey*, 98–106.

11 Trudeau had already told the premiers in 1976 that he thought unilateral action was an option; see J. Peter Meekison, "Introduction," in *Constitutional Patriation: The Lougheed-Lévesque Correspondence*, ed. J. Peter Meekison (Kingston: Institute of Intergovernmental Relations, 1999), 3.

12 On the following, see ibid., 1–10; and Russell, *Constitutional* Odyssey, 107–26. The most detailed account is Stephen Clarkson and Christina McCall, *Trudeau and Our Times*, vol. 1, *The Magnificent Obsession* (Toronto: McClelland and Stewart, 1991), 274–386.

The moment seemed opportune. The prime minister was riding high on his unexpected re-election, the Quebec Premier René Lévesque seemed weakened by the lost referendum, and according to the polls, Canadians liked the idea of an individual rights charter. Trudeau's package, with one exception, contained all the elements of constitutional change that were already familiar to everyone. Apart from the Charter, there would be a commitment to federal fiscal equalization, and the amendment formula would be based on the Victoria Charter with its provision of regional vetoes. The novelty was that such vetoes could be overridden by a subsequent national referendum.

If the individual rights charter mainly was an attack on Quebec's collective language legislation, the suggestion of a constitutional referendum overriding provincial veto powers was nothing less than a direct democratic – or populist – attack on all provinces. But it was the outrage over Trudeau's unilateralism that led to a concerted provincial counterattack. During a mid-October meeting in Toronto, only two provinces, Ontario and New Brunswick, supported Trudeau or at least stayed on the sidelines. The other eight provinces, soon to be dubbed the Gang of Eight, agreed on a triple strategy: They would challenge the constitutionality of unilateral federal action before the courts; they would propose their own plan for constitutional patriation; and they would try to convince the UK not to approve any request for constitutional change unless it came with federal–provincial agreement.

Provincial intervention in London was successful. In November 1980, the British Select Committee on Foreign Affairs decided to "inquire into the role of the United Kingdom regarding Canadian constitutional reform."[13] In January 1981, it released its report, the so-called Kershaw Report, named after the committee chair. The report held that "bearing in mind the federal character of the Canadian constitutional system," a Canadian constitutional patriation request should only be granted if it was supported by "as sufficient a level and distribution of Provincial concurrence" as the Canadians would require under the "least demanding of the formulae" put forward for their own post-patriation amendments.[14] It also affirmed that a patriated domestic constitution would not release the federal government from the Crown's treaty obligations to Indigenous peoples.[15] Even though dismissive of the report as an anachronistic act of imperial

13 Ronald J. Zukowsky, *Intergovernmental Relations in Canada: The Year in Review 1980* (Kingston: Institute of Intergovernmental Relations, 1981), 116.

14 Cited in ibid., 117.

15 Verelli, "Searching for an Amendment Formula," 34–5.

meddling in Canadian affairs, Trudeau was put on notice that he could not count on automatic support for his patriation plans.

The Gang of Eight also succeeded in agreeing on a patriation plan of its own. Unsurprisingly, there would be no Charter, and other controversial items, such as western calls for senate reform and Quebec's demands for wholesale power decentralization, were left aside. But there was agreement on an amendment formula, which was all the more remarkable since the two most powerful leaders of the group had been at opposite ends of the constitutional debate. While Peter Lougheed, the Conservative premier of Alberta, represented the western view of Confederation as a union of equal provinces, which allowed for an amendment formula based on some form of qualified majority rule, Quebec's René Lévesque obviously adhered to the view of Confederation as a compact of two nations, which in turn made a Quebec veto over constitutional amendments mandatory.

The eight provinces worked on a compromise. The 7/50 Fulton–Favreau formula would apply to most constitutional amendments. This meant that Lévesque would have to depart from Quebec's historical insistence on a veto. In order to make the 7/50 formula more palatable for Quebec, it included a provision according to which a two-thirds majority of a provincial legislature could opt out, with fiscal compensation, from an amendment affecting the division of powers. Because Lévesque had meanwhile called a provincial election for April 13, 1981, the premiers agreed to delay signing the agreement until after that date. Strengthened by a majority victory, the combative Quebec premier returned with last-minute demands. In order to save the agreement, the other premiers agreed that opting out would only require a simple rather than two-thirds majority in a provincial legislature. Publicly signed on April 16, 1981, in a cloakroom of the Château Laurier hotel in Ottawa, the agreement came to be known as the Cloakroom Agreement.

Finally, the Gang of Eight also secured success before the courts. The plan was that three provinces, Manitoba, Quebec, and Newfoundland, would ask their courts of appeal for a reference ruling on the constitutionality of unilateral federal action, which they did. Two courts, in Manitoba and Quebec, ruled in favour of the federal position. The Newfoundland court ruled in favour of the provinces. Trudeau agreed to delay final passage of his parliamentary resolution until the Supreme Court of Canada (SCC) had made the final ruling. With excited clusters of people gathered outside the Supreme Court building since the early morning hours, that ruling came on September 28, 1981. For the first time ever, the nine judges, appropriately attired in their scarlet robes for the occasion, rendered their decision on national television.

In fact, they rendered two decisions. By a seven to two majority, they held that "there is no legal requirement for provincial agreement to amendment of the Constitution." By a majority of six to three, however, they also concluded that proceeding with constitutional patriation "without such agreement would be unconstitutional in the conventional sense." In addition, the court elaborated that satisfying constitutional convention would require a "substantial measure of provincial consent." Yet while pointing out that the federal government's support by only two provinces certainly was not substantial by any measure, the court left it "for the political actors, not this Court, to determine the degree of provincial consent required."[16]

Far from speaking with a "forked tongue,"[17] the SCC rendered what can only be judged as a "political master stroke."[18] It first stated the obvious: The BNA Act does not contain any legal requirement for provincial consent on a federal resolution aiming at constitutional change when the power of approval still lies with the British government. Second, however, by acknowledging such a provincial consent requirement as a constitutional convention, the court provided a powerful affirmation of the federal principle: Neither order of government ought to be able to make unilateral decisions affecting the powers of the other. And playing the ball back to the political actors, finally, was not a cop-out but an admission of the limits of judicial power: It can overrule violations of the law but it cannot prescribe political behaviour under the law.

Even though he was convinced he had been given the legal right for unilateral action, and that Margaret Thatcher, the Conservative prime minister of the United Kingdom, would eventually let him have his way, the SCC ruling put Trudeau under political pressure to convene another and final constitutional conference for November 2, 1981. Although nobody dared say it aloud, the SCC ruling also meant that unanimity was no longer required, and an agreement without Quebec had come within the realm of possibility.[19]

What exactly happened during those four November days that followed, and for what reasons, has been told many times and in many different versions. For unrepentant defenders of a strong federal state, unbridled provincialism "triumphed" over national unity.[20] For Anglophone provincialists, it was a "historic"

16 *Re: Resolution to Amend the Constitution* [1981] 1 SCR 753.

17 Russell, *Constitutional Odyssey*, 118.

18 Clarkson and McCall, *Trudeau*, 354.

19 See Richard Simeon and Ian Robinson, *State, Society, and the Development of Canadian Federalism* (Toronto: University of Toronto Press, 1990), 278.

20 Garth Stevenson, *Unfulfilled Union: Canadian Federalism and National Unity* (Montreal: McGill-Queen's University Press, 2009), 258.

compromise marred only by "Quebec's unwillingness to sign."[21] For Quebec nationalists, it was a "major assault on Quebec's vision of federalism."[22]

For two days, the conference appeared destined for failure yet again as neither the prime minister nor the Gang of Eight would budge. Then, on the third day, November 4, 1981, the united front of the Gang of Eight began to show cracks. The Anglophone premiers felt betrayed when Trudeau reintroduced the idea of a referendum and Lévesque appeared to concur, even though the eight premiers previously had agreed to reject it. Lévesque, in turn, felt isolated when the NDP premier of Saskatchewan, Allan Blakeney, appeared to be towing Trudeau's line by presenting a new amendment formula proposal that neither gave Quebec a veto nor contained an opting-out provision. Lévesque wanted to end the conference without agreement right there and then. The other premiers wanted to rethink one more time.

In the evening of November 4, 1981, with Trudeau back in his residence and Lévesque ensconced in his hotel on the Quebec side of the Ottawa River, the attorney general of Ontario, Roy McMurtry, the attorney general of Saskatchewan, Roy Romanow, and the attorney general and justice minister of Canada, Jean Chrétien, worked out a new compromise package the elements of which had in fact all been proposed and discussed previously. In essence, the Anglophone premiers would get provincial equality by the adoption of the 7/50 formula for amendment; Quebec would get the opting-out provision, albeit without fiscal compensation; Trudeau would get his Charter, including minority language rights; concerns about Charter rights infringing upon provincial jurisdiction would be addressed by a so-called notwithstanding clause, whereby a provincial legislature could override certain Charter provisions; and there would be no referendum.

Because the agreement was concocted in the kitchen of the conference centre, it came to be known as the Kitchen Accord. And because everyone except the Quebec premier was kept up to date about what transpired in the kitchen conference, the night from November 4 to November 5, 1981, came to be known as the Night of the Long Knives.

During the evening, Trudeau was informed about the impending breakthrough. Unwilling to give up the idea of a referendum, he balked until the Conservative premier of Ontario, Bill Davis, threatened to withdraw

21 Meekison, "Introduction," 9–10.

22 Alain-G. Gagnon, "Québec–Canada's Constitutional Dossier," in *Québec: State and Society*, ed. Alain-G. Gagnon (Peterborough: Broadview Press, 2004), 139.

his long-standing loyal support for the prime minister. The next morning, Trudeau then insisted on modifications to the notwithstanding clause, which the Anglophone premiers accepted: in particular, it would not apply to minority language rights, and its invocation by a provincial legislature would have to be renewed after five years or lapse. Trudeau also insisted that the question of Indigenous rights, entirely abandoned during the negotiations, would be put on the agenda of another constitutional conference in the near future. Nine provincial premiers and the prime minister signed off on the modified Kitchen Accord. The Quebec delegation was already on its way back to Quebec City.

Before the final resolution was introduced to the Canadian parliament, the federal government and provinces agreed on two more modifications, hoping – in vain – that they might be sufficient to bring Quebec back into the constitutional fold. First, fiscal compensation was added to the opting-out provision, but only for matters of education and culture and not for much costlier social programs. Second, the right to have their children educated in English under the minority language provisions of the Charter would in Quebec only apply to citizens already educated in English in Canada, but not to immigrants.

Finally, under pressure from women's and Indigenous organizations, and with considerable support from the general public, two further changes were made before the final resolution was taken to London. Sexual equality was added to the list of Charter provisions to which the notwithstanding clause would not apply, and the recognition of "existing" Indigenous rights was added to the package. London gave its approval, and on April 17, 1982, in Ottawa and with Trudeau by her side, Queen Elizabeth II signed the Proclamation of the Constitution Act, 1982. Canada finally had become a fully sovereign country.

Fiscal equalization had already been a long-standing practice (see Chapter 5). The new Section 92A added to what would henceforth be called the Constitution Act, 1867, strengthened the regulatory and taxing power of the resource-owning provinces and was therefore celebrated as a major western victory because it was the only formal change in the division of powers contained in the final settlement.[23] But it did not dramatically change the existing power equation as the federal government retained paramountcy over what in economic terms is surely one of the most crucial aspects of natural resource management: export beyond provincial boundaries (Section 92A(3)). The more noteworthy

23 See J. Peter Meekison, Roy J. Romanow, and William D. Moull, *Origins and Meaning of 92A: The 1982 Constitutional Amendment on Resources* (Montreal: The Institute for Research on Public Policy, 1985).

changes pertained to amendment, the Charter of Rights and Freedoms, and Indigenous rights.

Amendment

The question of constitutional amendment in a federal system is a difficult one, and for good reason. Federal constitutions are foundational contracts about how to divide and share powers. In principle, any change to such a contract should require the approval of all constituent members of the federation. This is still so in the case of the European Union, which remains confederal in that unanimity of all member-states is required for treaty changes. In the established federal states, however, as pioneered by the Americans, some super majority is deemed sufficient to amend the constitution.[24] This super majority requirement is meant to balance autonomy and interdependence. On the one hand, the division of powers in a federation ought not be altered without substantive agreement by its members. On the other hand, the common bond of union ought to be strong enough so that individual members will tolerate the collective will of a super majority.

In Canada, the amendment issue is complicated by cultural asymmetry. Under the assumption that the collective will of nine Anglophone provinces may be fundamentally different from that of the one and only Francophone province, a balance of autonomy and interdependence cannot be achieved. The autonomy of Quebec, in other words, can only be safeguarded sufficiently by unanimity or, in other words again, by a Quebec veto. This conundrum explains both why it took the governments of Canada so long to find a domestic amendment formula and why in the end it was Quebec alone refusing to sign on. It also explains why, unique among all modern federations, Canada, in Part V of the Constitution Act, 1982, adopted not just one but five different constitutional amendment procedures. And because, as we shall see, the provinces have a powerful direct role to play in all but one of these procedures, the senate has been given only a suspensive veto, which parliament can override after 180 days.[25]

The first two of these constitutional amendment procedures are those governing all and any changes to the institutional and power relationship between

24 On the comparative dimension of the amendment question, see Thomas O. Hueglin and Alan Fenna, *Comparative Federalism: A Systematic Inquiry* (Toronto: University of Toronto Press, 2015), 275–307.

25 The Constitution Acts, 1867 and 1982, are available online at http://lois.justice.gc.ca/eng/Const/index.html.

the two orders of government. In other words, they are the ones primarily pertaining to federalism.

First, there is the general 7/50 procedure requiring approving resolutions of the federal House of Commons, the senate, and two-thirds (seven) of the provincial legislatures representing at least 50 per cent of the Canadian population (Section 38). If such an amendment "derogates" from provincial powers, the resolutions have to be supported by a majority of members in the house, senate, and the respective provincial assemblies. By majority of members also, a provincial legislature may declare "dissent" and opt out from an amendment. In the case of opting out from "education and other cultural matters," a dissenting province will receive "reasonable" fiscal compensation (Section 40). For obvious reasons, some matters are specifically excluded from the opting-out provision (Section 42). They include the principles of "proportionate" representation of the provinces in the House of Commons, senate powers, and the method of selecting senators.

Second, there is a unanimity procedure that requires approving resolutions in the House of Commons, the senate, and all provincial legislatures (Section 41). Matters specified under this procedure include Canada's link to the monarchy, a reduction in the number of provincial members in the House of Commons below the number of senators accorded to that province, the use of the English or French language (as specified in the Charter; see below), the composition of the Supreme Court, and amendment of the amendment procedure(s).

Right from the beginning, skepticism abounded as to whether these two procedures were of any practical use. As the high thresholds of approval would make Canada's constitution all but "unamendable," the only gain might therefore lie in the "satisfaction of psychic needs by giving Canadians the right to amend their own constitution."[26] And indeed, the 7/50 procedure has been used successfully only once, in 1983, for an amendment strengthening Indigenous rights to which the governments had already committed in principle at the November 1981 conference (see below). Achieving further constitutional change via unanimity was in turn attempted twice, and twice it failed (the Meech Lake Accord in 1987, and the Charlottetown Accord in 1992; see Chapter 8).

More successful, however, has been a third constitutional amendment procedure, which might be called a bilateral procedure because it involves only the federal government and one or several (but not all) of the provinces (Section 43). It requires approving resolutions by the House of Commons, the senate, and by

26 Richard J. Van Loon and Michael S. Whittington, *The Canadian Political System: Environment, Structure, and Process* (Toronto: McGraw-Hill Ryerson, 1984), 202.

the legislatures of the provinces to which the amendment applies. Provisions specified under this procedure include interprovincial boundary changes and changes to the use of the English or French language within a province. More generally, however, this amendment procedure can be applied to all provisions concerning individual provinces as entrenched either in the Constitution Acts, 1867 and 1982, or in the acts by which new provinces were admitted to the federation after 1867, which are part of the overall constitutional order.[27]

The bilateral, "special arrangements,"[28] or "some-but-not-all-provinces"[29] procedure has been more successful for two reasons: First, there are only two parties to the process, the federal government and the province(s) interested in the change; and second, whatever change is achieved does not pertain to federalism in that it would not change the division of powers. A "meaningful number" of constitutional amendments have been accomplished under this bilateral procedure.[30] Some of these amendments, such as the one replacing federal ferry services to Prince Edward Island with a bridge (1993), were only commonsensical. Others, such as ending the denominational school system in Newfoundland as well as Quebec (1997), or establishing status equality between the English and French linguistic communities in New Brunswick (1993), touched on some of the fundamental issues upon which Confederation had been built. However, since the impact of the amendments would not extend beyond the boundaries of the affected provinces, Section 43 has been accepted by governments and courts as giving legitimate expression to provincial diversity under the common constitutional bond.[31]

The fourth constitutional procedure allows the Parliament of Canada to change unilaterally constitutional provisions "in relation to the executive government of Canada or the Senate and House of Commons" (Section 44). While this procedure would appear straightforward in that it allows the federal government to change constitutional provisions pertaining only to its own operation, it has caused some controversy.

In 2006, Conservative Prime Minister Stephen Harper had come to power with a strong mandate to address long-standing western grievances about the

27 See Patrick Monahan, *Constitutional Law* (Toronto: Irwin Law, 2002), 179–80.

28 Ibid., 201.

29 Peter W. Hogg, *Constitutional Law of Canada* (Toronto: Carswell, 1998), 85.

30 Dwight Newman, "Understanding the Section 43 Bilateral Amending Formula," in Macfarlane, *Constitutional Amendment in Canada,* 147.

31 Ibid., 151.

undemocratic nature of the Canadian senate. With provincial consent on senate reform nowhere in sight, and endowed with a parliamentary majority since 2011, Harper asked the SCC whether some measure of senate reform might be achieved unilaterally. The crucial question in terms of Section 44 was whether the Parliament of Canada could amend Section 29 of the Constitution Act, 1867, by introducing term limits for senators.

The SCC denied the constitutionality of such a unilateral amendment. The "imposition of fixed senatorial terms," it held, would weaken "the security of tenure" that allowed senators to function as a regional second chamber of sober second legislative thought. Fixed senatorial terms would therefore affect provincial interests "by changing the fundamental nature or role of the Senate" as one of "Canada's foundational political institutions." The intended change to Section 29 of the Constitution Act, 1867, would therefore require the 7/50 general amendment procedure of Section 38.[32]

The decision not only raised questions about the future of senate reform, to which we shall return in Chapter 8, but also created a considerable measure of uncertainty about the ability of the Canadian parliament to make unilateral changes to anything that the court would consider part of the foundational architecture of Canada's federal system.[33] Effectively, Section 44 has only been used for uncontroversial housekeeping measures, such as periodic census-based adjustments of proportional parliamentary representation already granted to parliament previously under Section 52 of the Constitution Act, 1867.

Under the fifth and last constitutional amendment procedure, and with some explicit exception such as the use of French and English, the provinces can "exclusively make laws amending the constitution of the province" (Section 45). What exactly comprises provincial constitutions is not entirely certain, as only British Columbia has a document with the name "constitution" that "specifies the workings of its major institutions."[34] What falls under "provincial constitution" is generally thought to comprise sections of the Constitution Act, 1867, dealing with provincial institutions, such as Part V (Sections 58–90); constitution acts spelling out the conditions of admission into Confederation of other provinces later on; constitutional conventions as unwritten specifications of the mode of

32 *Reference re Senate Reform*, 2014 SCC 32.

33 See Emmett Macfarlane, "The Uncertain Future of Senate Reform," in Macfarlane, *Constitutional Amendment in Canada*.

34 On this and the following, see Emmanuelle Richez, "The Possibilities and Limits of Provincial Constitution-Making Power: The Case of Quebec," in Macfarlane, *Constitutional Amendment in Canada*, 164–70.

governance, such as "responsible government"; and statutory laws prescribing the functioning of governance, such as electoral laws and the like. When provinces – thus far unsuccessfully – have attempted to change their electoral systems, for instance, Section 45 provides the constitutional basis for doing so.

From any comparative perspective, this differentiated set of multilateral, bilateral, and unilateral amendment procedures satisfies one of the fundamental principles of modern federalism according to which the constituent members of a federal union should have significant co-decision powers over constitutional changes, which are understood as changes to the original and foundational agreement to establish and maintain such a union. It does not satisfy, of course, an understanding of federalism as a confederal compact, as has been prevalent among Quebec nationalists in particular.

Charter

As one of Canada's leading democratic theorists once noted, "Canada may be the only country where the primary role of the constitution is to maintain peace between governments."[35] This verdict is a bit unfair insofar as one of the primary roles of constitutions in federal systems is indeed to regulate the power relationship between two orders of government, both democratically elected to represent the interests of their respective constituencies, one national and the other provincial.

Yet the verdict rings true enough in that the original BNA Act was all about how the Dominion government would function in its relationship with the Crown and how the two orders of government would function in relation to one another. The individual rights of people making up the citizenry living under this new federal arrangement were not mentioned at all. In particular, there was no bill of rights of the kind the Americans had already adopted a century earlier.

Change came after the end of World War II. The Saskatchewan CCF government of Tommy Douglas adopted a provincial Bill of Rights 18 months before the United Nations' 1948 Universal Declaration of Human Rights.[36] In 1960, the Conservative government of John Diefenbaker followed suit with a federal Bill of Rights, which he thought would promote the idea of "one Canada," transcend regional identities, and apply to "all, including the poor, the dispossessed, the

35 Reginald Whitaker, "Democracy and the Canadian Constitution," in Banting and Simeon, *And No One Cheered*, 240.

36 Ian Greene, *The Charter of Rights and Freedoms: 30+ Years of Decisions that Shaped Canadian Life* (Toronto: James Lorimer, 2014), 40.

ignored, and the shut-out."[37] By 1975, Alberta and Quebec had adopted similar bills, and most other provinces had at least some form of protective legislation.

Apparently, Diefenbaker had first sought to entrench the federal Bill of Rights in the BNA Act but was unable to secure broad provincial consent for a constitutional amendment to that effect.[38] When Pierre Trudeau resurrected the idea of a constitutional charter, first as federal minister of justice in a 1968 policy paper,[39] he met with similar provincial resistance. That resistance very much had to do with the deeply engrained concept of parliamentary supremacy in the British and, by extension, Canadian political system.

Parliamentary or legislative supremacy in the British tradition goes back to the Glorious Revolution of 1688 when the bourgeois classes represented in parliament wrested absolute power from king and court.[40] For the British, it also meant that the courts would have to remain subservient to the will of parliament. Still today, British resentment of parliamentary subservience to the European Court of Justice has been one of the main arguments for leaving the European Union.

Under the merely statutory federal Bill of Rights, Canadian provinces had little to fear from judicial intrusions into their legislative prerogative since the courts generally respected the concept of parliamentary supremacy and were not prepared to forcefully defend individual rights infringements.[41] Under a constitutionally entrenched charter of rights, however, the Supreme Court of Canada would gain supremacy in the adjudication of such infringements.

What is the big deal, one might ask, since the courts had ruled on the constitutionality of provincial laws and regulations since Confederation? The answer is that while previous adjudication only pertained to the division of powers between the two orders of government, the courts would now be empowered to invalidate laws and regulations well within the provincial power domain if they were deemed to violate Charter rights. Of course, the same would be true for federal laws and regulations. However, at least in the opinion of some, this formal Charter "impartiality" would in practice strengthen national or Canadian values at the expense of provincial diversity.[42] In this way, a constitutionally

37 Cited in ibid, 23.

38 Ibid., 41.

39 Ibid., 57

40 See Christopher Hill, *The Century of Revolution 1603–1714* (New York: Norton, 1980).

41 See again Greene, *The Charter of Rights*, 42–3.

42 See Alan C. Cairns, *Charter versus Federalism: The Dilemma of Constitutional Reform* (Montreal: McGill-Queen's University Press, 1991), 76–7.

entrenched charter of individual rights could be seen as hollowing out the autonomous space given to the provinces under the property and civil rights clause of the old BNA Act.

The Charter of Rights and Freedoms as entrenched in 1982 "guarantees the rights and freedoms set out in it subject only to such reasonable limits prescribed by law as can be demonstrably justified in a free and democratic society" (Section 1). Within these limits, it also contains an explicit supremacy clause according to which "The Constitution of Canada is the supreme law of Canada, and any law that is inconsistent with the provisions of the Constitution is, to the extent of the inconsistency, of no force or effect" (Section 52(1), Constitution Act, 1982). Since the Charter is obviously part of that constitution, its provisions are indeed supreme and invalidate all provincial or federal laws, statutes, or regulations in violation of these provisions.[43]

As for its substantive content, the Canadian Charter of Rights and Freedoms can be regarded as one of the most detailed and extensive rights documents in modern constitutional history. It includes fundamental freedoms (Section 2), democratic rights (Sections 3–5), mobility rights (Section 6), legal rights (Sections 7–15), equality rights (Section 15), official bilingualism at the federal level and in the province of New Brunswick (Sections 16–22), and minority language education rights (Section 23).

Apart from the notwithstanding clause (see below), the Charter's most distinctive feature is Section 15, which stipulates equality before and under the law "without discrimination based on race, national or ethnic origin, colour, religion, sex, age or mental or physical disability." It also states that affirmative action measures for individuals or groups that are disadvantaged by any of these identity markers cannot be construed as discrimination against others. This affirmation of a diversity of collective group rights is a significant extension of conventional individual rights catalogues as first pioneered by the Americans.[44]

The emphasis on social rather than territorial diversity explains both the popularity of the charter idea even before its inception and the fear of provinces that the charter would infringe on their rights of social legislation in the name of intra-provincial uniformity. To assuage these fears, and mainly at the insistence of the three Prairie premiers,[45] the so-called notwithstanding clause was added

43 See Peter W. Hogg, "Supremacy of the Canadian Charter of Rights and Freedoms," *Canadian Bar Review* 61, no. 1 (1983).

44 See Cairns, *Charter versus Federalism*, 80.

45 Stevenson, *Unfulfilled Union*, 258.

to the Charter (Section 33). It allows any Canadian legislature to override certain sections of the Charter by means of a declaration that a particular law or provision enacted by that legislature "shall operate notwithstanding" these respective Charter sections. Overridden in this way can be Section 2 (fundamental freedoms) and Sections 7–15 (legal and equality rights). The override lapses after five years unless it is renewed by another declaration.

An absolute novelty in modern constitutionalism,[46] the idea that in order to pursue its policy objectives a legislature can simply override fundamental freedoms and legal or equality rights was not exactly greeted with enthusiasm by the principled defenders of modern democratic statehood. Rather, it was seen as one of those "undignified compromises" that had cobbled together the new Canadian constitution,[47] and at that a compromise that might nullify the entire meaning of having a charter to begin with.[48] One can also see the notwithstanding clause in a more positive light, however. By "declining to give judges the last word on fundamental rights,"[49] the notwithstanding clause has restored a measure of legislative supremacy. This supremacy, however, is not absolute. It can be invoked only for a period of five years at a time. This periodic review requirement adds a procedural and deliberative element to Canadian federalism.

In practice, until recently[50] Section 33 has been invoked only rarely on matters of political significance and, with one exception, without significant political consequences.[51] The exception came in 1988 when Liberal Quebec Premier Robert Bourassa used Section 33 to uphold Quebec's commercial sign language law after the SCC had ruled it a violation of Section 2 of the Charter (freedom of expression) and therefore unconstitutional.[52] Mainly directed at the predominantly Anglophone business sector in Montreal, the Parti Québécois's

46 See Robert C. Vipond, *Liberty and Community: Canadian Federalism and the Failure of the Constitution* (Albany: State University of New York Press, 1991), 192.

47 Stevenson, *Unfulfilled Union*, 258.

48 Whitaker, "Democracy," 257.

49 Melissa Williams, "Toleration, Canadian-Style: Reflections of a Yankee-Canadian," in *Canadian Political Philosophy*, ed. Ronald Beiner and Wayne Norman (Toronto: Oxford University Press, 2001), 217.

50 See the epilogue at the end of this book.

51 Greene, *The Charter of Rights*, 78–9.

52 See C. Michael MacMillan, "Rights in Conflict: Contemporary Disputes over Language Policy in Quebec," in *Contemporary Quebec: Selected Readings and Commentaries*, ed. Michael D. Behiels and Matthew Hayday (Montreal: McGill-Queen's University Press, 2011).

1977 Charter of the French Language, Bill 101, had decreed that all commercial signs in the province henceforth had to be in French only. The twofold rationale was simple and logical: Francophone Quebecers ought to be able to live their lives in French only, including when they went shopping, and new immigrants were to be visibly reminded that functioning in the province required learning French.

It was only a matter of time before the commercial sign law would be challenged under the new Charter. In its 1988 decision, the SCC as so often delivered a two-sided verdict.[53] On the one hand, it acknowledged that Quebec had a need and a right to protect the French language. On the other hand, it held that French-only signs were not necessary for this protection when bilingual signs would suffice. Under the gun from outraged Quebec nationalists, Bourassa also moved in a twofold way. On the one hand, the new language bill, Bill 178, toned down its language prescriptions: While outside commercial signs would still have to be French only, inside signs could be bilingual as long as French was displayed more prominently. On the other hand, Bourassa did invoke Section 33, the notwithstanding clause, to insulate the new bill from any further court challenges.

For a period of five years, that is. When the override expired in 1993, the Bourassa government elected not to renew it. Instead, it passed yet another language bill, Bill 86, which essentially granted shop owners the right to advertise in a second language of choice even on the outside of their premises, provided that French was twice as prominent than the other language. In part, this was a nod to a damning United Nations report that had found Bill 178 in violation of human rights. To a larger extent, however, it was a sign that the language issue had run its course.

There had been some degree of accommodation for both sides in the end, and the notwithstanding clause had played a crucial and constructive part. Paraphrasing Quebec's minister of education at the time, Claude Ryan, it had given Quebec some time to reconcile its collective aspirations with the liberal democratic principle of individual rights.[54] More generally, the possibility of overriding the courts can be seen as mitigating the legalism inherent in federalism. And the periodic review requirement adds a procedural and deliberative element to Canadian federalism. Pragmatic accommodation wins over abstract righteousness.

The same might be said also with regard to two other Charter provisions. One is mobility rights. In a federal union, it would seem, every citizen

53 *Ford v. Quebec* [1988] 2 SCR 712.

54 MacMillan, "Rights in Conflict," 408.

or permanent resident should have the right to move freely across provincial boundaries and seek employment or business opportunity in any part of the country without discrimination. Section 6(2) explicitly says so. However, subsection (4) allows provinces with unemployment rates above the national average to restrict employment opportunities for non-residents. It was added at the behest of Newfoundland, which wanted to make sure that local residents would be the main beneficiaries of the new jobs expected in the offshore oil fields. While free market purists – or even democrats – might cry foul over this constitutionally sanctioned form of labour market discrimination, it makes sense in the context of a federal system committed to fiscal equalization, because it substitutes transfer payments with taxable local income.

The other pragmatic Charter provision pertains to minority language education rights (Section 23). Language rights were the centrepiece in Pierre Trudeau's vision of a united liberal Canada. Official bilingualism, which his 1969 Official Languages Act had introduced as a federal practice, now became a constitutional right (Sections 16–22).[55] It was then only logical that the English-speaking minority in Quebec and French-speaking minorities in English Canada should have a constitutionally protected right to have their children educated in their mother tongue.

To this effect, and with the usual caveat of "where numbers warrant," the "mother tongue clause" of Section 23(1a) first extends this right to all Canadian citizens, and the "Canada Clause" of Section 23(1b) then extends it to all minority language parents in Canada as long as they received primary education in that language in Canada.

One would think that the "Canada Clause" of subsection 1b is superfluous in light of the fact that it is already contained in the "mother tongue clause" of subsection 1a. Yet the distinction is significant in that it allowed partial accommodation of Quebec's objection to anything but a "Quebec clause" that would extend minority language education rights only to the children of Anglophone parents who had received primary education in English in Quebec.[56] In a last-minute – yet unsuccessful – attempt at bringing Quebec back into the constitutional fold, Trudeau and the Anglophone premiers agreed on a provision whereby the mother tongue clause of Section 23(1a) would only take effect in Quebec after having been authorized by its legislature (Section 59, Constitution Act, 1982). Nobody expected such an authorization ever to be enacted. Quebec,

55 The Charter also constitutionalized official bilingualism in the province of New Brunswick.

56 See Greene, *The Charter of Rights*, 62–3 and 74–5.

in other words, had to live with the Canada Clause but got an exemption from the mother tongue clause.

In its explicit regulation of language and education rights, the Charter of Rights and Freedoms also broke new ground in modern constitutional history.[57] By allowing for asymmetry with regard to minority language education rights, it struck a compromise that was far from undignified. In a bilingual federal union worthy of its name, it seems entirely reasonable that Quebec should provide access to English public schools to all children with at least one parent educated in English "anywhere in Canada."[58] But it appears just as reasonable that Quebec should have the means to protect itself from cultural erosion by limiting English education rights for immigrant citizens.

Indigenous Rights

Thus far in this book, it has been difficult to integrate the history of Canada's Indigenous peoples with that of Canadian federalism because neither the Royal Proclamation of 1763 nor Confederation in 1867 recognized Indigenous rights as autonomous rights in the federal sense as a combination of self-rule and shared rule. The Royal Proclamation protected Indian lands only until "further Pleasure be known." The BNA Act, now the Constitution Act, 1867, subjected the inhabitants of these lands wholly to federal legislative fiat. Through the treaty process of land cessations, Indigenous peoples in Canada gained some rights of self-rule, such as traditional hunting rights, but they were not given any participatory role in the determination of what that meant and to whom it would apply (status Indians under the Indian Act).

The Constitution Act, 1982, was a first significant change in the relationship of Canada's Indigenous peoples and Canadian federalism because it recognized, in Section 35(1), "existing aboriginal and treaty rights," and in Section 35(2) extended these rights to "Indian, Inuit and Métis peoples." Thus far, however, it has remained rather unclear what exactly that means. Under Section 91 and 92 of the Constitution Act, 1867, all past, present, and future rights are lastingly and exclusively distributed among two orders of government, federal and provincial.

57 Paul-André Linteau, René Durocher, and Jean-Claude Robert, *Quebec since the 1930s* (Toronto: James Lorimer, 1991), 552.

58 See José Woehrling, "The Charter of Rights and Freedoms and Its Consequences," in *Contemporary Canadian Federalism: Foundations, Traditions, Institutions*, ed. Alain-G. Gagnon (Toronto: University of Toronto Press, 2009), 230–1.

The recognition of Indigenous rights means that these rights can only exist in addition to those exercised by the two orders of government.

Unless constitutional change would assign to Indigenous peoples some rights in exclusivity, these rights must inevitably lead to concurrence, overlap, and duplication,[59] as is routinely the case in federal–provincial relations as well. Contrary to federal–provincial relations, though, where each order of government has to deal with one other jurisdiction only, Indigenous peoples find themselves caught in between the rights claims of two jurisdictions.[60] In pursuit of their rightful interests, therefore, they are routinely confronted with a game of frisbee federalism, as rights may be challenged by either jurisdiction and obligations tossed back and forth between both.[61]

Despite prevailing ambiguities, the insertion of Section 35 into the Constitution Act, 1982, was a major achievement, and it was not least brought about by persistent Indigenous intervention. Concerns of Indigenous communities over their constitutional status had been on the rise since at least the infamous 1969 White Paper, in which Prime Minister Pierre Trudeau and Indian Affairs Minister Jean Chrétien had proposed to make Indians equal Canadian citizens by repealing the federal government's responsibilities under Section 94(24) of the BNA Act, as well as abolishing all special status provision for Indians, such as the Indian Act and existing treaties. The provision of social services in particular would entirely have been passed to the provinces. Under massive protest, the paper was withdrawn a year later, but Indigenous constitutional activism did not subside and would gradually grow in strength all the way to eventual constitutional patriation in 1982.[62]

When Trudeau introduced his constitutional patriation plans in 1978 with only vague references to Indigenous rights, the National Indian Brotherhood (NIB), forerunner to the Assembly of First Nations (AFN), threatened to intervene in London and ask the queen to block patriation if two basic demands were not met: entrenchment of Aboriginal and treaty rights in the constitution,

59 Patrick Macklem, *Indigenous Difference and the Constitution of Canada* (Toronto: University of Toronto Press, 2001), 176–7.

60 See James S. Frideres and René R. Gadacz, *Aboriginal Peoples in Canada* (Toronto: Pearson Prentice Hall, 2008), 269–70.

61 See Joyce Green, "Self-Determination, Citizenship, and Federalism: Indigenous and Canadian Palimpsest," in *Reconfiguring Aboriginal–State Relations*, ed. Michael Murphy (Montreal: McGill-Queen's University Press, 2005), 334–5.

62 This and the following is mainly based on Doug Saunders, "The Indian Lobby," in Banting and Simeon, *And No One Cheered*; see also Frideres and Gadacz, *Aboriginal Peoples*, 257–60.

and formal participation in the process of constitutional reform. Yet the three main Indigenous organizations – the NIB representing status Indians, the Native Council of Canada (NCC) representing non-status Indians and the Métis, and the Inuit Committee on National Issues (ICNI) representing the Inuit – were only given observer status at two subsequent First Ministers' Meetings, and in substance no more than a promise of "frank discussions" was forthcoming.[63] A large delegation of some 200 Indigenous people did indeed travel to London and, while unable to meet the queen, they nevertheless succeeded in raising national and international awareness of their concerns.

In the meantime, the short-lived Conservative government of Joe Clark had come and gone, and the first Quebec referendum on sovereignty-association had temporarily diverted attention from the constitution. After an April 1980 constitutional conference convened by the NIB and attended by an estimated 376 chiefs as well as 2,000 other Indigenous participants in Ottawa, there appeared to be general agreement that Indigenous rights provisions had to be part of the new constitution.[64] These provisions, however, would be left to a later stage of constitutional reform, and consequently they were omitted from Trudeau's unilateral patriation plans in October 1980.

The Indigenous reaction was swift and angry. From British Columbia, a "constitution express" with 500 Indigenous participants descended upon the nation's capital in November 1980. Shortly thereafter, another NIB–AFN meeting convened in Ottawa with again some 2,000 participants. Presentations by various Indigenous groups and organizations were made before parliament's Joint Committee on the constitution, at the United Nations in New York, and before the British Foreign Affairs Committee.[65]

Finally, the three federal parties and the three national Indigenous organizations, NIB, NCC, and ICNI, agreed on the constitutional entrenchment of "aboriginal and treaty rights of the aboriginal peoples of Canada," which were to include the "Indian, Inuit and Métis peoples." The agreement was concluded on Sunday, January 30, 1980, and lasted one day. On Monday, Indian Affairs Minister Jean Chrétien announced modifications to the effect that the Indigenous rights provisions would be amendable without Indigenous consent. The united Indigenous front collapsed, and the NIB retracted its agreement.[66]

---

63 Ibid., 305.

64 Ibid., 308–9.

65 Ibid., 313.

66 Ibid., 315–16.

Indigenous consent for future constitutional amendments concerning Indigenous rights became firmly entrenched in Indigenous demands, and it was just as firmly rejected by federal and provincial governments as it would have provided Indigenous peoples with de facto constitutional status as a third order of government in the federal system.

Then, finally, came the fateful November 1981 conference. When Trudeau announced the constitutional compromise on November 5, the Indigenous rights section had gone missing. It had not been part of the Gang of Eight's counterproposal to Trudeau's package, and it had not been part of the negotiations during the Night of the Long Knives. General finger pointing ensued. Chrétien said the section had been dropped because the "Indians" had opposed it; Trudeau said that seven premiers had opposed it.[67] Trudeau was closer to the truth. The constitutional entrenchment of Indigenous rights would make it harder for provincial governments to regulate matters such as hunting and fishing and, more ominously, it would strengthen future Indigenous land claims. In other words, the constitutional entrenchment of Indigenous rights would have an impact on provincial power.

Mass protests erupted across the country. In Vancouver, Indigenous people occupied the Museum of Anthropology, and 5,000 Indigenous people protested in front of the Alberta legislature. The federal government indicated its willingness to reinstate the Indigenous rights section, and the premiers eventually came around as well. When Alberta's Peter Lougheed signalled support if "existing" was added to "aboriginal and treaty rights," all the governments minus Quebec were finally in agreement.[68] Yet for future amendments to Section 35, the general 7/50 formula would apply. Canada's Indigenous peoples would not have any participatory role.

In a final attempt at preventing the inevitable, Indigenous organizations in Alberta, Saskatchewan, and British Columbia opposed to the constitutional package took their case to the courts in London, essentially arguing that patriation would deprive their treaty rights from further protection by the British Crown, thus making the Indigenous rights section vulnerable to Canadian repeal without Indigenous consent. Predictably, they lost. Treaty rights had long since become Canada's responsibility, and there was no reason for British judges to assume that the government of Canada would not honour its obligations. A moral victory of sorts came only when the British House of Commons finally debated – and

67 Ibid., 319.

68 Ibid., 321.

approved – the constitutional package, tabled as the "Canada Bill," and 27 out of 30 hours of the debate were spent on "Indian matters."[69] The fight over the constitutional entrenchment of Indigenous rights was over, but the fight over their meaning was only beginning.

In its 1990 precedent-setting *Sparrow* decision, the SCC provided clarification about just how far the protection of "existing" Indigenous rights under Section 35 would reach.[70] At issue were Indigenous fishing rights and the extent to which they were protected from government regulation. The SCC first affirmed that Section 35 applies to "rights in existence when the Constitution Act, 1982, came into effect; it does not revive extinguished rights." Implicitly, the SCC acknowledged in this way that previously existing Indigenous rights may have been extinguished. However, Section 35 protection now demands that the Crown must prove this by demonstrating that there was a "clear and plain intention" to do so. And as later court decisions clarified further, such demonstration is not only required for treaty rights but also for historical or cultural rights when no such treaties exist.[71]

The SCC then made a crucial distinction between "existing rights" and their "exercise."[72] The constitutional supremacy clause of Section 52 of the Constitution Act, 1982, it declared, does not shield existing Indigenous rights from government legislation or regulation. Government policy can regulate the exercise of Indigenous rights. The purpose of Section 35 is only "to demand the justification of any government regulation that infringes upon or denies aboriginal rights." As later court decisions elaborated, such justification may extend to almost the entire range of government objectives serving the interests of the "broader community as a whole," including environmental protection, conservation, and "general economic development."[73]

Widely celebrated for its affirmation of existing Indigenous rights as constitutionally protected rights as intended by Section 35, critics found little to laude in the *Sparrow* decision. Instead of taking Section 35 as an obligation to establish Indigenous rights as co-equal to those of the governments of Canada, the SCC interpreted it as the continuation of colonialism as first established in the

69 Ibid., 321–4.

70 *R. v. Sparrow*, [1990] 1 SCR 1075.

71 See Diana Ginn, "Indian Hunting Rights: *Dick v. R.*, *Jack and Charlie v. R.* and *Simon v. R.*," *McGill Law Journal* 31 (1986).

72 *R. v. Sparrow*.

73 Macklem, *Indigenous Difference*, 186–9.

Royal Proclamation of 1763.[74] The Royal Proclamation guaranteed Indigenous rights only until "further Pleasure be known." By distinguishing the exercise of Indigenous rights from their existence, and by making this exercise subservient to however-justified government infringement possibly amounting to outright denial, the Royal Proclamation's reservation of the Crown's ultimate extinguishment right had crept back into constitutional adjudication through the regulatory back door, so to speak.

In terms of federalism, Indigenous peoples in Canada remain caught in between Section 91(24) of the Constitution Act, 1867, according to the federal government exclusive power over "Indians, and Lands reserved for the Indians," and Section 92 assigning to the provinces a broad range of powers including healthcare, social services, and education in particular.[75] Federal governments have maintained in principle that Section 91(24) only gives them jurisdiction over Indigenous peoples but contains no obligation to exercise that jurisdiction. And in practice, federal governments have assumed responsibility for status Indians living on-reserve only. Provincial governments in turn have limited the provision of services to Indigenous people to urban and off-reserve areas.

Both orders of government have at times shirked their responsibilities, with provincial governments claiming that Section 91(24) means that the federal government is responsible for the entire range of services for Indigenous peoples, and the federal government insisting that the provinces are obligated to provide all provincial residents with a full range of services. Jurisdictional squabbles of this kind have doubtlessly contributed to Indigenous underfunding (see Chapter 5) as both orders of government have at times engaged in a game of "fiscal offloading."[76]

A case in point is Section 88 of the Indian Act. Added in 1951, it stipulates that all provincial laws are "applicable to and in respect of Indians in the province" (including on-reserve Indians) as long as these laws are "general" (i.e., pertaining to all provincial residents and not just singling out Indians, which only the federal government can do under its exclusive Section 91(24) powers) and as long as they do not contravene the terms of an existing treaty or a federal government act.[77] While

74 Menno Boldt, *Surviving as Indians: The Challenge of Self-Government* (Toronto: University of Toronto Press, 1993), 32–7.

75 On this and the following, see Government of Canada, "Volume Four: Perspectives and Realities," *Report of the Royal Commission on Aboriginal Peoples,* 1996, 400–6.

76 Ibid., 403.

77 The text of the Indian Act is available at http://laws-lois.justice.gc.ca/eng/acts/I-5/index.html.

clarifying how general provincial laws would also apply on reserves, a main purpose of Section 88 doubtlessly was to assign to the provinces the role of "primary delivery agent for reserve residents," including the responsibility "to pay part of the cost."[78]

One might in principle distinguish between a primary federal responsibility for matters of "aboriginality" – that is to say, support for whatever is necessary to maintain and strengthen the identity and life chances of Indigenous peoples as collectivities – and a primary provincial responsibility for providing "equity of services" to all provincial residents regardless of cultural, ethnic, or religious origin.[79] In practice today, both orders of government share in providing services to Indigenous peoples both on-reserve and off-reserve, although jurisdictional and fiscal squabbles continue.

Prior to 1982, the governments of Canada could play the game of Indigenous frisbee federalism almost with impunity. And it was by no means immediately clear what kind of change the affirmation of Indigenous rights in Section 35 of the Constitution Act, 1982, might bring about. For some, the landmark *Sparrow* decision demonstrated that change may not amount to much more than providing Canada's Indigenous peoples with some general constitutional leverage "to inconvenience government designs."[80] Governments can still ride roughshod over Indigenous interests and rights, only now they are required to give justifications for doing so. To be sure, Section 35 of the Constitution Act, 1982, which was mainly a result of sustained political pressure by Indigenous peoples themselves, has made it more difficult for the governments of Canada to shirk their cultural and social obligations toward Indigenous peoples. As we already saw in Chapter 6, however, the game of frisbee federalism is by no means over quite yet.

For others, the *Sparrow* decision seemed to invite a broader interpretation of Section 35. By recognizing fishing rights as cultural rights "worthy of constitutional protection," the SCC opened the door to an interpretation requiring governments to affirm such rights by ensuring their continued practice. Such affirmation in turn may result in legislation to conserve fisheries, but it also points to "certain social, fiscal, and institutional entitlements to Aboriginal people," which

78 Bradford Morse, "Government Obligations, Aboriginal Peoples and Section 91(24) of the *Constitution Act*, 1867," in *Aboriginal Peoples and Government Responsibility: Exploring Federal and Provincial Roles*, ed. David C. Hawkes (Ottawa: Carleton University Press, 1991), 70.

79 Alan Pratt, "Federalism in the Era of Aboriginal Self-Government," in Hawkes, *Aboriginal Peoples and Government Responsibility*, esp. 51–3.

80 Boldt, *Surviving as Indians*, 33.

are deemed "essential to the protection of interests associated with Aboriginal cultural difference." Failure to deliver on such entitlements would constitute "an infringement of Section 35."[81] Such entitlements not only raise the prospects of a right to Indigenous self-government,[82] they also, as the SCC would establish in a later string of decisions, include traditional land rights. We shall return to this issue in Chapter 8.

Flexible Renewal

Most would agree that the process of patriation was flawed. It is not so clear in what way and according to what principles. A general critique was that the process was a form of elite accommodation driven by bargaining politicians.[83] While this critique would dominate the process of constitutional politics for the next decade (see Chapter 8), it is not entirely convincing. Federalism is about power sharing, which inevitably means power sharing between governments representing their respective constituencies, national or provincial.

The process surely was flawed when a final agreement was reached during the Night of the Long Knives,[84] with the government of Quebec neither consulted nor informed and Indigenous rights unceremoniously dropped. While Indigenous rights at least belatedly were added back into the constitutional package, leaving Quebec out of the constitutional consensus was a "dangerous deed."[85] Just how dangerous would become clear in 1995 when the second Quebec referendum brought the country to the brink of separation by a hair's breadth (see again Chapter 8).

In terms of what the Constitution Act, 1982, actually contained, and what it meant for a federal system of divided and shared powers, even the assessments of the most seasoned federalism experts on either side of the cultural divide appear diametrically opposed. For Garth Stevenson (English Canadian), lamenting the state of Canadian federalism as one of "unfulfilled union," the amendment

81 Macklem, *Indigenous Difference*, 248–9.

82 Ibid., 249–52.

83 See Stevenson, *Unfulfilled Union*, 258.

84 This version of events has been challenged as inaccurate by former Newfoundland Premier Brian Peckford; see Postmedia News, "Peckford Rewrites History with New Account of 'Kitchen Accord' to Patriate Constitution," *National Post*, September 12, 2012.

85 Donald Smiley, "A Dangerous Deed: The Constitution Act, 1982," in Banting and Simeon, *And No One Cheered*.

formula with its "bizarre opting out provision" at least "symbolically" suggested that "the provinces were sovereign states whose powers could not be taken from them without their consent."[86] For François Rocher in turn (French Canadian), in search of an ideal form of federalism in which Quebec could find its proper place, the Charter ushered in a regime of "republican unitarism" in which "political sovereignty is exercised only be the general government."[87]

Both of these assessments miss the mark. As I want to argue, the Constitution Act, 1982, provided a basis for flexible renewal in the same way that the Constitution Act, 1867, had provided for a flexible beginning. Back in 1867, the contours of a constitutional order had been crafted that inevitably (even though unintentionally) left room for adjustment. The provincial rights movement of the nineteenth century did not happen against but within that constitutional order. Similarly, and even though overshadowed by the continuation of ultimately unsuccessful constitutional politics for another decade, the constitutional settlement of 1982 allowed for compromises and adjustments that perhaps can only be appreciated now, with the hindsight of almost four decades.

The idea of a charter of individual rights was popular even before it became a reality, and it remained popular across the country, including in Quebec.[88] And why would it not? Every modern democratic federation except Australia has one. Australia's various attempts at constitutional entrenchment of a bill of rights[89] mainly failed for the same reason that Canada's provincial premiers were opposed to the charter idea: the British tradition of parliamentary supremacy. A charter would divert parliamentary power to the judiciary. This may be so, but given the history of discrimination against marginalized groups, including women, a judicial check on the proper use of legislative power, provincial or federal, surely is not a bad thing.

The real question is whether the Charter has unduly changed the balance of power in Canada's federal system. The standard argument is that by protecting individual rights, the Charter promotes a national vision of universal citizenship and tilts the balance of power away from the provinces in their pursuit of

86 Stevenson, *Unfulfilled Union*, 257.

87 François Rocher, "The Quebec–Canada Dynamic or the Negation of the Ideal of Federalism," in Gagnon, *Contemporary Canadian Federalism*, 116.

88 David. E. Smith, *Federalism and the Constitution of Canada* (Toronto: University of Toronto Press, 2010), 129–30.

89 See Paul Kildea, "The Bill of Rights Debate in Australian Political Culture," *Australian Journal of Human Rights* 9, no. 1 (2003).

collective rights. Yet balancing the tension between individual and group rights is what federalism is all about.[90] What sometimes gets overlooked is that this tension exists across provinces and within. The 1988 SCC decision on Quebec's language charter, Bill 101, had it right by acknowledging both a collective right to protect the French language and an individual "freedom to express oneself in the language of one's choice."[91]

The Liberal Bourassa government responded with the inside-outside legislation of Bill 178, which it regarded as a suitable compromise. Just in case, it also invoked Section 33 of the Constitution Act, 1982, the notwithstanding clause, to insulate Bill 178 from further court challenges. In my opinion, the notwithstanding clause offered an ingenious way of dealing with the conundrum of conflicting rights. Effectively, it allowed the province to reclaim parliamentary sovereignty over its collective rights, albeit for a renewable five-year period only. After five years, however, the Bourassa government did not renew the override. Instead it opted to relax the province's language laws further by allowing less prominent English signs outside as well as inside of commercial premises.

Beyond the pivotal role it played in the affirmation and modification of Quebec's language laws, and the perhaps more controversial role it plays now in Quebec's ongoing affirmation of secularism, the notwithstanding clause gives expression to a constitutional rationale of Canadian federalism that is not grounded in a rigid either–or adjudication of rights as is the case in neighbouring American federalism. Instead, it allows and calls for a process of judicial and political deliberation about the boundaries between "fundamental rights and democratic will."[92]

A major comparative study has come to the conclusion that constitutional change, both formal and informal, is a "never-ending task" in federal systems, that this task should not be left to final adjudication by constitutional courts alone, and that federal systems therefore require mechanisms for "continuing constitutional negotiation."[93] The Canadian Charter of Rights and Freedoms, with its notwithstanding clause, has at least taken a step toward constitutionalizing such a mechanism.

---

90 See Daniel J. Elazar, *Exploring Federalism* (Tuscaloosa, AL: The University of Alabama Press, 1987), 91–8.

91 *Ford v. Quebec.*

92 Williams, "Toleration," 217; see also Vipond, *Liberty and Community*, 192–3.

93 Arthur Benz and Felix Knüpling, "Federalism and Constitutional Change: Lessons from Comparisons," in *Changing Federal Constitutions: Lessons from International Comparisons*, eds. Arthur Benz and Felix Knüpling (Opladen: Barbara Budrich, 2012), 411.

The opting-out provision with regard to formal constitutional amendment under the general 7/50 procedure is a different matter. What this provision means is that if a new power over a particular policy field were transferred to the federal government with the consent of seven provinces representing at least 50 per cent of the Canadian population, that federal government might not be able to exercise this power in one or several of the remaining three provinces opposed to the amendment and opting out from the power transfer. For Stevenson, this is a travesty of what he thinks of as "true" federalism because, unless the federal government is "willing to exercise powers in some parts of the country but not in others," it would have to secure consent from every single province – hence Stevenson's aforementioned reference to the provinces as "sovereign states."[94]

The true meaning of federalism is debatable, though, and as we have seen throughout this book so far, nowhere is this more true than in Canada. Opting out, or asymmetrical contracting, are deeply embedded traditions in Canadian federalism, from the Royal Canadian Mounted Police (RCMP), which began to provide provincial police services in some provinces but not others as early as 1906, to the asymmetrical tax rental agreements of the 1950s, to the general contracting- or opting-out provisions for cost-sharing programs in the 1960s. As McRoberts points out, the Liberal government of Lester Pearson negotiated contracting-out provisions with Quebec even in areas of exclusive federal jurisdiction, such as the youth allowance and student loan programs. The crowning achievement was the 1964 intergovernmental agreement by which provincial governments would be able to opt out from the Canada Pension Plan, which led to the establishment of a separate pension plan in Quebec. It was celebrated as a victory by Quebec's Liberal premier Jean Lesage but widely lauded as a triumph of cooperative federalism in English Canada as well.[95]

There is a difference, of course, between contracting out on a statutory basis grounded in intergovernmental agreement and the possibility of opting out from a reallocation of powers enshrined in the constitution by means of amendment. The latter creates formal constitutional asymmetry, repellent to those who continue to believe that a federal union must be based on symmetrical equality of all members. Yet the prospects of such permanently constitutionalized asymmetry would obviously not only suit those who think that the cultural difference between Quebec and the rest of the country requires such

94 Stevenson, *Unfulfilled Union*, 257.

95 Kenneth McRoberts, *Misconceiving Canada: The Struggle for National Unity* (Toronto: Oxford University Press, 1997), 40–1.

asymmetry,[96] but also those who prefer clear "constitutional rules" over the vagaries of intergovernmental accommodation.[97]

However, in an age of political, social, and economic hyper-complexity, the insistence on symmetry and constitutional clarity almost seems quixotic. In fact, one may be allowed to wonder whether some matters may simply have become too complicated to be constitutionalized in a clear-cut fashion.[98] Take, for instance, the expansion of provincial legislative powers over natural resources in Section 92A of the Constitution Act, 1867, which was part of the constitutional package deal of 1982. Section 92A was celebrated in the west as a major constitutional victory: "For the first time since Confederation, a constitutional amendment transferred legislative authority from Parliament to the provinces."[99] Yet at the same time, the addition of Section 92A did not in any way diminish federal powers over the same matter already in existence.[100] The pipeline war of 2018, pitting against each other the constitutional rights of two provinces with conflicting interests, the federal government, and various Indigenous communities, only goes to show that it was no more than an illusion to think that Section 92A would bring energy conflicts to a constitutional end.[101]

Similarly, the iconic constitutionalization of fiscal equalization as a federal commitment to "reasonably comparable levels of public services at reasonably comparable levels of taxation" in Section 36 of the Constitution Act, 1982, did not prevent equalization from becoming a matter of "fairly serious intergovernmental conflicts" during the 2000s,[102] and the meaning of "existing aboriginal and treaty rights" in Section 35 still awaits clarification regarding the "nature and scope" of

---

96 Alain-G. Gagnon, "Taking Stock of Asymmetrical Federalism in an Era of Exacerbated Centralization," in Gagnon, *Contemporary Canadian Federalism*, 267.

97 Alain-G. Gagnon and Raffaele Iacovino, *Federalism, Citizenship, and Quebec: Debating Multinationalism* (Toronto: University of Toronto Press, 2007), 157.

98 Smith, *Federalism and the Constitution*, 126.

99 J. Peter Meekison and Roy J. Romanow, "Western Advocacy and Section 92A of the Constitution," in Meekison, Romanow, and Moull, *Origins and Meaning of Section 92A*, 3.

100 William D. Moull, "The Legal Effect of the Resource Amendment – What's New in Section 92A?" in Meekison, Romanow, and Moull, *Origins and Meaning of Section 92A*, 61.

101 Gary Mason, "The Pipeline War That No Politician Will Win," *Globe and Mail*, February 2, 2018.

102 Daniel Béland et al., *Fiscal Federalism and Equalization Policy in Canada: Political and Economic Dimensions* (Toronto: University of Toronto Press, 2017), 48.

government obligations arising from the affirmation of these rights.[103] It is with regard to these rights, however, that the cautiously optimistic metaphor of flexible renewal does not apply. For Indigenous peoples in Canada, 1982 at best marked a beginning, not a renewal.

Federal constitutions rarely provide clarity. As already discussed in Chapter 1, they are best seen as a set of basic rules structuring the ongoing political process.[104] In light of this, it is misguided to begin a critical assessment of the Constitution Act, 1982, with the assumption that it "should have been the act of constitutional completion."[105]

To be sure, the process was flawed, and mainly so because Quebec was betrayed. The outcome of the process, however, in which Quebec did have a significant hand almost right to the end, in my assessment amounts to a compromise leaving the door open for all participants, Quebec included, to re-engage in an ongoing political process of flexible renewal. Social policy, so dear to Quebec's self-understanding, should have been included in the provision of fiscal compensation regarding constitutional amendments under the general 7/50 procedure. In a new age of slow economic growth, however, a federal appetite for exclusive power over another major social policy program is nowhere in sight.

Patriation was a turning point in Canadian federalism neither because it brought about constitutional completion nor because it amounted to constitutional failure. The pragmatic and flexible provisions with regard to constitutional amendment and the opting-out provision, and the entrenchment of individual rights and freedoms with the temporary override give adequate expression to Canadian complexity and diversity. Exacerbated centralization is nowhere in sight. Instead, the formal Canadian constitutional edifice, comprising the Constitution Acts, 1867 and 1982, give expression to a new kind of "postmodern" federalism for which the old model of a federal state with watertight constitutional rules and divided powers is no longer adequate.[106]

Given the political turmoil that ensued for more than a decade after the constitutional deed was done in 1982, the verdict of flexible constitutional renewal may be surprising. However, it is warranted for two reasons. First, all efforts to

103 Macklem, *Indigenous Difference*, 263.

104 Compare Jonathan A. Rodden, *Hamilton's Paradox: The Promise and Peril of Fiscal Federalism* (Cambridge: Cambridge University Press, 2006), 38, and the discussion in Chapter 1.

105 Smith, *Federalism and the Constitution*, 152.

106 See Peter J. Katzenstein, "Conclusion," in *The Culture of National Security: Norms and Identity in World Politics*, ed. Peter J. Katzenstein (New York: Columbia University Press, 1996), 518 (footnote 48).

better the 1982 deal have failed and the Constitution Act, 1982, therefore, is the constitution Canadians have to live with for the foreseeable future if not indefinitely. Second, what seemed to transpire after the dust settled on that tumultuous decade was the gradual realization that constitutional closure or completion was not to be had. The "true" nature of federalism, if there is such a thing, much more resembles an ongoing process than a final product, especially when there are deep disagreements about the dynamic and direction that process should take. In the following chapter, we shall follow the trajectory of Canadian federalism after 1982 and identify some of the main unresolved and probably unresolvable issues.

CHAPTER EIGHT

THE UNFINISHED BUSINESS OF CANADIAN FEDERALISM

Walking through a blizzard on February 29, 1984, Pierre Trudeau finally decided to call it quits. By no means did this mean that Canada's third-longest-serving prime minister[1] would not continue to loom large in the politics of Canadian federalism. As the opening sentence of an award-winning account of the "Trudeau phenomenon" summed it up six years later: "He haunts us still."[2] Trudeau's most formidable opponent in Quebec, René Lévesque, would be gone a year later, driven into resignation by hardline nationalists in his own party for whom he appeared not separatist enough.

First of all, it was the unfinished business of constitutional politics left behind by Trudeau and Lévesque that would haunt Canadians for another decade. In 1984, the Progressive Conservatives swept the federal election, winning a majority of seats in every region including Quebec. The new prime minister, Brian Mulroney, twice tried to bring about reconciliation with Quebec by means of a new constitutional amendment package negotiated with the provinces, and twice he failed. The Meech Lake Accord of 1987 collapsed because two provinces did not ratify in time. The Charlottetown Accord of 1992 was rejected by the

1 After Mackenzie King and John A. Macdonald.

2 Stephen Clarkson and Christina McCall, *Trudeau and Our Times*, vol. 1, *The Magnificent Obsession* (Toronto: McClelland and Stewart, 1991), 9–10.

people in a referendum. Mulroney was accused of bearing at least some of the blame because he was widely seen as no longer driven by a principled vision of federalism but as a dealmaker at any cost. "We are going to roll the dice" is how he himself explained his approach to last-minute efforts at rescuing the Meech Lake Accord.[3]

The political background for Mulroney's continued constitutional efforts was, of course, the looming spectre of Quebec secession. If constitutional amendment means changing the originally agreed-upon compact creating a federal union, then a member's withdrawal from that union is an extreme form of constitutional amendment. It can be seen as the continuation of constitutional politics by other means. None of the classical federal states have formal provisions for secession.[4] The search for clarity about how Quebec might lawfully secede from the rest of Canada, if it came to that, became a second matter of unfinished business in Canadian federalism.

In the wake of the Meech Lake debacle, Lucien Bouchard, one of Mulroney's key cabinet ministers and a close friend from university days, quit the Conservatives and founded the Bloc Québécois, a political party meant to represent the sovereigntist position in Ottawa by fielding candidates only in Quebec and only for federal elections. At the same time, the Reform Party, a new western conservative protest party under the leadership of Preston Manning, gave expression to western opposition to both Mulroney's introduction of a national Goods and Services Tax (GST) and to the Meech Lake and Charlottetown accords, which the west perceived as preferential and asymmetrical treatment of Quebec.

The rise of these two regional parties set the stage for the October 1993 federal election, the dramatic results of which made analysts wonder whether Canada's political party system was in a process of profound realignment.[5] Deeply unpopular and smelling defeat, Mulroney announced his retirement in February 1993 but stayed on until June, thus leaving his successor, Kim Campbell, precious little time for stepping out of her predecessor's shadow. The result was disastrous. Campbell lost her own seat. The Conservatives were decimated (from 151 to 2 seats), and the New Democratic Party imploded (from 44 to 9 seats). While the

3 Roy MacGregor, "Years Later, 'He Bugs Us Still,'" *Globe and Mail*, April 22, 2018.

4 The quasi-federal European Union was the first to adopt a formal withdrawal procedure in its 2007 Lisbon Treaty, which became the basis of Britain's "Brexit" in 2020.

5 Alain-G. Gagnon and A. Brian Tanguay, "Minor Parties in the Canadian Political System: Origins, Functions, Impact," in *Canadian Parties in Transition*, eds. A. Brian Tanguay and Alain-G. Gagnon (Toronto: Nelson, 1996), 107.

Liberals under Jean Chrétien won a majority government, the Reform Party took 52 seats, all but one in the west, and the Bloc took most of Quebec, 54 out of 75 ridings, an outcome resulting in the peculiar situation that a separatist party became Canada's official opposition with the second-most seats in the federal parliament, all of which came from one province.

A year later, Jacques Parizeau led the Parti Québécois back to power with an electoral promise to hold a second referendum on sovereignty within one year of the election. In case Canada was not willing to negotiate separation on Quebec's terms, Parizeau threatened with a unilateral declaration of independence. As we already know, Parizeau lost that referendum by the narrowest of margins, 49.5 per cent to 50.5 per cent. He was replaced by Bouchard, who declared that there would be another referendum when the conditions for victory were right. Seeing themselves as the only guardians of Canadian unity left in Ottawa, the Liberals set out to make sure this would not happen.

To this effect, Chrétien appointed a pro-federalist political science professor from Quebec, Stéphane Dion, as his new minister of intergovernmental affairs. Dion first sought assurance from the Supreme Court of Canada that unilateral separation of a province from the rest of Canada was unconstitutional, and then crafted a bill empowering the federal legislature to cast judgment upon the clarity of both a future referendum question and the numerical outcome of the referendum. Both outraged Quebec nationalists, but in the end it contributed to ending – at least for now – the most tumultuous chapter of constitutional politics in Canadian federalism.

The Liberals also tried to buy back Quebecers' Canadian loyalty with money. A so-called sponsorship program was established in 1996, dishing out money from a nearly open-ended slush fund to almost any cultural organization or community in Quebec as long as it was willing to fly the Canadian flag in return.[6] A 2003 report by the auditor general of Canada found program irregularities, including disregard for basic rules of parliamentary oversight and accountability.[7] The ensuing sponsorship scandal engulfed the government of Paul Martin, who had taken over from Chrétien in 2003, significantly contributing to Martin's electoral defeat in 2006.

6 See Antonia Maioni, "Showing the Flag – The Origins and Consequences of the Sponsorship Scandal," *Policy Options,* June 1, 2005.

7 Office of the Auditor General of Canada, "2003 November Report of the Auditor General of Canada: Chapter 3: The Sponsorship Program."

It was Martin who had unilaterally cut transfer payments to the provinces in 1995. But then, with federal finances dramatically improved, and perhaps also heeding calls for more cooperation and transparency laid down in the Social Union Framework Agreement (SUFA), Martin had negotiated the 2004 Health Accord with its promise of 10 years of predictable funding (see Chapter 5). And he was the driving force behind the 2005 Kelowna Accord, a series of intergovernmental agreements with Indigenous organizations meant to close the gap of socioeconomic inequality between Indigenous peoples and the rest of Canadians. It appeared as if Canadian federalism was back to its intergovernmental normal.

Not for long, though: The new Conservative prime minister, Stephen Harper, came to power declaring his intent to restore Canadian federalism to its classical form as intended by the British North America (BNA) Act of 1867: a strict separation of powers and only a minimum of intergovernmental cooperation.[8] And indeed, Harper only called two First Ministers' Meetings during his nine years in office, and when the Health Accord ran out in 2014, he short-circuited the intergovernmental negotiation process by replacing it with a new plan unilaterally.

Harper also brought to Ottawa a long-standing western disdain for the Canadian senate, not only because it is government appointed but moreover because the regional appointment formula seriously underrepresents the western provinces. He indicated that his intention was to either reform the senate or, preferably, abolish it altogether. By turning his back on two mechanisms conventionally thought crucial for the functioning of federalism – the informal mechanism of intergovernmental policymaking and the formal mechanism of regional representation in a second legislative chamber at the federal level – Harper reopened a debate about another and third area of unfinished business in Canadian federalism. This is a debate known in Canadian political science as the *intrastate* versus *interstate federalism* debate.

In order to understand this debate, we need to step back for a moment and review some federalism theory. Under the division of powers in federal systems, the governments of the federated entities – provincial governments in the Canadian case – have jurisdiction to make decisions that, notwithstanding externalities, only affect their own citizens. The federal government, on the other hand, has jurisdiction to make decisions that affect all citizens across provincial

---

8 Michael Behiels and Robert Talbot, "Stephen Harper and Canadian Federalism: Theory and Practice, 1987–2011," in *Challenges in Canadian Federalism*, eds. Michael Behiels and François Rocher (Ottawa: Invenire Books, 2011).

boundaries and therefore may also have an impact on provincial governance. For this reason, it is one of the core principles of federalism that the federated entities (provinces) should have some input into central decision making by means of a second or regional legislative chamber at the federal level. This is what is called *intrastate federalism*. The Canadian senate obviously qualifies poorly as such a chamber.

Intergovernmental relations (IGR), especially in the form of what Canadians call executive federalism, constitute a second mechanism of transmitting provincial input into central decision making. The prime minister and provincial premiers meet in so-called First Ministers' Conferences (FMCs) or Meetings (FMMs), either to exchange and coordinate views concerning shared policy concerns or to enter into intergovernmental agreements. This is what is called *interstate federalism*. It was not foreseen by the architects of the classical federal systems because the assumption was that the two orders of government would function independently within their respective spheres of jurisdiction.

As we have already seen in previous chapters, IGR has played a crucial role in Canadian federalism. The senate for the most part has not. The intrastate versus interstate federalism debate in essence is about whether one can be a substitute for or the other. By eschewing both, Harper seemed to favour governance in splendid isolation. His successor, Liberal Prime Minister Justin Trudeau, came to power suggesting improvement on both fronts. Yet while his promise of "sunnier ways" in intergovernmental relations thus far has turned out to be little more than naive optimism, his approach to senate reform contains possibilities of improving its performance as a regional chamber. Overall, however, the role of executive federalism in Canada's all but classical form of federalism remains as much unclear as substantive senate reform seems impossible.

Entirely unresolved as yet remains the question of how to accord Indigenous peoples in Canada equal and self-governing status within or parallel to the federal system. While recent court decisions affirming land rights certainly have made it more difficult to ignore this question altogether, and treaties have established self-governing rights in some important instances, Indigenous inclusion in the intergovernmental decision-making mechanisms and processes that are central to the functioning of Canadian federalism still appears tangential rather than substantial.

Finally, a book on federalism in Canada would be remiss if it did not at least make mention of what might seem a rather far-fetched question – and at that a question an answer to which would go way beyond the scope of this book. This is the question of whether nineteenth-century provincial and territorial boundaries are still adequate containers of regional identity. Embedded in this question is the further question of whether unitary governance in the provinces adequately reflects and represents the south–north urban–rural divide.

Constitutional Politics

Conservative Prime Minister Brian Mulroney had come to power in 1984 with the reputation as a skilled dealmaker and with the promise of achieving constitutional reconciliation with Quebec. His ambition to succeed where Pierre Trudeau had failed – by finding a place for Quebec within the Canadian system of federalism – contributed to the premature political demise of René Lévesque, who took the bait, calling it a *beau risque* (a risk worth taking). Led by Jacques Parizeau, the hardline separatists abandoned Lévesque, who resigned a year later. Lévesque's successor, Pierre-Marc Johnson, lasted only a couple of months as nine years of Parti Québécois rule in Quebec came to an end when Robert Bourassa's Liberals won the December 1985 provincial election.

Bourassa had also campaigned with the promise of seeking constitutional reconciliation,[9] and he lost little time taking the initiative. Five months after the election, his minister of intergovernmental affairs, Gil Rémillard, let the rest of Canada know the five conditions to be met if Quebec was to sign on to the Constitution Act, 1982: (1) explicit recognition of Quebec as a distinct society; (2) increased powers over immigration; (3) limitations on the federal spending power; (4) a veto on constitutional amendments; and (5) participation in the appointment of Supreme Court judges.[10]

Two rounds of intense intergovernmental negotiations later, the so-called Meech Lake Accord was signed by Canada's first ministers in the morning hours of June 3, 1987, after pulling an all-nighter. According to Rémillard, the accord had satisfied all of Quebec's five conditions.[11] The dealmaker Mulroney obviously was pleased as punch. But just how had it become possible to secure the agreement of the premiers of nine provinces who had always been suspicious of Quebec's special treatment in Confederation?

9 See Peter H. Russell, *Constitutional Odyssey: Can Canadians Become a Sovereign People?* (Toronto: University of Toronto Press, 2004), 133.

10 Gil Rémillard, "Quebec's Quest for Survival and Equality via the Meech Lake Accord," in *The Meech Lake Primer: Conflicting Views of the 1987 Constitutional Accord*, ed. Michael D. Behiels (Ottawa: University of Ottawa Press, 1989), 29.

11 Ibid., 30.

The remarkable feat was accomplished by means of making Quebec's asymmetrical demands de facto symmetrical:[12]

- a greater role in matters of immigration would be available to all provinces;
- the spending power would be reined in only insofar as any province could opt out from new cost-sharing programs with compensation;
- more veto power on constitutional amendments would be given to all provinces by extending the list of amendments requiring unanimity to senate reform and the creation of new provinces;
- fiscal compensation would now be available for all opt outs from centralizing amendments, not just education and culture;
- all provincial governments would have a say in Supreme Court appointments; and
- the clause recognizing Quebec as a distinct society would be couched in constitutional duality recognizing that French-speaking Canadians deserved protection outside Quebec as much as English-speaking Canadians deserved protection inside Quebec.

As soon as the contours of the agreement became public, Pierre Trudeau came out of retirement swinging. In two newspapers, Montreal's *La Presse* and the *Toronto Star*, he had a full-page denunciation published: The agreement between a bunch of provincial "snivelers" and a "weakling" of a prime minister would "render the Canadian state totally impotent."[13] Trudeau's outburst was only the beginning of what would quickly become a formidable chorus of opposition. Indigenous leaders rightly criticized not only that had they been entirely left out of the process yet again, but moreover that the new affirmation of constitutional duality left no space for Indigenous inclusion. And women's organizations, like other identity groups recognized under the Charter, feared that their hard-won equality rights might be jeopardized by the distinct society clause.[14]

12 The discussion of the Meech Lake Accord and its aftermath primarily relies on Russell, *Constitutional Odyssey*, 127–53.

13 Pierre Elliott Trudeau, "Say Goodbye to the Dream of One Canada," *Toronto Star*, May 27, 1987.

14 See the relevant chapters in Michael D. Behiels, ed., *The Meech Lake Primer: Conflicting View of the 1987 Constitutional Accord* (Ottawa: University of Ottawa Press, 1989).

In hindsight it is hard to appreciate what all the fuss was about. Neither did the Meech Lake Accord amount to a significant change in the division of powers between the two orders of government, nor did the distinct society clause affirm more than what the rest of Canada had already swallowed as inevitable ever since the beginning of the Quiet Revolution. Even Indigenous complaints were more procedural than substantive, since the accord, while not adding any Indigenous rights, also did not take anything away. Canada's first ministers had even added a clause to this effect.[15] The Meech Lake Accord died not from being fundamentally defective, but from a combination of procedural misfortune combined with hyperbolic constitutional righteousness.

While Pierre Trudeau had still been able to take his 1982 constitutional package to London without any parliamentary involvement back home, the new post-1982 amendment rules required provincial ratification. And since two of the Meech Lake constitutional changes pertaining to the Supreme Court and the amendment formula required unanimous provincial consent, Canada's political leaders not only decided to extend the unanimity rule to the entire accord but also chose the maximum time of three years for ratification to be achieved. This meant that there would inevitably be provincial elections before the June 1990 deadline, with the possibility of new leaders and parties coming to power. These in turn might not be willing to honour the pending agreement made by their predecessors. And that is exactly what happened.

By mid-1988, all but two provinces as well as the federal legislature had ratified the accord. The two holdouts were New Brunswick, where the newly elected Liberal premier, Frank McKenna, demanded further changes, and Manitoba, where the Conservatives under Gary Filmon had taken over from the New Democrats. Filmon was a lukewarm Meech supporter, but his minority government depended on the support of the Liberals, whose leader, Sharon Carstairs, was staunchly opposed to the accord. In an unfortunate coincidence of political manoeuvring, when the Bourassa government in Quebec passed the revised language bill (Bill 178) in December 1988 with the notwithstanding clause attached to it, English Canadian opponents of the accord saw their worst fears about a "distinct" Quebec confirmed and Filmon withdrew ratification from Manitoba's legislative agenda.

Then, in April 1989, the Liberals under Clyde Wells took over from the Conservatives in Newfoundland. Not coincidentally, with Trudeau-acolyte Deborah Coyne as his constitutional adviser, Wells took on the mantle as national defender of constitutional symmetry: equal rights for equal provinces. In April 1990, he rescinded Newfoundland's earlier support for the accord.

15 Russell, *Constitutional Odyssey*, 140.

The rest is history. Since Bourassa had ruled out any further changes to an agreement that Quebec had been first to ratify, McKenna suggested the idea of a companion accord. During a last-minute scramble, Canada's first ministers came up with an agreement promising wide-ranging further constitutional changes in the future meant to accommodate all outstanding grievances, senate reform in particular. Talks with Indigenous peoples about their constitutional status would resume as well.

McKenna had the accord ratified immediately. In order to do the same in time before the deadline, Filmon needed unanimous approval to speed up the legislative process. In one of the great ironies of Canadian history, the lone Indigenous member of the Manitoba legislature, Elijah Harper, holding up his eagle feather with the entire weight of Indigenous Canada behind him, refused to grant that approval. With hours to spare, Mulroney ventured that he would try to have the deadline extended by the Supreme Court if only Newfoundland ratified in time. Wells was offended that Newfoundland should have to act so that Indigenous peoples could be accommodated and had the legislature adjourn without a vote. On June 23, 1990, Meech was dead.

The next day, 200,000 Quebecers marched through the streets of Montreal calling for independence.[16] A month later, the images on national television of armed Mohawk "warriors" confronting police in riot gear – and eventually the Canadian army – during the Oka crisis drove home the lesson that Indigenous rights could no longer be pushed aside so easily.[17] English Canada, or what would now be called the Rest of Canada (ROC), remained deeply divided. This division was perhaps exemplified best by the fact that the Canadian senate, after a forceful and lengthy deposition by Pierre Trudeau during the committee hearings preceding ratification,[18] had refused to give its approval to the accord. As foreseen for constitutional amendments by Section 47 of the Constitution Act, 1982, the Meech Lake Accord had been ratified by the House of Commons only.

Quebec's reaction was swift and merciless.[19] Within barely half a year, in January 1991, the government released the report of the so-called Allaire

16 Ibid., 155.

17 *CBC News: The National,* "Oka Crisis: How It Started," September 24, 2015.

18 Pierre Elliott Trudeau, "Who Speaks for Canada? Defining and Sustaining a National Vision," in Behiels, *The Meech Lake Primer.*

19 The discussion of events leading up to the Charlottetown Accord again primarily relies on Russell, *Constitutional Odyssey,* 154–89; see also the useful overview in Nadia Verelli, "Negotiating the Charlottetown Accord in Canada," in *Changing Federal Constitutions: Lessons from International Comparison,* eds. Arthur Benz and Felix Knüpling (Opladen: Barbara Budrich, 2012), 161–89.

Committee, which had in fact begun to explore post-Meech options even before the accord's final demise. In essence, the Allaire report went back to Lévesque's sovereignty-association option a decade earlier, demanding full sovereignty over most social and economic policy fields within a Canadian economic and military union. At a Liberal Party convention in March 1991, the Bourassa government tried in vain to tone down the aggressively sovereigntist stance. Then, two months later, in March 1991, the multi-party Belanger-Campeau Committee reported. Since it included separatists as well as federalists, the Belanger-Campeau report did not spell out a definite constitutional path or option. Instead, it recommended a two-track path toward Quebec's constitutional future, which two months later, in May 1991, found its way into the Bourassa government's Bill 150:

- Quebec would hold a second referendum on sovereignty during the following year.
- At the same time, a legislative committee would explore whether the ROC might come up with a federalist option worth considering.
- The Bourassa government would no longer participate in the process.
- If an acceptable option was forthcoming, the door was open for a referendum on federalism rather than separation.

This was a formidable challenge, because it did not just come from hard-line nationalists – it had the backing of all major political parties in Quebec. Even more daunting, it was supported by a new and confident Francophone business community. And according to the polls, a whopping 64 per cent of Quebecers now favoured sovereignty over federalism.[20]

The federal government had no choice but to respond. It did so with a flurry of activities meant to demonstrate that it would now act on behalf of the people rather than steer the country toward another deal concocted among government leaders. Canada was on its way to the Charlottetown Accord. A flurry of proposals and recommendations were suggested, adopted, revised, dismissed, and reconsidered. Since the people in the end dismissed the whole package, the substantive details now are of less interest than the process.[21]

20 Verelli, "Negotiating the Charlottetown Accord," 163.

21 See ibid., 166–86.

A commission was set up to hold town hall meetings across the country. At the same time, a parliamentary committee explored alternatives to the 1982 constitutional amendment formula. Indigenous peoples were consulted for once. In an almost desperate attempt at leaving no one out, the federal government announced no less than 28 recommendations for further constitutional change to be studied by yet another parliamentary committee, which would hold five consultative conferences across the country yet again. As a result, the federal government's earlier 28 recommendations were dwindled down to six major proposals. These were then discussed during a round of intergovernmental meetings in which, as Bourassa had made clear from the outset, Quebec did not participate. An FMC, still without Quebec, agreed on a package that it offered to Quebec for consideration. Then, finally, with Bourassa at the table, all of Canada's first ministers began to negotiate what would eventually, on August 28, 1992, become the Charlottetown Accord. After all the inclusive and participatory hoopla, Canada was back to executive deals behind closed doors.

The outcome was a deal with far too many variables, widely criticized as giving something to everyone but not enough to anyone. The provisions on the division of powers, constitutional amendment, Supreme Court appointments, and the much-hated federal spending power received some jiggling and juggling, but in essence the accord did not fundamentally change anything. Yet even though it does not matter anymore, it is worth recalling two of the Charlottetown Accord's more extraordinary provisions and how they would have changed the fabric and operation of Canadian federalism for better or for worse.

One of these was the so-called Canada Clause, meant to make the recognition of Quebec as a distinct society more palatable to the ROC by likewise recognizing everything else thought of as part of Canada's "fundamental characteristics": parliamentary democracy; federalism; Indigenous self-government; French and English language minorities; racial, ethnic, and gender equality and diversity; individual and collective human rights; and the equality in principle of otherwise diverse provinces. The distinctiveness of Quebec was circumscribed as "including a French-speaking majority, a unique culture and a civil law tradition." The Canadian constitution henceforth was to be interpreted "in a manner consistent" with these characteristics. Furthermore, while Quebec's right to preserve and promote its distinctiveness was affirmed, nothing in the Canada Clause would change the division of powers or diminish Indigenous rights.[22]

22 The full text of the Charlottetown Accord is available at https://www.sqrc.gouv.qc.ca/documents/positions-historiques/positions-du-qc/part3/Document27_en.pdf.

On the one hand, the Canada Clause, if adopted, might well have created a judicial nightmare, forcing the courts to find a way of making constitutional interpretation consistent with this smorgasbord of competing and possibly conflicting claims and affirmations. On the other hand, however, one can also appreciate the Canada Clause as a genuine attempt at giving expression to the country's uniquely ambiguous mix of unity and diversity. Call it a postmodern manifesto.[23]

The other extraordinary result of the Charlottetown Accord was agreement on senate reform, which had never been a possibility before and is not likely to become one ever again. At the time, it transpired as a multiple tradeoff, part of a big-time gamble with unsatisfactory and uncertain consequences.[24] Yet again, a closer look at the way in which it came together provides an instructive summation of all the foundational grievances and tensions built into the Canadian federal system that are as inevitable as they are irresolvable.

The western provinces, Alberta in particular, as well as the Atlantic provinces to a lesser extent, had for a long time pushed for a so-called Triple-E senate: an *equal* number of senators per province rather than the regional formula of 1867 under which the two central provinces, Ontario and Quebec, were accorded almost half of all senate seats; provincially *elected* senators instead of appointment by the prime minister; and *effective* powers co-equal to the parliamentary chamber rather than self-imposed legislative restraint because of the lack of political legitimacy attributed to a government-appointed senate.[25] Such a Triple-E senate, so went the thinking, would address or at least ameliorate the twin grievances of Canada's peripheral provinces, the domination of politics by central Canadian interests, and what was perceived as the privileged status of Quebec in particular.

Since the failure of the Meech Lake Accord could be attributed at least in part to its one-sided focus on Quebec's grievances, it was inevitable that the Charlottetown approach would have to cast a much wider net of political accommodation. The principal tradeoff now was recognition of Quebec as a distinct society in return for some form of a Triple-E senate with six senators per province

---

23 Similarly, see Russell, *Constitutional Odyssey*, 203.

24 See Michael D. Behiels, "Charlottetown: The Anatomy of Mega-Constitutional Politics," *Policy Options*, December 1, 2002.

25 See Jack Stilborn, "Forty Years of Not Reforming the Senate – Taking Stock," in *Protecting Canadian Democracy: The Senate You Never Knew*, ed. Serge Joyal (Montreal: McGill-Queen's University Press, 2003); see also David E. Smith, *The Canadian Senate in Bicameral Perspective* (Toronto: University of Toronto Press, 2003).

(plus one for each of the three territories as well as an unspecified number yet to be determined for Indigenous peoples).

The next question was how an equal senate could be made acceptable to Ontario and Quebec, both of which would lose their privileged status of 24 senators each. Ontario's New Democratic Premier Bob Rae first signalled openness to compromise. Having come to power almost unexpectedly two years previously, and representing a new generation of Ontarians less committed to Burkean prescriptions of tried-tested-and-true, Rae suggested that Ontario would accept a fully equal senate if its powers were less than fully effective. In the end, as is consistent with the Westminster parliamentary tradition, the new senate would only have a 30-day suspensive veto over money bills, and a joint sitting of the senate and House of Commons would be able to overrule senatorial opposition to other bills.

This latter watering down of the Triple-E concept particularly aroused the ire of the western premiers, since proportional representation in the House of Commons would surely restore the kind of numerical central Canadian dominance during joint sittings that had just been taken away from the senate. Fearing for further legislative incursions into their resource economies, they insisted that the senate would be able to defeat tax bills related to natural resources on its own, and by simple majority.[26]

Bourassa, finally, was confronted with not only accepting an equal senate but also a Canada Clause in which Quebec's distinctiveness figured only as one of several of Canada's fundamental characteristics. What he got in return were three concessions meant to let Quebecers forgive and forget that Charlottetown was no longer just about *their* constitutional place, and perhaps not even primarily so.

First up, there was a somewhat peculiar double majority provision for senate approval of bills affecting French language or culture. Such bills would have to be approved by a majority of senators voting as well as a majority of Francophone senators voting. The defeat of such a bill could not be overridden by the House of Commons. Similar provisions had existed in bicultural Belgium since the 1970s.[27]

Second, Quebec would be guaranteed a minimum of 25 per cent of seats in the House of Commons. At the time, not least due to a declining birth rate

26 See Russell, *Constitutional Odyssey*, 209–10.

27 See Kris Deschouwer, "Ethnic Structure, Inequality and Governance of the Public Sector in Belgium," United Nations Research Institute for Social Development, January 2004.

(a side effect of the secularist thrust of the Quiet Revolution), the province was already at the margin of falling below the 25 per cent threshold, and it would do so soon thereafter. The 25 per cent guarantee would make Quebec representation in the House of Commons independent of its further demographic development, and it would give the province some assurance that it would retain a constant numerical presence in federal politics. According to the polls, it was this guarantee that of all the Charlottetown provisions was most soundly rejected in the ROC,[28] even though it was not nearly as peculiar as the double majority provision. After all, the old BNA Act of 1867, as amended in 1915 and as still in force as the Constitution Act, 1867, had already guaranteed to Prince Edward Island a number of parliamentary seats no less than its constitutionally accorded number of senate seats, regardless of demographics (see Chapter 2).

Thus far, none of the Charlottetown provisions would have dramatically changed the direction and operation of Canadian federalism. Some, such as the Canada Clause, were mostly symbolic in nature, and others, such as senate equality and the double majority provision, would not have affected the existing balance of powers in any substantial way. It was the third concession that Bourassa insisted on that might have upset the federal apple cart much more fundamentally: Instead of popular election of senators, provinces could also choose to have them elected by their own legislatures. This concession would have changed the direction of senate reform with potentially dramatic consequences, from a directly elected senate to an indirectly elected council of government delegates. Bourassa made no bones about the fact that Quebec senators would be expected to function in this way.[29]

The idea was not new and had repeatedly surfaced over the years in various government proposals under the label of "federal council" or "house of the provinces."[30] The only functioning second chamber of this kind among established federations is the German *Bundesrat*, which is indeed composed of *Länder* (provincial) delegates with a mandate to vote on behalf of their governments. The *Bundesrat*, however, operates under vastly different conditions. First, despite a significant east–west divide since German reunification in 1990, the main political conflict lines are social rather than regional and therefore less likely to become

28 Russell, *Constitutional Odyssey*, 226.

29 Ibid., 215.

30 See F. Leslie Seidle, "Senate Reform and the Constitutional Agenda: Conundrum or Solution?" in *Canadian Constitutionalism: 1791–1991*, ed. Janet Ajzenstat (Ottawa: Canadian Study of Parliament Group, 1991).

conflicts of federalism.[31] Second and more importantly, the German system of administrative federalism is characterized by a very different division of powers:[32] While most laws of importance are made at the federal level with co-equal participation of the *Bundesrat*, the *Länder* governments are then responsible for the implementation and administration of these laws. And since it is the *Länder* governments that are responsible for service delivery to their citizens in this way, they also have a strong incentive for coming to an agreement with the federal government. In a regionally and culturally divided federation like Canada, a senate of provincial government representatives might have been a dysfunctional disaster.

Since Bourassa had committed to a referendum in Bill 150, Canada's first ministers opted to have the fate of the Charlottetown Accord decided by countrywide referendums held in each province. On October 26, 1992, it was rejected in six provinces, including Quebec, as well as by 54 per cent of Canadian voters overall.[33] Charlottetown was as dead as Meech had been two years earlier.

Many explanations have been offered for Canada's sustained failure to come up with a universally acceptable constitutional reform package. Two stand out in particular. According to one, the Charter of Rights and Freedoms was to blame because it changed the country's "constitutional culture." By bringing the people into the orbit of constitutional politics, the executive game of deal making behind closed doors as the principal vehicle of constitutional change lost legitimacy.[34] According to the other explanation, the ultimate reason for failure was English Canada's refusal to give Quebec its due. While the Meech Lake Accord collapsed under the weight of English Canada's insistence on provincial equality, the Charlottetown Accord was doomed because it "remained devoid of any serious response to Quebec's agenda."[35]

---

31 See Petra Bendel and Roland Sturm, "Federal Republic of Germany," in *Diversity and Unity in Federal Countries*, eds. Luis Moreno and César Colino (Montreal: McGill-Queen's University Press, 2010), 167–99; the more recent rise of the right-wing populist Alternative für Deutschland (AfD) party does not change this assessment because it has been successful, albeit to different degrees, on both sides of the east–west divide.

32 On the difference between Canadian legislative and German administrative federalism, see Thomas O. Hueglin and Alan Fenna, *Comparative Federalism: A Systematic Inquiry* (Toronto: University of Toronto Press, 2015), 53–5.

33 Russell, *Constitutional Odyssey*, 227.

34 Alan C. Cairns, *Charter versus Federalism: The Dilemmas of Constitutional Reform* (Montreal: McGill-Queen's University Press, 1992), 96–126.

35 Kenneth McRoberts, *Misconceiving Canada: The Struggle for National Unity* (Toronto: Oxford University Press, 1997), 190–221.

While both explanations carry considerable merit, they miss the bigger picture. I would contend that the ultimate reason for the failure of Meech and Charlottetown was the misguided belief that there was a constitutional fix to be had for all that had ailed Canadian federalism ever since Confederation. Patriation in 1982 did not provide such a fix, and neither would have Meech or Charlottetown. As we have seen throughout this book and as we shall discuss more fully in the next and last chapter, Canadian federalism is grounded in competing and contested concepts of what federalism is or should be. No constitutional fix can successfully patch over that. The decade of constitutional politics from 1982 to 1992 should be remembered not so much as a lost opportunity of what might have been but as a painful clarification of what could not be.

Patriation in 1982 was necessary if Canada was ever to wean itself from British constitutional supervision. Even though at the time it was loathed by the defenders of provincial sovereignty, the Charter of Rights and Freedoms added an element of modern democracy that was universal rather than centralist, and, as we know now, it did not fundamentally alter the fabric and operation of Canadian federalism. At least with regard to the division of powers, the same can also be said about Meech and Charlottetown. When both failed, the question consuming Canadian politics for another decade was whether Quebec would ever be willing to simply make peace with the inevitable and accept the status quo.

Secession and Clarity

Two-thirds of Francophone voters in Quebec rejected the Charlottetown Accord.[36] A year later, Mulroney was gone and the Liberals were back in power led by Jean Chrétien – the same Jean Chrétien who had been Pierre Trudeau's justice minister and faithful point man for the federalist cause. A year later again, Bourassa was gone and the Parti Québécois was back in power led by Jacques Parizeau – the same Jacques Parizeau who had resigned as René Lévesque's finance minister when the wily premier appeared to soften his stance on sovereignty in the aftermath of the patriation debacle.

The stage was set for the final showdown between federalism and separatism. Even though we already know the outcome, and even though it does not matter anymore because Quebecers, in the October 30, 1995, referendum and by the slimmest of margins, once again opted for the status quo of federal union rather than separation, the traumatic experience of a country's near breakup raised

36 Ibid., 216.

existential questions about the conditions under which a constituent member of a federal union might lawfully secede from that union. One question was about clarity. English Canada's contention all along had been that there would never be a majority of Quebecers in favour of outright secession if the referendum question was clear and unmistakable: in or out? The other question was about unilateral withdrawal. Could Quebec decide for itself to separate, or did it have an obligation to reach an agreement on secession with the ROC? Chrétien's new point man for the federalist cause, Stéphane Dion, wasted no time taking up these questions.

The question of clarity had first arisen over Lévesque's opaque concept of sovereignty-association, which by many was understood as a concept of have-the-cake-and-eat-it-too. In 1980, knowing full well that a majority for outright independence was not to be had, the Parti Québécois formulated the referendum question "as cleverly as it could,"[37] asking Quebecers for a mandate to negotiate an agreement with the "rest of Canada" based on the "equality of nations." While such an agreement would have given Quebec full legislative sovereignty, the province would nevertheless remain in a Canadian economic and currency union. What exactly that meant remained for the most part unsaid.

Gearing up for the second referendum in 1995, Parizeau's inclination by comparison was blunt clarity. Hardly in office, he put before Quebec's National Assembly the proposal of a bill declaring that "Quebec is a sovereign country." It also contained the question to be asked in a June 1995 referendum: "Are you in favour of the Act passed by the National Assembly declaring the sovereignty of Quebec? Yes or No."[38] The problem was that there was still no majority for outright independence. After intervention by the more circumspect Bloc Québécois leader Lucien Bouchard, the question was changed to the old sovereignty-association formula and, in order to gain time for selling the new strategy, the referendum was postponed to October.

According to a June 12, 1995, agreement signed by Parizeau, Bouchard, and the leader of the soft-nationalist Action Démocratique du Québec, Mario Dumont, sovereignty for Quebec would now mean "to levy all of its taxes, pass all of its laws, [and] sign all of its treaties" within a framework of "joint institutions, including institutions of a political nature" shared with the ROC. Closely

37 Paul-André Linteau, René Durocher, and Jean-Claude Robert, *Quebec since 1930* (Toronto: James Lorimer, 1991), 537.

38 Cited in Robert A. Young, *Secession of Quebec and the Future of Canada* (Montreal: McGill-Queen's University Press, 1998), 268.

resembling the more confederal treaty framework of the European Union, those institutions would comprise an intergovernmental commission with mutual veto powers, an assembly of delegates from the legislatures on either side that would not possess legislative powers, and a conflict resolution tribunal.[39]

By late August, federalists and sovereigntists were almost tied in the polls. At the beginning of September, Parizeau made his move by introducing into the National Assembly Bill 1, to be passed directly after a positive referendum outcome. As the bill stipulated, Quebec would make a "formal offer of economic and political partnership with Canada," and it would declare itself a sovereign country either after a partnership treaty had been successfully negotiated with Canada and ratified by the National Assembly or unilaterally if the negotiations with Canada turned out to be "fruitless." In a simultaneous move, Parizeau also revealed the new referendum question: Quebecers were now asked to agree that "Quebec should become sovereign" after a "formal offer" had been made to Canada "within the scope" of both Bill 1 and the June 12 agreement.[40]

Quebecers, in other words, were asked to vote on a proposition contained in two lengthy and complicated documents. According to these documents, they were expected to approve something we might now call a "soft Quexit," assigning their collective future to an unfamiliar new set of partnership institutions and mechanisms with uncertain consequences. Had some 30,000 of them voted differently, that future might have become a reality. Or, in the case of "fruitless" negotiations followed by the ROC's refusal to accept unilateral withdrawal, the consequences might have been even more ominously unpredictable, including, as Stéphane Dion put it, "the violence we must fear."[41]

As Trudeau did before the first referendum, Chrétien made promises of federalism reform before the second. Quebec would be recognized as a distinct society after all, and its constitutional veto would be restored. After that second referendum, with the country in no mood for another round of constitutional politics, the prime minister had Quebec declared a distinct society unilaterally, by means of ordinary federal legislation. It did not impress anyone, least of all Quebecers. Neither did another piece of legislation aimed at placating Quebec's demand for a constitutional veto. The federal government would abstain from supporting constitutional change under the general 7/50 amendment formula unless there was regional approval analogous to the old Victoria formula.[42]

39 Ibid., 271–4.

40 Ibid., 277–8.

41 Ibid., 313.

42 On this and the following see Russell, *Constitutional Odyssey*, 237–40.

The English premiers and territorial leaders countered with the September 1997 Calgary Declaration, which, while acknowledging the "unique character" of Quebec, nevertheless flatly asserted that, no matter how diverse, all provinces were equal.[43] Lucien Bouchard, who had replaced Parizeau as premier of Quebec, declared that there would be another referendum only if there were winning conditions. Stéphane Dion, intent on shutting the door on any future attempt of Quebec to achieve separation on its own terms, asked the Supreme Court of Canada (SCC) for a reference on unilateral withdrawal.

More precisely, the federal government submitted three questions to the SCC: Is the unilateral secession of Quebec possible under the Canadian constitution? Is it possible as an act of self-determination under international law? If there are conflicting answers to the first two questions, which body of law takes precedence over the other? The SCC answered that under the Canadian constitution secession would require "principled negotiation with other participants in Confederation"; that there was no right to secede under international law because Quebecers were not denied self-determination in the sense of "meaningful access to government to pursue their political, economic, cultural and social development"; and that, consequently, there was no need to answer the third question.[44]

As the SCC elaborated, the Quebec government had a right to initiate secession if "a clear majority of Quebecers" had given it a mandate to do so based on "a clear question in favour of secession." Because secession must be regarded as a radical type of constitutional amendment, fundamentally changing the way in which the Canadian federation would operate henceforth, the court continued, all parties involved – the federal government, Quebec, and the other provinces – had an obligation to negotiate this secession amendment in good faith. These negotiations would be difficult and include everything from divvying up the national debt to boundary disputes and the protection of Indigenous rights.[45]

In other words, while the SCC had clearly slammed the door on any form of unilateralism, it did concede that Quebec had a right to secede in principle as long as the democratic will of Quebecers had been clearly expressed. It also made clear that in that case the ROC could not ignore the democratic will of Quebecers. As in its earlier patriation reference, however, when it left it to the politicians to decide what would constitute a "substantial measure of provincial support" (see Chapter 7), the court did not specify what it meant by a clear

43 See ibid., 238.

44 *Reference re Secession of Quebec*, [1998] 2 SCR 217.

45 Ibid.

question or a clear majority. But its emphasis on clarity nevertheless was a rebuke of both the legitimacy of a 50-plus-one referendum outcome and the attempt of fabricating winning conditions by fudging the referendum question.

Adding insult to injury, Stéphane Dion followed suit with the Clarity Act, which assigned to the House of Commons in Ottawa the right to determine what would be a clear question and a clear majority. Worse, the act did not spell out what clarity should mean. The House of Commons would decide whether it found the question or the outcome clear enough after the fact, unilaterally and by taking into consideration "any views it considers to be relevant." Minimally, a clear question had to be about outright independence and nothing else, and a clear majority certainly had to be more than 50 per cent plus one of valid votes cast, specifically also taking into consideration the level of eligible voter participation.[46]

The Bouchard government in Quebec countered with Bill 99, a long-winded rebuttal of the Clarity Act, which in essence stated that no one but Quebecers themselves would decide "on the political regime and legal status of Quebec," that they alone would determine "the mode and exercise" of doing so, and that, if the exercise was a referendum, "fifty percent of the valid votes cast plus one" would be sufficient.[47]

What might have been the opening salvos of yet another round of "constitutional warfare"[48] turned out to be not much more than the last two gasps of self-righteous constitutional petulance. Bouchard's winning conditions never came. Quebecers, as Canadians elsewhere, finally appeared to have enough of constitutional politics. The Parti Québécois lost the 2003 provincial election to the Liberals, and after briefly returning to power with a minority government in 2012, lost official party status in the 2018 election. The Bloc Québécois in turn, while losing official party status in the 2011 federal election, rebounded from 10 to 32 seats in the 2019 federal election.

There is no way of telling whether Canada will have to deal with another bout of Quebec separatism in the future. For a small island of French-speaking people surrounded by a sea of Englishness, in Canada, in North America, and in a globalizing world of popular culture, academia, trade, and commerce, defensive survival instincts will always be closely under the collective skin. But that

46 *An Act to give effect to the requirement for clarity as set out in the opinion of the Supreme Court of Canada in the Quebec Secession Reference*, [2000] SC 26.

47 *An Act respecting the exercise of the fundamental rights and prerogatives of the Québec people and the Québec State*, Bill 99, c. 46, 2000.

48 Russell, *Constitutional Odyssey*, 246.

mentality has been muted by the obvious success of the Quiet Revolution and the process of mutual adjustment in Canadian federalism it triggered. The three objectives that André Bernard had identified at the beginning of that process – national survival, economic well-being, and the idea of a homeland[49] – have been met at least in part.

Quebec's language policies, temporarily aided by the notwithstanding clause, have worked. The "ethnic vote," which Parizeau blamed for the 1995 referendum outcome, will remain opposed to Quebec leaving Canada, but allophones are now strengthening rather than weakening the French factor in the province. According to Quebec's language watchdog, the *Office québécois de la langue française*, French school enrolment of allophones in Montreal, where most of them live, has gone up from 15 per cent in 1971 to nearly 90 per cent in 2015. French school attendance by Anglophones also has gone up by 20 per cent during the same time period.[50]

Pierre Trudeau's vision of a fully bilingual country also has done its work, not in the English-speaking provinces, to be sure, but where it matters most, at the federal level of government and administration. Francophones constitute 23 per cent of the Canadian population, but they now make up 26 per cent of the Canadian public service and occupy 31 per cent of executive positions in the Canadian public service. There are complaints that federal government and administration nevertheless function predominantly in English. But it surely is no longer so, as André Bernard once observed, that Francophones are not in the loop about what is going on in Ottawa.[51] The disproportionate number of Francophones in federal public service with bilingual proficiency requirements is also not surprising, as the rate of bilingualism in Quebec is 42.6 per cent as compared to a Canadian average of 17.9 per cent.[52]

When it comes to economic well-being, the record may be mixed, but Quebec most certainly no longer fits the cliché of an agricultural hinterland dominated by an English commercial elite in Montreal. Quebec's impressive

49 André Bernard, *What Does Quebec Want?* (Toronto: James Lorimer, 1978).

50 Government of Québec, "Langue et educatión au Québec," Office Québécoise de la Langue Française, 2017.

51 Bernard, *What Does Quebec Want?*, 85–6.

52 See Government of Canada, "The Next Level: Normalizing a Culture of Inclusive Linguistic Duality in the Federal Public Service Workplace," Privy Council Office, 2017.

strategy of *rattrapage* (catching up),[53] state-led economic modernization since the 1960s, has resulted in rates of economic growth that until recently lagged behind Canada by only a few percentage points[54] but may have pulled even with the province's economic arch rival, Ontario, at the present time.[55] Moreover, to the extent that the nationalist project in Quebec as first carried forward by the Parti Québécois has also been one of social democratic amelioration,[56] both relative poverty and income inequality have consistently been lower in Quebec than in the rest of Canada.[57]

Numbers never show the whole picture, but, as mentioned before, it is the homeland objective that most clearly defies quantitative assessment. According to André Bernard again, belonging to a homeland for Quebecers is defined by "the French language, the territorial symbols of Quebec, and Quebec-based institutions."[58] With the French language secure and the Quebec flag flying over undisputed territorial boundaries, it is the role Quebec-based institutions play in the context of Canadian federalism that continues to fuel nationalist discontent. To be sure, there is also discontent in other provinces, mostly over fiscal relations with Ottawa, the federal spending power, and the degree of federal unilateralism that remains possible, with the 1995 fiscal transfer cuts as the most dramatic point of reference. But for hardline nationalists in Quebec, the discontent goes much deeper.

With wholesale separation out of reach, the new nationalist mantra is asymmetry. This might be surprising given the fact that it has long since become standard practice to grant Quebec de facto asymmetry by including opting-out provisions without fiscal disadvantage in shared-cost and other intergovernmental agreements, such as the 2004 Health Accord, provisions which then have been

53 See Luc Bernier, "The Beleaguered State: Québec at the End of the 1990s," in *The Provincial State in Canada: Politics in the Provinces and Territories*, eds. Keith Brownsey and Michael Howlett (Peterborough, ON: Broadview Press, 2001), 140–4.

54 See Peter Graefe, "Quebec Nationalism and Quebec Politics, from Left to Right," in *Transforming Provincial Politics: The Political Economy of Canada's Provinces and Territories in the Neoliberal Era*, eds. Bryan M. Evans and Charles W. Smith (Toronto: University of Toronto Press, 2015), 141.

55 See Graeme Hamilton, "'It's Raining Money': Quebec's Economy Crawled Out of the Doghouse. Now, It's a Powerhouse," *National Post*, July 28, 2017.

56 See Kenneth McRoberts, *Quebec: Social Change and Political Crisis* (Toronto: McClelland and Stewart, 1988), 247–58.

57 Graefe, "Quebec Nationalism," 141.

58 Bernard, *What Does Quebec Want?*, 77.

used by Quebec alone.[59] Moreover, the low level of dependency on federal fiscal transfers, the lowest among OECD federations,[60] together with the imposition of only mild (and rarely enforced) national standards in the costliest of shared policy fields, healthcare,[61] has not stood in the way of Quebec's use of social policy as a "tool of nation building."[62]

Not good enough, object Quebec nationalists. This de facto asymmetry is just an agreement of convenience that only prevents further de facto power encroachments and is moreover open to all provinces. Real asymmetry must be a power transfer "entrenched in the Constitution," and it must be available only to Quebec because Quebec otherwise "does not have special status within the Canadian federation." The "symmetrical application of asymmetry" to all provinces effectively shuts the door to any substantive power transfer, because federal governments will be ever more "reluctant" to grant a power transfer to Quebec when this transfer is also available to "all of the other provinces."[63]

Yet a counternarrative also seems to be emerging among what might be called Quebec post-nationalists. After "forty years of quiet revolution," according to this narrative, Quebec occupies a "central and unique place in the Canadian federation," which cannot be denied any longer. That being so, Canada "cannot progress or fulfill itself without the acceptance and sometimes the ad hoc recognition of its structural duality." This "dialectic" between the "desire" to put Quebec "back in the Canadian box" and the impossibility to do so "means that Canada is one of the most accommodating federations in the world."[64]

What remains of Quebec's discontent in terms of its special place in Confederation is the memory of conquest in 1759 and of constitutional isolation in 1982. The former did not lead to assimilation. The BNA Act of 1867, now the Constitution Act, 1867, recognized duality as the underlying cause of federation. The Constitution Act, 1982, did not change that. With the notwithstanding clause

59 Michael M. Atkinson et al., *Governance and Public Policy in Canada: A View from the Provinces* (Toronto: University of Toronto Press, 2013), 13–14.

60 Ibid., 12.

61 Ibid., 13.

62 Ibid., 21.

63 Michel Seymour, "Not Finding Our Way: The Illusory Reform of the Canadian Federation," in *Contemporary Canadian Federalism: Foundations, Traditions, Institutions*, ed. Alain-G. Gagnon (Toronto: University of Toronto Press, 2009), 196–7.

64 Jocelyn Létourneau, *A History for the Future: Rewriting Memory and Identity in Quebec* (Montreal: McGill-Queen's University, 2004), 139–40.

as a temporary buffer,[65] the Charter of Rights and Freedoms did not undermine Quebec's Francophone collectivity. Patriation without Quebec's signature, and Quebec's repeated symbolic affirmations of "non-adherence" to the Constitution Act, 1982, in 2002, 2007, and again in 2011,[66] are of no political or legal consequence. After all, Germany's arguably most powerful federated entity, Bavaria, did not sign the West German constitution of 1949 either.

Interstate Federalism and Intrastate Federalism

All federal systems require intergovernmental relations (IGR) for the sake of policy coordination between the different orders of government. Consisting of hundreds if not thousands of meetings and other forms of communication every year, this form of IGR is typically conducted among policy specialists in the ministries and civil service of both orders of government.[67]

As we have already seen in this chapter and in previous chapters, Canada in addition relies heavily on a qualitatively different form of IGR, aimed at policymaking rather than policy coordination. As criticized early on by Donald Smiley, this form of "executive federalism" entails intergovernmental negotiations at the political level, typically culminates in so-called First Ministers' Conferences, and is aided if not driven by "intergovernmental affairs specialists" organized in separate ministries or departments "not responsible for particular programs but rather the relations between jurisdictions."[68] Richard Simeon's iconic characterization of policymaking in Canadian federalism as "federal–provincial diplomacy" has likened it to the diplomatic relations among sovereign states in the international arena.[69]

65 See ibid.

66 Government of Québec, *Quebecers, Our Way of Being Canadian: Policy on Québec Affirmations and Canadian Relations* (Québec: Secrétariat aux Affaires Intergouvernementales Canadiennes, 2017), 33 and endnote 75.

67 See Johanne Poirier, Cheryl Saunders, and John Kincaid, eds., *Intergovernmental Relations in Federal Systems: Comparative Structures and Dynamics* (Toronto: Oxford University Press, 2015).

68 Donald V. Smiley, "An Outsider's Observations of Federal–Provincial Relations among Consenting Adults," in *Perspectives on Canadian Federalism*, ed. R.D. Olling and M.W. Westmacott (Toronto: Prentice-Hall, 1988), 282–3.

69 Richard Simeon, *Federal–Provincial Diplomacy: The Making of Recent Policy in Canada* (Toronto: University of Toronto Press, 2006).

This kind of high-level executive (interstate) federalism was not foreseen to play such a dominant role in Canadian federalism, and it has been widely criticized as a secretive and conflictive way of conducting public business, one step removed from direct parliamentary accountability.[70] This was the criticism levelled against the way in which the Meech Lake Accord was negotiated, and it was the same criticism that led to efforts of transparency and public inclusion in the case of the Charlottetown Accord. As we saw earlier in this chapter, however, the Charlottetown Accord was in the end negotiated as usual, behind closed doors.

Canada's heavy reliance on executive interstate federalism has been attributed to the lack of intrastate federalism, the appropriate representation of provincial interests in central policy making, particularly with regard to the senate, the members of which are appointed by the federal government rather than elected directly.[71] The argument often draws on a comparison with the neighbouring United States, which has a directly elected senate and lacks executive federalism in the form of direct negotiations between presidents and state governors.

This comparative argument is flawed for two reasons, however. First of all, legislative chambers of the senate kind rarely represent regional or provincial interests at the central level of government.[72] Second, the reason for the absence of executive federalism in the United States is not its elected senate but the presidential system of federalism with its separation of executive and legislative powers. While Canada's first ministers can usually rely on supportive majorities in their respective parliamentary chambers, there is no point for presidents and governors to negotiate policy when opposing majorities in their respective legislatures can simply block it.

More importantly, intrastate federalism and interstate federalism serve different purposes. The intrastate rationale for the Canadian senate would be that provincial interests should have some institutionalized form of representation at the federal level because federal legislation affects all citizens regardless of the division of powers. The interstate rationale for IGR is that policy cooperation is required because most powers are overlapping regardless of the division of powers. Regional representation in a second chamber at the federal level and IGR in the form of executive federalism, in other words, follow complementary

70 Smiley, "An Outsider's Observations," 279–80.

71 See the critical discussion in Donald V. Smiley and Ronald L. Watts, *Intrastate Federalism in Canada* (Toronto: University of Toronto Press, 1985), 17–35.

72 See Hueglin and Fenna, *Comparative Federalism*, 205–37.

rationales. One cannot simply substitute one for the other. The crux of the intrastate–interstate conundrum in Canadian federalism is that while the senate is institutionalized but not effective in terms of federalism, executive federalism has been crucial in the operation of Canadian federalism but lacks institutional strength.

Beginning with the first Dominion–Provincial Conference in 1906, there have always been FMCs in Canada, and from the very beginning they were mostly about fiscal and social relations.[73] Yet the Canadian preoccupation with executive federalism at the first ministers' level only began for real during the 1960s. While there had been 19 FMCs between 1900 and 1959, the number rose to 39 for the 1959–84 period.[74] A number of reasons account for this increase.

First, politics had become more complicated. Financing shared-cost programs in particular became a contentious issue of political bargaining. IGR was more generally overshadowed by the deepening conflict lines opening up at the time between Quebec nationalism, pan-Canadian nation-building in Ottawa, and western discontent.[75]

Second, the prolonged conflict over constitutional patriation inflated the number of FMCs that would have been held otherwise. These FMCs were occasioned by the incompleteness of the BNA Act of 1867 with regard to a domestic constitutional amendment formula, and they came to an end as a regular occurrence with the demise of the Charlottetown Accord in 1992.

Third, in line with Smiley's criticism (see above), executive federalism was accompanied by an ever-denser network of intergovernmental specialists. As first pioneered by Quebec in 1961, all governments established separate departments or ministries of intergovernmental relations.[76] The number of federal–provincial committees and other intergovernmental bodies mushroomed from 190 in 1968 to almost 800 by 1975.[77] By the mid-1980s, Canadian federalism apart from the major fiscal transfers (see Chapter 5) had come to rely on 99 cost-sharing

---

73 Roger Gibbins, *Regionalism: Territorial Politics in Canada and the United States* (Toronto: Butterworths, 1982), 90.

74 Kathy Brock, "Executive Federalism: Beggar Thy Neighbour?" in *New Trends in Canadian Federalism*, eds. François Rocher and Miriam Smith (Toronto: University of Toronto Press, 2003), 73.

75 See David J. Elkins and Richard Simeon, *Small Worlds: Provinces and Parties in Canadian Political Life* (Toronto: Methuen, 1980), 299–306.

76 Richard Simeon and Ian Robinson, *State, Society, and the Development of Canadian Federalism* (Toronto: University of Toronto Press, 1990), 203.

77 Gibbins, *Regionalism*, 91.

agreements, 50 intergovernmental transfer agreements, 93 joint initiatives, and 60 other intergovernmental arrangements.[78]

The Quiet Revolution, with its quest for a more autonomous and confident place in Confederation, was the main driver of all these developments in several ways. Quebec's Premier Jean Lesage not only established the first department of intergovernmental affairs, he also proposed to institutionalize FMCs as an annual event, together with a permanent intergovernmental secretariat, and he initiated the practice of annual Premiers Conferences.[79] Apart from interprovincial policy coordination, the main purpose of the latter clearly was to organize a common front against "federal dominance" as had already been the case with earlier interprovincial conferences dating all the way back to 1887.[80]

Alongside already existing regional forums of cooperation, the Western Premiers Conference, the Council of Maritime Premiers, and the Council of Atlantic Premiers, the pan-Canadian Premiers Conferences were institutionalized as the Council of the Federation (CoF) in 2003. This was yet another Quebec initiative, this time by Liberal Premier Jean Charest, as a belated response to Paul Martin's unilateral transfer cuts in 1995. As the CoF's founding agreement emphasized, the general objectives of this new forum for provincial–territorial cooperation were "adequate financial resources," "respect" for the constitutional division of powers, and "exercising leadership on national issues of importance to provinces."[81]

While the "proactive" nature of the CoF doubtlessly has provided some leadership in federal–provincial relations, it has not been successful in establishing itself as a major force in Canadian federalism, and not least so because success or failure remain "contingent in the individual leaders involved."[82] In particular, that also applies to the prime minister. Already the first interprovincial conference in 1887, while an "impressive indication" of the provinces' rising importance,[83] came

78 Brock, "Executive Federalism," 73.

79 Simeon and Robinson, *State, Society, and the Development of Canadian Federalism*, 202.

80 Gibbins, *Regionalism*, 93.

81 Council of the Federation, "Council of the Federation Founding Agreement," Charlottetown, Prince Edward Island, December 5, 2003.

82 Marc-Antoine Adam, Josée Bergeron and Marianne Bonnard, "Intergovernmental Relations in Canada: Competing Visions and Diverse Dynamics," in Poirier, Saunders, and Kincaid, *Intergovernmental Relations*, 149.

83 Donald Creighton, *Canada's First Century* (1970; repr., Toronto: Oxford University Press, 2012), 67.

to nothing because the prime minister, John. A. Macdonald, simply ignored it.[84] Had he accepted the invitation and attended, it would have been the first federal–provincial conference.[85] Federal participation and involvement was also part of Quebec's original plan for the CoF, but it was opposed by other provinces.[86] The effectiveness of a coordinated voice of provinces and territories in Canadian federalism nevertheless is co-determined by the degree to which the prime minister of the day is willing to pay attention to its communications.

With so much focus on the vertical dynamic of executive federalism, between the federal government and the provincial/territorial governments, the importance of interprovincial policy coordination sometimes flies under the radar. This horizontal form of executive federalism, as Jennifer Wallner demonstrated in the case of public schooling, not only serves obvious objectives of policy harmonization across provincial boundaries, but by doing so also obviates possible federal intervention.[87] To the extent that the provinces are able to self-organize desirable national policy objectives, in other words, they may be able to avert or even reverse centralizing power tilts. It is also worth noting, as Nicole Bolleyer does, how much of Canadian intergovernmentalism was in fact initiated by Quebec, usually thought of as the main source of conflict in Canadian IGR.[88]

With the end of constitutional politics after 1992, the frequency and importance of FMCs, already demoted symbolically to First Ministers' Meetings (FMMs) rather than conferences, declined. Finance Minister Paul Martin's unilateral cuts to social transfers in 1995 triggered a number of contentious FMMs culminating in the 2004 Health Accord and its promise of 10 years of increased and stable funding (see Chapter 5). Along the way, in 1999, all governments of Canada except Quebec also signed on to the SUFA, which essentially aimed at tying the federal government into a predictable social policy framework of intergovernmental transparency and cooperation.[89] By most accounts, however, its

84 Garth Stevenson, *Ex Uno Plures: Federal–Provincial Relations in Canada 1867–1896* (Montreal: McGill-Queen's University Press, 1997), 189.

85 Ibid.

86 Nicole Bolleyer, *Intergovernmental Cooperation: Rational Choices in Federal Systems and Beyond* (Oxford: Oxford University Press, 2009), 77.

87 Jennifer Wallner, *Learning to School: Federalism and Public Schooling in Canada* (Toronto: University of Toronto Press, 2014).

88 Bolleyer, *Intergovernmental Cooperation*, 77.

89 Canadian Intergovernmental Conference Secretariat, "Agreement: A Framework to Improve the Social Union for Canadians," First Ministers' Meeting, Ottawa, February 4, 1999.

practical impact has been marginal at best.[90] The Quebec government of Lucien Bouchard did not sign on to begin with because it did not want to give credence to the legitimacy of the federal spending power in areas of provincial jurisdiction. And in Ottawa, when the Conservatives took over from the Liberals in 2006, the new prime minister, Stephen Harper, while not outright repudiating it, for the most part simply ignored it.

Harper also turned his back on executive federalism. While intergovernmental cooperation and coordination remained business as usual in most policy areas,[91] Harper's intention to return to classical or what he now called "open" federalism mainly meant that he would shun meetings with his provincial counterparts. It is for this reason that he had his finance minister, Jim Flaherty, simply announce a new federal funding plan for healthcare when the 2004–2014 Health Accord ran out. In this way, Harper not only avoided submitting himself to an arduous and conflictive negotiation process with his provincial and territorial counterparts, he also largely escaped criticism because the plan in essence continued with previous funding levels and did not contain any new conditions.[92] Call it aloof federalism rather than open federalism. The two FMMs Harper did call during his nine years in office, in November 2008 and January 2009, were emergency meetings occasioned by the 2008 world financial crisis.

Harper's Liberal successor, Justin Trudeau, campaigning for sunnier ways in intergovernmental relations, quickly found out once in office that at least some of his provincial colleagues had not exactly waited for a new federal embrace. His attempts at bringing about intergovernmental agreement on carbon pricing in order to meet international environmental commitments were met with fierce opposition by newly elected Conservative governments in Ontario, Saskatchewan, and Alberta, and his enthusiasm for forging a new common Health Accord ended up in a series of bilateral agreements that few provincial premiers thought were particularly sunny.

It is the informality of executive federalism that makes success or failure particularly vulnerable to agency, to the whim of office holders at any given

90 See the critical discussion in Sarah Fortin, "From the Canadian Social Union to the Federal Social Union 1990–2006," in Gagnon, *Contemporary Canadian Federalism*, 315–19.

91 For a thorough discussion, see James Bickerton, "Deconstructing the New Federalism," *Canadian Political Science Review* 4, no. 2–3 (2010).

92 See Jennifer Wallner, "Ideas and Intergovernmental Relations in Canada," *PS: Political Science & Politics* 50, no. 3 (2017): 719–20.

time.[93] How otherwise could it be that FMCs (or FMMs) have been singled out as "one of the most crucial institutions of Canadian federalism,[94] yet at the same time have been questioned as the "weakest link" in Canadian IGR?[95]

Calls to formalize federal–provincial conferences go all the way back to the Rowell-Sirois Commission. Because "cooperation between the autonomous governments of the federal system has today become imperative," the commissioners concluded, federal–provincial conferences should be "regularized" as annual events and should be provided with a "permanent secretariat."[96] A permanent secretariat serving all intergovernmental activities was created in 1973.[97] And the Charlottetown Accord of 1992 contained a provision calling for the constitutionalization of FMCs.

Formal institutionalization of FMCs with a statutory or even constitutional set of rules still would not eliminate the vicissitudes of agency, but they would pose constraints on actors.[98] At best and over time, annual FMCs might establish or improve patterns of cooperation and transparency not unlike those envisaged in the SUFA. Minimally, a formalized annual FMC requirement would take away a good deal of prime ministerial discretion over the level and intensity of intergovernmental cooperation. As it stands, the fate of interstate federalism in Canada remains tied to political happenstance rather than deliberate design.

Then what about intrastate federalism? Smiley and Watts describe it as threefold regional representation in the institutions of the federal government:

---

93 See more generally Jennifer Wallner, "Empirical Evidence and Pragmatic Explanations: Canada's Contributions to Comparative Federalism," in *The Comparative Turn in Canadian Political Science*, eds. Linda A. White et al. (Vancouver: University of British Columbia Press, 2008), 171.

94 Donald V. Smiley, *Canada in Question: Federalism in the Eighties* (Toronto: McGraw-Hill Ryerson, 1980), 98.

95 Martin Papillon and Richard Simeon, "The Weakest Link? First Ministers' Conferences in Canadian Intergovernmental Relations," in *Reconsidering the Institutions of Canadian Federalism*, eds. J. Peter Meekison, Hamish Telford, and Harvey Lazar (Montreal: McGill-Queen's University Press, 2004).

96 Joseph Sirois and Newton Wesley Rowell, "Section G, Abstract of the Leading Recommendations," *Report of the Royal Commission on Dominion–Provincial Relations* (Ottawa: Privy Council Office, 1940), 275.

97 See Canadian Intergovernmental Conference Secretariat (CICS) website, available at http://www.scics.ca/en.

98 See Paul Pierson, *Politics in Time: History, Institutions, and Social Analysis* (Princeton: Princeton University Press, 2004), 34.

in the executive, in the parliamentary legislative chambers, and in the senate.[99] However, all democratic political systems, federal or unitary, elect representatives from all parts of the country, and the political leaders, wanting to be elected by voters in all parts of the country, will wisely strive for regional diversity in cabinet and other executive institutions. The quintessential federal institution at the national level of government is a second legislative chamber meant to give the federated entities a co-deciding voice in central decision making.

Even though formally endowed with powers all but equal to those of the House of Commons, the Canadian senate has never been able to perform this function because it lacks political legitimacy in two ways: Senators are appointed by the prime minister, and the regional formula of representation adopted in 1867 violates the principle first pioneered by the Americans according to which proportional representation of the people in the parliamentary chamber should be complemented by equal representation of the federated entities in the regional chamber.

Recent calls for senate reform or outright abolition have come particularly from the west, which sees itself as Canada's new economic powerhouse yet commands fewer seats in the senate than Atlantic Canada.[100] The populist Reform Party renewed calls for a Triple-E senate. When he became prime minister in 2006, Stephen Harper carried these western senate grievances with him. Transforming the existing senate into a Triple-E senate would require a constitutional amendment under the general 7/50 procedure. Knowing full well that sufficient provincial support for such an amendment was not to be had, and in order to get persistent western calls for senate reform off his back, Harper introduced into the legislature a more modest reform package aiming at voluntary provincial senate elections and nine-year term limits for senators.[101]

He then asked the SCC for a reference on whether either could be accomplished unilaterally by the parliament of Canada. As widely expected, and possibly by Harper himself, the court essentially held that both measures would amount to changes of the existing constitutional order serious enough to require amendment under the general 7/50 formula.

In the midst of a scandal over dubious expense claims by a number of senators, which led to widespread calls for senate abolition across the country,

99 Smiley and Watts, *Intrastate Federalism in Canada*, 40–59.

100 See Loleen Berdahl and Roger Gibbins, *Looking West: Regional Transformation and the Future of Canada* (Toronto: University of Toronto Press, 2014).

101 Ibid., 53.

Harper also asked the SCC whether abolition could be achieved under the general 7/50 formula. Again, the court denied. Senate abolition, the judges argued, falls outside the scope of matters addressed by Part V of the Constitution Act, 1982, concerning constitutional amendment. To include abolition therefore amounts to an amendment of Part V, for which unanimity is required.[102]

Notwithstanding the unlikely event that the entire country should come to one mind about senate reform, then, it seems that Canadians are saddled with their senate as it is. Or perhaps not. Recent developments may have opened the door for pragmatic change below the level of formal amendment.

According to the founders' intentions in 1867, the senate was to be both a chamber of sober second thought and a chamber of regional representation. By most counts, the Canadian senate has fulfilled its first role, fine-tuning and sometimes correcting legislative drafts coming from the House of Commons and initiating independent investigations on a variety of policy issues.[103] It has nevertheless become a second partisan chamber. Tied to their political parties' caucuses, senators have rarely strayed from party loyalty, and party loyalty is the prime reason for their appointment by the prime minister of the day to begin with. Any meaningful sense of representing regional interests has all but fallen by the wayside.

Already before coming to power in 2015, the current prime minister, Justin Trudeau, severed the ties between Liberal senators and the Liberal Party caucus. Liberal senators, he announced, would henceforth have to sit as independents. Once in office, Trudeau proceeded to form an independent advisory board for senate appointments, and he has since then only made non-partisan and merit-based senate appointments. As it stands, a majority of senators now belong to the so-called Independent Senators Group.[104]

These were politically expedient moves at a time when the senate scandal had brought to light that prominent senators had filed travel expenses for conducting senate business while in reality campaigning for their parties, and when polls showed that perhaps as many as 90 per cent of Canadians favoured senate reform or outright abolition.[105] Whether a more independent senate will improve its role as a chamber of second thought is an open question.

---

102 *Reference re Senate Reform*, 2014 SCC 32.

103 For an overall assessment, see Serge Joyal, ed., *Protecting Canadian Democracy: The Senate You Never Knew* (Montreal: McGill-Queen's University Press, 2003).

104 Senate of Canada, "Senators."

105 *CBC News*, "Majority Wants Senate Changed or Abolished, Poll Suggests," June 20, 2013.

But, as has been suggested by two former senators with impeccable credentials, Michael Kirby and Hugh Segal, one possibility for a senate freed from partisan shackles might be finding its way "back to regional roots" by reorganizing itself in regional caucuses.[106] Senators would still be government appointed. Kirby and Segal therefore recommend that, with the exception of "money bills and certain constitutional provisions," the senate should exercise self-restraint by limiting its powers to a six-month suspensive veto.

As stated at the outset of this section, intrastate and interstate federalism are complementary forces in the Canadian federal system, and they follow different rationales. One cannot expect, therefore, that regional reorganization of the Canadian senate would lead to less reliance and emphasis on executive federalism. In fact, a recent comparative study suggests the opposite: A stronger regional voice in national decision making might lead to the need for stronger intergovernmental structures.[107]

Indigenous Land Rights and Self-Government

As we just saw in Chapter 7, Indigenous peoples and organizations were alarmed about the prospects of losing the "Crown's" protection once Canada had adopted a domestic constitutional amendment formula. Since that amendment formula did not provide for any Indigenous co-decision rights, the fear was that it might be used to abrogate the hard-won recognition of Indigenous rights in Section 35 of the Constitution Act, 1982. Indigenous peoples had reason to be fearful. While there has been no attempt to meddle with Section 35, Canadian governments had to be pushed every step of the way by the courts to give it meaning and substance.

Contrary to most Canadians, Indigenous peoples still attach considerable symbolic weight to the "Crown." It was the Crown's Royal Proclamation of 1763 that had recognized, albeit ambiguously, a nation-to-nation relationship with Indigenous peoples. When the Canadian state took over that relationship in 1867, it became one of assimilation. Already in 1857, John A. Macdonald had introduced into the legislature of the Province of Canada a Gradual Civilization Bill aiming at the "enfranchisement" of Indians so long as they were "sufficiently advanced in the elementary branches of education" as well as "of good moral

106 Michael Kirby and Hugh Segal, "A House Undivided: Making Senate Independence Work," Public Policy Forum, September 22, 2016.

107 Bolleyer, *Intergovernmental Cooperation*, 50.

character and free from debt."[108] After 1867, Macdonald's Electoral Franchise Act of 1885 was guided by the same assimilationist approach, even though further restrictions applied due to massive opposition in parliament.[109]

A whole century later, Canada's official policy of assimilation both culminated and came to an end with Pierre Trudeau's infamous 1969 White Paper. Macdonald's approach to Indian policy had been (mis)guided by nineteenth-century notions of European cultural superiority. Trudeau's approach essentially was the same as his response to Quebec nationalism: The only road to the just society he envisaged for all Canadians was one of individual liberalism – the prioritization of "'individual rights' over 'peoples' rights."[110]

As presented to parliament by Trudeau's minister of Indian affairs and northern development, Jean Chrétien, the White Paper was meant to bring about equality by repealing the Indian Act, closing the Department of Indian Affairs, effectively ending treaty relations by settling outstanding claims, handing back to Indians title and control of reserve lands, and reassigning social policy responsibilities to the provinces as in the case of other Canadians. "To be an Indian must be to be free – free to develop Indian cultures in an environment of legal, social and economic equality with other Canadians."[111]

In Thomas King's eloquent recount, Trudeau "blithely intimated that there was no such thing as Indian entitlement to land or Native rights and suggested that it was in the best interests of First Nations people to give up their reserves and assimilate into Canadian society."[112] The response was "fast and furious."[113] Indigenous groups and organizations across the country countered,

---

108 *An Act to encourage the gradual Civilization of the Indian Tribes in this Province, and to amend the Laws respecting Indians,* 1857, CAP 26.

109 See Wendy Moss and Elaine Gardner-O'Toole, "Aboriginal People: History of Discriminatory Laws" (Ottawa: Government of Canada Publications, 1991); note that the Indian Act of 1876 was enacted by the Liberal government of Alexander Mackenzie during Macdonald's temporary fall from power because of the railway scandal.

110 Menno Boldt, *Surviving as Indians: The Challenge of Self-Government* (Toronto: University of Toronto Press, 1993), 83–4.

111 "Statement of the Government of Canada on Indian policy (The White Paper, 1969)," (Ottawa: Queen's Printer, 1969).

112 Thomas King, *The Inconvenient Indian: A Curious Account of Native People in North America* (Toronto: Anchor Canada, 2013), 73.

113 Thomas J. Courchene, *Indigenous Nationals Canadian Citizens: From First Contact to Canada 150 and Beyond* (Montreal: McGill-Queen's University Press, 2018), 68.

in the words of Thomas King again, that "whatever the problems were with the Indian Act and with the Department of Indian Affairs, Native people were sure that giving up their land and their treaty rights was not the answer."[114] After a year, the White Paper was withdrawn.

Yet the White Paper did mark a crucial turning point in Indigenous–Canadian relations. Realizing that nothing less than "their very existence as Indians" was at stake, "Indians began to organize."[115] The importance of a new level of Indigenous activism, from Harold Cardinal's famous response to the White Paper in 1969[116] all the way to the Idle No More Movement almost half a century later,[117] cannot be overstated.[118] Just as the Judicial Committee of the Privy Council in the nineteenth century was pushed by the provincial rights movement (see Chapter 3), and just as it took the decisive actions of a separatist government in Quebec for the SCC to acknowledge that Quebec had a right to protect the French language (see Chapter 7), so it was not belated enlightenment on the part of Canada's political and legal classes that led to the eventual recognition of Indigenous rights, but instead, as already noted in Chapter 7, organized pressure coming from Indigenous peoples themselves.

Equipped with the 1973 *Calder* decision, in which the SCC had for the first time declared as "wholly wrong" the assumption that Indigenous peoples had had no rights prior to "conquest or discovery" and therefore had "no rights at all except those subsequently granted or recognized by the conqueror or discoverer,"[119] Canada's First Nations began to press for land claim settlements. After the Constitution Act, 1982, had recognized "existing aboriginal and treaty rights" in Section 35(1), that pressure could no longer be ignored. Between 1973 and 2016, the governments of Canada signed off on 26 comprehensive land claim agreements with First Nations. About a hundred more are in the process of being negotiated.[120] Among the most important settlements thus far concluded are the

114 King, *Inconvenient Indian*, 73.

115 Donald Purich, *Our Land: Native Rights in Canada* (Toronto: James Lorimer, 1986), 186.

116 Harold Cardinal, *The Unjust Society: The Tragedy of Canada's Indians* (Edmonton: Hurtig, 1969).

117 See Idle No More website, available at http://www.idlenomore.ca.

118 I owe this emphasis on Indigenous activism as the driving force of change to a conversation with Chris Alcantara.

119 *Calder et al. v. Attorney-General of British Columbia*, [1973] SCR 313.

120 Government of Canada, "Comprehensive Claims" (Ottawa: Crown–Indigenous Relations and Northern Affairs Canada, 2016).

James Bay Agreements in northern Quebec (1975–8), the Yukon First Nation Agreements (1993), and the Nisga'a Agreement in northern British Columbia (1999),[121] as well as several agreements with the Inuit in Canada's north, most significantly including the creation of Nunavut as a third northern territory (1999).[122]

That Indigenous peoples have rights under the treaties they concluded, for better or for worse, with the governments of Canada is not under dispute in principle, although the history of these treaties is in practice littered with betrayal and broken commitments. Even under the more recent treaty agreements, such as the Nisga'a Final Agreement, for instance, Canadian governments might "use financing arrangements as means to control Nisga'a government."[123] An entirely different and far more legally protracted question, however, is what rights Indigenous peoples possess in the case that no written documents in the form of treaty agreements can be produced to show such rights.

One of the most persistent colonialist assumptions has been that Indigenous rights could only be acquired through interactions with the "Crown" – such as by means of treaties. Behind that assumption loom two further and rather grotesque assumptions: that what the white settlers found upon their arrival in the "New World" was *terra nullius*, an empty land occupied and owned by no one, and that, therefore, Indigenous peoples had no rights at all unless the "Crown" had established such rights.

Presumably, and in spite of the *Calder* decision mentioned above, this was also the rationale behind Alberta Premier Peter Lougheed's insistence that the recognition of Indigenous rights in Section 35 of the Constitution Act, 1982, should be limited to "existing" rights – rights that had already been recognized under Canadian law but not rights that might be invoked from "outside the Canadian constitutional order."[124] Lougheed, in other words, was worried that a more general recognition of Indigenous rights might become a challenge for provincial control of land and resources.

121 See for details Courchene, *Indigenous Nationals*, 182–200.

122 See ibid., 221–31.

123 Michael Asch, "Self-Government in the New Millennium," in *Nation to Nation: Aboriginal Sovereignty and the Future of Canada*, eds. John Bird, Lorraine Land, and Murray MacAdam (Toronto: Irwin Publishing, 2002), 69.

124 Kiera Ladner, "An Indigenous Constitutional Paradox: Both Monumental Achievement and Monumental Defeat," in *Patriation and its Consequences: Constitution Making in Canada*, eds. Lois Harder and Steve Patten (Vancouver: University of British Columbia Press, 2015), 274.

As it turned out, Lougheed had every reason to worry. Notwithstanding his insistence on "existing" rights, the courts would soon establish that Indigenous rights had indeed existed before the "Crown" had claimed sovereignty, and that they existed still. In 1993, the British Columbia Court of Appeal had to deal with a case that would mark the beginning of a dramatic change in Canadian–Indigenous legal relations. It was also the last time that Indigenous land rights would be denied out of hand – in the name of Canadian federalism.

Fifty-one hereditary chiefs of the Gitksan and Wet'suwet'en peoples had gone to court claiming that they still had title to and jurisdiction over their traditional lands, some 58,000 square kilometres, because, as in most of British Columbia, that land had never been signed away by means of a treaty. The court of appeal denied these rights with two main arguments. One of these was that oral history was not sufficient proof of historical land use and ownership. The other argument was that Indigenous jurisdiction was not possible because "British Columbia's entry into Canada in 1871 exhaustively distributed legislative power between the province and the federal government."[125] On further appeal, however, the SCC in its 1997 *Delgamuukw* decision, allowed oral history as evidence of existing land title rights, which it affirmed.[126]

Two further decisions then turned from the issue of traditional Indigenous rights to the obligations of Canadian governments in the face of it.[127] In its 2004 *Haida* decision, the SCC affirmed that if the "Crown" wanted to make use of land claimed as traditional Indigenous land, it had a duty "to consult with Aboriginal peoples and accommodate their interests" even when the existence of "title has not yet been legally recognized."[128] And in its 2014 *Tsilhqot'in* decision, it held that in the case of legally existing land title rights, the governments of Canada seeking to use that land "must obtain the consent of the Aboriginal title holders" and, if that consent is denied, can only proceed by "demonstrating both a compelling and substantial governmental objective."[129]

Lougheed's worst nightmares came true in 2018 when the courts halted or at least delayed construction of an interprovincial oil pipeline extension

125 Cited in *Delgamuukw v. British Columbia*, [1997] 3 SCR 1010.

126 Ibid.

127 See the overview in Courchene, *Indigenous Nations*, 150–6.

128 *Haida Nation v. British Columbia (Minister of Forests)*, 2004 SCC 73.

129 *Tsilhqot'in Nation v. British Columbia*, 2014 SCC 44. This demonstration involves the so-called *Sparrow* test first set out in *R. v. Sparrow*, [1990] 1 SCR 1075. The criteria are not unlike those applied to cases of expropriation in Canadian society; see Courchene, *Indigenous Nationals*, 150.

on grounds that the federal government had not adequately consulted with Indigenous peoples; and again two years later when nationwide Indigenous and non-Indigenous protests erupted over the arrest and removal of hereditary chiefs blockading construction of an intra-provincial gas pipeline on land to which they owned title and for which they had denied the provincial government consent.[130] We shall return to these issues in the epilogue at the end of the book.

With the claim to landownership came the quest for self-government to get out from under the demeaning confines of the Indian Act. As of 2018, the Canadian government has concluded 22 self-government agreements with 43 "Indigenous communities," and about another 50 are pending. Self-government means that Indigenous peoples can autonomously make laws and policies on a variety of "matters internal to their communities and integral to their cultures and traditions" and "in harmony with federal and provincial laws." The extent of self-government varies from agreement to agreement. There are also separate self-governing agreements pertaining only to education.[131]

Self-government means powers and financial means to be self-sufficient. While the Yukon Agreements have gone furthest by providing the Yukon First Nations with "the full range of provincial-cum-municipal regulatory powers,"[132] the Nisga'a Agreement, contrary to most other settlements, provides full ownership of natural resources – albeit on a territory that comprises only 8 per cent of traditional Nisga'a lands. In most other cases, self-sufficiency is nowhere in sight.

In a federal system, self-government also means having a seat and voice at the intergovernmental negotiation table. In 1990, Elijah Harper had blocked the last-minute passage of the Meech Lake Accord in the Manitoba legislature in protest and on behalf of Indigenous peoples all across the country because they had been entirely left out of the negotiation process. As he explained it later: "These settler people and their governments didn't recognize us as a Nation, and as a government and that's why we opposed the Meech Lake Accord."[133]

While the accord would have recognized Quebec as a distinct society, it made no mention at all of Canada's First Nations. A few years later, when the Charlottetown Accord was negotiated, Indigenous organizations for the first

130 In this instance, that government was the government of British Columbia, but Lougheed would have been concerned just the same.

131 Government of Canada, "Self-Government" (Ottawa: Crown–Indigenous Relations and Northern Affairs Canada, 2016).

132 Courchene, *Indigenous Nationals*, 192.

133 Elijah Harper, cited in Courchene, *Indigenous Nationals*, 95.

time were fully included in the process. As a result, the accord this time around contained far-reaching provisions that would have included Indigenous representation in almost all Canadian political institutions and processes. In particular, as was also a central recommendation by the Royal Commission on Aboriginal Peoples,[134] it would have recognized an inherent right of Indigenous self-government as a third tier of government in the Canadian federal system.[135]

With explicit constitutional recognition of an inherent right of self-government falling by the wayside with the demise of the Charlottetown Accord, the Liberal government of Jean Chrétien embarked on a different path. In a 1995 position paper, it declared that an Indigenous right of self-government was already contained in the constitution, implicitly, under Section 35(1) with its recognition of "existing aboriginal and treaty rights,"[136] a position also echoed by SCC decisions shortly thereafter.[137]

As the position paper also stated, financing Indigenous self-government would be considered a "shared responsibility" to be negotiated "among federal, provincial and territorial governments, and Aboriginal governments and institutions."[138] This was the rationale behind Paul Martin's 2005 intergovernmental–Indigneous Kelowna Accord, which would have committed $5.1 billion of additional funding for Indigenous issues over a five-year period.[139] It, too, fell by the wayside when Martin's successor Stephen Harper reneged on the financial commitment.

As in the case of executive federalism more generally, agency obviously plays a major part in negotiating a financially secure path toward Indigenous self-government. Recognizing in principle an Indigenous right of self-governance has made that path less "unilateral." Its outcome thus far has been described as "increasingly becoming a multilevel, trilateral reality."[140] More than trilateral

134 See Courchene, *Indigenous Nationals*, 99–101.

135 Alan C. Cairns, *Citizens Plus: Aboriginal Peoples and the Canadian State* (Vancouver: University of British Columbia Press, 2018), 81–3.

136 Government of Canada, "The Government of Canada's Approach to Implementation of the Inherent Right and the Negotiation of Aboriginal Self-Government" (Ottawa: Crown–Indigenous Relations and Northern Affairs Canada, 1995).

137 See Patrick Macklem, *Indigenous Difference and the Constitution of Canada* (Toronto: University of Toronto Press, 2001), 173–4.

138 Government of Canada, "The Government of Canada's Approach."

139 See Courchene, *Indigenous Nationals*, 103–4.

140 Martin Papillon, "Canadian Federalism and the Emerging Mosaic of Aboriginal Multilevel Governance," in *Canadian Federalism: Performance, Effectiveness, and Legitimacy*, eds. Herman Bakvis and Grace Skogstad (Toronto: Oxford University Press, 2012), 298.

in fact: As the federal government's 1995 position paper notes, multilevel negotiations also seek to provide "municipalities and third parties with meaningful opportunities to have input into negotiation processes that may directly affect their interests."[141]

In sum, there is no clear picture of what Indigenous governance might look like in the future. Current visions amount to a muddled mix of options ranging all the way from a subordinate municipality-like status with a limited range of delegated powers to a third tier of government with equal status and participation in the institutions and processes of Canadian federalism.[142] Two things, however, seem utterly clear. First, the most quintessentially Indigenous option, the return to a nation-to-nation relationship not unlike the sovereignty-association option envisaged for Quebec by René Lévesque, is not an option that is likely. Canada's governments will not have it, and Canada's diverse Indigenous community of some 600 bands and nations will not muster the necessary amount of political cohesion to force it. Second, as long as Canada's Indigenous peoples remain junior partners in a federal system where constitutionally guaranteed sovereignty rights are only accorded to federal and provincial governments, a meaningful form of self-government and autonomous policymaking will remain out of reach.[143]

Shifting Identities

In almost every way, this book has been an account of federalism in Canada driven by path-dependent predictability. It has dealt with the issues and dynamics that have animated – or plagued – Canadian federalism ever since Confederation. The main drivers were the everlasting duality of English and French Canada, the more than occasional tensions between central Canada and the west as a resource-rich hinterland, and the intergovernmental power game between the two orders of government more generally. At the end of this account, a twenty-first century book on federalism in Canada should at least raise the question about the extent to which this conventional structuration of

141 Government of Canada, "The Government of Canada's Approach."

142 See Frances Abele and Michael J. Prince, "Four Pathways to Aboriginal Self-Government in Canada," *The American Review of Canadian Studies* 36, no. 4 (2006).

143 See Christopher Alcantara and Zachary Spicer, "A New Model for Making Aboriginal Policy? Evaluating the Kelowna Accord and the Promise of Multilevel Governance in Canada," *Canadian Public Administration* 59, no. 2 (2016).

Canadian politics and federalism still aligns with new fault lines of interests, conflicts, and identity.

At least for now, Quebec's distinctiveness has lost some of its lustre as a beacon of transformative politics.[144] And while the west is no longer the resource hinterland it was meant to be in Confederation, intra-regional divisions have at the present time deepened over questions of resource extraction and environmental protection.[145] Finally, the legitimacy of provincial structures may be questioned more generally in light of the fact that the urban–rural divide within provinces may be more significant than the interprovincial divide. Of the roughly 37 million Canadians, more than one-third live in the three largest metropolitan areas, Toronto, Montreal, and Vancouver.[146] Arguably, these and other large cities have more in common with one other than with the rural and northern parts of the provinces they happen to be located in. Does this mean that the territorial boundaries of Canadian federalism ought to be redrawn?

In terms of political will and possibility, this is obviously a merely rhetorical question. But it points to further questions of political legitimacy. The conventional justification of Canadian federalism has always been that it serves "small worlds" of diversity discernible on an east–west axis of provincial and regional politics and identity, from socioeconomic alienation in the west, to central Canadian dominance and hubris, to sociocultural distinctiveness in Quebec, and to disaffected dependency in the east.[147] As more recent research has shown, however, there is also a significant "north–south dimension" of politics and identity within and across provincial and regional boundaries, which can be roughly summarized by a divide between (sparsely populated) northern/rural, and (more densely populated) southern/urban/suburban identity clusters.[148]

There is, in other words, some degree of incongruency between political boundaries and, broadly speaking, sociological identity. Driven by the imperatives of party competition and majority rule, governments are always in danger

144 See Daniel Salée, "Transformative Politics, the State, and the Politics of Social Change in Quebec," in *Changing Canada: Political Economy as Transformation*, eds. Wallace Clement and Leah F. Vosko (Montreal: McGill-Queen's University Press, 2003).

145 See Loleen Berdahl and Roger Gibbins, *Looking West: Regional Transformation and the Future of Canada* (Toronto: University of Toronto Press, 2014).

146 Statistics Canada, "Section 1: Census Metropolitan Areas," 2018.

147 See Elkins and Simeon, *Small Worlds*.

148 Ailsa Henderson, "Regional Political Cultures in Canada," *Canadian Journal of Political Science* 37, no. 3 (2004), 604.

of becoming insensitive to diversity. At the federal level, the institutions and mechanisms of intrastate and interstate federalism, however weak and informal, are meant to constrain regionally insensitive dictates of majority rule. At the provincial level, no such constraints are in place. The idea of federalism as a balance of shared rule and self-rule does not find expression within the confines of provincial boundaries. As are most other federal systems, Canadian federalism is incomplete in this way.

Just as the commercial and financial interests in central Canada meant to control what they considered to be their western resource hinterland, so do the commercial and financial southern centres mean to control the northern resource hinterland within provincial boundaries. And especially since they already and increasingly have to consult and accommodate Indigenous peoples living on desirable northern resource land, provinces would resist any attempt of providing northern interests with more shared rule – let alone grant any form of self-rule.

It is in this context that the creation of Nunavut in 1999 merits a brief concluding reflection.[149] Proposals and negotiations for a separate territory for the Inuit population living in the central and eastern Canadian Arctic had been going on since the 1970s. In a 1982 referendum, the population of the Northwest Territories (NWT) approved the idea of dividing the territory and establishing the eastern half as the new territory of Nunavut, an area of roughly 2 million square kilometres inhabited by some 30,000 people, 85 per cent of which are Inuit. The federal government insisted that the creation of Nunavut had to be preceded by a settlement of Inuit land claims. Over a period of 10 years, the 1993 Nunavut Land Claims Agreement was negotiated with the legal representative of the Inuit in the NWT, the Tunngavik Federation of Nunavut (TFN), which thereafter became Nunavut Tunngavik Inc. (NTI).

Under the agreement, as signed in 1991 by the federal government, the TFN, and the NWT government, the Inuit would retain title to about 18 per cent of selected lands, including all resource rights. In addition, they would also receive a modest share of mineral royalties collected by the government of Canada from the vast remaining lands, and they would be accorded another $1.73 billion in cash over a period of 14 years. The agreement also contained a commitment in principle to establish Nunavut as a separate territory.

149 The following draws from André Légaré, "An Assessment of Recent Political Development in Nunavut: The Challenges and Dilemmas of Inuit Self-Government," *Canadian Journal of Native Studies* 18, no. 2 (1998): 274–7; and Courchene, *Indigenous Nationals*, 224–7.

After another decade of negotiations between the federal government, the NWT government, and NTI, Nunavut came into existence on April 1, 1999. In a way, the new territory had gotten itself two governments. One is the territorial government of Nunavut that represents all of Nunavut's people, a Westminster-style parliamentary government combined with consensus-oriented characteristics rooted in the Inuit tradition.[150] The other de facto government is NTI, representing the Inuit people and managing Inuit land and resources. The government of Nunavut in fact owns no land outside municipal boundaries. It has no access to resource revenue, and depends almost entirely on federal transfers to the tune of a whopping $40,000 per capita. As Tom Courchene dryly remarks, however, that amount would quickly become secondary if Nunavut was given ownership of natural resources as is the case for the provinces of Canada.[151]

Insofar as it resulted, as Ailsa Henderson has shown, in "the emergence of a distinct political culture" combining Inuit tradition with Canadian political practice,[152] the creation of Nunavut is indeed a remarkable incidence of boundary change with the objective of establishing self-rule for a new government within the Canadian federal system. It is doubtful, however, as to whether it can be regarded as a model or template for future adjustments of identity shifts. To begin with, the creation of Nunavut was not a response to shifting identities but a belated recognition of Inuit identity already in existence and neglected for far too long. Further, what has been created is a territory, not a province. Just like the other two territories, Yukon and NWT, Nunavut is represented in Ottawa by one elected member of parliament and one senator. The vested interests of Canada's governments in the intergovernmental power game are hardly affected. And finally, the governments negotiating the deal did not have to give up much. The federal government still owns most of the new territory's resources since the NWT government had not owned them to begin with.

150 See Government of Nunavut, "Consensus Government."

151 Courchene, *Indigenous Nationals*, 227; the other territories are in a similar situation.

152 Ailsa Henderson, *Nunavut: Rethinking Political Culture* (Vancouver: University of British Columbia Press, 2007), 1–2.

CHAPTER NINE

CONTESTED CONCEPTS OF CANADIAN FEDERALISM

From a comparative perspective, the most remarkable characteristic of federalism in Canada is not intergovernmental tension and conflict, western alienation, or even Quebec separatism. Regional governments have wrestled with central dominance and fiscal superiority almost everywhere, socioeconomic diversity and inequality across regional boundaries are a ubiquitous feature of capitalist market economies, and separatist movements have existed or are persisting to this day in many countries.

No, the most remarkable characteristic of federalism in Canada is, as I have tried to show throughout the preceding chapters, that all through its history there have been and still are deep disagreements about the meaning of federalism, its objectives, and its operation. By comparison, in the United States, even though it appears today as a federation deeply divided along regional lines as well as state boundaries, the nature and operation of federalism itself are rarely contested. The constitution is sacrosanct, and what it means is left to the courts. In other established federations such as Germany, disagreements about the proper functioning of federalism does lead to constitutional revision from time to time. But in order to be successful, constitutional reform requires broad "political consensus among decision-makers on all orders of government."[1] Typically, such consensus is lacking in Canada.

1 Arthur Benz and Felix Knüpling, "Federalism and Constitutional Change: Lessons from Comparison," in *Changing Federal Constitutions: Lessons from International Comparison*, eds. Arthur Benz and Felix Knüpling (Berlin: Barbara Budrich, 2012), 410.

The precondition for consensus is agreement on a set of basic concepts providing the parameters within which inevitable differences about both constitutional meaning and constitutional change can be addressed and accommodated. In Canada, such agreement rarely if ever has existed. The reasons are easy to see. Confederation not so much constituted a universal agreement on first principles as it was a working compromise allowing for different interpretations for each of the participants. It was not even clear who the original participants were: four provinces agreeing on union; two "races" agreeing on mutually autonomous coexistence; or colonial entities released into subordinate provincehood by a union government acting on behalf of the imperial mother country.

Some of the interpretations of Canadian federalism that grew out of these uncertainties about the nature of the union can be put to rest. First among these is a "centralist concept" according to which "the whole of the Canadian people constitutes the only legitimate source of sovereign authority."[2] If this was John A. Macdonald's nation-building concept of a faux federalism, then it was put to rest, with considerable assistance from the Judicial Committee of the Privy Council (JCPC) in Westminster, by the nineteenth-century provincial rights movement.

To be sure, the Canadian war efforts during the first half of the twentieth century, and the somewhat belated construction of a modern welfare state thereafter, reintroduced a centralizing and nation-building dynamic to Canadian federalism. This dynamic was countered, however, by what came to be known as "province-building," a reassertion of provincial power and jurisdiction led by Quebec's Quiet Revolution and mainly seconded by the resource-rich western provinces.[3] Both nation-building and province-building were driven by the imperatives of modern economic and social management, and they led to the growth of government at both levels of the federation.

Doubtlessly, a recalibration of Canadian federalism took place with the overall result that the federal government became more active in matters that had originally been assigned to exclusive provincial jurisdiction. But to speak of Canadian federalism in its current form as characterized by "exacerbated centralization"[4] appears

2 Edwin R. Black, *Divided Loyalties: Canadian Concepts of Federalism* (Montreal: McGill-Queen's University Press, 1975), 15–16.

3 See Robert A. Young, Philippe Faucher, and André Blais, "The Concept of Province-Building: A Critique," *Canadian Journal of Political Science* 17, no. 4 (1984).

4 Alain-G. Gagnon, "Taking Stock of Asymmetrical Federalism in an Era of Exacerbated Centralization," in *Contemporary Canadian Federalism: Foundation, Traditions, Institutions*, ed. Alain-G. Gagnon (Toronto: University of Toronto Press, 2009).

possible only from a sovereigntist-nationalist perspective that is as incompatible with the idea of federalism as a balanced sharing of sovereignty as was Macdonald's centralist concept.

It is likewise unnecessary to revisit the old debate about conflicting visions of Canadian society, an individualist vision of liberty for all citizens and a collectivist vision of provincial community. This debate was at the heart of the conflict between Pierre Trudeau's pan-Canadian liberalism and René Lévesque's nationalist aspirations. I believe, however, that mutual animosity has stood in the way of rationality in the characterization of either side of the debate. Lévesque's humanist nationalism did not defy individual liberty, and neither did Trudeau's anti-nationalist federalism aim at eradicating Quebec as a cultural community. Moreover, more importantly and more generally, as Robert Vipond has shown conclusively, liberty and community are not mutually exclusive concepts but have accompanied Canadian federalism all through its historical trajectory as complementary concepts of being and belonging.[5]

Finally, at least for me, there is also no need to engage in a debate about nationalism and multinationalism.[6] Canada is not a nation-state. It is a federation of provinces and territories. In Canada's federal system, Quebec is a province, not a nation. Because it is the only province with a Francophone majority, it is distinct, a province unlike the others. Cultural duality complicates the conventional scheme of federation as a union among equal members. The process that began with the Quiet Revolution in the 1960s was entirely legitimate in that it sought to rectify disadvantages that had resulted from that duality. More than half a century later, it would appear that the Canadian federation is capable of accommodating, and willing to accommodate, Quebec's distinctiveness, and that Quebec has been provided with sufficient political strength to guard against further disadvantage or discrimination.

It has become commonplace to call countries like Canada, Switzerland, Belgium, Spain, and India "multinational."[7] There is nothing wrong with that so long as "multinational" serves as a descriptor of territorially bounded cultural plurality coexisting within one country. Federalism is a political form that can

5 Robert C. Vipond, *Liberty and Community: Canadian Federalism and the Failure of the Constitution* (Albany: State University of New York Press, 1991).

6 See Alain-G. Gagnon and Raffaele Iacovino, *Federalism, Citizenship, and Quebec* (Toronto: University of Toronto Press, 2007).

7 See Alfred Stepan, "Federalism and Democracy: Beyond the U.S. Model," *Journal of Democracy* 10, no. 4 (1999), 20.

accommodate such plurality. As Alfred Stepan has pointed out, democratic "multinational" polities are all federations.[8] I believe, however, that federalism cannot accommodate nationalism if nationalism is to be understood, as John Stuart Mill recognized early on, as a collective "identity of race and descent" embedded in a "community of recollections" as its strongest driving force, ultimately aiming at "government by themselves … exclusively."[9]

To take a comparative perspective, as long as the European Union remains a multinationalist enterprise, it will remain incomplete as a federation. Federalism requires a level of socioeconomic integration and solidarity that must transcend nationalism. That was the European project after 1945. It never quite succeeded, and the greatest danger for Europe now is neo-nationalist retrenchment. It is therefore not helpful to insist on Canadian federalism as a multinationalist enterprise. Multinationalism fails as a project of political accommodation if the objective is a federation with shared values strong enough to withstand neo-nationalist retrenchment.

If multinationalism fails as an antidote to pan-Canadian nationalism, what can replace it? Samuel LaSelva has suggested to start from the other end, by replacing the idea of pan-Canadian nationalism with George-Étienne Cartier's notion of a pan-Canadian "political nationality," the sharing of a political identity "with which 'neither the national origin, nor the religion of any individual would interfere.'"[10] Political nationality is in this way a notion or concept not unlike "constitutional patriotism," which proposes to detach political allegiance and collective identity from insistence on a national culture and to focus instead on shared constitutional norms, values, and democratic procedures.[11] In this way, as Cartier imagined, the "two races" can compete not "against each other" but "for the general welfare."[12] For the country as a whole this would require accepting that generally uniform solutions for all its parts are not necessary in all instances and for all matters. For Quebec it would mean replacing emotional nationalist discourse grounded in the memory of injustice

8 Ibid.

9 From John Stuart Mill, *Considerations on Representative Government*, in *Political Ideologies*, eds. Matthew Festenstein and Michael Kenny (Oxford: Oxford University Press, 2005), 271.

10 Cited in Samuel V. LaSelva, *The Moral Foundations of Canadian Federalism: Paradoxes, Achievements, and Tragedies of Nationhood* (Montreal: McGill-Queen's University Press, 1996), 25.

11 See Jan-Werner Müller and Kim Lane Scheppele, "Constitutional Patriotism: An Introduction," *International Journal of Constitutional Law* 6, no. 1 (2008).

12 Cited in LaSelva, *Moral Foundations*, 25.

with a rational discourse on the institutional and procedural requirements of cultural difference.[13]

The image of Canada as a multinational federation replaced the older image of English–French duality when Indigenous rights of existence could no longer be ignored. I believe, however, that multinationalism also fails as a concept of Indigenous inclusion. The notion of nationalism is alien to Indigenous culture. Indigenous organizations only began in the 1980s to refer to themselves as "First Nations" as a strategic political move in response to the "Canadian rhetoric about the 'two founding nations.'"[14] There is no generic Indigenous "nation," and the idea of whittling the more than 600 Indigenous bands in Canada down to some 60 to 80 "nation-governments," as the Royal Commission on Aboriginal Peoples (RCAP) suggested,[15] strikes me as a strangely alienating concession to political acculturation.

The self-understanding of Indigenous collective identity is in fact much closer to the concept of constitutional patriotism than to nationalism. As the Great Law of the Haudenosaunee or Iroquois Confederacy states: "If any man or any nation outside the Five Nations shall obey the laws of the Great Peace … they shall be welcomed to take shelter beneath the Tree of the Long Leaves."[16]

What remains, then, in terms of contested concepts about the meaning and functioning of Canadian federalism, are two sets of deep disagreements, one foundational and one operational.

The foundational disagreement is about whether Confederation came about as a compact among equal provinces or as a compact between two nationalities. Neither one of these views is exactly borne out by historical fact or the way in which Confederation came into existence, yet both allow each opposing camp to sustain a powerful narrative about how Confederation ought to be thought of and how it ought to function.

The operational disagreement is about whether Canadian federalism should be constitutional federalism maximizing autonomy on the basis of

---

13 See similarly John Erik Fossum, "Deep Diversity versus Constitutional Patriotism," *Ethnicities* 1, no. 2 (2001).

14 James S. Frideres and René R. Gadacz, *Aboriginal Peoples in Canada* (Toronto: Pearson Prentice Hall, 2008), 22.

15 See Alan C. Cairns, *Citizens Plus: Aboriginal Peoples and the Canadian State* (Vancouver: University of British Columbia Press, 2018), 138.

16 A.C. Parker, *The Constitution of the Five Nations or The Iroquois Book of the Great Law* (1916; repr., Ohsweken: Iroqrafts, 2006), 30 (provision 2).

strictly separated powers or procedural federalism in its acceptance of high-level interdependence on the basis of interjurisdictional cooperation. As I shall argue, and as should be obvious from previous chapters in this book, these views and concepts are in reality more complementary than mutually exclusive.

Finally, mention must be made of the Indigenous concept of treaty federalism, which stands apart from both the constitutional and the procedural concept of federalism in its *a priori* claim of full sovereignty. Not unlike the concept of sovereignty-association, treaty federalism therefore aims at a "domestic version of a mini-international system."[17] Also like sovereignty-association, the Indigenous concept of treaty federalism falls outside the parameters of federalism as a combination of self-rule and shared rule. As they were not part of the original federal compact, however, Indigenous peoples have the right not to enter it now.[18] Whether it is possible to escape the confines of interdependence under conditions of modern governance complexity, however, is another question.

A Plural Compact of Provinces or a Dual Compact of Nationalities?

The way the foundational story of the classical federations is told is that previously independent entities come together as equal members to form a union for mutual economic and security benefit. Canada's foundational story is different. John A. Macdonald and other founders indeed had in mind a continental union for economic and security purposes. The parts of that union, however, were not exactly meant to be equal. The west, in the words of Clifford Sifton, Wilfrid Laurier's interior minister, was to "give a vast and profitable traffic to its railways and steamship lines" and to "furnish a steady and remunerative business to the manufacturers of eastern Canada."[19] And in central Canada, the principal task at hand was not to forge a union so much as to disentangle the already existing and dysfunctional dual union of Canada East and Canada West that had been decreed in 1841. Equality and duality were contested concepts of the Canadian federal compact from the very beginning.

17 Cairns, *Citizens Plus*, 135.

18 In order not to be misunderstood: If they have a clear will to do so, Quebecers are of course free to negotiate leaving the compact. But leaving an already existing compact is not the same as not entering it to begin with.

19 Cited from a 1904 speech in Winnipeg, in John F. Conway, *The Rise of the New West: The History of a Region in Confederation* (Toronto: James Lorimer, 2014), 26–7.

Also from the very beginning, English and French Canadians had a different assessment of what exactly Confederation meant. Macdonald obviously thought that he had ascertained for the union all the powers necessary for the sovereign control of peace, order, and good government. To grant provinces powers over property and civil rights was a minimum concession to Quebec that was not meant to amount to anything of political importance let alone sovereign substance. French Canadians saw it differently. The federal compact was meant to give them everything that the autonomy and survival of French Canada required: language, religion, education, land and resource ownership, and municipal affairs; in fact, as the French Canadian newspaper *La Minerve* declared on Confederation day in 1867, these powers would amount to everything "dearest and most precious to us."[20]

These different assessments were not contradictory. In their attempt to construct a continental economy, Macdonald and the English merchant class had little if any concern for local affairs. French Canadians in turn were not interested in economic modernization. Social policy for the most part was left to municipalities and the church. The French Canadian understanding of Confederation primarily was one of disentanglement. The future relationship of Quebec with the federal government was of little concern. As Quebec businessman and politician Joseph Cauchon put it, there was "no delegation of power either from above or from below" because both orders of government would receive their respective powers from the imperial parliament.[21] French Canadians wanted to be on their own, in their own province, as much as possible.

So, increasingly, did English Canadians in Ontario and some of the other provinces, Nova Scotia in particular. What emerged in conjunction with the provincial rights movement spearheaded by Ontario was the so-called compact theory of Confederation most prominently enunciated by a retired Quebec judge T.J.J. Loranger.[22] Emulating the founding story of American federalism and downplaying the effective legal status of the new constitution as a British statute, this theory in essence insisted that Confederation had come about as an agreement among equal provinces, and that this agreement therefore had been merely ratified by the imperial parliament. Accordingly, while all provincial powers were original powers retained by the provinces, the federal government

20 Cited in Arthur I. Silver, *The French-Canadian Idea of Confederation 1864–1900* (Toronto: University of Toronto Press, 1982), 42.

21 Cited in ibid., 43.

22 For the following see Black, *Divided Loyalties*, 151–7.

as a creation of the provincialist compact only held powers ceded to it by that compact.

The provincialist compact theory became the dominant theory of Confederation among those seeking to protect provincial powers and autonomy from federal encroachment.[23] It also fuelled western demands for provincial equality,[24] and it provided the ideological backdrop for those opposed to granting Quebec any kind of special or distinct status.[25] In Quebec, however, where it had surfaced first, the provincialist compact theory soon became superimposed by the idea of Confederation as a dual compact between the English and the French.

Duality had been the de facto organizing principle of governance during the years of legislative union prior to Confederation.[26] Canada East and Canada West had kept much of their separate administrative structures, which meant that that there had to be double ministries, one French and one English, including the dualized prime ministry. Even the capital and seat of the united legislature alternated between English and French Canada. The passage of bills routinely (but not always) required double majority approval from Canada East and Canada West members. Since each side was further divided along party lines between conservatives (Canada West and East), reformers (Canada West), and radicals (Parti Rouge, Canada East), governments were unstable and governance unworkable. For the English Canadians, Confederation meant escape from this stifling dualism. For French Canadians it meant trading federal duality for provincial autonomy.

The British North America (BNA) Act, now the Constitution Act, 1867, had not entirely done away with duality. Section 93 had upheld existing separate school education for cultural and religious minorities in all provinces. Section 94 had implicitly acknowledged legal duality by a provision of amalgamating (common) civil law in the English-speaking provinces into one uniform body of civil law under federal jurisdiction that was obviously juxtaposed to the continued existence of (statutory) civil law in Quebec. And Section 133 had ascertained bilingual services and rights at the federal level of government and in Quebec.

Yet it was only when virulent anti-Catholicism combined with attacks on French school education occurred in some of the other provinces, New

---

23 See Vipond, *Liberty and Community*, 6.

24 See Loleen Berdahl and Roger Gibbins, *Looking West: Regional Transformation and the Future of Canada* (Toronto: University of Toronto Press, 2014), 19–21.

25 See Kenneth McRoberts, *Misconceiving Canada: The Struggle for National Unity* (Toronto: Oxford University Press, 1997), 199.

26 See on the following ibid., 6–9.

Brunswick, Ontario, and Manitoba in particular,[27] that French Canadians fully took to the idea that only an understanding of Confederation as a dual compact between two founding nations would guarantee their cultural survival. As most prominently enunciated by Henri Bourassa at the beginning of the twentieth century, Confederation comprised a "double contract," one "concluded between the French and the English of the old province of Canada," the other to "bring together the scattered colonies of British North America."[28] This formulation presupposes that membership equality in the Canadian federation must be guaranteed in two different ways, as equality among provinces and as equality between two cultural groups. The problem is that each of these equality guarantees leads to different conclusions about the nature and organization of Canadian federalism.

The theory of Confederation as a compact among equal provinces demands symmetry with regard to three central tenets of federalism: the distribution of powers, regional representation, and constitutional amendment.

First, no member in the federation must have rights or powers the others do not have. From this supposition stems much of English Canada's opposition to the recognition of Quebec as a distinct society even when this recognition for the most part would have been symbolic only. Having been denied resource ownership like the other provinces until 1930, the symmetrical equality argument also fuels long-standing suspicions of being treated as second-class members in the three western Prairie provinces.

Second, regional representation in Canada's second legislative chamber, the senate, must be equal or at least fair. During the Confederation debates, the question of regional representation was more hotly contested than even the distribution of powers. The outcome, 24 senators each for Ontario, Quebec, and the Maritimes, seemed fair enough: parity with Ontario for Quebec even though its population had already fallen behind, and overrepresentation for the Maritimes which, with a combined population of roughly half of Quebec's, still pulled considerable economic weight.[29] Symmetry, equality, and fairness only became an issue with the entrance of the western provinces into Confederation. The entire west was again treated as a region and accorded 24 senators in all: hence the insistence on senate reform mostly coming from that region. At the beginning of the twenty-first century, the west's 24 senators represent 31 per cent of the Canadian

27 Ibid., 17–19; also in greater detail in Silver, *The French-Canadian Idea*, 150–217.

28 Cited in McRoberts, *Misconceiving Canada*, 20.

29 See the 1861 Census, available at https://www66.statcan.gc.ca/eng/1867/186700160016_The%20Census.pdf.

population, whereas all of Atlantic Canada (the three Maritime provinces plus Newfoundland and Labrador) can boast 30 senators representing a mere 7 per cent of Canadians.[30] Not to mention economic weight: Between 1981 and 2010, the gross domestic product (GDP) of the four western provinces has oscillated between 40 and 50 per cent of Canada's total.[31]

Third, constitutional amendments, which make changes to the original compact, must in principle require the approval of all federated members. This means that all members are equal in having a veto over constitutional change. Treaty changes in the European Union, for instance, require such unanimous approval. In the classical federations, however, as pioneered by the Americans and to avoid almost certain deadlock, procedures have been devised that require super majorities rather than unanimity. Constitutional change should be difficult but not impossible. The 7/50 default procedure for constitutional amendment in Canada established in Section 38 of the Constitution Act, 1982, requiring the approval of two-thirds of the provinces representing at least 50 per cent of the Canadian population, formally satisfies principles of symmetry and equitability.

In sharp contrast, the theory of Confederation as a dual compact between the English and French makes different and asymmetrical demands on federalism. These demands of asymmetry have become more strident over time in Quebec, as the lone predominantly Francophone province saw itself confronted not only with nine predominantly Anglophone provinces rather than the original four or five, but also with a declining population rate, which stands below 25 per cent of the Canadian population at the moment. The rise of the dual compact theory in Quebec was in many ways a response to fears of marginalization in a federation numerically dominated by the English.

It is the dual compact theory that makes Quebec asymmetrical in terms of federalism because, vis-à-vis the other provinces, it logically implies that Quebec should have powers that the other provinces will not need and therefore will not have,[32] that senate reform essentially amounts to an Anglophone imposition of provincial equality,[33] and that to protect its position as a founding nation Quebec must retain a veto over constitutional amendments.[34]

---

30 Berdahl and Gibbins, *Looking West*, 38.

31 Conway, *The Rise of the New West*, 16.

32 See Michel Seymour, "On Not Finding Our Way: The Illusory Reform of the Canadian Federation," in Gagnon, *Contemporary Canadian Federalism*, 196–9.

33 See McRoberts, *Misconceiving Canada*, 210–11.

34 See Alain-G. Gagnon, "Québec–Canada's Constitutional Dossier," in *Québec: State and Society*, ed. Alain-G. Gagnon (Peterborough: Broadview Press, 2004), 139–40.

Under the long shadow of a double compact meant to guarantee both provincial equality and cultural duality, Canadian federalism inevitably must remain caught in an uneasy truce of competing visions about what it should be and how it should function. Essentially, it is a truce between federalism and confederalism. Modern federalism assumes that changes to the agreed-upon constitutional order by means of qualified majority rule are justified. The enabling condition for such majority rule is provincial equality in an existential sense: No member of the federation is considered to be so much of an outsider with such a divergent set of interests that majority rule would put that member into a position of permanent minority status and marginalization. Confederalism in turn insists that differences are so significant that each member of the federation needs to retain a veto over all collective changes.

It is possible, however, as I want to argue, that the two contested concepts – a federalism of provincial equality and a confederalism of cultural duality – can not only be reconciled, but also that the Constitution Act, 1982, does in fact provide for such reconciliation at least in principle. In order to make that argument, I am taking recourse to the early seventeenth-century German theorist of federalism Johannes Althusius,[35] who declared that in a composite commonwealth decisions "may be made according to the judgments of the more numerous or larger part in the things that concern all [members] together, but not in those that concern them separately."[36] In other words, Althusius thought that whereas matters of universal concern for the entire commonwealth could be decided by majority vote, matters particular to individual members should require approval of these members.

Similarly, the Constitution Act, 1982, provides for a constitutional amendment procedure based on qualitative majority approval for matters deemed to be affecting all provinces equally in Section 38, and for a constitutional amendment procedure based on unanimity for matters considered existential for each province in its own right in Section 41. Moreover, Section 38 also allows a dissenting province to opt out from an amendment affecting its powers, and Section 40 provides for fiscal compensation if the opting out occurs in areas of education or culture more generally.

In practice, one may well disagree with what the Constitution Act, 1982, considers to be matters requiring unanimity or with the limitation of fiscal

35 See Thomas O. Hueglin, *Early Modern Concepts for a Late Modern World: Althusius on Community and Federalism* (Waterloo: Wilfrid Laurier University Press 1999).

36 Johannes Althusius, *Politica* (1614; Indianapolis: Liberty Fund, 1995), 65.

compensation to education and culture only. In principle, however, the Canadian amendment provisions point to an Althusian solution, or at least compromise, of the symmetry versus asymmetry conundrum. It is no longer contested which path Canadian federalism ought to take in exclusivity. What remains contested instead is the meaning and understanding of what is universal and what is particular.

That question obviously also pertains to the extant division of powers in the Canadian federal system. Quebec nationalists, governments, and political parties have all demanded at different times to return Canadian federalism closer to the original formula of 1867. In the aftermath of the failed Meech Lake Accord, and short of outright separation, the Quebec Liberal Party's 1991 Allaire report probably went furthest. It suggested not only that the province should have exclusive power over the entire field of social policy, including healthcare and unemployment insurance, but moreover that the Supreme Court of Canada (SCC) should no longer have jurisdiction over Quebec, and especially not so with regard to Charter challenges.[37]

The Allaire report was perhaps a less than entirely sincere attempt of politically capitalizing on post-Meech anger in Quebec.[38] However, it also gave genuine expression to a retrograde understanding of federalism inferred from a narrow reading of the 1867 Confederation settlement that routinely animates complaints about federal meddling in provincial jurisdiction. The Canadian founders left social policy to the provinces because it was not perceived to be an important matter for the creation of a successful political, social, and economic union. As discussed in Chapter 4, the crisis of capitalism and federalism during the interwar years dramatically changed this perception.[39] It became clear that the stability of the capitalist market required government intervention, and that such intervention essentially had to include social policy measures aiming at both individual social security and, as the Rowell-Sirois Commission had already pointed out, interprovincial equitability.[40]

---

37 McRoberts, *Misconceiving Canada*, 205; Peter H. Russell, *Constitutional Odyssey: Can Canadians Become a Sovereign People?* (Toronto: University of Toronto Press, 2004), 159–60.

38 See A. Brian Tanguay, "Sclerosis or a Clean Bill of Health? Diagnosing Québec's Party System in the Twenty-First Century," in Gagnon, *Québec*, 159–60.

39 See Keith G. Banting, *The Welfare State and Canadian Federalism*, 2nd ed. (Montreal: McGill-Queen's University Press, 1987), 47–8.

40 See Joseph Sirois and Newton Wesley Rowell, *Report of the Royal Commission on Dominion–Provincial Relations, Book I* (Ottawa: Privy Council Office, 1940), chapter VI, 160.

As the Rowell-Sirois Commission had also pointed out, such equitability by means of "desirable" standards of "uniformity" went beyond the scope of the provinces as social policy actors individually.[41] In a 1981 publication, the government of Canada made no bones about what this had meant, a nearly "revolutionary" challenge to the constitutional division of powers because the distinction between economic and social policy had become "blurred" and because social security therefore had to be considered as an important and legitimate policy "instrument" for the federal government.[42] To the extent, then, that it is instrumental for Canadian economic stability, and in accordance with the pith and substance doctrine first developed by the JCPC in the nineteenth century, one might say that social policy has become an overlapping responsibility and power in Canadian federalism.

The most important consequence of this change in the understanding of Canadian federalism was the development of healthcare and social assistance as shared-cost programs. While the Quebec government's 1954 Tremblay report had bravely called for the opposite with the return of social security policy into the exclusive domain of the provinces,[43] the federal scheme proved extremely popular across all parts of Canada. Healthcare in particular took on the iconic status of a pan-Canadian citizenship right.[44]

As explained in Chapter 5, the federal government imposed some general conditions for the uniform delivery of healthcare by the provinces: the delivery had to be public, comprehensive, universal, portable, and accessible. For some, this kind of federal imposition amounts to a move away from classical federalism with its assumption of strictly divided powers, and toward a regime of "administrative" federalism whereby the provinces are in danger of becoming "administrative agents" of the federal government.[45] Administrative federalism is the hallmark of German federalism, where the *Länder* administrations are indeed obliged

41 Ibid., chapter IX, 249.

42 Government of Canada, *Federalism and Decentralization: Where Do We Stand?* (Ottawa: Minister of Supply and Services Canada, 1981).

43 David Kwavnick, ed., *The Tremblay Report* (Toronto: McClelland and Stewart, 1973), 216–17.

44 See Gerard W. Boychuk, *National Health Insurance in the United States and Canada: Race, Territory, and the Roots of Difference* (Washington DC: Georgetown University Press, 2008), 141–53.

45 See Marc-Antoine Adam, Josée Bergeron, and Marianne Bonnard, "Intergovernmental Relations in Canada: Competing Visions and Diverse Dynamics," in *Intergovernmental Relations in Federal Systems: Comparative Structures and Dynamics*, eds. Johanne Poirier, Cheryl Saunders, and John Kincaid (Toronto: Oxford University Press, 2015), 165.

to carry out federal law.[46] This is not the case in Canada, however. Instead, as exemplified by healthcare, I would argue that the management of overlapping powers in Canadian federalism has by and large followed the Althusian distinction of universal and particular matters of public policy.

Compared to most other federations, the general conditions for public policy delivery imposed by the federal government in return for cost sharing are "minimal."[47] Where they are indeed more onerous, as in the case of healthcare, for instance, equitability and portability requirements across the country may be seen as a universal civic code much in the same sense that Cartier understood "political nationality" as a pan-Canadian rallying point "for the general welfare."[48] Provinces in turn do not just carry out or administer federal law. The generality of the conditions leaves plenty of room for particular program design and delivery.[49]

Only the insistence on healthcare delivery as universally public, even though widely supported across the country, has in fact resulted in occasional political controversy because it pits a social democratic understanding of healthcare as a common public good against neoliberal notions of healthcare as a private good that can be traded in a free market. Ironically, support for public-only healthcare is lowest in Quebec, even though it purportedly is the most social democratic province in the country. And, more than elsewhere, to appease its dualist insistence on asymmetry Quebec's violations of the public delivery condition have been tolerated with regard to new and costly diagnostic services such as MRI and CT scans and ultrasound.[50]

How Much Autonomy or Interdependence?

The foundational disagreement over Confederation either as a provincial compact among equal provinces or as a dual compact among two founding nations obviously is a disagreement mainly if not exclusively between Quebec and the

---

46 See Thomas O. Hueglin and Alan Fenna, *Comparative Federalism: A Systematic Inquiry* (Toronto: University of Toronto Press, 2015), 148–55.

47 Robin Boadway, "Canada," in *The Practice of Fiscal Federalism: Comparative Perspectives*, ed. Anwar Shah (Montreal: McGill-Queen's University Press, 2007), 119.

48 See LaSelva, *Moral Foundations*, 25.

49 See Keith Banting, "Canada: Nation-Building in the Federal Welfare State," in *Federalism and the Welfare State: New World and European Experiences*, eds. Herbert Obinger, Stephan Leibfried, and Francis G. Castles (Cambridge: Cambridge University Press, 2005), 113.

50 See Boychuk, *National Health Insurance*, 150–2.

English-speaking rest of the country. Quebec's insistence on dualist asymmetry also is a potent driver in the quest to keep the federal government out of provincial affairs. Put simply, if you want to do things differently, you need to do them by yourself, without outside interference.

This points to the other and operational disagreement between the adherents of a classical form of constitutional federalism according to which each order of government should be able to carry out its responsibilities under the constitution autonomously, that is to say without interference from the other order, and the adherents of cooperative or procedural federalism according to which the proper functioning of the Canadian federal system requires cooperative interaction between the two orders of government to the effect that both become interdependent upon each other.

These are of course ideal-typical distinctions. As already noted by the JCPC in its 1881 *Parsons* decision (see Chapter 3), the classical form of federalism with its assumption of powers cleanly divided between the two orders of government never existed. More often than not, the powers written into Section 91 and Section 92 of the BNA Act turned out to be overlapping in practice. By the same token, as just discussed in the previous section about healthcare, the proper functioning of the Canadian federal system has never meant a complete loss of autonomy. What it comes down to, then, is a disagreement about where to strike the balance.

According to François Rocher, the corner posts of the disagreement are occupied by the two commission reports that have assumed iconic character in pre-formulating the federal vision of English and French Canada, respectively. For English Canada it is the 1940 report of the Rowell-Sirois Commission. Faced with the crisis of the 1930s, when neither order of government appeared capable of responding adequately to the catastrophic social ills of the Great Depression, the Rowell-Sirois report recommended interdependence at the expense of autonomy, thus undermining, as Rocher contends, a core principle of federalism in the name of efficiency. For Quebec in turn, it was the 1956 report of the Tremblay Commission. Concerned with what had by then become English Canada's mantra of functioning federalism – ever more federal intervention in areas formally under provincial jurisdiction – the Trembley report, according to Rocher again, by insisting on provincial autonomy as the only important political objective gave short shrift to the inevitability of interdependence and thus also neglected an important normative aspect of federalism as a cooperative partnership.[51]

51 See François Rocher, "The Quebec–Canada Dynamic or the Negation of the Ideal of Federalism," in Gagnon, *Contemporary Canadian Federalism*.

For Rocher, herein lies the crux of the Canadian federalism conundrum: mutual negation of what he would consider an ideal form of federalism from either end, so to speak. The English Canadian understanding of federalism, according to his argument, has become entirely efficiency driven. Quebec's position in turn has never strayed far from insisting on a degree of autonomy amounting to almost complete dissociation from the rest of Canada. The argument is compelling by clearly identifying underlying concepts often obscured by fuzzy political language. Yet suggesting a starkly dichotomous Quebec–Canada dynamic as a perennial characteristic of Canadian federalism appears somewhat overdrawn.

While the Tremblay report may have given expression to Quebec's most innate political instincts (autonomy as the overriding principle safeguarding dualism and distinctiveness), Quebec politics has by no means been oblivious to the necessities of cooperation. It was the Quebec government of Jean Lesage that first established a specialized department of intergovernmental affairs in 1961. Still in 2017, the Quebec government's intergovernmental department, meanwhile renamed Secrétariat aux affaires intergouvernementales canadiennes, produced a programmatic vision of Canadian federalism in which cooperative federalism is acknowledged as a "flexible way" of adapting to the "current reality," which is characterized by "increasingly complex" intergovernmental relations.[52] The political goal of maximizing autonomy to the point of dissociation appears moderated by the acknowledgement of interdependence as inevitable and ultimately beneficial.

English Canada in turn has not always – if ever – shared a uniformly homogenous vision of interdependence as the most efficient form of federalism. Western provinces in particular have resented interdependence as a form of hinterland dependency. In the 1982 constitutional patriation settlement, the west pressed for, and gained, more autonomy over natural resources. The Reform Party's 1988 slogan "The West Wants In" did not aim at interdependence at the expense of autonomy. It aimed at a stronger regional voice in central decision making – itself a core concept of federalism. And western Conservative Prime Minister Stephen Harper's "open federalism," if it amounted to much at all, followed a rationale of disentanglement seeking to place more emphasis on autonomy as formally prescribed by the constitution.[53]

52 Government of Québec, *Quebecers, Our Way of Being: Policy on Québec Affirmations and Canadian Relations* (Quebec: Secréteriat aux Affaires Intergouvernementales Canadiennes, 2017), 115.

53 See Institute of Intergovernmental Relations, *Open Federalism: Interpretations, Significance* (Kingston: Institute of Intergovernmental Relations, 2006).

Ultimately, the autonomy versus interdependence dynamic in Canadian federalism is all about political legitimacy. As we saw in Chapter 5, with the onset of the modern welfare state the federal government took on, and wanted to take on, a significant part of the legitimation function, balancing as it were the capitalist market with social stabilization policies. This set it on a course of conflict with the provinces, Quebec in particular, which were adamant about retaining control of the legitimation function as their exclusive prerogative under the constitution. As first suggested by David Easton,[54] however, there are two kinds of political legitimacy: input legitimacy and output legitimacy. Input legitimacy is about voice, participation, and inclusion. In a federal system, it is also about which order of government legitimately represents voice, participation, and inclusion with regard to policy matters divided under the constitution. Output legitimacy is about satisfactory policy and program delivery.

The autonomy versus interdependence dynamic in Canadian federalism can in this way be reformulated as an input–output dynamic: Autonomy prioritizes input legitimacy, the proper assignment of responsibility and accountability under the constitution. Interdependence, to the extent that it is efficiency driven in Rocher's terms, prioritizes output legitimacy. Arguably, however, English Canada became captivated by efficiency considerations as the overriding concern only twice, first during and after the social catastrophe of the Great Depression, as reflected in the recommendations of the Rowell-Sirois Commission, and again after decades of constitutional wrangling had shifted considerable attention to normative considerations in the aftermath of the Meech and Charlottetown Accord debacle. A general sense of federalism fatigue set in, and political scientists indeed focused on "performance, effectiveness, and [output] legitimacy" as their overriding concern.[55] In Quebec, of course, the negative outcome of Meech and Charlottetown triggered the opposite – deepened autonomy concerns – and a similar occurrence of federalism fatigue only set in after the 1995 referendum when it became clear that the status quo would not be changeable any time soon.

Fatigue, perhaps, but not a lack of vigilance. As the Quebec government's intergovernmental Secrétariat under the direction of then Liberal Premier Philippe Couillard noted in 2017, "the temptation to centralize is always present in our federal system." And in reference to the SCC's 2011 *Securities* reference (see Chapter 3), which had called for a flexible form of cooperative federalism that

---

54 See David Easton, *A Systems Analysis of Political Life* (New York: Wiley, 1965).

55 See Herman Bakvis and Grace Skogstad, *Canadian Federalism: Performance, Effectiveness, and Legitimacy* (Toronto: Oxford University Press, 2012).

would not, however, erode the constitutional balance of powers, the Secrétariat affirmed that "cooperative federalism must not be used as a pretext to push aside the division of powers."[56]

The question, then, is yet again how to understand and interpret "division of powers." A literalist reading of the BNA Act of 1867 is of little help once it is accepted that its formulations are sufficiently vague to allow for different interpretations. The BNA Act mentions hospitals, asylums, and charities as provincial powers, but not medicare or universal healthcare. The intention of the founders clearly was to limit provincial powers to matters of local concern. That was a travesty of federalism, and it was corrected by the rulings of the JCPC. But if social policy can be said to have become a matter of national concern, as it arguably did after the 1930s crisis of capitalism (see Chapter 4), then extrapolating from the limited meaning of the BNA Act with regard to provincial social policy powers that the provinces should now nevertheless have exclusive control over social policy would appear not only as a misreading of the founders' intentions but also a travesty of federalism.

The problem of overlapping powers is inevitable as it eludes constitutional certainty. Classical federalism with its assumption of cleanly divided powers has been as much an illusion as nation-state sovereignty. Both were grounded in assumptions about a modern world that could be compartmentalized in a binary fashion. Political reality has been messier. Federal constitutions, it has been argued, are essentially incomplete contracts providing no more than basic rules that need to be complemented by an ongoing process of intergovernmental contracting.[57] That process is itself inevitably embedded in contested arguments and assumptions.

The debate about the SCC's 2011 *Securities* decision is a case in point. Securities regulation is about investors' protection and the stability of financial markets.

For some, the essence of the decision was that it denied the federal government a wholesale takeover of securities regulation. In the hands of 13 provincial and territorial regulators, the system has been considered one of the best in the world.[58]

56 Government of Québec, *Quebecers*, 115–16.

57 Jonathan A. Rodden, *Hamilton's Paradox: The Promise and Peril of Fiscal Federalism* (Cambridge: Cambridge University Press, 2006), 37–8.

58 Stéphane Rousseau, "The Provinces' Competence over Securities Regulation in Canada: Taking Stock of the Supreme Court's Opinion," in *What's Next for Canada? Securities Regulation after the Reference*, ed. Anita Anand (Toronto: Irwin Law, 2012), 284.

As proposed, federal regulation would only duplicate what was already in place and functioning well.[59] Moreover, given the regionalized character of Canadian financial markets, investors might be served more efficiently by decentralization.[60] In this way, the federal government's general trade and commerce power should not displace what was essentially deemed local regulation in much the same way that the JCPC had argued almost a century and a half earlier in the case of fire insurance.[61]

For others, however, the essence of the decision was the opposite in that the court did find room for a federal role in securities regulation. The 2008 financial crisis had shown that there had at least been the possibility of a "financial meltdown of an entire economic system."[62] Arguably, this was a systemic risk well beyond the scope of a decentralized securities regulation regime with different standards and non-mandatory cooperation.[63] As such, it constituted a national concern and therefore called for federal imposition of "common standards" to prevent financial market "disturbance" in one provincial jurisdiction from spreading across the country. The argument is not unlike that of the Rowell-Sirois Commission half a century earlier, according to which social problems such as mass unemployment had become systemic threats that went beyond the scope of a merely local policy response.[64]

These are obviously efficiency-driven and output-oriented arguments. As arguments based on different rationales, however, they do not *a priori* negate the underlying principles of divided powers and autonomy. The federal government can act only if its imposition of common standards does not merely duplicate what the provinces can achieve on their own. The pith and substance of federal involvement in securities regulation must be national concern beyond provincial efficacy. The constitutional intention of distinguishing between matters of general and particular concern is not violated.

In terms of the division and balance of powers, the leading question is not who should do what but instead who should do how much of what. To be sure, this amounts to a "decompartmentalization" that was not foreseen or intended

59 Ibid., 283.

60 Jeffrey G. MacIntosh, "A National Securities Commission? The Headless Horseman Rides Again," in Anand, *What's Next for Canada?*, 257–9.

61 In the 1881 *Parsons* case; see Chapter 3.

62 Anita Anand, "After the Reference: Regulating Systemic Risk in Canadian Financial Markets," in Anand, *What's Next for Canada?*, 221.

63 Ibid., 205–12.

64 See the discussion in Chapter 4.

by the designers of modern classical federalism.[65] However, such decompartmentalization must not necessarily translate into a distortion of the power balance between general and particular so long as systemic risk concerns do not spill over into unilateral assertions of federal paramountcy.

In its latest ruling on the matter of securities regulation, concerning a 2013 revised proposal for a Cooperative Capital Markets Regulatory System (CCMRS) most vigorously contested by Quebec, the SCC found that this was not the case because an opt-in provision would leave choice of participation to individual provinces.[66] While the fate of the CCMRS remains unclear to date, it is likely that only Quebec and Alberta will want to remain outside. Whether this rather open-ended approach to a national form of securities regulation will prove to be effective remains to be seen. By the same token, if there were a systemic risk indicating the possibility of a general meltdown of Canadian capital markets, it is hard to see how individual provinces could remain on the outside.

What seems to be clear is that the classical conception of Canadian federalism as the political organization of divided and shared rule needs to be rethought. Autonomy is no longer a pristine space of sheltered self-rule, if it ever was. Instead, it is negotiated space with flexible and overlapping boundaries. In this way, whether federalism remains grounded in the principle of "non-subordination"[67] largely depends on a process of political negotiation with "clear and consensual rules."[68] From a provincialist perspective, such rules are lacking with regard to the federal spending power in particular (see Chapter 5). Its exercise, however, has not rendered the balance of power obsolete. The constitution continues to provide the foundational backbone for the Canadian federal system precisely because autonomy and interdependence remain contested concepts.

Treaty Federalism

For Indigenous peoples in Canada, federalism has mainly meant being caught between a rock and a hard place, often being simultaneously subjected to federal legislation and provincial regulation. By intuition, Canada's Indigenous peoples

65 Rocher, "The Quebec–Canada Dynamic," 114.

66 *Reference re Pan-Canadian Securities Regulation*, 2018 SCC 48.

67 Rocher, "The Quebec–Canada Dynamic," 119.

68 Alain Noël, "Social Justice in Overlapping Sharing Communities," in *Dilemmas of Solidarity: Rethinking Redistribution in the Canadian Federation*, eds. Sujit Choudhry, Jean-François Gaudreault-DesBiens, and Lorne Sossin (Toronto: University of Toronto Press, 2006), 67.

have rejected federalism and instead looked to the Crown as the only legitimate counterpart in a difficult and poorly defined relationship, which they saw and still see essentially as a nation-to-nation relationship between two sovereign parties. They could draw support for this view from the Royal Proclamation of 1763, in which the Crown addressed them as "several Nations or Tribes of Indians" who should live "unmolested" on their lands.[69] At least in hindsight, of course, it seems clear that the Crown had no intention of honouring that pledge, and particularly not so once the Crown's powers over Indians had been passed on to the Canadian government.

The BNA Act of 1867 formally subjected Indigenous peoples to federal legislation, and the Indian Act of 1876 made them powerless wards of the Crown. The Constitution Act, 1982, while recognizing "existing and aboriginal treaty rights" in Section 35, still continued to subject Indigenous peoples to the Canadian constitutional order. Not least because Indigenous peoples had at best non-voting observer status in the deliberations leading up to the 1982 constitutional settlement, Indigenous scholars began to think about an alternative that would do justice to their traditional insistence on the Indigenous relationship with the Canadian state as a nation-to-nation relationship. The result was a reformulation of that relationship as treaty federalism.[70]

As particularly elaborated by James Youngblood Henderson, there are two parallel federalisms in Canada: constitutional federalism regulating the relationship between the federal government and the provinces and treaty federalism as the basis for the relationship between the Crown and Indigenous peoples.[71] Treaty federalism is asymmetrical because of the plurality of treaties, each establishing a distinct relationship with each individual nation.[72] It is also confederal rather than federal in that there is no emphasis on dualized or common citizenship.[73]

While the Indigenous peoples' understanding of treaty federalism as an expression of their relationship with Canadian politics and society is relatively new, the main underlying principle of decision making by mutual

69 Government of Canada, "250th Anniversary of the Royal Proclamation of 1763."

70 See Kiera Ladner, "Treaty Federalism: An Indigenous Vision of Canadian Federalisms," in *New Trends in Canadian Federalism*, eds. François Rocher and Miriam Smith (Toronto: University of Toronto Press, 2012).

71 James (sákéj) Youngblood Henderson, "Empowering Treaty Federalism," *Saskatchewan Law Review* 58 (1994).

72 See Ladner, "Treaty Federalism," 174.

73 See Cairns, *Citizens Plus*, 182–4.

agreement guiding this understanding is very old. A case in point is the ancient Haudenosaunee or Iroquois Confederacy, which still exists on Canada's largest reserve in southwestern Ontario.[74] Based on oral tradition for centuries, the Great Law of the Confederacy was brought into its current written English form only at the beginning of the twentieth century.[75]

It would be simplistic to qualify the Great Law as a federal constitution or the confederacy as a democracy.[76] According to the Great Law, the confederacy is governed by the hereditary chiefs of 50 clans. The number of chiefs is uneven across the five participating nations of the Mohawk, Seneca, Cayuga, Oneida, and Onondaga. So is the distribution of power and influence. All decisions ultimately require unanimity, but by deliberating and proposing a decision first the Mohawk clearly are in a dominant position.[77] The important underlying principle, however, is not so much unanimity as it is a procedural commitment to reach agreement.[78] It is this commitment to the process that respects the sovereignty of each nation.

The process can perhaps best be compared to treaty deliberations in the European Union. Treaty changes require agreement of all member-states. Large member-states like Germany or France clearly dominate the agenda. Smaller member-states are doubtlessly under pressure to tag along. Their formal veto power, however, prevents their particular interests from being ignored. In order to reach agreement, the larger member-states will make concessions.[79] Crucial for the success of the process is an "effort to create the necessary institutional preconditions for deliberation."[80] The Great Law's elaborate provisions for deliberation in a climate of mutual respect constitute such an effort. Everyone gets to

---

74 See the Haudenosaunee Confederacy's website, available at https://www.haudenosauneeconfederacy.com.

75 Parker, *The Constitution of the Five Nations*; a sixth nation, the Tuscarora, was admitted to the confederacy later and without participatory rights in the system.

76 See Donald S. Lutz, "The Iroquois Confederation Constitution: An Analysis," *Publius: The Journal of Federalism* 28, no. 2 (1998): 99–127.

77 Parker, *The Constitution of the Five Nations*, provision 10.

78 Ibid., provisions 5–14.

79 See Clive Church and David Phinnemore, "From the Constitutional Treaty to the Treaty of Lisbon and Beyond," in *European Union Politics*, eds. Michelle Cini and Nieves Pérez-Solórzano Borragán (Oxford: Oxford University Press, 2010), 47.

80 Jürgen Neyer, "Discourse and Order in the EU: A Deliberative Approach to Multi-Level Governance," *Journal of Common Market Studies* 41, no. 4 (2003): 688.

speak, everyone is heard out in full, and there is even a provision to use wood for the council fire that does not spark so that the proceedings might not be disrupted.[81]

Because they were based on mutual agreement, the decisions taken at the confederacy's council fire can be interpreted as treaty agreements. This was also the Indigenous peoples' approach to dealing with the European settler societies, most famously expressed by the so-called Two Row Wampum belt. Serving as symbolic aids of understanding when a written language was not available, wampum belts are patterns of beads made from shells and sown on strips of hide. The Two Row Wampum belt, first presented to the Dutch by the Haudenosaunee at Fort Albany in 1613, shows two parallel lines of dark beads against a background of light beads. In the words of Indigenous teacher and scholar Leroy Little Bear, the meaning is clear and simple: "It means two sovereigns jointly occupying a territory … Both are equal. Neither dominates the other … However, if action or undertaking by one is going to affect the other, they treat about it. They negotiate a settlement or an understanding."[82]

After the British took over from the Dutch in 1664 and from the French in 1763, treaty relationships unfolded between various Indigenous peoples on one side and the Crown on the other. Two phases can be distinguished.[83] During the eighteenth century, treaties for the most part were still peace and friendship treaties with mutual rights and obligations aimed at securing space for European settlement on shared territory. Treaty negotiations followed traditional Indigenous protocol, and Indigenous peoples were referred to as "nations and tribes of Indians." After 1871, with the advent of the numbered treaties and the Canadian government now negotiating on behalf of the Crown, Indigenous peoples were addressed as "Her Majesty's subjects," negotiations enforced English protocol, and treaties became acts of massive land surrender. And with the surrender of land also came the surrender of rights.

It is against this historical backdrop that the concept of treaty federalism was developed as a confederal relationship in which each side would retain full sovereignty and parallel to the federal relationship of shared sovereignty between

81 Parker, *The Constitution of the Five Nations*, provision 3.

82 Personal communication.

83 See Thomas O. Hueglin, "Exploring Concepts of Treaty Federalism: A Comparative Perspective," paper prepared for the Royal Commission on Aboriginal Peoples, 1994.

the federal government and provinces under the Canadian constitution. Treaty federalism became the main conceptual starting point for the recommendations of RCAP in 1996.[84] In order to regain sovereignty, Indigenous peoples would have to form land-based nations of their own, have a parliament of their own, and regain almost complete policymaking authority funded by sufficient levels of fiscal transfers from the Canadian state. While Indigenous involvement in the institutions and processes of Canadian federalism were recognized as crucial, Indigenous representatives would have to be elected from Indigenous constituencies only, and their relationship with the Canadian state would amount to the quasi-diplomatic interactions of Indigenous delegates.

It is probably at least in part because of this noble attempt at a wholesale rewriting of history that the recommendations of RCAP effectuated little change and the Indian Act is still in place. There are at least three major obstacles standing in the way of a full realization of treaty federalism. First, as the RCAP final report acknowledged, different Indigenous communities themselves have different visions about their future relationship with the Canadian state.[85] Second, with about half of the Canadian Indigenous population living off-reserve and in urban environments, it is far from clear how many would want to see themselves in a nation-to-nation relationship with the rest of Canadian society.[86] Third, the kind of socioeconomic policy power disentanglement that RCAP envisaged for its version of treaty federalism is as unrealistic as it proved to be for the Canadian federal system.

Treaty federalism nevertheless is as important a conceptual guidepost for Indigenous relations with the Canadian settler and immigrant society as the two-founding-nations concept has been for Quebec's relationship with English Canada. In my own research contribution to RCAP, I had likened Indigenous and Althusian concepts of treaty federalism. Both essentially point to a form of council governance among autonomous communities with the objective of reaching common ground by mutual agreement.[87] I would add now that there is one difference: the Althusian distinction of what is general and what is particular.

84 See the analysis in Cairns, *Citizens Plus*, 116–60.

85 Government of Canada, "Volume Two: Restructuring the Relationship," *Report of the Royal Commission on Aboriginal Peoples*, 1996, 108–11.

86 Cairns, *Citizens Plus*, 73–4.

87 See Hueglin, "Exploring Concepts."

As already discussed above, this distinction implies the acceptance that matters of general concern can be decided by qualified majority rule. This is a distinction that, I believe, must also guide Indigenous–Canadian treaty relations. It is a concession to inevitable interdependence and governance efficiency to be sure. As a corollary, however, it might facilitate a path toward a form of partial autonomy that can focus on and secure cultural survival.

EPILOGUE

STILL A FEDERAL COUNTRY

In 1980, Donald Smiley began the third edition of his seminal contribution to the study of Canadian federalism, *Canada in Question*, by stating that "Canada is in the most elemental way a federal country, and it seems that it is becoming increasingly so."[1] The reasons for this diagnosis, which he describes and explains throughout the remainder of the book, were socioeconomic and cultural: regional economies with conflicting objectives and the English–French divide underpinned by different visions of how to live together, both resulting in a weak sense of national identity. Central political institutions were ineffective in dealing with these conflicts. American corporate and government impositions further weakened the federal government's ability to steer a coherent national economic course. As a consequence, as Smiley concluded, there was a "compounded crisis of Canadian federalism" threatening the country's survival as a sustainable political community.[2]

Three decades later, in 2009, Garth Stevenson ended the fifth edition of his equally seminal contribution to the study of Canadian federalism, *Unfulfilled Union*, with a "tentative forecast" pointing in the opposite direction. Provincially

1 Donald V. Smiley, *Canada in Question: Federalism in the Eighties* (Toronto: McGraw-Hill Ryerson, 1980), 1.

2 Ibid., 252–303.

bounded differences would become less important due to a number of factors, including the shift from a resource to a service economy, a gradual decline of Quebec's distinct impact on the dynamic of Canadian federalism, the growth of a multicultural immigrant society increasingly populating metropolitan areas across the country, and the Charter of Rights and Freedoms as a leveller of collective difference. Moreover, a protracted economic crisis foreseeable in the aftermath of the 2008 financial crisis would strengthen the federal government's macroeconomic hand as the crisis of the 1930s had done before.[3]

Smiley's sombre assessment came in the midst of what was at least a dual crisis confronting national unity: the rising tide of separatism in Quebec and the energy conflict playing out between Ottawa and the west. While the collapse of oil prices brought the energy conflict to an end within a few years, Smiley's pessimism with regard to national unity came precariously close to fruition with the second Quebec referendum in 1995.

During the first decade of the new millennium, the storms of federal–provincial conflict had calmed, and Stevenson's somewhat more upbeat forecast was entirely plausible. The year 1995 turned out to be a turning point for Quebec nationalism. At least for the foreseeable future, outright separatism seemed off the agenda. Instead, Canada was admired around the globe as a multicultural success story. To the satisfaction of the west, oil prices had steadily risen, and they had at least stabilized again after a sudden drop caused by the 2008 financial crisis. Stephen Harper's "open federalism" had promised restraining federal intervention in areas of provincial jurisdiction. There would not be another attempt at a national energy policy.

All seemed well, then, but not for long. Harper's open federalism turned out to be a disguise for an ideological attack on social spending that not only left provinces in the lurch but moreover soured intergovernmental relations because important decisions were made unilaterally yet again.[4] And when Justin Trudeau came to power in 2015 with the promise of "sunnier ways," it did not take long before the state of Canadian federalism appeared closer to Smiley's assessment than to Stevenson's forecast. Energy prices were in a freefall yet again, and any attempt to provide coherent federal leadership appeared more futile than ever. If Canada's problem in the past had been its overbearing neighbour to the south,

3 Garth Stevenson, *Unfulfilled Union: Canadian Federalism and National Unity*, 4th ed. (Montreal: McGill-Queen's University Press, 2009), 267–85.

4 See Julián Castro-Rea, "Harper's Legacy on Federalism: 'Open Federalism' or Hidden Agenda?" *Review of Constitutional Studies* 21, no. 2 (2016).

it now found itself being squeezed by the rivalry of two world powers: China in ascendance and the United States in decline.

Unsurprisingly, energy policy became the lighting rod once more, this time combined with environmental concerns. During the electoral campaign, Trudeau had promised to combat climate change. Hardly in office, he had taken along provincial premiers to the Paris Climate Conference in December 2015. He then announced that in order to reach the Paris climate targets, he would impose a carbon tax on all provinces without a policy of their own that would gradually match federal emission targets. Except for Saskatchewan, governed since 2007 by the conservative Saskatchewan Party, most provinces raised few if any objections.

This changed when three conservative provincial governments were elected, replacing the New Democratic Party (NDP) in Manitoba (2016) and the Liberals in New Brunswick and Ontario (2018). Liberal Ontario in particular had been supportive of Trudeau's plans. When the Conservative Doug Ford government took over, he first cancelled the provincial cap-and-trade regime already in place and then, together with Saskatchewan, went to court for a reference to have the federal carbon tax ruled unconstitutional. While the federal government claimed that the tax was a national concern under the constitution's peace, order, and good government (POGG) clause, the provinces not only rejected this claim but moreover argued that the carbon tax regime violated constitutional principles because it did not apply equally to all provinces.[5] The courts in Ontario and Saskatchewan affirmed the constitutionality of Trudeau's carbon tax, but the question has now been referred to the Supreme Court of Canada.[6]

All the while, a multidimensional conflict has been brewing over pipelines. At the same time when the Liberals came to power in Ottawa, the province of Alberta elected an NDP majority government. After more than four decades in power, Alberta's conservatives had finally run out of steam. In addition, they also had to split votes with the breakaway conservative Wildrose Party. The new premier, Rachel Notley, promised to balance the province's dependence on energy exports with environmental concerns. Effectively, she made a deal with Justin Trudeau. If the federal government supported and brought along the construction of pipelines to Canada's west coast, she would in turn comply with the Liberal's carbon scheme.

5 See Arthur White-Crummey, "Carbon Tax Court Primer: Who Are the Players at This Week's Reference Case?" *Regina Leader-Post*, February 11, 2019.

6 See Maham Abedi, "2 Provincial Courts Sided with Trudeau's Carbon Tax – What Happens Next?" *Global News*, June 28, 2019.

Alberta is a landlocked province. In order to get its oil and gas to the west coast and hence to lucrative Asian markets, the pipelines have to cross the province of British Columbia, which hugs the western coastline. Along the way, the pipelines' path inevitably crosses traditional Indigenous territory. The construction and operation of such pipelines, in other words, is a major challenge to federalism and its division of powers. While overall approval falls under the federal government's trade and commerce power, the provinces have jurisdiction over local regulation and environmental protection. Moreover, as various court rulings have established, Indigenous peoples not only need to be consulted if their existing and treaty rights are affected, their consent is *required* when they hold title to traditional lands.

The main pipeline under consideration, the Kinder Morgan or Trans Mountain pipeline, would run parallel to an already existing pipeline, more than doubling the capacity to pump oil from Alberta to the ship terminals in British Columbia. In 2017, British Columbians elected an NDP minority government that requires support from three elected members of the Green Party to remain in office. Half a year after taking office, in January 2018, the new premier of British Columbia, John Horgan, announced that his government would block increased oil shipments over environmental concerns. A trade war erupted with fellow NDP Premier Notley in Alberta, who even took the dramatic step of banning the import of much-coveted British Columbia wine into the province.

Half a year later, British Columbia's Court of Appeal revoked the federal approval of the pipeline expansion because Indigenous peoples had not been consulted sufficiently. Rather than taking the decision to the Supreme Court, the Trudeau government vowed to reopen proper consultations with the Indigenous communities involved. Notley, under pressure from the reunited conservatives and an upcoming election, accused the federal government of not being active enough on the pipeline file and revoked her commitment to the federal carbon scheme. In April 2019, Notley was thoroughly defeated in Alberta's provincial election, and in the October federal election of the same year, Trudeau's Liberals did not win a single seat in the province. Alberta's new conservative premier, Jason Kenney, wasted no time rekindling sentiments of western alienation that included threats of separation ("Wexit").

Controversy also engulfed another pipeline, which is meant to transport natural gas from northern British Columbia to a newly built terminal on the coast. In this case, the provincial government had approved the project. Since benefit agreements had been signed with all First Nations along the pipeline's projected path, it came as a surprise when Indigenous protesters nevertheless appeared on the scene and blocked access roads. After a standoff with the RCMP in January 2019, 14 protesters, including a number of hereditary chiefs of the Wet'suwet'en nation, were arrested. It should not have been surprising at all.

As discussed in Chapter 2, Canada's Indigenous peoples were forced under the Indian Act to adopt western-style band council elections. This imposition effectively created a dualized form of Indigenous governance with divided loyalties. On the one hand, there are First Nations with elected band councils and chiefs. On the other hand, there are the hereditary chiefs who still command authority over traditional lands and the Indigenous people living on them. Band council governance depends on government money under the Indian Act, and it is not surprising that First Nations would be inclined to sign benefit agreements with the pipeline developers in the hopes of bringing additional money and jobs. Federal and provincial governments approving the gas pipeline only negotiated with First Nations. The hereditary chiefs, who had been accorded title to the land in the Supreme Court of Canada's 1997 *Delgamuukw* decision (see Chapter 8), were opposed to the project, and they were not consulted.[7]

Contrary to Stevenson's forecast, then, the socioeconomic differences animating Canadian federalism have not diminished or gone away. Moreover, working out these differences has become even more difficult because of Indigenous rights, which Stevenson did not take into consideration at all and which cannot simply be ignored any longer. In fact, these rights also cast a potentially divisive shadow on Indigenous communities themselves.

When the Wet'suwet'en hereditary chiefs were arrested, "progressive" voices across the country erupted in support. When it was pointed out that perhaps a majority of the Indigenous communities in the area, those represented by the First Nations band councils, were in support of the gas pipeline, which promised jobs and income, the standard answer of the same "progressives" was that band council support did not mean a thing as it had obviously been given under duress, accepting some scraps falling from the tables of profit-seeking capitalist enterprises, with the government in cahoots.

All true, yet it is not just Indigenous peoples and communities that are under that kind of duress, and it is condescending to expect Indigenous peoples to hold up the torch for the rest of us. Thus, if a majority of Indigenous peoples wish to participate in capitalist and even environmentally dubious endeavours for personal gain, it is not for us to wag the finger. And if perhaps a majority of Indigenous peoples wish to somehow join capitalism to escape the ravages of

7 See Carey Newman, "There Are Two Kinds of Indigenous Governance Structures, but Canada Has Been Listening to Just One," *CBC News*, January 11, 2019.

colonialism, then the question arises about the legitimacy of hereditary chiefs adamant about stemming the tide. However, how to square traditional hereditary authority with modern governance is a question that Indigenous peoples must figure out for themselves.

In my view, a possible answer to this question inevitably points to one of the quintessential cooperative mechanisms of federalism, bicameralism.[8] Hereditary chiefs would form a second or upper legislative chamber with the power to block or at least suspend band council decisions affecting traditional customs or rights entrusted to them. Bicameralism as a combination of elected and hereditary governance is not without precedent. The constitution of Yap, one of the four member-states of the Federated States of Micronesia in the South Pacific, accords to traditional chiefs' councils the right to "disapprove" legislation when such legislation "adversely affects tradition and custom or the role or function of a traditional leader as recognized by tradition and custom."[9]

Cultural differences may be on the rise again elsewhere as well, once again setting Quebec apart from the rest of the country. The issue is public display of religious symbols, and it pits Quebec against the rest of the country in a reversal of fortune: The province once entirely dominated by Catholicism is now fiercely secularist with the lowest church attendance in all of North America.[10]

In 2013, the last and short-lived Parti Québécois government led by Pauline Maurois introduced a highly controversial Quebec Charter of Values (also called a Charter of Secularism in the original French version) that banned the wearing of conspicuous religious symbols (such as turbans or head scarves) for public-sector employees (including teachers and healthcare workers), as well as requiring that faces have to be uncovered during public service interactions. In 2014, the Parti Québécois government was defeated, but the Liberal government of Philippe Couillard introduced and passed an equally controversial Bill 62, which essentially disallowed face coverings in all public spaces (potentially including city buses).

The bill was opposed by both opposition parties, the Parti Québécois and the new nationalist right-wing Coalition Avenir Québec (CAQ), as not going far

8 See Thomas O. Hueglin, "Exploring Concepts of Treaty Federalism: A Comparative Perspective," paper prepared for the Royal Commission on Aboriginal Peoples, 1994.

9 Federated States of Micronesia, Legal Information System, *Constitution of the State of Yap*, Article V, Section 16.

10 The following relies on David M. Rayside, Gerald Sabin, and Paul E. Thomas, *Religion and Canadian Party Politics* (Vancouver: University of British Columbia Press, 2017), 269–310.

enough. Courts have thus far halted the implementation of Bill 62 for potential Charter violations. After the 2018 provincial election, however, with the CAQ winning a majority of seats, the government of François Legault not only promised to make the bill's provisions even stricter, but moreover that he would invoke the notwithstanding clause of Section 33 of the Charter of Rights and Freedoms to insulate the bill from further court challenges under the Charter. The new Bill 21 has meanwhile been passed, and the notwithstanding clause has been invoked. Court challenges are pending nevertheless.[11]

No such sustained efforts aiming at religious neutrality exist elsewhere in the country. The main explanation for the difference is Quebec's commitment to secularism. Ever since the Quiet Revolution renounced Catholicism's oppressive grip on the province, Quebecers have remained suspicious of religious interference with the public sphere. In this way they are more European than North American, as France and other European countries have introduced similar laws at least with regard to veiled faces. What distinguishes French-speaking Quebec from English Canada yet again may indeed be grounded in a different conception of liberalism. While liberalism in English-speaking Canada includes freedom of religious expression in the public sphere, liberalism for French-speaking Quebecers more likely means the opposite, the restriction of religious symbols in the public sphere.[12]

The point is that Quebec will remain a distinct province regardless of whether separatism has subsided for good or not. Its governments are still suspicious of the kind of liberal individualism enshrined in the Charter of Rights and Freedoms, which they continue to see as an attack on Quebec's right to preserve itself as a cultural community.

One of the oldest questions about Canadian federalism has been whether the dynamic of conflict and accommodation animating it is owed to underlying sociological differences across provinces and regions or shaped by the institutionalized power of governments.[13] The obvious answer is that it is both.

---

11 See *CTV News*, "Bill 21: Quebec Bans Religious Symbols for Government Employees," June 17, 2019.

12 See Luc Turgeon et al., "A Tale of Two Liberalisms? Attitudes toward Minority Religious Symbols in Quebec and Canada," *Canadian Journal of Political Science* 52, no. 2 (2019).

13 See the classical argument in Alan C. Cairns, "The Governments and Societies of Canadian Federalism," *Canadian Journal of Political Science* 10, no. 4 (1977).

There is no doubt that the institutions of Canadian federalism, and the political forces operating through them, have played a decisive role in its evolution and direction over time. The provincial rights movement in the nineteenth century corrected the centralist power imbalance intended by the founders. That had little or nothing to do with sociological difference. In the twentieth century, then, the involvement in two world wars and the need for welfare after the capitalist crisis of the 1930s created a stronger sense of national unity and thus allowed the federal government to assume a participating or even leadership role in policy areas originally meant to be left in the exclusive power domain of the provinces. Again, it is hard to see how the dynamic of Canada's modern welfare federalism had anything to do with regional difference, sociological or otherwise.

Institutions do matter. Yet sociological difference was the reason why Canada became a federation to begin with. Cultural and socioeconomic difference also shaped the big debates and conflicts during the second half of the twentieth century, including Quebec's quest to secure language and culture and the west's concerted effort to overcome its status as Canada's resource hinterland. And it is socioeconomic and cultural difference that continues to shape the dynamic of Canadian federalism. Notwithstanding the obvious rise of a pan-Canadian service industry, the socioeconomic tension between western and central Canadian interests will persist to the extent that western economies remain resource based and hence dependent on the vagaries of world commodity markets.[14] And notwithstanding the fact that Quebec's role as a state-led socioeconomic "counter-paradigm" has been weakened by the hegemonic forces of neoliberalism and globalization,[15] it will hardly succumb to "Angloconformity"[16] in terms of defining its own distinct identity.

No doubt, then, that Canada will remain, as Smiley put it, a federal country in a "most elemental way."[17] And the dynamic of how Canadian federalism might unfold in practice will no doubt remain overshadowed by deep conceptual

---

14 See Loleen Berdahl, "The West in Canada: Assessing the West's Role in the Post-2011 Federal System," in *The Changing Federal Environment: Rebalancing Roles,* ed. Nadia Verelli (Montreal: McGill-Queen's University Press, 2014).

15 See Daniel Salée, "Transformative Politics, the State, and the Politics of Social Change in Quebec," in *Changing Canada: Political Economy as Transformation*, eds. Wallace Clement and Leah F. Vosko (Montreal: McGill-Queen's University Press, 2003).

16 Yasmeen Abu-Laban, "Diversity in Canadian Politics," in *Canadian Politics,* 6th ed., eds. James Bickerton and Alain-G. Gagnon (Toronto: University of Toronto Press, 2014), 308.

17 See Smiley, *Canada in Question*, 1.

differences about how it should. According to one view, Canadians themselves do not really understand federalism because they "prefer a sharing of power and responsibility" instead of insisting on a "clear demarcation of what each order of government does."[18] From such an ideal-type perspective of classical federalism, this may be an indication that Canadians are "not particularly strong federalists."[19] Another view, however, points to modern federalism as a dynamic form of divided and shared governance oscillating between the rigidity of constitutional federalism and the flexibility of procedural federalism.[20] According to that view, Canadians understand their federal system quite well.

Constitutional rigidity guarantees a division of powers in principle on the basis of member equality. One only needs to look at how unitary states treat local government or how Canadian provinces treat municipalities to appreciate how important this guarantee is. Constitutional rigidity is what makes federalism different from other forms of multilevel governance where members are at best protected by weak mechanisms of arbitration, and where, as the famous saying goes, the strong do what they can and the weak suffer what they must.[21]

Constitutional guarantees are upheld by an independent judiciary. Court judgments inevitably produce winners and losers. However, the Supreme Court of Canada, as well as the British Judicial Committee of the Privy Council before it, have been guided by genuine considerations of these constitutional guarantees and their meaning rather than becoming a polarized battleground over ideological difference, as has the Supreme Court of the neighbouring United States. Herein, I would argue, lies the greatest strength of the Canadian federal system.

Procedural flexibility in turn – the intergovernmental process of cooperation – is an inevitable concession to the complexity of modern governance. As the Judicial Committee of the Privy Council already noted in in its earliest decisions, the idea of a watertight separation of powers in most instances turns out to be an illusion. Under conditions of modern governance complexity, it becomes

18 See Patrick Fafard, François Rocher, and Catherine Côté, "The Presence (or Lack Thereof) of a Federal Culture in Canada: The Views of Canadians," *Regional and Federal Studies* 20, no. 1 (2010), 28.

19 Ibid.

20 See Thomas O. Hueglin, "Comparing Federalisms: Variations or Distinct Models?" in *Federal Dynamics: Continuity, Change, and the Varieties of Federalism*, eds. Arthur Benz and Jörg Broscheck (Oxford: Oxford University Press, 2013).

21 The Athenians to the Melians, cited in Thucydides, *The Peloponnesian War* (New York: The Modern Library, 1934), chapter 17, 331.

impossible altogether. Policymaking increasingly depends on negotiated agreement, working around constitutional rigidity without, however, violating the constitution's fundamental stipulations about what each order of government can do without the consent of the other. Yet the boundaries between autonomy and interdependence are fluid. Herein lies the greatest ambiguity of the Canadian federal system.

Contrary to classical assumptions, federalism means more than legalism. Squaring constitutional intention with the complexities of modern governance is a balancing act. This balancing act requires federal comity: As outlined in Chapter 1, all governments in a federal system ought to act in a pro-federal manner, respectful of each other's rights, interests, and needs. However, appeals to good behaviour in a federal system driven by competing strategies of political expediency may ring hollow in provincial ears when federal governments can use superior fiscal clout and the spending power for unilateral action. Good behaviour therefore requires reliable and binding procedural rules and institutionalized mechanisms securing or at least facilitating intergovernmental cooperation. These are for the most part lacking in the Canadian federal system, and herein lies its greatest weakness.

BIBLIOGRAPHY

Abedi, Maham. "2 Provincial Courts Sided with Trudeau's Carbon Tax – What Happens Next?" *Global News*, June 28, 2019. Available at https://globalnews.ca/news/5438730/carbon-tax-trudeau-provincial-courts.

Abele, Frances, and Michael J. Prince. "Four Pathways to Aboriginal Self-Government in Canada." *The American Review of Canadian Studies* 36, no. 4 (2006): 568–94.

Abu-Laban, Yasmeen. "Diversity in Canadian Politics." In *Canadian Politics*, 6th ed., edited by James Bickerton and Alain-G. Gagnon, 395–418. Toronto: University of Toronto Press, 2014.

Acheson, T.W. "The National Policy and the Industrialization of the Maritimes, 1880–1910." In *Industrialization and Underdevelopment in the Maritimes, 1880–1930*, edited by T.W. Acheson, David Frank, and James D. Frost. Toronto: Garamond Press, 1985.

Adam, Marc-Antoine, Josée Bergeron, and Marianne Bonnard. "Intergovernmental Relations in Canada: Competing Visions and Diverse Dynamics." In *Intergovernmental Relations*, edited by Johanne Poirier, Cheryl Saunders, and John Kincaid. Toronto: Oxford University Press, 2015.

Aitken, H.G.H. "Defensive Expansionism: The State and Economic Growth in Canada." In *Approaches to Canadian Economic History*, edited by W.T. Easterbrook and M.H. Watkins, 183–221. Toronto: Gage Publishing, 1980.

Ajzenstat, Janet, Ian Gentles, Paul Romney, and William D. Gairdner, eds. *Canada's Founding Debates*. Toronto: Stoddart, 1999.

Albo, Gregory, and Jane Jensen. "A Contested Concept: The Relative Autonomy of the State." In *The New Canadian Political Economy*, edited by Wallace Clement and Glen Williams, 180–211. Toronto: Gage Publishing, 1980.

Alcantara, Christopher, and Zachary Spicer. "A New Model for Making Aboriginal Policy? Evaluating the Kelowna Accord and the Promise of Multilevel Governance in Canada." *Canadian Public Administration* 59, no. 2 (2016): 183–203.

Alexander, David G. *Atlantic Canada and Confederation: Essays in Canadian Political Economy*. Toronto: University of Toronto Press, 1983.

Althusius, Johannes. *Politica*. 1614. Indianapolis, IN: Liberty Fund, 1995.

———. *Politica Methodice Digesta*. 1614. Aalen: Scientia, 1981.

Anand, Anita. "After the Reference: Regulating Systemic Risk in Canadian Financial Markets." In *What's Next for Canada? Securities Regulation after the Reference*, edited by Anita Anand. Toronto: Irwin Law, 2012.

Arban, Erika. "La Subsidiarité en Droit Européen et Canadien: Une Comparaison." *Canadian Public Administration* 56, no. 2 (2013): 219–34.

Asch, Michael. "Self-Government in the New Millennium." In *Nation to Nation: Aboriginal Sovereignty and the Future of Canada*, edited by John Bird, Lorraine Land, and Murray MacAdam, 65–84. Toronto: Irwin Publishing, 2002.

Atkinson, Michael M., Daniel Béland, Gregory P. Marchildon, Kathleen McNutt, Peter W.B. Phillips, and Ken Rasmussen. *Governance and Public Policy in Canada: A View from the Provinces*. Toronto: University of Toronto Press, 2013.

Bacchus, Barua, Milagros Palacios, and Joel Emes. "The Sustainability of Health Care Spending in Canada 2017." Vancouver, BC: Fraser Institute, March 2017. Available at https://www.fraserinstitute.org/sites/default/files/sustainability-of-health-care-spending-in-canada-2017.pdf.

Baier, Gerald. "The Courts, the Constitution, and Dispute Resolution." In *Canadian Federalism: Performance, Effectiveness, and Legitimacy*, 3rd ed., edited by Herman Bakvis and Grace Skogstad, 79–95. Toronto: Oxford University Press, 2012.

———. "The Law of Federalism: Judicial Review and the Division of Powers." In *New Trends in Canadian Federalism*, 2nd ed., edited by François Rocher and Miriam Smith. Toronto: University of Toronto Press, 2012.

Bakvis, Herman, Gerald Baier, and Douglas Brown. *Contested Federalism: Certainty and Ambiguity in the Canadian Federation*. Toronto: Oxford University Press, 2009.

Bakvis, Herman, and Grace Skogstad, eds. *Canadian Federalism: Performance, Effectiveness, and Legitimacy*. Toronto: Oxford University Press, 2012.

Banting, Keith G. "Canada: Nation-Building in a Federal Welfare State." In *Federalism and the Welfare State: New World and European Experiences*, edited by Herbert Obinger, Stephan Leibfried, and Francis G. Castles, 89–137. Cambridge, UK: Cambridge University Press, 2005.

———. "The Three Federalisms Revisited: Social Policy and Intergovernmental Decision-Making." In *Canadian Federalism*, edited by Herman Bakvis and Grace Skogstad, 137–60. Toronto: Oxford University Press, 2012.

———. *The Welfare State and Canadian Federalism.* 2nd ed. Montreal, QC: McGill-Queen's University Press, 1987.

Banting, Keith G., and Richard Simeon, eds. *And No One Cheered: Federalism, Democracy and the Constitution Act.* Toronto: Methuen, 1983.

Behiels, Michael D. "Charlottetown: The Anatomy of Mega-Constitutional Politics." *Policy Options*, December 1, 2002. Available at http://policyoptions.irpp.org/magazines/kyoto/charlottetown-the-anatomy-of-mega-constitutional-politics.

———, ed. *The Meech Lake Primer: Conflicting Views of the 1987 Constitutional Accord.* Ottawa: University of Ottawa Press, 1989.

———. *Prelude to Quebec's Quiet Revolution: Liberalism versus Neo-Nationalism, 1945–1960.* Montreal, QC: McGill-Queen's University Press, 1985.

Behiels, Michael D., and Robert Talbot. "Stephen Harper and Canadian Federalism: Theory and Practice 1987–2011." In *Challenges for Canadian Federalism,* edited by Michael Behiels and François Rocher, 15–86. Ottawa: Invenire Books, 2011.

Béland, Daniel, and André Lecours. "Canada's Equalization Policy in Comparative Perspective." *IRPP Insight* 9 (2016): 1–18. https://irpp.org/research-studies/insight-no9.

———. "Equalization at Arm's Length." Mowat Centre, University of Toronto, March 2012. Available at https://tspace.library.utoronto.ca/bitstream/1807/99225/1/Béland_Lecours_2012_Equalization_at_Arm%27s.pdf.

Béland, Daniel, and Melanee Thomas. "Jason Kenney's Case of Quebec Envy." *Policy Options*, November 2019. Available at https://policyoptions.irpp.org/magazines/november-2019/jason-kenneys-case-of-quebec-envy.

Béland, Daniel, André Lecours, Gregory P. Marchildon, Haizhen Mou, and M. Rose Olfert. *Fiscal Federalism and Equalization Policy in Canada.* Toronto: University of Toronto Press, 2017.

Bendel, Petra, and Roland Sturm. "Federal Republic of Germany." In *Diversity and Unity in Federal Countries*, edited by Luis Moreno and César Colino, 167–99. Montreal, QC: McGill-Queen's University Press, 2010.

Benz, Arthur. "German Dogmatism and Canadian Pragmatism? Stability and Constitutional Change in Federal Systems." Hagen: FernUniversität Hagen, 2008.

Benz, Arthur, and Felix Knüpling. "Federalism and Constitutional Change: Lessons from Comparisons." In *Changing Federal Constitutions: Lessons from International Comparisons*, edited by Arthur Benz and Felix Knüpling, 395–412. Opladen: Barbara Budrich, 2012.

Berdahl, Loleen. "The West in Canada: Assessing the West's Role in the Post-2011 Federal System." In *Canada: The State of the Federation, 2011; The Changing Federal Environment: Rebalancing Roles*, edited by Nadia Verrelli, 45–64. Montreal, QC: McGill-Queen's University Press, 2014.

Berdahl, Loleen, and Roger Gibbins. *Looking West: Regional Transformation and the Future of Canada.* Toronto: University of Toronto Press, 2014.

Bernard, André. *What Does Quebec Want?* Toronto: Lorimer, 1978.

Bernier, Luc. "The Beleaguered State: Québec at the end of the 1990s." In *The Provincial State in Canada: Politics in the Provinces and Territories*, edited by Keith Brownsey and Michael Howlett, 139–62. Peterborough, ON: Broadview Press, 2001.

Bickerton, James. "Deconstructing the New Federalism." *Canadian Political Science Review* 4, no. 2–3 (2010): 56–72.

———. "Regionalism in Canada." In *Canadian Politics*, edited by James Bickerton and Alain-G. Gagnon, 209–38. Peterborough, ON: Broadview Press, 1999.

Bird, John, Lorraine Land, and Murray Macadam, eds. *Nation to Nation: Aboriginal Sovereignty and the Future of Canada*. Toronto: Irwin, 2001.

Black, Edwin R. *Divided Loyalties: Canadian Concepts of Federalism*. Montreal, QC: McGill-Queen's University Press, 1975.

Black, Errol, and Jim Silver. *Equalization: Financing Canadians' Commitment to Sharing and Social Solidarity*. Winnipeg, MB: Canadian Centre for Policy Alternatives, 2004.

Blöchlinger, Hansjörg and Claire Charbit. "Fiscal Equalization." *OECD Economic Studies* 44 (2008).

Block, Fred. "The Fiscal Crisis of the Capitalist State." *Annual Review of Sociology* 7 (1981): 1–27.

Boadway, Robin. "Canada." In *The Practice of Fiscal Federalism: Comparative Perspectives,* edited by Anwar Shah, 99–124. Montreal, QC: McGill-Queen's University Press, 2007.

Boldt, Menno. *Surviving as Indians: The Challenge of Self-Government*. Toronto: University of Toronto Press, 1993.

Bolger, Francis W.P. "Prince Edward Island and Confederation, 1863–1873." *Canadian Catholic Historical Association*, Report 28, 1961. Available at http://umanitoba.ca/colleges/st_pauls/ccha/Back%20Issues/CCHA1961/Bolger.pdf.

Bolleyer, Nicole. *Intergovernmental Cooperation: Rational Choices in Federal Systems and Beyond*. Oxford, UK: Oxford University Press, 2009.

Borins, Sandford F. *The Language of the Skies: The Bilingual Air Traffic Control Conflict in Canada*. Montreal, QC: McGill-Queen's University Press, 1983.

Bothwell, Robert, Ian Drummond, and John English. *Canada, 1900–1945*. Toronto: University of Toronto Press, 1987.

Boucher, François, and Jocelyn Maclure. "The Equalization Program Does not Subsidize Quebec's Welfare State." *In Due Course* (Canadian Public Affairs blog), September 4, 2014. Available at http://induecourse.ca/the-equalization-program-does-not-subsidize-quebecs-welfare-state.

Boychuk, Gerard W. *National Health Insurance in the United States and Canada: Race, Territory, and the Roots of Difference*. Washington, DC: Georgetown University Press, 2008.

Brock, Kathy L. "Executive Federalism: Beggar Thy Neighbour?" In *New Trends in Canadian Federalism*, 2nd ed., edited by François Rocher and Miriam Smith. Toronto: University of Toronto Press, 2012.

———. "Open Federalism, Section 94, and Principled Federalism: Contradictions in Vision." Paper presented at the Annual Meeting of the Canadian Political Science Association, Saskatoon, May 2007.

———. "Striving for Fairness: First Nations, Current Reforms and Provincial Interests." In *Canadian Fiscal Relations: What Works, What Might Work Better*, edited by Harvey Lazar, 227–50. Montreal, QC: McGill-Queen's University Press, 2005.

Brodie, Janine. *The Political Economy of Canadian Regionalism*. Toronto: Harcourt Brace Jovanovich, 1990.

Brooks, Stephen, and A. Brian Tanguay. "Quebec's *Caisse de dépôt et placement*: Tool of nationalism?" *Canadian Public Administration* 28, no. 1 (1985): 99–119.

Broschek, Jörg. "Historical Institutionalism and the Varieties of Federalism in Germany and Canada." *Publius: The Journal of Federalism* 42, no. 4 (2012): 662–87.

Brouillet, Eugénie. "Canadian Federalism and the Principle of Subsidiarity: Should We Open Pandora's Box?" *Supreme Court Law Review* 54, no.2 (2011): 601–32.

Brunet-Jailly, Emmanuel. "The Governance and Fiscal Environment of First Nations' Fiscal Intergovernmental Relations in Comparative Perspectives." Victoria, BC: National Centre for First Nations Governance 2008. Available at http://fngovernance.org/ncfng_research/emmanual_brunet-jailley.pdf.

Bryden, P.E. "The Obligations of Federalism: Ontario and the Origins of Equalization." In *Framing Canadian Federalism: Essays in Honour of John T. Saywell*, edited by Dimitri Anastakis and P.E. Bryden, 75–94. Toronto: University of Toronto Press, 2009.

Buckley, Kenneth. "Capital Formation in Canada, 1896–1930." In *Approaches to Canadian Economic History*, edited by W.T. Easterbrook and M.H. Watkins, 169–83. Toronto: Gage Publishing, 1980.

Burke, Sara Z., and Patrice Milewski, eds. *Schooling in Transition: Readings in Canadian History of Education*. Toronto: University of Toronto Press, 2012.

Burns, R.M. *The Acceptable Mean: The Tax Rental Agreements, 1941–1962*. Toronto: Canadian Tax Foundation, 1980.

Bushnell, Ian. *The Captive Court: A Study of the Supreme Court of Canada*. Montreal, QC: McGill-Queen's University Press, 1992.

Bzdera, André. "Comparative Analysis of Federal High Courts: A Political Theory of Judicial Review." *Canadian Journal of Political Science* 26, no. 1 (1993): 3–29.

Cairns, Alan C. *Charter versus Federalism: The Dilemma of Constitutional Reform*. Montreal, QC: McGill-Queen's University Press, 1991.

———. *Citizens Plus: Aboriginal Peoples and the Canadian State*. Vancouver, BC: University of British Columbia Press, 2018.

———. "The Governments and Societies of Canadian Federalism." *Canadian Political Science Review* 10, no. 4 (1977): 695–725.

———. "The Judicial Committee and Its Critics." *Canadian Journal of Political Science* 4, no. 3 (1971): 301–45.

———. "The Politics of Constitutional Conservatism." In *And No One Cheered: Federalism, Democracy and the Constitution Act*, edited by Keith Banting and Richard Simeon. Toronto: Methuen, 1983.

Canadian Institute of Health Information. "National Health Expenditure Trends, 1975 to 2016." 2016. Available at https://secure.cihi.ca/free_products/NHEX-Trends-Narrative-Report_2016_EN.pdf.

Canadian Intergovernmental Conference Secretariat. "Agreement: A Framework to Improve the Social Union for Canadians." First Minister's Meeting. Ottawa, ON, February 4, 1999. Available at http://scics.ca/en/product-produit/agreement-a-framework-to-improve-the-social-union-for-canadians.

Cardinal, Harold. *The Unjust Society: The Tragedy of Canada's Indians*. Edmonton, AB: Hurtig, 1969.

Caron, Jean-François, Guy Laforest, and Catherine Vallières-Roland. "Canada's Federative Deficit." In *Contemporary Canadian Federalism*, edited by Alain-G. Gagnon, 132–62. Toronto: University of Toronto Press, 2012.

Carter, Sarah. *Lost Harvests: Prairie Indian Reserve Farmers and Government Policy*. Montreal, QC: McGill-Queen's University Press, 1990.

Castro-Rea, Julián. "Harper's Legacy on Federalism: 'Open Federalism' or Hidden Agenda?" *Review of Constitutional Studies* 21, no. 2 (2016): 257–75.

CBC News. "Majority Wants Senate Changed or Abolished, Poll Suggests." June 20, 2013. Available at https://www.cbc.ca/news/politics/majority-wants-senate-changed-or-abolished-poll-suggests-1.1398046.

CBC News: The National. "Oka Crisis: How It Started." September 24, 2015. Available at https://www.youtube.com/watch?v=fShsLqN01A0.

Church, Clive, and David Phinnemore. "From the Constitutional Treaty to the Treaty of Lisbon and Beyond." In *European Union Politics*, edited by Michelle Cini and Nieves Pérez-Solórzano Borragán, 41–58. Oxford, UK: Oxford University Press, 2010.

Clarkson, Stephen. "The Multi-Level State: Canada in the Semi-Periphery of both Continentalism and Globalization." *Review of International Political Economy* 8, no. 3 (September, 2001): 501–527. Available at https://doi.org/10.1080/09692290110055858.

Clarkson, Stephen, and Christina McCall. *Trudeau and Our Times*. Vol. 1, *The Magnificent Obsession*. Toronto: McClelland and Stewart, 1991.

Clement, Wallace. "The Corporate Elite, the Capitalist Class, and the Canadian State." In *The Canadian State: Political Economy and Political Power*, edited by Leo Panitch, 225–48. Toronto: University of Toronto Press, 1977.

Conlan, Tim. "From Cooperative to Opportunistic Federalism: Reflections in the Half-Century Anniversary of the Commission on Intergovernmental Relations." *Public Administration Review* 66, no. 5 (2006): 663–76.

Conway, John F. *The Rise of the New West: The History of a Region in Confederation*. Toronto: Lorimer, 2014.

———. *The West: The History of a Region in Confederation*. Toronto: Lorimer, 1983.

Council of the Federation. "Council of the Federation Founding Agreement." Charlottetown, Prince Edward Island, December 5, 2003. Available at http://canadaspremiers.ca/wp-content/uploads/2013/03/cof_founding-agreement.pdf.

Courchene, Thomas J. *Indigenous Nationals Canadian Citizens: From First Contact to Canada 150 and Beyond*. Montreal, QC: McGill-Queen's University Press, 2018.

Craig, Gerald M., ed. *Lord Durham's Report*. 1839. Toronto: McClelland and Stewart, 1963.

Creighton, Donald. *Canada's First Century*. 1970. Reprint, Toronto: Oxford University Press, 2012.

———. *The Empire of the St. Lawrence*. Toronto: Macmillan, 1970.

CTV News. "Bill 21: Quebec Bans Religious Symbols for Government Employees." June 17, 2019. Available at https://montreal.ctvnews.ca/bill-21-quebec-bans-religious-symbols-for-government-employees-1.4469041.

Dardanelli, Paolo, and John Kincaid, eds. *Dynamic De/Centralization in Federations*. Special issue, *Publius: The Journal of Federalism* 49 (2019).

Daschuk, James. *Clearing the Plains: Disease, Politics of Starvation and the Loss of Indigenous Life*. Regina, SK: University of Regina Press, 2019.

Descartes, René. "Discourse on the Method." 1637. In *The Philosophical Writings of Descartes*. Vol I. Cambridge, UK: Cambridge University Press, 1985.

Deschouwer, Kris. "Ethnic Structure, Inequality and Governance of the Public Sector in Belgium." *United Nations Research Institute for Social Development*, January, 2004. Available at http://www.unrisd.org/unrisd/website/document.nsf/(httpPublications)/EC506A59176BE044C1256E9E003077C3?OpenDocument.

Dicey, A.V. *An Introduction to the Study of the Law of the Constitution*. 1885. London: Macmillan, 1915.

Dickinson, John, and Brian Young. *A Short History of Quebec*. Montreal, QC: McGill-Queen's University Press, 2008.

Di Matteo, Livio. *A Federal Fiscal History: Canada, 1867–2017*. Toronto: Fraser Institute, 2017. Available at https://www.fraserinstitute.org/sites/default/files/federal-fiscal-history-canada-1867–2017.pdf.

The Economist. "Canada's Example to the World: Liberty Moves North." October 29, 2016. Available at https://www.economist.com/leaders/2016/10/29/liberty-moves-north.

Eisen, Ben, Milagros Palacios, Fred McMahon, and Alex Whalen. "Catching Up With Canada: A Prosperity Agenda for Atlantic Canada." Fraser Institute, 2019. Available at https://www.fraserinstitute.org/sites/default/files/catching-up-with-canada-prosperity-agenda-for-atlantic-canada.pdf.

Elazar, Daniel J. *Exploring Federalism*. Tuscaloosa, AL: University of Alabama Press, 1987.

Elkins, David J., and Richard Simeon, eds. *Small Worlds: Provinces and Parties in Canadian Political Life*. Toronto: Methuen, 1980.

English, John. *Citizen of the World*. Toronto: Knopf Canada, 2006.

Fafard, Patrick, François Rocher, and Catherine Côté. "The Presence (or Lack Thereof) of a Federal Culture in Canada: The Views of Canadians." *Regional and Federal Studies* 20, no. 1 (2010): 19–43.

Federated States of Micronesia, Legal Information System. *Constitution of the State of Yap*. Available at http://fsmlaw.org/yap/constitution/index.htm.

Feehan, Jim. "Canada's Equalization Formula: Peering Inside the Black Box … and Beyond." *School of Public Policy Research Papers* 7, no. 24 (2014): 1–27.

Feeley, Malcolm, and Edward L. Rubin. *Federalism: Political Identity and Tragic Compromise*. Ann Arbor, MI: University of Michigan Press, 2008.

Ferguson, Nelson. "From Coal Pits to Tar Sands: Labour Migration between an Atlantic Canadian Region and the Athabasca Oil Sands." *Just Labour: A Canadian Journal of Work and Society* 17&18 (2011): 106–18.

Finkel, Alvin. "Origins of the Welfare State in Canada." In *The Canadian State: Political Economy and Political Power*, edited by Leo Panitch, 344–70. Toronto: University of Toronto Press, 1977.

Fortin, Sarah. "From the Canadian Social Union to the Federal Social Union of Canada." In *Contemporary Canadian Federalism: Foundation, Traditions, Institutions*, edited by Alain-G. Gagnon, 303–29. Toronto: University of Toronto Press, 2012.

Fortin, Sarah, Alain Nöel, and France St-Hilaire, eds. *Forging the Canadian Social Union: SUFA and Beyond*. Montreal, QC: Institute for Research on Public Policy, 2003.

Fossum, John Erik. "Deep Diversity versus Constitutional Patriotism." *Ethnicities* 1, no. 2 (2001): 179–206.

Fowke, V.C. "The National Policy – Old and New." *Canadian Journal of Economics and Political Science* 18, no. 3 (1952): 271–86. Reprinted in *Approaches to Canadian Economic History*, edited by W.T. Easterbrook and M.H. Watkins, 237–58. Toronto: Gage Publishing, 1980.

Fox, Kevin. "Canada's Largest Shipyard Closes." *Globe and Mail*, June 27, 2003. Available at https://www.theglobeandmail.com/news/national/canadas-largest-shipyard-closes/article22617919.

Franks, C.E.S. "The Senate in Modern Times." In *Protecting Canadian Democracy: The Senate You Never Knew*, edited by Serge Joyal, 158–65. Montreal, QC: McGill-Queen's University Press, 2003.

Frideres, James S., and René R. Gadacz. *Aboriginal Peoples in Canada*. Toronto: Pearson Prentice Hall, 2008.

Frost, James D. "The 'Nationalization' of the Bank of Nova Scotia, 1880–1910." In *Industrialization and Underdevelopment in the Maritimes, 1880–1930*, edited by T.W. Acheson, David Frank, and James D. Frost. Toronto: Garamond Press, 1985.

Gagnon, Alain-G. "Federal-Provincial and Intergovernmental Relations in Canada." In *Contemporary Canadian Federalism*, edited by Alain-G. Gagnon, 251–4. Toronto: University of Toronto Press, 2012.

———. "Québec–Canada's Constitutional Dossier." In *Québec: State and Society*, edited by Alain-G. Gagnon, 127–50. Peterborough, ON: Broadview Press, 2004.

———. "Taking Stock of Asymmetrical Federalism in an Era of Exacerbated Centralization." In *Contemporary Canadian Federalism: Foundations, Traditions, Institutions*, edited by Alain-G. Gagnon, 255–72. Toronto: University of Toronto Press, 2012.

Gagnon, Alain-G., and Raffaele Iacovino. *Federalism, Citizenship, and Quebec*. Toronto: University of Toronto Press, 2007.

Gagnon, Alain-G., and A. Brian Tanguay. "Minor Parties in the Canadian Political System: Origins, Functions, Impact." In *Canadian Parties in Transition*, edited by Alain-G. Gagnon and A. Brian Tanguay, 106–34. Toronto: Nelson, 1996.

Gaudreault-DesBiens, Jean-François. "The Irreducible Federal Necessity of Jurisdictional Autonomy, and the Irreducibility of Federalism to Jurisdictional Autonomy." In *Dilemmas of Solidarity: Rethinking Redistribution in the Canadian Federation*, edited by Sujit Choudhry, Jean-François Gaudreault-DesBiens, and Lorne Sossin, 185–205. Toronto: University of Toronto Press, 2006.

Gauvreau, Michael. "From Rechristianization to Contestation: Catholic Values and Quebec Society, 1931–1970." In *Contemporary Quebec: Selected Readings & Commentaries*, edited by Michael D. Behiels and Matthew Hayday, 126–56. Montreal, QC: McGill-Queen's University Press, 2011.

Gibbins, Roger. *Regionalism: Territorial Politics in Canada and the United States*. Toronto: Butterworths, 1982.

Ginn, Diana. "Indian Hunting Rights: *Dick v. R.*, *Jack and Charlie v. R.* and *Simon v. R.*" *McGill Law Journal* 31 (1986): 527–50.

Government of Canada. "The 2003 Accord on Health Care Renewal." 2004. Available at https://www.canada.ca/en/health-canada/services/health-care-system/health-care-system-delivery/federal-provincial-territorial-collaboration/first-ministers-meeting-year-plan-2004/2003-accord-health-care-renewal-progress.html.

———. *2008 December Report of the Auditor General of Canada to the House of Commons*. Ottawa: Office of the Auditor General of Canada, 2008. Available at http://www.oag-bvg.gc.ca/internet/English/parl_oag_200812_01_e_31825.html.

———. "250th Anniversary of the Royal Proclamation of 1763." Indigenous and Northern Affairs Canada. Available at https://www.aadnc-aandc.gc.ca/eng/1370355181092/1370355203645.

———. "A Brief History of the Canada Health and Social Transfer." Ottawa: Department of Finance, 2004.

———. Canada Health Act (RSC 1985, c. C-6). Available at http://laws.justice.gc.ca/eng/acts/C-6/page-2.html#docCont.

———. "Comprehensive Claims." Ottawa: Crown–Indigenous Relations and Northern Affairs Canada, 2016. Available at https://www.aadnc-aandc.gc.ca/eng/1100100030577/1100100030578.

———. *Federalism and Decentralization: Where Do We Stand?* Ottawa: Minister of Supply and Services Canada, 1981. Available at http://publications.gc.ca/collections/collection_2016/bcp-pco/CP46-3-8-eng.pdf.

———. "The Government of Canada's Approach to Implementation of the Inherent Right and the Negotiation of Aboriginal Self-Government." Ottawa: Crown–Indigenous Relations and Northern Affairs Canada, 1995. Available at https://www.rcaanc-cirnac.gc.ca/eng/1100100031843/1539869205136.

———. "History of Health and Social Transfers." 2014. Available at https://www.canada.ca/en/department-finance/programs/federal-transfers/history-health-social-transfers.html.

———. The Indian Act (RSC 1985, c. I-5). Available at http://laws-lois.justice.gc.ca/eng/acts/i-5.

———. "Information on the Tax Exemption under Section 87 of the Indian Act." 2019. Available at https://www.canada.ca/en/revenue-agency/services/aboriginal-peoples/information-indians.html.

———. "Major Federal Transfers, 2017." Department of Finance. Available at https://www.canada.ca/en/department-finance/programs/federal-transfers/major-federal-transfers.html.

———. "The Next Level: Normalizing a Culture of Inclusive Linguistic Duality in the Federal Public Service Workplace." Privy Council Office, 2017. Available at https://www.canada.ca/en/privy-council/corporate/clerk/publications/next-level/next-level.html.

———. *The Quebec Resolutions (The 72 Resolutions)*. Ottawa: Library and Archives Canada, October 1864. Available at https://www.bac-lac.gc.ca/eng/discover/politics-government/canadian-confederation/Pages/copyright-sources-documents.aspx#4.

———. "Self-Government." Ottawa: Crown–Indigenous Relations and Northern Affairs Canada, 2016. Available at https://www.rcaanc-cirnac.gc.ca/eng/1100100032275/1529354547314.

———. "Statement of the Government of Canada on Indian Policy (The White Paper, 1969)." Ottawa: Queen's Printer, 1969. Available at https://www.aadnc-aandc.gc.ca/eng/1100100010189/1100100010191.

———. "Treaties and Agreements." Crown–Indigenous Relations and Northern Affairs Canada. Available at https://www.rcaanc-cirnac.gc.ca/eng/1100100028574/1529354437231

———. "Volume One: Looking Forward, Looking Back." *Report of the Royal Commission on Aboriginal Peoples*, 1996. Available at http://www.bac-lac.gc.ca/eng/discover/aboriginal-heritage/royal-commission-aboriginal-peoples/Pages/final-report.aspx.

———. "Volume Two: Restructuring the Relationship." *Report of the Royal Commission on Aboriginal Peoples*, 1996. Available at http://data2.archives.ca/e/e448/e011188230-02.pdf.

———. "Volume Four: Perspectives and Realities." *Report of the Royal Commission on Aboriginal Peoples*, 1996. Available at http://data2.archives.ca/e/e448/e011188230-04.pdf.

Government of Nunavut. "Consensus Government." Available at https://www.gov.nu.ca/consensus-government.

———. "Main Estimates 2017–2018." Iqaluit, NU: Department of Finance, February 2017. Available at https://www.gov.nu.ca/sites/default/files/files/Finance/Budgets/main_estimates_2017-2018_english.pdf.

Government of Québec. "Fiscal Imbalance in Canada: Historical Background." Commission on Fiscal Imbalance, Supporting Document 1, 2002. Available at http://www.groupes.finances.gouv.qc.ca/desequilibrefiscal/en/pdf/historique_en.pdf.

———. "For a Fair Share of Federal Health Funding." Quebec, QC: Budget 2017–2018. Available at http://www.budget.finances.gouv.qc.ca/budget/2017-2018/en/documents/Budget1718_Health.pdf.

———. "Langue et educatión au Québec." Office Québécoise de la Langue Française, 2017. Available at https://www.oqlf.gouv.qc.ca/ressources/sociolinguistique/2017/20170331_etude1.pdf.

———. *Quebecers, Our Way of Being Canadian: Policy on Québec Affirmations and Canadian Relations.* Québec: Secrétariat aux Affaires Intergouvernementales Canadiennes, 2017. Available at https://www.sqrc.gouv.qc.ca/documents/relations-canadiennes/politique-affirmation-en.pdf.

———. "Québec's Historical Position on the Federal Spending Power 1944–1998." Secrétariat aux affaires intergouvernementales canadiennes, Direction des politiques institutionnelles et constitutionnelles, Ministère du Conseil exécutif, July 1998. Available at https://www.sqrc.gouv.qc.ca/documents/institutions-constitution/position-en.pdf.

Graefe, Peter. "Quebec Nationalism and Quebec Politics, from Left to Right." In *Transforming Provincial Politics: The Political Economy of Canada's Provinces and Territories in the Neoliberal Era*, edited by Bryan M. Evans and Charles W. Smith, 137–61. Toronto: University of Toronto Press, 2015.

Gramsci, Antonio. *Prison Notebooks*. 3 vols. New York: Columbia University Press, 2011.

Granatstein, J.L., et al. *Nation: Canada since Confederation*. Toronto: McGraw-Hill Ryerson, 1990.

Green, Joyce. "Self-Determination, Citizenship, and Federalism: Indigenous and Canadian Palimpsest." In *Canada: The State of the Federation 2003, Reconfiguring Aboriginal–State Relations*, edited by Michael Murphy, 329–52. Montreal, QC: McGill-Queen's University Press, 2005.

Greene, Ian. *The Charter of Rights and Freedoms: 30+ Years of Decisions that Shaped Canadian Life.* Toronto: James Lorimer, 2014.

Gunnarson, Maja. "Jurisdictional Disputes and Indigenous Health: The Emergence of Jordan's Principle," *McGill Journal of Law and Health*, November 2018. Available at https://mjlh.mcgill.ca/2018/11/20/jurisdictional-disputes-and-indigenous-health-the-emergence-of-jordans-principle.

Gwyn, Richard. *Nation Maker, Sir John A. Macdonald: His Life, Our Times.* Vol. 2, *1867–1891.* Toronto: Random House, 2011.

Hamilton, Alexander, John Jay, and James Madison. *The Federalist.* Indianapolis, IN: Liberty Fund, 2001.

Hamilton, Graeme. "'It's Raining Money': Quebec's Economy Crawled Out of the Doghouse. Now, It's a Powerhouse." *National Post*, July 28, 2017. Available at https://nationalpost.com/news/canada/from-the-doghouse-to-a-powerhouse-quebecs-economy-has-rebounded.

Harrington, Denise. "Who Are the Separatists?" In *Western Separatism: The Myths, Realities & Dangers*, edited by Larry Pratt and Garth Stevenson. Edmonton, AB: Hurtig Publishers, 1981.

Hayek, Friedrich. "The Economic Conditions of Interstate Federalism." 1935. In *Individualism and Economic Order,* edited by Friedrich Hayek, 255–72. Chicago, IL: Chicago University Press, 1980.

Heard, Andrew. *Canadian Constitutional Conventions: The Marriage of Law and Politics.* Toronto: Oxford University Press, 2014.

Heilbroner, Robert L. *The Nature and Logic of Capitalism.* New York: Norton, 1985.

Helliwell, John F., and Robert N. McRae. "Resolving the Energy Conflict: From the National Energy Program to the Energy Agreements." *Canadian Public Policy* 8, no. 1 (1982): 14–23.

Henderson, Ailsa. *Nunavut: Rethinking Political Culture.* Vancouver, BC: University of British Columbia Press, 2007.

———. "Regional Political Cultures in Canada." *Canadian Journal of Political Science* 37, no. 3 (2004): 55–81.

Henderson, James (sákéj) Youngblood. "Empowering Treaty Federalism." *Saskatchewan Law Review* 58 (1994): 241–329.

Higgins, Jenny. "The 1985 Canada–Newfoundland Atlantic Accord." Heritage Newfoundland and Labrador, 2012. Available at http://www.heritage.nf.ca/articles/politics/atlantic-accord.php.

Hill, Christopher. *The Century of Revolution, 1603–1714.* New York: Norton, 1982.

Hobbes, Thomas. *Leviathan.* 1651. Cambridge: Cambridge University Press, 1992.

Hogg, Peter W. *Constitutional Law of Canada.* Toronto: Carswell, 1998.

———. "Is the Supreme Court of Canada Biased in Constitutional Cases?" *The Canadian Bar Review* 57, no. 4 (1979): 721–39.

———. "Supremacy of the Canadian Charter of Rights and Freedoms." *Canadian Bar Review* 61, no. 1 (1983): 69–80.

Howlett, Karen, and Jane Taber. "Ontario to Lose Equalization Payments as Alberta's Economic Fortunes Fall." *Globe and Mail*, December 17, 2016. Available at https://www.theglobeandmail.com/news/politics/ontario-to-lose-equalization-payments-as-albertas-economic-fortunes-fall/article27831080.

Howlett, Michael, Alex Netherton, and M. Ramesh. *The Political Economy of Canada: An Introduction.* Toronto: Oxford University Press, 1999.

Hueglin, Thomas O. "Comparing Federalisms: Variations or Distinct Models?" In *Federal Dynamics: Continuity, Change, and the Varieties of Federalism,* edited by Arthur Benz and Jörg Broschek, 27–47. Oxford, UK: Oxford University Press, 2013.

———. *Early Modern Concepts for a Late Modern World: Althusius on Community and Federalism.* Waterloo, ON: Wilfrid Laurier University Press 1999.

———. "Exploring Concepts of Treaty Federalism: A Comparative Perspective." Paper prepared for the Royal Commission on Aboriginal Peoples, 1994. Available at http://publications.gc.ca/site/archivee-archived.html?url=http://publications.gc.ca/collections/collection_2016/bcp-pco/Z1-1991-1-41-38-eng.pdf.

———. "Federalism and Democracy: A Critical Reassessment." In *The Global Promise of Federalism,* edited by Grace Skogstad et al., 17–42. Toronto: University of Toronto Press, 2013.

———. "From Constitutional to Treaty Federalism: A Comparative Perspective." *Publius: The Journal of Federalism* 30, no. 4 (2000): 137–52.

Hueglin, Thomas O., and Alan Fenna. *Comparative Federalism: A Systematic Inquiry.* Toronto: University of Toronto Press, 2015.

Imai, Shin. "The Structure of the Indian Act: Accountability in Governance." Comparative Research in Law & Political Economy Research Paper No. 35 (2012). Available at http://digitalcommons.osgoode.yorku.ca/clpe/8.

Innis, Harold. *The Fur Trade in Canada: An Introduction to Canadian Economic History.* 1930. Toronto: University of Toronto Press, 1999.

Institute of Intergovernmental Relations. *Open Federalism: Interpretations, Significance.* Kingston, ON: Institute of Intergovernmental Relations, 2006.

Irving Shipbuilding. "Our History." Available at http://www.irvingshipbuilding.com/irving-shipbuilding-about-us-our-history.aspx.

Janigan, Mary. *Let the Eastern Bastards Freeze in the Dark: The West versus the Rest in Confederation.* Toronto: Vintage Canada, 2013.

Jenkin, Michael. *The Challenge of Diversity: Industrial Policy in the Canadian Federation.* Ottawa: Science Council of Canada, 1983.

Joyal, Serge, ed. *Protecting Canadian Democracy: The Senate You Never Knew.* Montreal, QC: McGill-Queen's University Press, 2003.

Katzenstein, Peter J. "Conclusion." In *The Culture of National Security: Norms and Identity in World Politics*, edited by Peter J. Katzenstein, 498–537. New York: Columbia University Press, 1996.

Kildea, Paul. "The Bill of Rights Debate in Australian Political Culture." *Australian Journal of Human Rights* 9, no. 1 (2003): 65–118.

Kincaid, John. "The Rise of Coercive Federalism in the United States." In *The Future of Australian Federalism: Comparative and Interdisciplinary Perspectives*, edited by Gabrielle Appleby, Nicholas Aroney, and Thomas John, 157–79. Cambridge, UK: Cambridge University Press, 2012.

King, Thomas. *The Inconvenient Indian: A Curious Account of Native People in North America.* Toronto: Anchor Canada, 2013.

Kirby, Michael, and Hugh Segal. "A House Undivided: Making Senate Independence Work." Public Policy Forum, September 22, 2016. Available at https://medium.com/@PPForum/a-house-undivided-making-senate-independence-work-b773ad28b786.

Kitchen, Harry. "Canadian Municipalities: Fiscal Trends and Sustainability." *Canadian Tax Journal* 50, no. 1 (2002): 156–80.

Kwavnick, David, ed. *The Tremblay Report.* Toronto: McClelland and Stewart, 1973.

Ladner, Kiera. "An Indigenous Constitutional Paradox: Both Monumental Achievement and Monumental Defeat." In *Patriation and its Consequences: Constitution Making in Canada,* edited by Lois Harder and Steve Patten, 267–89. Vancouver, BC: University of British Columbia Press, 2015.

———. "Treaty Federalism: An Indigenous Vision of Canadian Federalisms." In *New Trends in Canadian Federalism,* edited by François Rocher and Miriam Smith. Toronto: University of Toronto Press, 2012.

Lajoie, Andrée. "The Federal Spending Power and Fiscal Imbalance in Canada." In *Dilemmas of Solidarity: Rethinking Redistribution in the Canadian Federation,* edited by Sujit Choudhry, Jean-François Gaudreault-DesBiens, and Lorne Sossin, 145–66. Toronto: University of Toronto Press, 2006.

———. "Federalism in Canada: Provinces and Minorities – Same Fight." In *Contemporary Canadian Federalism: Foundations, Traditions, Institutions,* edited by Alain-G. Gagnon, 163–86. Toronto: University of Toronto Press, 2012.

Lane, Robert E. "The Politics of Consensus in an Age of Affluence." *American Political Science Review* 59 (1965): 874–95.

LaSelva, Samuel V. *The Moral Foundations of Canadian Federalism: Paradoxes, Achievements, and Tragedies of Nationhood.* Montreal, QC: McGill-Queen's University Press, 1996.

Laski, Harold J. "The Obsolescence of Federalism." *The New Republic* 98, no. 1274 (1939): 367–9.

Latouche, Daniel. "The Constitutional Misfire of 1982." In *And No One Cheered: Federalism, Democracy and The Constitution Act,* edited by Keith Banting and Richard Simeon, 96–118. Toronto: Methuen, 1983.

Lavoie, Josée G. "Medicare and the Care of First Nations, Métis and Inuit," *Health Economics, Policy and Law* 13 (2018): 280–98.

Lazar, Harvey. "Foreword." In *Canadian Fiscal Relations: What Works, What Might Work Better,* edited by Harvey Lazar, v–vi. Montreal, QC: McGill-Queen's University Press, 2005.

———. "The Social Union Framework Agreement and the Future of Fiscal Federalism." In *Towards a New Mission Statement for Canadian Fiscal Federalism,* edited by Harvey Lazar, 99–128. Montreal, QC: McGill-Queen's University Press, 2000.

———. "Trust in Intergovernmental Fiscal Relations." In *Canadian Fiscal Relations: What Works, What Might Work Better,* edited by Harvey Lazar, 3–36. Montreal, QC: McGill-Queen's University Press, 2005.

Leadbeater, David. "An Outline of Capitalist Development in Alberta." In *Essays on the Political Economy of Alberta,* edited by David Leadbeater, 4–20. Toronto: New Hogtown Press, 1984.

Leavitt, Kieran. "Alberta's Equalization Referendum 'Political Science Fiction,' Experts Say." *Star Edmonton,* August 20, 2019. Available at https://www.thestar.com/edmonton/2019/08/20/albertas-equalization-referendum-political-science-fiction-experts-say.html.

Légaré, André. "An Assessment of Recent Political Development in Nunavut: The Challenges and Dilemmas of Inuit Self-Government." *Canadian Journal of Native Studies* 18, no. 2 (1998): 271–99.

Leslie, John, and Ron Maguire, eds. *The Historical Development of the Indian Act.* Ottawa: Indian and Northern Affairs, 1978..

Létourneau, Jocelyn. *A History for the Future: Rewriting Memory and Identity in Quebec.* Montreal, QC: McGill-Queen's University Press, 2004.

Levitt, Kari. *Silent Surrender: The Multinational Corporation in Canada.* Toronto: Macmillan of Canada, 1970.

Linteau, Paul-André, René Durocher, and Jean-Claude Robert. *Quebec: A History 1867–1929.* Toronto: James Lorimer, 1983.

———. *Quebec since 1930.* Toronto: James Lorimer, 1991.

Lister, Frederick K. *The Early Security Confederations: from the Ancient Greeks to the United Colonies of New England.* Westport, CT: Greenwood, 1999.

Locke, John. *Second Treatise of Government.* 1690. Indianapolis, IN: Hacket, 1980.

Locke, Wade. "Cutting through the Gordian Knot: An Objective Assessment of the Equalization Implications for Newfoundland and Labrador of the 2007 Federal Budget." *Newfoundland Quarterly* 100, no. 2 (2007): 48–51.

Lutz, Donald S. "The Iroquois Confederation Constitution: An Analysis." *Publius: The Journal of Federalism* 28, no. 2 (1998): 99–127.

Macfarlane, Emmett. "The Uncertain Future of Senate Reform." In *Constitutional Amendment in Canada*, edited by Emmett Macfarlane, 228–47. Toronto: University of Toronto Press, 2016.

MacGregor, Roy. "Years Later, 'He Bugs Us Still.'" *Globe and Mail*, April 22, 2018. Available at https://www.theglobeandmail.com/news/national/years-later-he-bugs-us-still/article738737.

MacIntosh, Jeffrey G. "A National Securities Commission? The Headless Horseman Rides Again." In *What's Next for Canada? Securities Regulation after the Reference*, edited by Anita Anand, 223–77. Toronto: Irwin Law, 2012.

MacKinnon, Janice. "Equalization: Its Problems and the 2007 Federal Budget." In *Transitions: Fiscal and Political Federalism in an Era of Change*, edited by John R. Allan, Thomas J. Courchene, and Christina Leuprecht, 73–88. Kingston, ON: Institute of Intergovernmental Relations, 2009.

———. *Minding the Public Purse: The Fiscal Crisis, Political Trade-offs, and Canada's Future.* Montreal, QC: McGill-Queen's University Press, 2003.

Macklem, Patrick. *Indigenous Difference and the Constitution of Canada.* Toronto: University of Toronto Press, 2001.

MacLennan, Hugh. *Two Solitudes.* 1945. Toronto: McClelland and Stewart, 1957.

MacMillan, C. Michael. "Rights in Conflict: Contemporary Disputes over Language Policy in Quebec." In *Contemporary Quebec: Selected Readings and Commentaries*, edited by Michael D. Behiels and Matthew Hayday, 393–417. Montreal, QC: McGill-Queen's University Press, 2011.

Magnet, Joseph Eliot. "The Constitutional Distribution of Taxation Powers." *Ottawa Law Review* 10 (1978): 473–534.

Magnusson, Warren. "Are Municipalities Creatures of the Provinces?" *Journal of Canadian Studies* 39, no. 2 (2005): 5–29.

Maioni, Antonia. "Health Care." In *Canadian Federalism: Performance, Effectiveness, and Legitimacy,* edited by Herman Bakvis and Grace Skogstad, 165–82. Toronto: Oxford University Press, 2012.

———. "Showing the Flag: The Origins and Consequences of the Sponsorship Scandal." *Policy Options,* June 1, 2005. Available at http://policyoptions.irpp.org/magazines/the-gomery-effect/showing-the-flag-the-origins-and-consequences-of-the-sponsorship-scandal.

Manitoba Métis Federation. "Budget Continues Trudeau's Commitment to Reconciliation with the Métis Nation." News release, March 2019. Available at http://www.mmf.mb.ca/news_details.php?news_id=355.

Martel, Marcel and Martin Pâquet. *Speaking Up: A History of Language and Politics in Canada and Quebec.* Toronto: Between the Lines, 2012.

Mason, Gary. "The Pipeline War That No Politician Will Win." *Globe and Mail,* February 2, 2018. Available at https://www.theglobeandmail.com/opinion/the-pipeline-war-no-politician-will-win/article37818150.

Matthews, Ralph. *The Creation of Regional Dependency.* Toronto: University of Toronto Press, 1983.

McKay, Todd. "Are You a Province that Doesn't Want to Develop Its Resources? Equalization Has a Nice, Juicy Payout Just for You." *Financial Post,* January 12, 2017. Available at https://business.financialpost.com/opinion/are-you-a-province-that-doesnt-want-to-develop-its-resources-equalization-has-a-nice-juicy-payout-just-for-you.

McLachlin, Beverley. "Canada's Legal System at 150: Democracy and the Judiciary." Speech, Empire Club of Canada, Toronto, ON, June 3, 2016. Available at https://www.scc-csc.ca/judges-juges/spe-dis/bm-2016-06-03-eng.aspx.

McRoberts, Kenneth. *Misconceiving Canada: The Struggle for National Unity.* Toronto: Oxford University Press, 1997.

———. *Quebec: Social Change and Political Crisis.* Toronto: McClelland and Stewart, 1988.

McRoberts, Kenneth, and Dale Posgate. *Quebec: Social Change and Political Crisis.* Toronto: McClelland and Stewart, 1980.

Meekison, J. Peter. "Introduction." In *Constitutional Patriation: The Lougheed-Lévesque Correspondence,* edited by J. Peter Meekison, 1–12. Kingston, ON: Institute of Intergovernmental Relations, 1999.

Meekison, J. Peter, and Roy Romanow. "Western Advocacy and Section 92A of the Constitution." In *Origins and Meaning of 92A: The 1982 Constitutional Amendment on Resources,* edited by J. Peter Meekison, Roy Romanow, and William D. Moull, 3–32. Montreal, QC: The Institute for Research on Public Policy, 1985

Meekison, J. Peter, Roy J. Romanow, and William D. Moull. *Origins and Meaning of 92A: The 1982 Constitutional Amendment on Resources.* Montreal, QC: The Institute for Research on Public Policy, 1985.

Milke, Mark. "Facts about Aboriginal Funding in Canada." Calgary: Fraser Institute, 2016. Available at https://www.fraserinstitute.org/article/facts-about-aboriginal-funding-canada.

Mill, John Stuart. *Considerations on Representative Government.* In *Political Ideologies*, edited by Matthew Festenstein and Michael Kenny, 271–3. Oxford, UK: Oxford University Press, 2005.

Miller, J.R. *Compact, Contract, Covenant: Aboriginal Treaty-Making in Canada.* Toronto: University of Toronto Press, 2009.

Monahan, Patrick. *Constitutional Law.* Toronto: Irwin Law, 2002.

Montesquieu. *The Spirit of the Laws.* 1748. Cambridge: Cambridge University Press, 1989.

Montreal Gazette. "Quebec Remained the Most-Taxed Province in 2017, Report Shows," January 11, 2019. Available at https://montrealgazette.com/news/local-news/quebec-remained-the-most-taxed-province-in-2017-report-shows.

Morse, Bradford. "Government Obligations, Aboriginal Peoples and Section 91(24) of the *Constitution Act*, 1867." In *Aboriginal Peoples and Government Responsibility: Exploring Federal and Provincial Roles*, edited by David C. Hawkes, 59–91. Ottawa: Carleton University Press, 1991.

Morton, Desmond. *A Short History of Canada.* Edmonton, AB: Hurtig Publishers, 1983.

Morton, W.L. "Introduction." In *Manitoba: The Birth of a Province*, Vol 1, edited by W.L. Morton, ix–xxx. Canada: Manitoba Record Society Publications, 1965. Available at http://www.mhs.mb.ca/docs/books/mrs01.pdf.

Moss, Wendy, and Elaine Gardner-O'Toole. "Aboriginal People: History of Discriminatory Laws." Ottawa: Government of Canada Publications, 1991. Available at http://publications.gc.ca/Collection-R/LoPBdP/BP/bp175-e.htm#2.%20Restricted%20Right%20to%20Sell%20Agricultural%20Products(txt).

Moull, William D. "The Legal Effect of the Resource Amendment – What's New in Section 92A?" In *Origins and Meaning of 92A: The 1982 Constitutional Amendment on Resources*, edited by J. Peter Meekison, Roy J. Romanow, and William D. Moull, 33–66. Montreal, QC: The Institute for Research on Public Policy, 1985.

Müller, Jan-Werner, and Kim Lane Scheppele. "Constitutional Patriotism: An Introduction." *International Journal of Constitutional Law* 6, no. 1 (2008): 1–32.

Neatby, H. Blair. *The Politics of Chaos: Canada in the Thirties.* 1972. Ottawa: The Golden Dog Press, 2003.

Nelles, H.V. "Canadian Energy Policy 1945–80: A Federalist Perspective." In *Entering the Eighties: Canada in Crisis*, edited by R. Kenneth Carty and W. Peter Ward, 91–117. Toronto: Oxford University Press, 1980.

Newman, Carey. "There are Two Kinds of Indigenous Governance Structures, but Canada Has Been Listening to Just One." *CBC News*, January 11, 2019. Available at https://www.cbc.ca/news/opinion/gaslink-pipeline-1.4973825.

Newman, Dwight. "Understanding the Section 43 Bilateral Amending Formula." In *Constitutional Amendment in Canada*, edited by Emmett Macfarlane, 147–63. Toronto: University of Toronto Press, 2016.

Neyer, Jürgen. "Discourse and Order in the EU: A Deliberative Approach to Multi-Level Governance." *Journal of Common Market Studies* 41, no. 4 (2003): 687–706.

Nietzsche, Friedrich. "Socrates und die Tragoedie." 1871. In *Kritische Studienausgabe*, Vol. 1. Berlin: de Gruyter, 1999.

Noël, Alain. "Balance and Imbalance in the Division of Financial Resources." In *Contemporary Canadian Federalism: Foundations, Traditions, Institutions*, edited by Alain-G. Gagnon, 273–302. Toronto: University of Toronto Press, 2012.

———. "Social Justice in Overlapping Sharing Communities." In *Dilemmas of Solidarity: Rethinking Redistribution in the Canadian Federation*, edited by Sujit Choudhry, Jean-François Gaudreault-DesBiens, and Lorne Sossin, 57–72. Toronto: University of Toronto Press, 2006.

O'Connor, James. *The Fiscal Crisis of the State*. New York: St. Martin's Press, 1973.

Office of the Auditor General of Canada. "2003 November Report of the Auditor General of Canada: Chapter 3: The Sponsorship Program." Available at http://www.oag-bvg.gc.ca/internet/English/parl_oag_200311_03_e_12925.html.

———. "2011 June Status Report of the Auditor General of Canada." Available at http://www.oag-bvg.gc.ca/internet/English/parl_oag_201106_04_e_35372.html#hd4a.

Official Debates of the House of Commons of the Dominion of Canada. Vol. 12 (1882). Available at https://www.canadiana.ca/view/oocihm.9_07185_8/2?r=0&s=3.

Official Report of the Debates of the House of Commons of the Dominion of Canada. Vol. 20 (1885). Available at https://www.canadiana.ca/view/oocihm.9_07186_3_4/2?r=undefined&s=undefined.

Owram, Doug. "Reluctant Hinterland." In *Western Separatism: The Myths, Realities and Dangers*, edited by Larry Pratt and Garth Stevenson. Edmonton, AB: Hurtig Publishers, 1981.

Pal, Leslie A. *State, Class, and Bureaucracy: Canadian Unemployment Insurance and Public Policy*. Montreal, QC: McGill-Queen's University Press, 1988.

Panitch, Leo, ed. *The Canadian State: Political Economy and Political Power*. Toronto: University of Toronto Press, 1977.

Papillon, Martin. "Canadian Federalism and the Emerging Mosaic of Aboriginal Multilevel Governance." In *Canadian Federalism: Performance, Effectiveness, and Legitimacy*, edited by Herman Bakvis and Grace Skogstad, 284–301. Toronto: Oxford University Press, 2012.

———. "Why We Need a New Kelowna Accord." *Ottawa Citizen*, April 4, 2016. Available at http://ottawacitizen.com/opinion/columnists/papillon-why-we-need-a-new-kelowna-accord.

Papillon, Martin, and Richard Simeon. "The Weakest Link? First Ministers' Conferences in Canadian Intergovernmental Relations." In *Reconsidering the Institutions of Canadian Federalism*, edited by J. Peter Meekison, Hamish Telford, and Harvey Lazar, 113–40. Montreal, QC: McGill-Queen's University Press, 2004.

Parker, A.C. *The Constitution of the Five Nations or the Iroquois Book of the Great Law*. 1916. Reprint, Ohsweken: Iroqrafts, 2006.

Paul, Daniel N. *We Were Not the Savages*. Halifax, NS: Nimbus, 1993.

Peach, Ian. "Prime Minister Trudeau Needs to Have a Serious Discussion with the Provinces about the Substance and the Process of Making Good National Policies in a Federal State." *Policy Options*

(July 2016). Available at https://policyoptions.irpp.org/magazines/july-2016/national-policy-making-must-respect-federalism.

Perry, David B. *Financing the Canadian Federation 1867 to 1995: Setting the Stage for Change.* Toronto: Canadian Tax Foundation, 1997.

Phillips, Paul. *Regional Disparities.* Toronto: Lorimer, 1982.

Pierson, Paul. *Politics in Time: History, Institutions, and Social Analysis.* Princeton, NJ: Princeton University Press, 2004.

Pius XI. *Quadragesimo Anno.* Papal Encyclical, May 15, 1931. Available at http://www.papalencyclicals.net.

Plourde, André. "Oil and Gas in the Canadian Federation." Working paper No. 2010-01, Department of Economics, University of Alberta, 2010. Available at https://sites.ualberta.ca/~econwps/2010/wp2010-01.pdf.

Poirier, Johanne, and Cheryl Saunders. "Conclusion: Comparative Experiences of Intergovernmental Relations in Federal Systems." In *Intergovernmental Relations in Federal Systems*, edited by Johanne Poirier, Cheryl Saunders, and John Kincaid, 440–98. Toronto: Oxford University Press, 2015.

Poirier, Johanne, Cheryl Saunders, and John Kincaid, eds. *Intergovernmental Relations in Federal Systems: Comparative Structures and Dynamics.* Toronto: Oxford University Press, 2015.

Polanyi, Karl. *The Great Transformation: The Political and Economic Origins of our Time.* 1944. Boston, MA: Beacon Press, 2001.

Porter, John. *The Vertical Mosaic: An Analysis of Social Class and Power in Canada.* 1965. Toronto: University of Toronto Press, 1981.

Postmedia News. "Peckford Rewrites History with New Account of 'Kitchen Accord' to Patriate Constitution." *National Post*, September 12, 2012. Available at https://nationalpost.com/news/politics/kitchen-accord-downgraded-former-premier-rewrites-constitutional-history.

Pratt, Alan. "Federalism in the Era of Aboriginal Self-Government." In *Aboriginal Peoples and Government Responsibility: Exploring Federal and Provincial Roles*, edited by David C. Hawkes, 19–58. Ottawa: Carleton University Press, 1989.

Prince, Michael J., and Frances Abele. "Funding an Aboriginal Order of Government in Canada: Recent Developments in Self-Government and Fiscal Relation." In *Toward a New Mission Statement for Canadian Fiscal Federalism*, edited by Harvey Lazar, 337–67. Montreal, QC: McGill-Queen's University Press, 2000.

Prins, Harald E.L. *The Mi'kmaq: Resistance, Accommodation, and Cultural Survival.* Orlando, FL: Harcourt Brace, 1996.

Purich, Donald. *Our Land: Native Rights in Canada.* Toronto: Lorimer, 1986.

Pusey, Merlo J. *Charles Evans Hughes.* New York: Macmillan, 1951.

Rayside, David M., Gerald Sabin, and Paul E. Thomas. *Religion and Canadian Party Politics.* Vancouver, BC: University of British Columbia Press, 2017.

Rémillard, Gil. "Quebec's Quest for Survival and Equality via the Meech Lake Accord." In *The Meech Lake Primer: Conflicting Views of the 1987 Constitutional Accord*, edited by Michael D. Behiels, 28–42. Ottawa: University of Ottawa Press, 1989.

Resnick, Philip. *Parliament vs. People: An Essay on Democracy and Canadian Political Culture.* Vancouver: New Star Books, 1984.

Richards, John, and Larry Pratt. *Prairie Capitalism: Power and Influence in the New West.* Toronto: McClelland and Stewart, 1979.

Richez, Emmanuelle. "The Possibilities and Limits of Provincial Constitution-Making Power: The Case of Quebec." In *Constitutional Amendment in Canada,* edited by Emmett Macfarlane, 164–84. Toronto: University of Toronto Press, 2016.

Rocher, François. "The Quebec–Canada Dynamic or the Negation of the Ideal of Federalism." In *Contemporary Canadian Federalism: Foundations, Traditions, Institutions,* edited by Alain-G. Gagnon, 81–131. Toronto: University of Toronto Press, 2012.

Rodden, Jonathan. *Hamilton's Paradox: The Promise and Peril of Fiscal Federalism.* Cambridge, UK: Cambridge University Press, 2006.

Romanow, Roy J. "Building on Values: The Future of Health Care in Canada." Commission on the Future of Health Care in Canada, November 2002. Available at http://publications.gc.ca/collections/Collection/CP32-85-2002E.pdf.

Romney, Paul. "Provincial Equality, Special Status and the Compact Theory of Canadian Federalism." *Canadian Journal of Political Science* 32, no. 1 (1999): 21–39.

Rousseau, Stéphane. "The Provinces' Competence over Securities Regulation in Canada: Taking Stock of the Supreme Court's Opinion." In *What's Next for Canada? Securities Regulation after the Reference,* edited by Anita Anand. Toronto: Irwin Law, 2012.

Russell, Peter H. *Constitutional Odyssey: Can Canadians Become a Sovereign People?* Toronto: University of Toronto Press, 2012.

———. *Leading Constitutional Decisions.* Ottawa: Carleton University Press, 1982.

Sacouman, R. James. "The Differing Origins, Organization, and Impact of Maritime and Prairie Co-Operative Movements to 1940." In *Underdevelopment and Social Movements in Atlantic Canada,* edited by Robert J. Brym and R. James Sacouman, 37–58. Toronto: New Hogtown Press, 1979.

Salée, Daniel. "Transformative Politics, the State, and the Politics of Social Change in Quebec." In *Changing Canada: Political Economy as Transformation,* edited by Wallace Clement and Leah F. Vosko, 25–50. Montreal, QC: McGilll-Queen's University Press, 2003.

Sancton, Andrew. *Canadian Local Government: An Urban Perspective.* Toronto: Oxford University Press, 2011.

Saunders, Doug. "The Indian Lobby." In *And No One Cheered: Federalism, Democracy and the Constitution Act,* edited by Keith Banting and Richard Simeon, 301–32. Toronto: Methuen, 1983.

Saywell, John T. *The Lawmakers: Judicial Power and the Shaping of Canadian Federalism.* Toronto: University of Toronto Press, 2002.

Scharpf, Fritz W. *Föderalismusreform.* Frankfurt: Campus, 2009.

———. "The Joint-Decision Trap: Lessons from German Federalism and European Integration." *Public Administration* 66, no. 3 (1988): 239–78.

Scholey, Lucy. "'Incomprehensible Failure:' Auditor General Says Federal Government Not Improving Life for Indigenous People," *APTN News,* May 29, 2018. Available at https://aptnnews.ca/2018

/05/29/incomprehensible-failure-auditor-general-says-federal-government-not-improving-life-for-indigenous-people.

Schutter, Helder de. "Federalism as Fairness." *Journal of Political Philosophy* 19, no. 2 (2011): 167–89.

Schwartz, David. "How Does Native Funding Work?" *CBC News*, February 8, 2013. Available at http://www.cbc.ca/news/canada/how-does-native-funding-work-1.1301120.

Seidle, Leslie F. "Senate Reform and the Constitutional Agenda: Conundrum or Solution?" In *Canadian Constitutionalism: 1791–1991*, edited by Janet Ajzenstat, 90–122. Ottawa: Canadian Study of Parliament Group, 1991. Available at http://cspg-gcep.ca/pdf/1991_11-e.pdf.

Senate of Canada. "Senators." Available at https://sencanada.ca/en/senators.

Seymour, Michel. "Not Finding Our Way: The Illusory Reform of the Canadian Federation." In *Contemporary Canadian Federalism: Foundations, Traditions, Institutions,* edited by Alain-G. Gagnon, 187–212. Toronto: University of Toronto Press, 2012.

Shaffer, Ed. "The Political Economy of Oil in Alberta." In *Essays on the Political Economy of Alberta,* edited by David Leadbeater, 174–93. Toronto: New Hogtown Press, 1984.

Shah, Anwar. "Introduction: Principles of Fiscal Federalism." In *The Practice of Fiscal Federalism: Comparative Perspectives,* edited by Anwar Shah, 3–42. Montreal, QC: McGill-Queen's University Press, 2007.

Silver, Arthur I. *The French Canadian Idea of Confederation 1864–1900.* Toronto: University of Toronto Press, 1982.

Simeon, Richard. *Federal–Provincial Diplomacy: The Making of Recent Policy in Canada.* Toronto: University of Toronto Press, 2006.

Simeon, Richard, and Ian Robinson. *State, Society, and the Development of Canadian Federalism.* Toronto: University of Toronto Press, 1990.

Sirois, Joseph, and Newton Wesley Rowell. *Report of the Royal Commission on Dominion–Provincial Relations. Book I, Canada, 1867–1939.* Ottawa: Privy Council Office, 1940. Available at http://www.solon.org/Constitutions/Canada/English/Committees/Rowell-Sirois.

Smiley, Donald V. *Canada in Question: Federalism in the Eighties.* Toronto: McGraw-Hill Ryerson, 1980.

———. "A Dangerous Deed: The Constitution Act, 1982." In *And No One Cheered: Federalism, Democracy and The Constitution Act,* edited by Keith Banting and Richard Simeon, 74–95. Toronto: Methuen, 1983.

———. "An Outsider's Observations of Federal–Provincial Relations among Consenting Adults." In *Perspectives on Canadian Federalism*, edited by R.D. Olling and M.W. Westmacott, 105–11. Toronto: Prentice-Hall, 1988.

———. "The Political Context of Resource Development in Canada." In *Natural Resource Revenues: A Test of Federalism*, edited by Anthony Scott, 61–72. Vancouver, BC: University of British Columbia Press, 1976.

———, ed. *The Rowell-Sirois Report.* Toronto: Macmillan, 1978.

Smiley, Donald V., and Ronald L. Watts. *Intrastate Federalism in Canada.* Toronto: University of Toronto Press, 1985.

Smith, David E. *The Canadian Senate in Bicameral Perspective.* Toronto: University of Toronto Press, 2003.

———. *Federalism and the Constitution of Canada.* Toronto: University of Toronto Press, 2010.

Smith, Jennifer. *Federalism.* Vancouver, BC: University of British Columbia Press, 2005.

Sprague, D.N. *Canada and the Métis, 1869–1885.* Waterloo, ON: Wilfrid Laurier University Press, 1988.

Standing Senate Committee on Legal and Constitutional Affairs. "The Extraordinary Federal Powers and a Genuine Federation." In *Report to the Senate of Canada.* Ottawa: 1980. Available at http://www.solon.org/Constitutions/Canada/English/Committees/Goldenberg.

Starr, Richard. *Equal as Citizens: The Tumultuous and Troubled History of a Great Canadian Idea.* Halifax, NS: Formac Publishing, 2014.

Statistics Canada, "Section 1: Census Metropolitan Areas." 2018. Available at https://www150.statcan.gc.ca/n1/pub/91-214-x/2018000/tbl/tbl-1.1-eng.htm.

———. "Unemployment Rate by Province." January 2018. Available at https://www.statcan.gc.ca/daily-quotidien/180209/cg-a003-eng.htm.

Stepan, Alfred. "Federalism and Democracy: Beyond the U.S. Model." *Journal of Democracy* 10, no. 4 (1999): 19–34.

Stevenson, Garth. *Ex Uno Plures: Federal–Provincial Relations in Canada 1867–1896.* Montreal, QC: McGill-Queen's University Press, 1997.

———. "Federalism and the Political Economy of the Canadian State." In *The Canadian State: Political Economy and Political Power*, edited by Leo Panitch, 71–100. Toronto: University of Toronto Press, 1977.

———. "Fiscal Federalism and the Burden of History." Institute of Intergovernmental Relations working paper. Queen's University, September 28–9, 2006.

———. *Unfulfilled Union: Canadian Federalism and National Unity.* 5th ed. 1982. Montreal, QC: McGill-Queen's University Press, 2009.

Stilborn, Jack. "Forty Years of Not Reforming the Senate – Taking Stock." In *Protecting Canadian Democracy: The Senate You Never Knew*, edited by Serge Joyal, 31–66. Montreal, QC: McGill-Queen's University Press, 2003.

Story, Rod, and Tolga R. Yalkin. *Expenditure Analysis of Criminal Justice in Canada.* Ottawa: Office of the Parliamentary Budget Officer, 2013. Available at http://pbo-dpb.gc.ca/web/default/files/files/files/Crime_Cost_EN.pdf.

Streeck, Wolfgang. *Buying Time: The Delayed Crisis of Democratic Capitalism.* London, UK: Verso, 2014.

Summers, Valerie A. "Newfoundland between a Rock and a Hard Place: Regime Change in Newfoundland." In *The Provincial State in Canada: Politics in the Provinces and Territories*, edited by Keith Brownsey and Michael Howlett, 23–47. Peterborough, ON: Broadview Press, 2001.

Swinton, Katherine. "Federalism, the Charter, and the Courts; Rethinking Constitutional Dialogue in Canada." In *Rethinking Federalism: Citizens, Markets, and Governments in a Changing World*, edited by Karen Knop et al., 294–315. Vancouver, BC: University of British Columbia Press, 1995.

———. "Federalism under Fire: The Role of the Supreme Court of Canada." *Law and Contemporary Problems* 55, no. 1 (1992): 121–45.

Tanguay, A. Brian. "Sclerosis or a Clean Bill of Health? Diagnosing Québec's Party System in the Twenty-First Century." In *Québec: State and Society*, edited by Alain-G. Gagnon, 221–43. Peterborough, ON: Broadview Press, 2004.

Thompson, John Herd, with Allen Seager. *Canada 1922–1939.* Toronto: McClelland and Stewart, 1985.

Thucydides. *The Peloponnesian War.* New York: The Modern Library, 1934.

Tilly, Charles. "Western State-Making and Theories of Political Transformation." In *The Formation of National States in Western Europe*, edited by Charles Tilly, 601–38. Princeton, NJ: Princeton University Press, 1975.

Trudeau, Justin. "New Process for Judicial Appointments to the Supreme Court of Canada." August 2, 2016. Available at http://pm.gc.ca/eng/news/2016/08/02/new-process-judicial-appointments-supreme-court-canada.

Trudeau, Pierre Elliott. "Established Program Financing: A Proposal Regarding the Major Shared-Cost Programs in the Fields of Health and Post-Secondary Education." In *Canadian Federalism: Myth or Reality*, 3rd ed., edited by J. Peter Meekison, 246–8. Toronto: Methuen, 1977.

———. *Federalism and the French Canadians.* 1968. Reprint, Toronto: Macmillan, 1977.

———. *Federal-Provincial Grants and the Spending Power of Parliament.* Working paper. Ottawa: Government of Canada Working Paper on the Constitution, 1969.

———. "Say Goodbye to the Dream of One Canada." *Toronto Star*, May 27, 1987. Available at https://www.solon.org/Constitutions/Canada/English/Arguments/trudeau-star-87.html.

———. "Who Speaks for Canada? Defining and Sustaining a National Vision." In *The Meech Lake Primer: Conflicting Views of the 1987 Constitutional Accord*, edited by Michael D. Behiels, 60–99. Ottawa: University of Ottawa Press, 1989.

Truth and Reconciliation Commission of Canada. *Final Report of the Truth and Reconciliation Commission of Canada.* Vol. 1, *Summary.* Toronto: James Lorimer, 2015.

Turgeon, Luc, Antoine Bilodeau, Stephen E. White, and Ailsa Henderson. "A Tale of Two Liberalisms? Attitudes toward Minority Religious Symbols in Quebec and Canada." *Canadian Journal of Political Science* 52, no. 2 (2019): 247–65.

Turgeon, Luc, and Jennifer Wallner. "Adaptability and Change in Federations: Centralization, Political Parties, and Taxation Authority in Australia and Canada." In *The Global Promise of Federalism,* edited by Grace Skogstad, David Cameron, Martin Papillon, and Keith Banting, 188–213. Toronto: University of Toronto Press, 2013.

"The Union Act: An Act to Reunite the Provinces of Upper and Lower Canada, and for the Government of Canada." 3 & 4 Vict., c. 35 (U.K.), July 23, 1840. Available at http://www.solon.org/Constitutions/Canada/English/PreConfederation/ua_1840.html

Van Loon, Richard J., and Michael S. Whittington. *The Canadian Political System: Environment, Structure, and Process.* Toronto: McGraw-Hill Ryerson, 1984.

Veltmeyer, Henry. "The Capitalist Underdevelopment of Atlantic Canada." In *Underdevelopment and Social Movements in Atlantic Canada*, edited by Robert J. Brym and R. James Sacouman, 17–35. Toronto: New Hogtown Press, 1979.

Verrelli, Nadia. "Negotiating the Charlottetown Accord in Canada." In *Changing Federal Constitutions: Lessons from International Comparison*, edited by Arthur Benz and Felix Knüpling, 161–89. Opladen: Barbara Budrich, 2012.

———. "Searching for an Amendment Formula: The 115-Year Journey." In *Constitutional Amendment in Canada*, edited by Emmett Macfarlane, 19–41. Toronto: University of Toronto Press, 2016.

Vickers, Jill. "Why Should Women Care About Federalism?" In *Canada: The State of the Federation*, edited by Douglas M. Brown and Janet I. Hiebert, 135–52. Kingston: McGill-Queen's University Press, 1994.

Vipond, Robert C. *Liberty and Community: Canadian Federalism and the Failure of the Constitution*. Albany, NY: State University of New York Press, 1991.

Waite, P. B. *The Life and Times of Confederation 1864–1867: Politics, Newspapers, and the Union of British North America*. Toronto: University of Toronto Press, 1962.

Wallner, Jennifer. "Empirical Evidence and Pragmatic Explanations: Canada's Contributions to Comparative Federalism." In *The Comparative Turn in Canadian Political Science*, edited by Linda A. White, Richard Simeon, Robert Vipond, and Jennifer Wallner, 158–76. Vancouver, BC: University of British Columbia Press, 2008.

———. "Ideas and Intergovernmental Relations in Canada." *PS: Political Science & Politics* 50, no. 3 (2017): 717–22.

———. *Learning to School: Federalism and Public Schooling in Canada*. Toronto: University of Toronto Press, 2014.

Watkins, M.H. "A Staples Theory of Economic Growth." In *Approaches to Canadian Economic History*, edited by W.T. Easterbrook and M.H. Watkins, 49–73. Toronto: Gage Publishing, 1980.

Watts, Ronald L. *The Spending Power in Federal Systems: A Comparative Study*. Kingston, ON: Institute of Intergovernmental Relations, 1999.

Wheare, K. C. *Federal Government*. 1946. Reprint, New York: Oxford University Press, 1963.

Whitaker, Reginald. "Democracy and the Canadian Constitution." In *And No One Cheered: Federalism, Democracy and The Constitution Act*, edited by Keith Banting and Richard Simeon. Toronto: Methuen, 1983.

———. *Federalism and Democratic Theory*. Kingston: Institute of Intergovernmental Relations, 1983.

White-Crummey, Arthur. "Carbon Tax Court Primer: Who Are the Players at This Week's Reference Case?" *Regina Leader-Post*, February 11, 2019. Available at https://leaderpost.com/news/politics/constitutional-question-primer-whos-who-and-what-are-they-on-about.

Williams, Glen. *Not for Export*. 3rd ed. 1983. Toronto: McClelland and Stewart, 1994.

Williams, Melissa. "Toleration, Canadian-Style: Reflections of a Yankee-Canadian." In *Canadian Political Philosophy*, edited by Ronald Beiner and Wayne Norman, 216–31. Toronto: Oxford University Press, 2001.

Wilson, Beth, with Carly Steinman. *Hunger Count 2000: A Surplus of Hunger*. Toronto: Canadian Association of Food Banks, 2000.

Woehrling, José. "The Charter of Rights and Freedoms and Its Consequences." In *Contemporary Canadian Federalism: Foundations, Traditions, Institutions,* edited by Alain-G. Gagnon, 224–50. Toronto: University of Toronto Press, 2012.

Young, Iris Marion. *Justice and the Politics of Difference.* Princeton, NJ: Princeton University Press, 1990.

Young, Robert A. *Secession of Quebec and the Future of Canada.* Montreal, QC: McGill-Queen's University Press, 1998.

Young, Robert A., Philippe Faucher, and André Blais. "The Concept of Province-Building: A Critique." *Canadian Journal of Political Science* 17, no. 4 (1984): 783–818.

Zukowsky, Ronald J. *Intergovernmental Relations in Canada: The Year in Review 1980.* Kingston, ON: Institute of Intergovernmental Relations, 1981.

Court Cases and Legislation

An Act respecting the exercise of the fundamental rights and prerogatives of the Québec people and the Québec State, Bill 99, c. 46, 2000. Available at http://www2.publicationsduquebec.gouv.qc.ca /dynamicSearch/telecharge.php?type=5&file=2000C46A.PDF.

An Act to encourage the gradual Civilization of the Indian Tribes in this Province, and to amend the Laws respecting Indians, 1857, CAP 26. Available at http://caid.ca/GraCivAct1857.pdf.

An Act to give effect to the requirement for clarity as set out in the opinion of the Supreme Court of Canada in the Quebec Secession Reference, [2000] SC 26. Available at https://laws-lois.justice.gc.ca/eng /acts/c-31.8/page-1.html.

The Attorney General for Ontario v. The Attorney General for the Dominion of Canada (Canada) [1896] UKPC 20 (9 May 1896).

The Attorney General of Canada (Appeal No. 103 of 1920) v. The Attorney General of Alberta and others (Canada) [1921] UKPC 107 (8 November 1921).

The Attorney General of Canada (Appeal No. 101 of 1936) v. The Attorney General of Ontario and others (Canada) [1937] UKPC 7 (28 January 1937).

The Attorney-General of Ontario and others (Appeal No. 2 of 1940) v. The Canada Temperance Federation (Ontario) [1946] UKPC 2 (21 January 1946).

Calder et al. v. Attorney-General of British Columbia, [1973] SCR 313. Available at https://scc-csc.lexum .com/scc-csc/scc-csc/en/item/5113/index.do.

Canada Ltée (Spraytech, Société d'arrosage) v. Hudson (Town), 2001 SCC 40.

Canadian Western Bank v. Alberta, 2007 SCC 22.

Central Canada Potash Co. Ltd. et al. v. Government of Saskatchewan, [1979] 1 SCR 42.

Charles Russell v. The Queen, (New Brunswick) [1882] UKPC 33 (23 June 1882).

CIGOL v. Saskatchewan, [1978] 2 SCR 545.

The Citizens Insurance Company of Canada and The Queen Insurance Company v. Parsons (Canada) [1881] UKPC 50 (26 November 1881).

Daniels v. Canada (Indian Affairs and Northern Development), 2016 SCC 12.

Delgamuukw v. British Columbia, [1997] 3 SCR 1010.

Ford v. Quebec, [1988] 2 SCR 712. Available at https://scc-csc.lexum.com/scc-csc/scc-csc/en/item/384/index.do.

General Motors of Canada Ltd. v. City National Leasing, [1989] 1 SCR 641.

Haida Nation v. British Columbia (Minister of Forests), 2004 SCC 73.

Labatt Breweries of Canada Ltd. v. Attorney General of Canada, [1980] 1 SCR 914.

Public Service Board et al. v. Dionne et al., [1978] 2 SCR 191.

R. v. Crown Zellerbach Canada Ltd., [1988] 1 SCR 401.

R. v. Sparrow, [1990] 1 SCR 1075.

Reference re Assisted Human Reproduction Act, 2010 SCC 61.

Reference re Firearms Act, [2000] 1 SCR 783.

Reference re Pan-Canadian Securities Regulation, 2018 SCC 48. Available at https://scc-csc.lexum.com/scc-csc/scc-csc/en/item/17355/index.do

Reference re Secession of Quebec, [1998] 2 SCR 217. Available at https://scc-csc.lexum.com/scc-csc/scc-csc/en/item/1643/index.do.

Reference re Securities Act, 2011 SCC 66.

Reference re Senate Reform, 2014 SCC 32. Available at https://scc-csc.lexum.com/scc-csc/scc-csc/en/item/13614/index.do.

Re: Resolution to Amend the Constitution, [1981] 1 SCR 753. Available at https://scc-csc.lexum.com/scc-csc/scc-csc/en/item/2519/index.do.

Rewe-Zentral AG v. Bundesmonopolverwaltung für Branntwein (Germany) 120/78 [1979] 20 February 1979.

Severn v. The Queen, [1878] 2 SCR 70.

St. Ann's Island Shooting and Fishing Club v. The King, [1950] SCR 211.

The Toronto Electric Commissioners (Appeal No. 99 of 1924) v. Colin G. Snider and others (Ontario) [1925] UKPC 2 (20 January 1925).

Tsilhqot'in Nation v. British Columbia, 2014 SCC 44.

Index

www.ingramcontent.com/pod-product-compliance
Lightning Source LLC
LaVergne TN
LVHW020436080826
844660LV00033B/1298
* 9 7 8 1 4 4 2 6 3 6 4 5 3 *